HARCOURT
· T R O P H I E S ·

A HARCOURT READING/LANGUAGE ARTS PROGRAM

TEACHER'S EDITION

SENIOR AUTHORS
Isabel L. Beck ◆ Roger C. Farr ◆ Dorothy S. Strickland

AUTHORS
Alma Flor Ada ◆ Marcia Brechtel ◆ Margaret McKeown
Nancy Roser ◆ Hallie Kay Yopp

SENIOR CONSULTANT
Asa G. Hilliard III

CONSULTANTS
F. Isabel Campoy ◆ David A. Monti

⬳Harcourt

Orlando Boston Dallas Chicago San Diego

Visit *The Learning Site!*

www.harcourtschool.com

Program Authors
SENIOR AUTHORS

Isabel L. Beck
Professor of Education and Senior Scientist at the Learning Research and Development Center, University of Pittsburgh

Research Contributions: Reading Comprehension, Beginning Reading, Phonics, Vocabulary

Roger C. Farr
Chancellor's Professor of Education and Director of the Center for Innovation in Assessment, Indiana University, Bloomington

Research Contributions: Instructional Assessment, Reading Strategies, Staff Development

Dorothy S. Strickland
The State of New Jersey Professor of Reading, Rutgers University

Research Contributions: Early Literacy, Elementary Reading/Language Arts, Writing, Intervention

AUTHORS

Alma Flor Ada
Director of Doctoral Studies in the International Multicultural Program, University of San Francisco

Research Contributions: English as a Second Language, Bilingual Education, Family Involvement

Marcia Brechtel
Director of Training, Project GLAD, Fountain Valley School District, Fountain Vally California

Research Contributions: English as a Second Language, Bilingual Education

Margaret McKeown
Research Scientist at the Learning Research and Development Center, University of Pittsburgh

Research Contributions: Reading Comprehension, Vocabulary

Nancy Roser
Professor, Language and Literacy Studies, University of Texas, Austin

Research Contributions: Early Literacy, Phonics, Comprehension, Fluency

Hallie Kay Yopp
Professor, Department of Elementary Bilingual and Reading Education, California State University, Fullerton

Research Contributions: Phonemic Awareness, Early Childhood

SENIOR CONSULTANT

Asa G. Hilliard III
Fuller E. Callaway Professor of Urban Education, Department of Educational Foundations, Georgia State University, Atlanta

Research Contributions: Multicultural Literature and Education

CONSULTANTS

F. Isabel Campoy
Former President, Association of Spanish Professionals in the USA

Research Contributions: English as a Second Language, Family Involvement

David A. Monti
Professor, Reading/Language Arts Department, Central Connecticut State University

Research Contributions: Classroom Management, Technology, Family Involvement

Research clearly shows that phonemic awareness is one of the primary predictors of success in learning to read and instruction in phonemic awareness significantly supports students' reading and writing achievement.

Phonemic awareness is the awareness of sounds in spoken language. It is recognizing and understanding that speech is made up of a series of individual sounds, or phonemes, and that the individual sounds can be manipulated. A phonemically aware child can segment and blend strings of isolated sounds to form words. Phonemic awareness falls under the umbrella of phonological awareness, which also includes recognizing and manipulating larger units of sound, such as syllables and words. Phonemic awareness can be difficult for young children to attain because it demands a shift in attention from the *content* of speech to the *form* of speech. It requires individuals to attend to the sounds of speech separate from their meanings. Primary grade teachers will find that a handful of children enter school with well-developed phonemic awareness. Other children have only a rudimentary sense of the sound structure of speech. With extended exposure to a language-rich environment, most children develop phonemic awareness over time.

Research has shown that phonemic awareness is significantly related to success in learning to read and spell. The relationship is one of reciprocal causation or mutual facilitation. That is, phonemic awareness supports reading and spelling acquisition, and instruction in reading and spelling, in turn, supports further understanding of the phonemic basis of our speech. The relationship is so powerful that researchers have concluded the following:

- Phonemic awareness is the most potent predictor of success in learning to read (Stanovich, 1986, 1994).
- The lack of phonemic awareness is the most powerful determinant of the likelihood of failure to learn to read (Adams, 1990).
- Phonemic awareness is the most important core and causal factor separating normal and disabled readers (Adams, 1990).

Phonemic awareness is central in learning to read and spell because English and other alphabetic languages map speech to print at the level of phonemes. Our written language is a representation of the *sounds* of our spoken language. It is critical to understand that our speech is made up of sounds. Without this insight, written language makes little sense.

Direct instruction in phonemic awareness helps children decode new words and remember how to read familiar words. Growth and improvement in phonemic awareness can be facilitated through instruction and practice in phonemic awareness tasks such as these:

- **Phoneme isolation,** which requires students to recognize individual sounds in words. For example, "What is the last sound in *hop*?" (/p/)
- **Phoneme matching,** which requires students to recognize the same sound in different words. For example, "Which two words begin with the same sound—*bed, bike, cat*?" (*bed, bike*)
- **Phoneme blending,** which asks students to form a recognizable word after listening to separately spoken sounds. For example, "What word is /a/ -/p/ -/l/?" (*apple*)
- **Phoneme segmentation,** which has students break a word into its individual sounds. For example, "What sounds do you hear in the word *dog*?" (/d/-/ô/-/g/)
- **Phoneme deletion,** which requires students to identify what word remains when a specific phoneme has been removed. For example, "Say *spin* without /s/." (*pin*)
- **Phoneme addition,** which requires the identification of a word when a phoneme is added. For example, "Say *row* with /g/ at the beginning." (*grow*)

Q **What types of phonemic awareness activities or tasks are children exposed to in the program?**

A Phonemic awareness instruction in *Trophies* is strongly supported by the finding that phonemic awareness is one of the most potent predictors of success in learning to read. Activities for stimulating phonemic awareness are incorporated throughout the program. There are two types of phonemic awareness instruction in *Trophies.* The first is word-play activities that draw attention to sounds in spoken language, recited poems, and read-aloud literature. The second type is more formal instruction that focuses on single phonemes to prepare students for studying the letter-sound correspondences for those phonemes.

Q **What phonemic awareness skills are taught in kindergarten and grade 1?**

A Phonemic awareness instruction in *Trophies* follows a systematic, developmental sequence progressing in difficulty from an awareness of words, syllables, and onset/rimes to isolating medial phonemes, substituting phonemes, and other manipulating tasks.

> **" A growing number of studies indicate that phonemic awareness is not simply a strong predictor, but that it is a necessary prerequisite for success in learning to read. "**
>
> — **Hallie Kay Yopp**
> Professor
> Department of Elementary
> Bilingual and Reading Education,
> California State University,
> Fullerton

Phonemic Awareness Skills Sequence

- Word Segmentation
- Rhyme Recognition and Production
- Syllable Blending
- Syllable Segmentation
- Syllable Deletion
- Onset and Rime Blending
- Initial Phoneme Isolation

- Final Phoneme Isolation
- Medial Phoneme Isolation
- Phoneme Blending
- Phoneme Segmentation
- Phoneme Substitution
- Phoneme Addition
- Phoneme Deletion

Q **How do the phonemic awareness lessons relate to the phonics lessons in *Trophies*?**

A In kindergarten and grade 1, each phonemic awareness lesson is tied to a phonics lesson. A phonemic awareness lesson, for example, could focus on blending phonemes in words with the /i/ sound, featuring such words as *sit, lip,* and *if.* The subsequent phonics lesson would be the short sound of the letter *i.*

Look for

✓ **Daily phonemic awareness lessons in Kindergarten and Grade 1**
✓ **Additional Support Activities to Reteach and Extend**
✓ **Point-of-use suggestions for Reaching All Learners**

EXPLICIT, SYSTEMATIC PHONICS

Decoding is the process of translating written words into speech. Phonics instruction gives students the knowledge of letter-sound correspondences and strategies they need to make the translations and to be successful readers.

Explicit, systematic phonics instruction can help children learn to read more effectively. Current and confirmed research shows that systematic phonics instruction has a significant effect on reading achievement. Research findings clearly indicate that phonics instruction in kindergarten and first grade produces a dramatic impact on reading achievement. In phonics instruction letter-sound correspondences are taught sequentially and cumulatively and are then applied. The individual sounds represented by letters are blended to form words, and those words appear in decodable text. At grade 2, more complex letter patterns are introduced and practiced. This type of instruction allows students to continually build on what they learn.

Word Blending and Word Building are essential aspects of phonics instruction. Word Blending is combining the sounds represented by letter sequences to decode and pronounce words. In phonics instruction beginning in kindergarten or first grade, students are explicitly taught the process of blending individual sounds into words. They begin with VC or CVC words, such as *at* or *man,* and progress to words with consonant blends, as in *tent* and *split.* In contrast to Word Blending, which focuses on decoding a particular word, Word Building allows students to practice making words by using previously taught letter-sound relationships. Word Building activities require children to focus attention on each letter in the sequence of letters that make up words. This helps children develop a sense of the alphabetic system of written English.

As students progress through the grades, they receive direct instruction in decoding multisyllabic words. Direct instruction in recognizing syllables will help students develop effective strategies to read longer, unfamiliar words. Research shows that good readers chunk letter patterns into manageable units in order to read a long, unfamiliar word. Effective strategies include

- identifying syllable boundaries
- identifying syllable types
- isolating affixes
- applying phonics knowledge to blend syllables in sequence

Direct instruction in these strategies helps students recognize word parts so they can apply phonics generalizations to decode unfamiliar words.

“ Decoding is important because this early skill accurately predicts later skill in reading comprehension. ”

— Isabel L. Beck
Professor of Education and Senior Scientist at the Learning Research and Development Center, University of Pittsburgh

Q **How is Word Blending taught in *Trophies*?**

A The purpose of Word Blending instruction is to provide students with practice in combining the sounds represented by letter sequences to decode words. *Trophies* employs the cumulative blending method, which has students blend sounds successively as they are pronounced.

Q **How does *Trophies* use Word Building to help students with decoding (reading) and encoding (spelling)?**

A In the decoding portion of Word Building, teachers first tell students what letters to put in what place. For example, students are told to put *c* at the beginning, *a* after *c,* and *t* at the end. They are asked to read the word *cat* and then are asked to change *c* to *m* and read the new word, *mat.* In Word Building activities that help encoding, students are asked which letter in the word *cat* needs to change to make the word *mat.* This encoding approach is used to build spelling words throughout the first grade program.

Q **How are students taught to decode multisyllabic words?**

A Students are taught to see words as patterns of letters, to identify long words by breaking them down into syllable units, and to blend the syllables to form and read long words. Decoding lessons throughout grades 2–6 directly and explicitly provide students with various strategies, including understanding syllable types and patterns and recognizing such word structures as prefixes, suffixes, and root words, to decode multisyllabic words.

Look for

✓ **Phonics and spelling lessons**
✓ **Word Blending**
✓ **Word Building**
✓ **Decoding/Phonics lessons in Grades 2–6**
✓ **Additional Support Activities to reteach and extend**

PROFESSIONAL BIBLIOGRAPHY See the research citations in the Additional Resources section.

READING ALOUD

Reading aloud to students contributes to their motivation, comprehension, vocabulary, fluency, knowledge base, literary understanding, familiarity with academic and literary terms, sense of community, enjoyment, and perhaps to a lifetime love of literature.

Sharing and responding to books during read-aloud time helps develop communication and oral language skills and improves comprehension. Literature that is read aloud to students serves as the vehicle for developing literary insights, including sensitivity to the sounds and structure of language. Students learn how powerful written language can be when fluent readers read aloud, interpreting a text through appropriate intonation, pacing, and phrasing. Comprehension skills are developed as students ask and answer questions and share their personal understandings. More advanced students who are read to and who get to talk with others about the best of written language learn both to discuss texts knowingly and to interpret their meaning expressively.

Reading aloud exposes students to more challenging texts than they may be able to read independently. Vocabulary development is fostered by listening to both familiar and challenging selections read aloud. Texts read aloud that are conceptually challenging for students can effectively improve language and comprehension abilities. Listening to challenging texts also exposes students to text structures and content knowledge that are more sophisticated than they may encounter in their own reading.

Listening skills and strategies are greatly improved during read-aloud activities. When students are encouraged to respond to stories read aloud, they tend to listen intently in order to recall relevant content. When students listen responsively and frequently to literature and expository texts, they hone critical-thinking skills that will serve them in many other contexts. In summary, reading aloud

- models fluent reading behavior
- builds students' vocabularies and concepts
- creates an interest in narrative structures
- builds background knowledge by introducing children to new ideas and concepts and by expanding on what is familiar to them
- exposes students to different text structures and genres, such as stories, alphabet books, poetry, and informational books

" Sharing literature with children increases their vocabulary and their understanding of how language works. Sharing stories, informational books, and poetry with children has become increasingly valued for its cognitive contribution to children's literary development. "

— **Dorothy S. Strickland**
The State of New Jersey
Professor of Reading,
Rutgers University

Q **How does *Trophies* provide opportunities for teachers to read aloud to their students?**

A *Trophies* provides a comprehensive collection of read-aloud selections for all levels of instruction. In kindergarten through grade 2, include read-aloud options for students every day. In grades 3–6, a read-aloud selection accompanies every lesson in the *Teacher's Edition.* Read-aloud selections are available in *Read-Aloud Anthologies* for kindergarten through grade 2, the *Library Books Collections* for kindergarten through grade 6 and in several other formats.

Q **What genres can students meet through read-alouds?**

A Students encounter a wide variety of literary genres and expository texts through read-aloud selections in all grades. Expository nonfiction becomes more prevalent as students move up the grades. Other genres include poetry, finger plays, folktales, myths, and narrative nonfiction. In lessons in grades 3-6 with Focus Skills, such as narrative elements or text structure, the genre of the read-aloud selection matches the genre of the reading selection.

Q **What kind of instruction accompanies read-aloud selections in *Trophies*?**

A In kindergarten and grade I, the instruction that accompanies Sharing Literature includes three options:
- Build Concept Vocabulary
- Develop Listening Comprehension
- Listen and Respond

In grade 2, options include Developing Listening Comprehension, Set a Purpose, and Recognize Genre. The instructional focus in kindergarten centers on concepts about print and beginning narrative analysis (characters, setting, important events). In kindergarten through grades 2, students are taught more complex literary skills, such as following the structure of stories, recognizing their beginnings, middles, and endings, and even occasionally generating alternative endings. In grades 3–6, read-alouds also serve as a vehicle for exploring expository text structures.

Look for

✓ **Daily "Sharing Literature" acitivities in Kindergarten through Grade 2**
✓ **Read-aloud selections and instruction with every lesson in Grades 2–6**
✓ **Library Books Collections at all grades**
✓ **Read-Aloud Anthologies in Kindergarten through Grade 2**

COMPREHENSION

Reading comprehension is the complex process of constructing meaning from texts. Recent comprehension research has been guided by the idea that the process is strategic and interactive.

Comprehension is the construction of meaning through an interactive exchange of ideas between the text and the reader. Comprehension strategies are interactive processes that allow readers to monitor and self-assess how well they understand what they are reading. These processes include determining the purpose or purposes for reading, such as to obtain information or to be entertained. After the purpose is determined, readers activate prior knowledge about the content of the text and its structure. Research has shown that the more readers know about the content of a particular text, the more likely they will understand, integrate, and remember the new information. Familiarity with the genre or text structure also fosters comprehension.

Most students need explicit instruction in comprehension skills and strategies. Research shows that comprehension skills and strategies are necessary for student success and that they do not develop automatically in most students. Without explicit instruction and guidance, many readers fail to acquire automatic use of these skills and strategies and show little flexibility in applying them to understand a variety of texts. Research shows that poor readers who are directly taught a particular strategy do as well as good readers who have used the strategy spontaneously. Typically, direct instruction consists of

- an explanation of what the skill or strategy is and how it aids comprehension
- modeling how to use the skill or strategy
- working directly with students as they apply the skill or strategy, offering assistance as needed
- having students apply the skill or strategy independently and repeatedly

Students need extensive direct instruction, guidance, and cumulative practice until they can independently determine the method of constructing meaning that works for them.

Students need to learn strategies for comprehending a wide variety of texts, including both fiction and nonfiction. In kindergarten, students should be taught to understand narrative structure. They should learn to identify the beginning, middle, and ending of a story and other literary elements, such as characters and setting. Then they can use their knowledge of these elements to retell stories they have listened to. In first through third grade, readers deepen their knowledge of these narrative elements and interact with others as book discussants and literary meaning makers. They learn to use the specific language of literature study, such as *point of view* and *character trait*. By grades 4–6, students must have the skills, strategies, and knowledge of text structures to comprehend complex nonfiction texts, including those in the classroom content areas. Students need to be explicitly and systematically taught the organizational structure of expository text, e.g., compare/contrast, cause/effect, and main idea and details. These organizational structures should be taught systematically and reviewed cumulatively.

> **❝ One of the fundamental understandings about the nature of reading is that it is a constructive act. Specifically, a reader does not extract meaning from a page, but constructs meaning from information on the page and information already in his/her mind. ❞**
>
> **— Isabel L. Beck**
> Professor of Education and Senior Scientist at the Learning Research and Development Center, University of Pittsburgh

Q How does *Trophies* provide explicit instruction in comprehension?

A *Trophies* features systematic and explicit comprehension instruction grounded in current and confirmed research. Comprehension instruction in kindergarten focuses on helping students construct meaning from stories read to them. From the earliest grades, teachers guide students before, during, and after reading in the use of strategies to monitor comprehension. Guided comprehension questions ask students to apply a variety of comprehension skills strategies appropriate to particular selections. Each tested skill is introduced, reinforced, assessed informally, retaught as needed, reviewed at least twice, and maintained throughout each grade level.

Q How does comprehension instruction in *Trophies* build through the grades?

A Comprehension instruction in *Trophies* is rigorous, developmental, and spiraled. Students gain increasingly sophisticated skills and strategies to help them understand texts successfully. In the instructional components of the earliest grades, emergent and beginning readers develop use of strategies as they respond to texts read by the teacher, and more advanced students begin to apply skills and strategies to texts they read themselves. Students demonstrate their comprehension through asking and answering questions, retelling stories, discussing characters, comparing stories, and making and confirming predictions. As students progress through the grades, they build upon their existing skills and read a more extensive variety of texts.

Q How is instruction in genres and text structures developed in the program?

A The foundation of *Trophies* is a wide variety of fiction and nonfiction selections, including many paired selections to promote reading across texts. Instruction in both the *Pupil Edition* and *Teacher's Edition* helps students develop a thorough understanding of genre characteristics and text structures. In kindergarten, students explore story elements, such as characters, setting, and important events. As students move up the grades, they analyze both literary elements and devices and expository organizational patterns, such as cause/effect and compare/constrast, to understand increasingly difficult texts.

Look for

- ✔ Focus Strategies and Focus Skills
- ✔ Diagnostic Checks
- ✔ Additional Support Activities
- ✔ Guided Comprehension
- ✔ Strategies Good Readers Use
- ✔ Ongoing Assessment
- ✔ *Comprehension Cards*

VOCABULARY

A large and flexible vocabulary is the hallmark of an
educated person. The more words students acquire, the
better chance they will have for success in reading,
writing, and spelling.

Students acquire vocabulary knowledge through extensive reading in a variety of texts. The amount of reading students do in and out of school is a strong indicator of students' vocabulary acquisition. Research supports exposing students to rich language environments through listening to literature and reading a variety of genres independently. Their vocabulary knowledge grows when they hear stories containing unfamiliar words. As students progress through the grades, their reading of books and other materials contributes more significantly to vocabulary knowledge than viewing television, participating in conversations, or other typical oral language activities. In other words, increasing students' volume of reading is the best way to promote vocabulary growth.

Students need multiple encounters with key vocabulary words in order to improve comprehension. Current and confirmed research has shown that students need to encounter a word several times before it is known well enough to facilitate comprehension. Direct instruction in vocabulary has an important role here because learning words from context is far from automatic. After being introduced to new words, students need opportunities to see those words again in their reading and to develop their own uses for the words in a variety of different contexts, in relationship to other words, and both inside and outside of the classroom. For instruction to enhance comprehension, new words need to become a permanent part of students' repertoires, which means instruction must go well beyond providing information on word meanings.

Students can benefit from direct instruction in vocabulary strategies. Although estimates of vocabulary size and growth vary, children likely learn between 1,000 and 5,000 words per year—and the average child learns about 3,000 words. Since wide reading provides a significant source for increasing word knowledge, it is imperative that students learn key strategies to help them learn new words as they are encountered. Vocabulary strategies students should know by third grade include

- using a dictionary and other reference sources to understand the meanings of unknown words
- using context to determine the meanings of unfamiliar words
- learning about the relationships between words (synonyms, antonyms, and multiple-meaning words)
- exploring shades of meaning of words that are synonyms or near-synonyms
- using morphemic analysis—breaking words into meaning-bearing components, such as prefixes and roots

At grades 3 and above, morphemic analysis becomes an even more valuable dimension of vocabulary instruction. For example, learning just one root, *astro,* can help students unlock the meanings of such words as *astronaut, astronomy, astrology,* and *astrological.*

❝ Research on vocabulary shows that for learners to come to know words in a meaningful way, they need to engage with word meanings and build habits of attending to words and exploring their uses in thoughtful and lively ways. ❞

— **Margaret C. McKeown**
Research Scientist
Learning Research and Development Center,
University of Pittsburgh

Q How does *Trophies* provide exposure to a wide variety of texts?

A *Trophies* provides students with a wealth of opportunities to read a rich variety of texts. The *Pupil Editions,* the nucleus of the program in Grades 1–6, feature a variety of high-quality literature selections that help students build vocabulary. *Trophies* also provides students with extensive reading opportunities through such components as these:

- *Big Books* (kindergarten and grade 1)
- *Read-Aloud Anthologies* (kindergarten through grade 2)
- *Library Books Collections* (kindergarten through grade 6)
- *Books for All Learners* (grades 1–6)
- *Intervention Readers* (grades 2–6)
- *Teacher's Edition* Read-Aloud Selections (grades 2–6)

Q How does the program provide multiple exposures to key vocabulary?

A Students are given many rich exposures to key vocabulary through the following program features:

- Vocabulary in context on *Teaching Transparencies*
- *Pupil Edition* and *Teacher's Edition* Vocabulary Power pages
- *Pupil Edition* main selections
- Word Study pages of the *Teacher's Edition* (grades 3–6)
- Additional Support Activities in the *Teacher's Edition*
- *Practice Books*
- *Books for All Learners*
- *Intervention Readers*

Q How does *Trophies* facilitate the teaching of vocabulary-learning strategies?

A Lessons include explicit teaching and modeling of vocabulary strategies. Specific lessons in both the *Pupil Edition* and *Teacher's Edition* provide direct instruction that helps enable students to increase their vocabulary every time they read. Strategies include using a dictionary, using context to determine word meaning, and understanding word structures and word relationships.

Look for

✔ **Building Background and Vocabulary**
✔ ***Big Book* lessons**
✔ **Listening Comprehension**
✔ **Word Study (Grades 3–6)**
✔ **Lessons on word relationships and word structure (Grades 3–6)**
✔ **Additional Support Activities**

FLUENCY

Research recognizes fluency as a strong indicator of efficient and proficient reading. A fluent reader reads with accuracy at an appropriate rate, attending to phrasing. When the reading is oral, it reflects a speech-like pace.

Oral fluency is reading with speed, accuracy, and prosody—meaning that the reader uses the stress, pitch, and juncture of spoken language. Researchers have repeatedly demonstrated the relationship between fluency and reading comprehension. If a reader must devote most of his or her cognitive attention to pronouncing words, comprehension suffers. It follows then that students who read fluently can devote more attention to meaning and thus increase their comprehension. This is why oral reading fluency is an important goal of reading instruction, especially in the elementary grades. Word recognition must be automatic—freeing cognitive resources for comprehending text. If word recognition is labored, cognitive resources are consumed by decoding, leaving little or no resources for interpretation. In Kindergarten and at the beginning of grade 1, oral reading may sound less like speech because students are still learning to decode and to identify words. Nevertheless, with appropriate support, text that "fits," and time to practice, students soon begin to read simple texts in a natural, more fluent manner. By the beginning of grade 2, many students have come to enjoy the sounds of their own voices reading. They choose to read and to reread with the natural sounds of spoken language and have few interruptions due to inadequate word attack or word recognition problems.

Fluent readers can
- recognize words automatically
- group individual words into meaningful phrases
- apply strategies rapidly to identify unknown words
- determine where to place emphasis or to pause to make sense of a text

Fluency can be developed through directed reading practice, opportunities for repeated reading, and other instructional strategies. The primary method to improve fluency is directed reading practice in accessible texts. Practice does not replace instruction; it provides the reader the opportunity to gain speed and accuracy within manageable text. One form of directed reading practice is repeated reading, which gives a developing reader more time and chances with the same text. Repeated reading
- provides practice reading words in context
- produces gains in reading rate, accuracy, and comprehension
- helps lower-achieving readers

" Children gain reading fluency when they can read at a steady rate, recognizing words accurately and achieving correctness in phrasing and intonation. "

— **Nancy Roser**
Professor, Language and Literacy Studies
The University of Texas at Austin

Q **How does *Trophies* teach and assess oral reading fluency?**

A Toward developing fluent readers, *Trophies* provides explicit, systematic phonics instruction to build word recognition skills that enable students to become efficient decoders. (See the Phonics section of these pages for more information.) *Trophies* also provides the following tools that enable teachers to assess student progress on an ongoing basis:

- Oral reading passages in the back of each *Teacher's Edition* (Grades 2-6)
- Guidelines to help teachers use these passages (Grades 2-6)
- *Oral Reading Fluency Assessment*

Q **How does *Trophies* provide intervention for students who are not developing oral reading fluency at an appropriate pace?**

A In the grades 2-6 *Intervention Resource Kit,* every day of instruction includes a fluency builder activity. Students are assigned repeated readings with cumulative texts. These readings begin with word lists, expand to include multiple sentences, and eventually become extended self-selected passages. Fluency performance-assessment activities are also provided in the *Intervention Teacher's Guides.*

Q **How does *Trophies* provide opportunities for repeated readings?**

A In grades 1–6, the Rereading for Fluency features offer a wide variety of engaging activities that have students reread with a focus on expression, pacing, and intonation. These activities include

- **Echo Reading**—Students repeat (echo) what the teacher reads aloud.
- **Choral Reading**—Students read aloud with the teacher simultaneously.
- **Repeated Reading**—The teacher models, and students reread several times until fluency is gained.
- **Readers Theatre**—Students assume roles and read them aloud from the text.

Look for

- ✔️ **Rereading for Fluency**
- ✔️ **Oral reading passages in the *Teacher's Edition***
- ✔️ ***Oral Reading Fluency Assessment***
- ✔️ ***Intervention Teacher's Guides***

ASSESSMENT

Assessment is integral to instruction. By choosing the appropriate assessment tools and methods, you can find out where your students are instructionally and plan accordingly.

Assessment is the process of collecting information in order to make instructional decisions about students. Good decisions require good information and to provide this information, assessment of students and their learning must be continuous. Because the reading process is composed of many complex skills, such as comprehension, word attack, and synthesis of information, no one assessment tool can evaluate completely all aspects of reading. Teachers need to gather information about their students in many ways, both formally and informally. Assessment helps them plan instruction, and ongoing assessments throughout the instructional process should guide their decisions and actions.

Assessment must systematically inform instruction and help teachers differentiate instruction. The first tool the classroom teacher requires is an entry-level assessment instrument to identify students' instructional level and potential for participating in grade-level instruction. This diagnostic instrument should be sensitive to gaps and strengths in student learning. After placement, teachers need differentiation strategies that are flexible and that can be easily adapted according to continual monitoring of student progress.

Assessments for monitoring progress should be used to determine ongoing priorities for instruction. The use of both formal and informal tools and strategies, including formative and summative assessments, provides a comprehensive picture of students' achievement as they progress through an instructional program. Informal assessments encourage teachers to observe students as they read, write, and discuss. These assessments provide immediate feedback and allow teachers to quickly determine which students are having difficulty and need additional instruction and practice. Formal assessments

provide opportunities for teachers to take a more focused look at how students are progressing. Whether formal or informal, monitoring instruments and activities should be

- frequent
- ongoing
- easy to score and interpret

Teachers should be provided with clear options for monitoring and clear pathways for providing intervention and enrichment as needed. Less frequent summative assessments may be used to gauge long-term growth.

Student progress needs to be communicated to parents and guardians on a regular basis. As students become more accountable for their learning through standards-based testing, teachers are becoming more accountable not only to administrators but also to families. A complete instructional program should offer means for teachers to communicate with families about how their students are progressing and how families can contribute to students' growth.

> **❝ Knowing how well a student can use literacy skills such as reading, writing, listening, and speaking is vital to effective instruction. ❞**
>
> **— Roger Farr**
> Chancellor's Professor and Director of the
> Center for Innovation in Assessment,
> Indiana University, Bloomington

Q How does *Trophies* integrate entry-level group and individual assessments with instruction?

A The *Placement and Diagnostic Assessment* provides an overview of specific diagnostic information about prerequisite skills for each grade level. In addition, *Reading and Language Skills Assessment* pretests can be used to determine whether students need additional instruction and practice in phonics, comprehension skills, vocabulary, writing, and writing conventions.

Q What monitoring instruments are included with *Trophies*?

A Formative assessments that facilitate monitoring student progress include

- Diagnostic Checks at point of use for immediate assessment of understanding, with follow-up Additional Support Activities in the *Teacher's Edition*
- Ongoing Assessment to assess and model the use of reading strategies, in the *Teacher's Edition*
- *Intervention Assessment Book*
- Performance Assessment activities in the *Teacher's Edition*
- *End-of-Selection Tests* to monitor students' comprehension of each selection

In each theme's *Teacher's Edition*, the Theme Assessment to Plan Instruction section provides a clear road map for using assessment to adapt instruction to student needs.

Q What other assessment instruments are used in *Trophies*?

A The *Reading and Language Skills Assessment*, which includes posttests for end-of-theme assessment and Mid-Year and End-of-Year Tests, provides information about students' mastery of reading skills. Other assessments instruments in *Trophies* include

- *Holistic Assessment*, which uses authentic, theme-related passages and provides a more global, holistic evaluation of students' reading and writing ability
- *Oral Reading Fluency Assessment*, which monitors accuracy and rate
- *Assessment Handbook* (Kindergarten)

Look for

In the *Teacher's Edition*
✓ **Diagnostic Checks**
✓ **Ongoing Assessment**
✓ **Performance Assessment**
✓ **Theme Assessment to Plan Instruction**

Other Components
✓ *Placement* and *Diagnostic Assessments*
✓ *Reading and Language Skills Assessment (Pretests and Posttests)*
✓ *Holistic Assessment*
✓ *Oral Reading Fluency Assessment*
✓ *Assessment Handbook (Kindergarten)*

WRITING

Good writing skills are critical both to students'
academic achievement and to their future success
in society.

Writing instruction should incorporate explicit modeling and practice in the conventions of written English. All students can benefit from systematic instruction and practice in spelling, grammar, usage, mechanics, and presentation skills, such as handwriting and document preparation. Mastering these conventions enables students to communicate their ideas and information clearly and effectively.

- In kindergarten, children should use their growing knowledge of language structure and the conventions of print to begin expressing their ideas through words and pictures and putting these ideas into writing, with words spelled phonetically.

- In grades 1–3, students should continue to transfer their developing reading skills to writing conventions by using their knowledge of word structure and phonics to spell new words. They should learn and apply the fundamentals of grammar, mechanics, and sentence structure.

- In grades 4–6, instruction should build advanced spelling, grammar, and mechanics skills and should apply them in student writing of narratives, descriptions, and other extended compositions. Students should be systematically taught to apply writing conventions in purposeful writing activities.

Students should learn about and practice the process skills that good writers use. Many students do not realize, until they are told, that most stories and articles are not written in one sitting. Good writers plan, revise, rewrite, and rethink during the process of writing. Instruction in writing processes can spring from author features and interviews with the writers whose works students are reading. The teacher's modeling of effective prewriting, drafting, revising, proofreading, and publishing techniques should build upon this understanding. Particular attention should systematically be paid to revision strategies such as adding, deleting, clarifying, and rearranging text. Students

should apply these strategies to their own work repeatedly and should learn new techniques gradually and cumulatively.

Systematic instruction in writer's craft skills should be applied to the process. Students should be taught that, whatever the form of their writing, they must determine a clear focus, organize their ideas, use effective word choice and sentence structures, and express their own viewpoint. These writer's craft skills should be taught through focused exercises and writing tasks and should be reinforced cumulatively in lessons that teach the elements of longer writing forms.

> **Effective writing is both an art and a science. The ability to generate interesting ideas and a pleasing style characterizes the art side; mastering the craft and its conventions characterizes the science side. Good instruction judiciously attends to both.**
>
> — **Dorothy S. Strickland**
> The State of New Jersey
> Professor of Reading,
> Rutgers University

Q **How does *Trophies* provide instruction and practice in the conventions of written English?**

A *Trophies* provides systematic, explicit instruction and abundant practice in spelling, grammar, usage, and mechanics in daily, easy-to-use lessons. Transparencies, activities, and practice sheets are provided for modeling and practice. Presentation skills are also formally taught, with an emphasis on handwriting at the lower grades. Spelling instruction, especially at the primary grades, is closely linked to phonics instruction. All skills of conventions are applied in purposeful writing activities.

Q **How does *Trophies* teach the process of writing?**

A From the earliest grades, students using *Trophies* learn that good writers plan and revise their writing. Students are guided through the prewriting, drafting, revising, and proofreading stages with models, practice activities, graphic organizers, and checklists. Instruction in presentation skills, such as handwriting and speaking, guides the publishing stage. Teacher rubrics for evaluation are provided at point of use, and reproducible student rubrics are provided in the back of the *Teacher's Edition*.

Q **How does *Trophies* apply writer's craft instruction to the writing process?**

A In kindergarten, students begin to write sentences and brief narratives about familiar experiences. Students also engage in shared and interactive writing in kindergarten through grade 2. In grades 1 and 2, instruction in story grammar and sentence types becomes more sophisticated, with students learning about and applying one component, such as capitalization, at a time. In grades 2–6, explicit writer's craft lessons are built into the writing strand and follow this format:

- Weeks 1 and 2 of the unit present writer's craft skills, such as organizing, choosing words, and writing effective sentences. Students complete targeted exercises and apply the craft in relatively brief writing forms.
- Weeks 3 and 4 present longer writing forms, emphasizing the steps of the writing process. The writer's craft skills learned in Weeks 1 and 2 are applied in longer compositions.
- In grades 3–6, Week 5 presents a timed writing test in which students apply what they have learned.

Look for

- ✔ Writer's Craft lessons
- ✔ Writing Process lessons
- ✔ Timed or Tested Writing lessons
- ✔ 5-day grammar and spelling lessons
- ✔ Traits of good writing

LISTENING AND SPEAKING

Increasingly, young people must comprehend, and
are expected to create, messages that are oral and visual
rather than strictly written. Listening and speaking skills are
essential to achievement in both reading and writing.

Listening to narratives, poetry, and nonfiction texts builds thinking and language skills that students need for success in reading and writing. The domains of the language arts (listening, speaking, reading, and writing) are closely connected. Listening instruction and speaking instruction are critical scaffolds that support reading comprehension, vocabulary knowledge, and oral communication skills. Classroom instruction must be focused on these skills and must also strategically address the needs of students with limited levels of language experience or whose language experiences are primarily in languages other than English.

Listening instruction and speaking instruction should progress developmentally through the grades. In the primary grades, instruction should focus on

- listening to and retelling stories, with an emphasis on story grammar (setting, characters, and important events)
- explicit modeling of standard English structures, with frequent opportunities to repeat sentences and recite rhymes and songs
- brief oral presentations about familiar topics and experiences
- developing familiarity with academic and literary terms

As students move up the grades, they should develop increasingly sophisticated listening and speaking skills, including the more complex production skills. By grades 4–6, students should be increasingly capable of

- delivering both narrative and expository presentations using a range of narrative and rhetorical devices
- modeling their own presentations on effective text structures they have analyzed in their reading
- orally responding to literature in ways that demonstrate advanced understanding and insight
- supporting their interpretations with facts and specific examples
- interpreting and using verbal and nonverbal messages
- analyzing oral and visual messages, purposes, and persuasive techniques

“ Oral response activities encourage critical thinking and allow students to bring their individuality to the process of responding to literature. **”**

— **Hallie Kay Yopp**
Professor
Department of Elementary Bilingual
and Reading Education,
California State University, Fullerton

Q **How does *Trophies* provide rich listening experiences that build understanding of language structures and texts?**

A From the very first day of kindergarten through the end of grade 6, *Trophies* provides abundant and varied texts, support, and modeling for listening instruction. With resources such as *Big Books, Read-Aloud Anthologies,* and Audiotext of the reading selections, the teacher has every type of narrative and expository text available. *Trophies* also provides direct instruction and engaging response activities so that teachers can use each listening selection to its full advantage. The *English-Language Learners Resource Kit* provide additional opportunities for students with special needs to develop an understanding of English language structure, concept vocabulary and background, and listening comprehension skills.

Q **How does *Trophies* develop listening through the grades?**

A Listening is developed through the Sharing Literature features in kindergarten through grade 2 with such options as Build Concept Vocabulary, Developing Listening Comprehension, and Listen and Respond and through the *Read-Aloud Anthologies.* In grades 3–6, read-alouds serve as a vehicle for setting a purpose for listening and they develop listening comprehension and listening strategies.

Q **How does *Trophies* provide instruction in speaking and in making presentations?**

A *Trophies* provides instruction to guide students in making both narrative and expository presentations. In kindergarten, each lesson offers formal and informal speaking opportunities through the Share Time feature. In grades 1 and 2, speaking activities are included in the Rereading for Fluency and in the Wrap-Up sections of the lesson. The Morning Message feature in kindergarten through grade 2 provides additional informal speaking opportunities. In grades 3–6, presentation skills become more sophisticated. Students are asked to make such presentations as extended oral reports, multimedia presentations, debates, and persuasive speeches.

Look for

- ✔ Developing Listening Comprehension
- ✔ Daily "Sharing Literature" activities (Kindergarten–Grade 2)
- ✔ Read-Aloud selections and instruction with every lesson (Grades 2–6)
- ✔ Morning Message (Kindergarten–Grade 2)
- ✔ Author's Chair presentations in (Kindergarten–Grade 2)
- ✔ Rereading for Fluency
- ✔ Listening and Speaking Lessons (Grades 3–6)
- ✔ Presentation Rubrics (Grades 2–6)
- ✔ Read-Aloud Anthologies (Kindergarten–Grade 2)

RESEARCH AND INFORMATION SKILLS

Today's increasing amount of accessible information and ideas mandates an explicit approach to research and information skills and strategies.

Information is more widely available to the general public than ever before, and having the skills and strategies to effectively access and produce information is increasingly important. Evaluating and producing electronically transmitted information is becoming a basic literacy skill, as well as a skill that can lead to a more rewarding working life. Students who do not receive instruction in information skills are at a clear disadvantage. The goal of such instruction should be to prepare students to carry these skills into many areas so that students can be independent seekers, consumers, and providers of information throughout their lives.

Instruction in research and information skills should begin at an early age. By grade 2, students should be learning to choose reference sources for specific purposes, such as to clarify word meanings or to find colorful, exact words for their own writing. In grade 3, students should refine their dictionary skills and become familiar with the structure of other reference sources, such as atlases and encyclopedias. In grade 4 and above, students should become more proficient with

- using a variety of print and electronic information media, such as newspapers, almanacs, library catalogs, and other online sources
- basic keyboarding and word processing skills
- computer usage skills, such as efficient Internet searching and document creation
- using tables of contents, indexes, and other document features to locate information
- taking notes efficiently
- evaluating the quality of information
- finding information in a library
- using references sources as an aid to writing

As students move up the grades, they should learn to produce and deliver increasingly lengthy, well-researched informational reports. Because the language arts domains (reading, writing, listening, and speaking) are closely interrelated, the text structures students learn through their reading become structures they can use to effectively present their own research. Students should be able to compose, revise, edit, and publish their research findings by using a computer. Other skills for students in the upper grades include substantive inquiry, framing questions to develop the research logically, identifying and securing multiple reference sources, analyzing and synthesizing information, and summarizing and evaluating the research results.

Q **How does *Trophies* provide instruction in using reference sources, including computer-based resources?**

A Direct instruction is provided through explicit skill lessons. Instruction includes such skills as recognizing authoritative sources and evaluating information. These lessons include

- Using a Dictionary
- Locating Information: Online Information
- Locating Information: Text Features/Book Parts
- Locating Information: Newspapers, Magazines, and Reference Sources
- Search Techniques

Q **What technological resources are available for use by students with *Trophies*?**

A *The Learning Site* (www.harcourtschool.com) offers, among many other features, motivating, interactive activities that challenge students to practice and apply skills taught in the *Pupil Edition* and *Teacher's Edition.*

Other resources available for students include

- Writing Express ™ *CD-ROMs* (activities that provide reinforcement of language and writing skills)
- *Mission: Comprehension*™ *Reading Skills Practice* (practice and reinforcement of comprehension skills)
- *Phonics Express*™ *CD-ROM* (captivating games and activities that reinforce phonics skills)
- *Media Literacy and Communication Skills Package*™ (a set of videotapes and accompanying Teacher's Guides that reinforce listening, speaking, viewing and presentation skills)

Q **How are students taught to develop research reports and other informational projects?**

A In grades I–2, the Making Connections sections in the *Pupil's Editions* and the Cross-Curricular Centers in the *Teacher's Editions* offer activities that rerquire students to gather and present information. In grades 3–6, students engage in a full theme's worth of instruction in all stages of writing a research report, including gathering information, note-taking, outlining, drafting, revising, and publishing. Students also have the opportunity to use information and research skills to complete a theme project, which involves formulating research questions and recording and presenting their research findings.

Look for

✔ **Skill lessons with Teaching Transparencies**
✔ **Research Report Writing lessons**
✔ **Theme Projects**
✔ **Presentation Rubrics**
✔ **Technology integrated with the lesson plans**

REACHING ALL LEARNERS

Students come to school with diverse experiences and language backgrounds. Teachers, who are charged with providing universal access to high-quality instruction, require specially designed plans and materials to help all students meet or exceed grade-level standards.

Curriculum and instruction must be carefully planned to provide for students who need varying levels of intervention and challenge. Students require additional instruction, practice, and extension at different times and in different degrees. Some students need occasional reteaching and slight modifications in pacing, while others are at greater risk and require more intensive intervention. Research shows that students with learning difficulties need more review and practice to perform a new task automatically. Instruction should cumulatively integrate simpler or previously learned tasks with newer, more complex activities. In addition, research shows the following:

- Reading difficulties can stem from inaccuracy in identifying words.
- Intervention should be geared toward a student's level of reading development.
- Diagnostic testing results should show what students know and what they need to know; frequent assessment is critical.
- Instruction should be direct and explicit.

Curriculum and instruction must be structured to meet the needs of English-language learners. The 2000 U.S. Census confirmed what many educators already knew: more and more students do not speak English as their first language. Widely ranging levels of English proficiency in mainstream classrooms present special challenges and opportunities for teachers. Depending on their level of English acquisition and their grade placement, English-language learners need varying degrees of additional support in areas such as oral language, English phonology, vocabulary, background information, and the academic language of school.

Students who already meet or exceed grade-level expectations need opportunities for enrichment or acceleration. They need to be challenged by vocabulary extension study and exposure to sophisticated literature in a variety of genres. Students may also be encouraged to carry out investigations that extend their learning. Such activities should promote sustained investigative skills: raising questions, researching answers, and organizing information. Several research studies have shown the importance of setting high standards for advanced learners. An instructional program that clearly provides for differentiation at a variety of levels can be the tool teachers need to provide universal access to high-level standards.

> **❝** In the process of helping students learn, we want to support them in discovering that each person is unique and has a unique contribution to make towards creating a better world for all. **❞**
>
> — **Alma Flor Ada**
> Director of Doctoral Studies in the International Multicultural Program University of San Francisco
>
> — **F. Isabel Campoy**
> Former President, Association of Spanish Professionals in the USA

Q **How does** *Trophies* **provide differentiated instruction at a variety of levels?**

A *Trophies* was designed to accommodate a diverse student population, with tiers of differentiation for different needs. Diagnostic Checks, with brief activities, are positioned at point of use within each lesson in the *Teacher's Edition* so that specific needs of students can be identified and addressed. Additional Support Activities, tied closely to the lessons, are provided for further differentiation. The three types of activities address below-level readers, advanced students, and English-language learners. In addition, Alternative Teaching Strategies are provided for students who perform below level on the *Reading and Language Skills Assessments.* The *Library Books Collections* and the *Books for All Learners* also provide students at all levels with a wealth of reading opportunities in a variety of genres.

Q **What additional support does** *Trophies* **provide?**

A An *Intervention Resource Kit* and an *English-Language Learners Resource Kit* are available for students with greater needs.
Both kits
- align closely with the core program
- provide rigorous daily lessons
- provide abundant cumulative, spiraled practice

For below-level readers, the *Intervention Resource Kit* preteaches and reteaches the same skills and concepts that are taught in the core program. The *English-Language Learners Resource Kit* builds background, vocabulary and concepts, academic language, comprehension, and language arts. Finally, to guide teachers in making instructional decisions, *Trophies* provides a complete assessment program, with instruments for entry-level assessment, monitoring of progress, and summative assessment. (See the Assessment section of these pages for more information.)

Look for

✔ **Reaching All Learners**
✔ **Diagnostic Checks**
✔ **Additional Support Activities**
✔ **Practice pages for all levels**
✔ *Books for All Learners*
✔ *Intervention Resource Kit*
✔ *English-Language Learners Resource Kit*
✔ *Library Books Collections*
✔ *Placement and Diagnostic Assessments*

CLASSROOM MANAGEMENT

The task of managing the classroom is becoming increasingly complex. Teachers are seeking to maximize instructional effectiveness for students with a diverse range of skills and backgrounds.

Classroom management is a critical variable related to student achievement. Research shows that the more time teachers spend dealing with student behavior and interruptions in instruction, the more student achievement suffers. A classroom environment that promotes student growth and learning results from making effective decisions about the organization and scheduling of instruction and the physical arrangement of the classroom.

Effective organization includes differentiating instruction to engage all students in instructional-level activities. Grouping strategies are important for addressing diverse needs, but grouping must never be treated as an aim in itself. Flexible grouping can help ensure that all students meet instructional goals, and it can be effective in helping students participate and contribute in a learning environment. Grouping should be fluid and temporary, varying according to individual students' progress and interests and should allow time for students to function independently and be responsible for their own work. The types of instruction that are most successful in the major grouping patterns include

Whole Group
- Sharing literature
- Developing concepts
- Providing modeling
- Presenting new knowledge

Small Group
- Developing skills
- Practicing processes
- Collaborating on projects
- Providing challenge activities

After flexible work groups are established, effective classroom organization should focus on scheduling classroom activities and creating a classroom arrangement that facilitates learning. Initially, teachers might establish one or two learning centers based on tasks that are familiar to students. Then teachers can develop other centers and routines as needed. Before beginning a routine, teachers should introduce students to the procedures for using each area, ensuring that students understand what they are to do and how much time they should spend in each area. A rotation schedule should be established so that students can easily move from one area to another as tasks are completed. Helping students become familiar with schedules and routines enables the teacher to devote more time to individual and small-group instruction.

> **" The organization of the classroom should provide students with many opportunities to share with teachers and other students the things they are reading and writing. "**
>
> — **Roger Farr**
> Chancellor's Professor and Director of the
> Center for Innovation in Assessment,
> Indiana University, Bloomington

Q **How can teachers keep other students engaged in meaningful experiences while providing instruction to students with special needs?**

A *Trophies* provides an abundance of productive materials and ideas for independent and small-group work

- Managing the Classroom sections in the back of the *Teacher's Editions* provide clear instructions in arranging the classroom with centers or stations, using a Work Board with center incons to help organize routines and schedules, and tracking student progress.
- Classroom Management and Reading and Writing Routines sections in the *Teacher's Editions* (grades 1–2) provide suggestions for individual, whole-group, and small-group activities.
- Cross-Curricular Centers and Stations with pacing suggestions regulate student participation.
- Content is integrated from social studies, science, and other content areas.
- *Books for All Learners* allow students to read independently at their own level.
- Practice pages are included for students with diverse skills and language backgrounds.
- Theme Projects are included for extended group work.
- *Comprehension Cards, Library Books Collections,* and other resources facilitate group and independent reading.

Q **How does *Trophies* help teachers manage its instructional pathways for classrooms with diverse learners?**

A *Trophies* provides a clear, manageable system of diagnostic assessment checkpoints, ongoing formal assessment and performance-based opportunities, and instructional pathways for teachers to follow based on results. In addition to easy-to-use lesson planners that include suggested pacing, the system provides

- Diagnostic Checks and customized activities at point of use
- Additional Support Activities to reinforce, reteach, and extend key concepts in every lesson
- *Intervention Resource Kits* and *English-Language Learners Resource Kits* for more intensive instruction
- Alternative Teaching Strategies for additional options to modify instruction

For more information, see Theme Assessment to Plan Instruction in each *Teacher's Edition.*

Look for

✓ **Diagnostic Checks**
✓ **Cross-Curricular Centers or Stations**
✓ **Workboards**
✓ ***Books for All Learners***
✓ ***Library Books Collections***
✓ **Practice pages**
✓ **Theme Projects**
✓ **Comprehension Cards**
✓ **Managing the Classroom**

Contents

Theme 7: Bug Surprises

Consonants *Bb, Kk*
Short Vowel *Oo*

Theme 8: Animal Adventures

Consonants /w/*w*, /ks/*x*

Reference Materials

THEME 5

Family Ties

Living, working, and playing are ties that bind families and friends together. Children will discover what it means to care for one another and how to help each other learn and grow.

Theme Resources

READING MATERIALS

Big Book

◀ *Off We Go!*
by Jane Yolen
illustrated by Laurel Molk

Library Books

◀ *A Birthday Basket for Tía*
by Pat Mora
illustrated by Cecily Lang

◀ *Dear Juno*
by Soyung Pak
illustrated by Susan
Kathleen Harthung

Big Book of Rhymes and Songs

◀ *Winter Birds*
◀ *The Very Nicest Place*

Read-Aloud Anthology

◀ *Let's Go, Froggy!* by Jonathan London
◀ *The Three Bears* retold by Anne Rockwell
◀ *Grandfather and I* by Helen E. Buckley
◀ *The Three Little Pigs* retold by Anne Rockwell
◀ *Jamaica's Find* by Juanita Havill

Independent Readers

▲*Pop-Pop*   ▲*Play Cake*   ▲*Too Little*

PHONICS

**Theme 5
Practice Book**

**Phonics
Practice Book**

Pre-decodable Books

▲*The Park*   ▲*Sit on My Chair*   ▲*My Pig*

Alphabet Patterns

gate, fish, igloo
pages TI3-TI5

Phonics Express™ CD-ROM

Level A

TEACHING TOOLS

Big Alphabet Cards

Gg, Ff, Ii

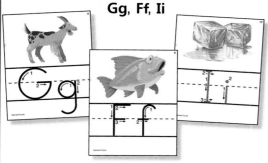

Letter and Sound Charts

Charts 23, 2, and 17

Letter and Sound Chart Sentence Strips

23, 2 , 17

Wiggle, giggle, Geese in the sun.

High-Frequency Word Cards

on, to

Picture/Word Cards

Teacher's Resource Book

pages 73, 52, 67

Oo-pples and Boo-noo-noos

English-Language Learners Kit

Intervention Kit

MANIPULATIVES

Tactile Letter Cards

Write-On/Wipe-Off Board
Letters and Sounds Place Mat

Word Builder and Word Builder Cards

Magnetic Letters

Aa Bb Cc

ASSESSMENT

Assessment Handbook
Group Inventory
Theme 5 Test

Big Book ▶

Library Book ▶

Week 1

	Week 1
• **Sharing Literature** • **Listening Comprehension**	**Big Book:** *Off We Go!* **Library Book:** *A Birthday Basket for Tia* **Read-Aloud Anthology:** *"Let's Go, Froggy!"* **Big Book of Rhymes and Songs:** *"Winter Birds"*
• **Phonemic Awareness** • **Phonics** • **High-Frequency Words**	Consonant /g/*g* **T** Consonant /f/ *f* **T** Review Consonants *Gg, Ff* **T** High-Frequency Words *on, to* **T**
• **Reading**	**Pre-decodable Book 12:** *The Park* **Independent Reader 12:** *Pop-Pop*
• **Writing**	**Shared Writing** Naming Words List **Interactive Writing** Sentences Birthday Message **Independent Writing** Captions
• **Cross-Curricular Centers**	👑 **Manipulatives** Family Puzzles ABC **Letters and Words** Letter Match 🌐 **Math** Four and Five 👑 **Manipulatives** Long and Short ☕ **Cooking** A Birthday Party

T = tested skill

Week 2

	Week 2
	Big Book: *Off We Go!* **Library Book:** *Dear Juno* **Read-Aloud Anthology:** *"The Three Bears"* **Big Book Rhymes and Songs:** *"The Very Nicest Place"*
	Short Vowel /i/ *i* **T** Blending /i/ - /t/ Words with /i/ and /t/
	Pre-decodable Book 13: *Sit on My Chair* **Independent Reader 13:** *Play Cake*
	Shared Writing Letter Story **Interactive Writing** Opposites Story **Independent Writing** Animals Sentence
	👑 **Manipulatives** Animal Sort ✏️ **Writing** Dotted *i*'s 🎭 **Drama** Puppet Play 🧱 **Block** My Dream House 🎧 **Listening** Audiotext

Library Book ▶

Week 3

Big Book: *Off We Go!*

Library Book: *Dear Juno*

Read-Aloud Anthology: *"Jamaica's Find"*
"Grandfather and I"
"The Three Little Pigs"

Review Consonant /g/g,
Short Vowel /I/i T

Blending /i/ - /g/

Words with /i/ and /g/ g

Review Blending /i/ - /g/

Pre-decodable Book 14: *My Pig*

Independent Reader 14: *Too Little*

Shared Writing
Writing Process:
Write a Story

 Science
Call Me on My Phone

 Social Studies
"I Like You" Bracelets

 Math
A House for Me

 Social Studies
My Family Tree

 Literacy
Let's Read

Theme Organizer
Half-Day Kindergarten

Use the following chart to help organize your half-day kindergarten schedule. Choose independent activities as time allows during your day.

ORAL LANGUAGE

Morning Message
Phonemic Awareness
Sharing Literature
- Big Book: Off We Go!
- Library Book: *A Birthday Basket for Tía*
- Library Book: *Dear Juno*
- *Read-Aloud Anthology*
- *Big Book of Rhymes and Songs*

LEARNING TO READ

Phonics
Pre-decodable Books 12–14
- *The Park*
- *Sit on My Chair*
- *My Pig*

High-Frequency Words

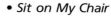 **Independent 12–14**
- *Pop-Pop*
- *Play Cake*
- *Too Little*

LANGUAGE ARTS

Shared Writing
Interactive Writing
Independent Writing
Writing Every Day

INDEPENDENT ACTIVITIES

Sharing Literature
Respond to Literature
Phonics
Independent Practice
Handwriting
Practice Book pages
High-Frequency Words
Independent Practice
Practice Book pages

About the
Authors and Illustrators

Jane Yolen

Author of *Off We Go!*
Jane Yolen is an award-winning author of many books. Her titles include *The Girl in the Golden Bower,* and *Child of Faerie, Child of Earth.* Yolen and her husband have homes in Massachusetts and in Scotland.

Laurel Molk

Illustrator of *Off We Go!*
Laurel Molk has an assortment of animals like the ones described in *Off We Go!* at her home in Massachusetts. She illustrated *Beneath the Ghost Moon,* also written by Jane Yolen.

Pat Mora

Author of *A Birthday Basket for Tía*
Pat Mora grew up in El Paso, Texas. The Mexican American community where she grew up has influenced her writing. Her work has been published in textbooks, anthologies, and her own collections of poetry. Mora has also written *Pablo's Tree,* which is illustrated by Cecily Lang.

Soyung Pak

Author of *Dear Juno*
Soyung Pak was born in Korea and grew up outside Philadelphia. As an adult, she visited family members in Korea and took photographs to give to the illustrator of *Dear Juno,* her first book.

Susan Kathleen Hartung

Illustrator of *Dear Juno*
Susan Kathleen Hartung earned a BFA at the School of Visual Arts in New York City. She now lives in Brooklyn with her dog, cat, and goldfish. Dear Juno is her first book.

Cecily Lang

Illustrator of *A Birthday Basket for Tía*
Cecily Lang was born and raised in New York City, where she currently works as an illustrator.

Theme Assessment

MONITORING OF PROGRESS

After completing the theme, most children should show progress toward mastery of the following skills:

Concepts of Print
- ❑ Identify the front cover, back cover, and title page of a book.
- ❑ Follow words from left to right and from top to bottom on the printed page.

Phonemic Awareness
- ❑ Blend vowel consonant sounds orally to make words or syllables.
- ❑ Track auditorily each word in a sentence and each syllable in a word.

Phonics and Decoding
- ❑ Match all consonant sounds and short-vowel sounds to appropriate letters.
- ❑ Read one-syllable and High-Frequency Words.
- ❑ Understand that as letters of words change, so do the sounds.

Vocabulary and High-Frequency Words
- ❑ Read High-Frequency Words *on* and *to.*
- ❑ Identify and sort common words in basic categories.
- ❑ Learn words associated with the calendar.

Comprehension
- ❑ Connect to life experiences the information and events in texts.
- ❑ Understand a story problem and solution.

Literary Response
- ❑ Identify characters, settings, and important events.
- ❑ Identify different types of everyday print materials.

Writing
- ❑ Use letters and phonetically spelled words to write about experiences, stories, people, objects, or events.
- ❑ Write uppercase and lowercase letters of the alphabet independently, attending to the form and proper spacing of the letters.

Listening and Speaking
- ❑ Recite and act out a short poem.
- ❑ Relate an experience or creative story in a logical sequence.

Assessment Options

Assessment Handbook
- Group Inventory
- Phonemic Awareness Inventory
- Theme Skills Assessment
- Concepts About Print Inventory
- Observational Checklists

Reaching All Learners

■ BELOW-LEVEL

Levels of Support

Point-of-use Notes in the Teacher's Edition

pp. 23, 25, 35, 39, 41, 43, 49, 55, 59, 61, 63, 69, 73, 85, 91, 93, 95, 99, 101, 103, 107, 109, 115, 119, 129, 133, 137, 141, 145, 149, 153, 155, 156

Additional Support Activities

High-Frequency Words:
pp. S2–S3

Comprehension and Skills:
pp. S12–S13, S18–S19

Phonemic Awareness:
pp. S4–S5, S10–S11, S14–S15

Phonics:
pp. S6–S7, S8–S9, S16–S17

Intervention Resource Kit

■ ENGLISH-LANGUAGE LEARNERS

Levels of Support

Point-of-use Notes in the Teacher's Edition

pp. 51, 53, 55, 59, 65, 71, 73, 83, 87, 95, 99, 103, 109, 111, 117, 129, 141, 149, 155, 163, 165

Additional Support Activities

High-Frequency Words:
pp. S2–S3

Comprehension and Skills:
pp. S12–S13, S18–S19

Phonemic Awareness:
pp. S4–S5, S10–S11, S14–S15

Phonics:
pp. S6–S7, S8–S9, S16–S17

 Visit *The Learning Site!* at
www.harcourtschool.com
See Language Support activities

English-Language Learners Resource Kit

■ ADVANCED

Levels of Challenge

Point-of-use Notes in the Teacher's Edition

pp. 25, 35, 45, 55, 59, 63, 71, 73,87, 95, 99, 103, 107, 109, 115, 119, 129, 131, 139, 141, 147, 149, 155, 156, 161, 165

Additional Support Activities

High-Frequency Words:
pp. S2–S3

Comprehension and Skills:
pp. S12–S13, S18–S19

Phonemic awareness:
pp. S4–S5, S10–S11, S14–S15

Phonics:
pp. S6–S7, S8–S9, S16–S17

Accelerated Instruction

Use higher-grade-level materials for accelerated instruction.

Theme Project, pp. 12

Combination Classrooms
Buddy Reading
Have children spend their independent reading time reading with a partner. Try to include an advanced reader and a beginning reader in each pair, regardless of their age or grade. Encourage each pair to record titles of books they enjoyed.

Students with Special Needs
Building Confidence
Children with special needs may need extra support in reading. Provide many opportunities for children to read and reread texts they can successfully read. Once children gain confidence in their reading ability, challenge them to read new texts and support them in their efforts.

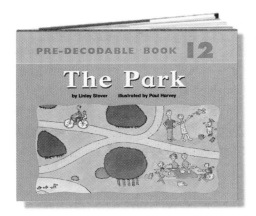

Recommended Reading

Below are suggestions for reading materials that will meet kindergarten children's diverse needs. Books that are on a child's level provide support for new skills. Advanced books give children an opportunity to stretch and challenge their reading potential. Read-aloud books are important because they expose children to story language and vocabulary.

■ BELOW-LEVEL

Do You Want to Be My Friend? by Eric Carle. Crowell, 1988. A little mouse tries hard to find a friend and finally finds one in this nearly wordless book.

A Boy, a Dog, and a Frog by Mercer Mayer. Dial, 1967. A wordless book of a boy's adventures.

We Are Playing by Jan Pritchett. Rigby, 2003. Read about children playing and many kinds of fun.

Pancakes for Breakfast by Tomie dePaola. Harcourt, 1978. A lady attempts to have pancakes for breakfast, but she doesn't have enough supplies.

■ ON-LEVEL

Goodnight Moon by Margaret Wise Brown. HarperCollins, 1991. A young rabbit says goodnight to everything in his room before going to sleep.

Look What I Can Do by Jose Aruego. Aladdin, 1998. Two water buffalo show off the things they can do, leading to a bigger adventure than they expected.

Just Like Daddy by Frank Asch. Aladdin.,1981. A young bear describes all the activities he does during the day which are just like his daddy's.

Henry by F.R. Robinson. Instant Reader, Harcourt, 1997. Henry is a little different from the other members of his family.

■ ADVANCED

We Eat Rice by Min Hong. Lee & Low, 2000. A family finds many different ways to eat their favorite food—rice.

Snazzy Aunties by Nick Sharrat. Candlewick, 1996. A boy has many aunts who are very different from one another.

Best Friends by Marcia Leonard. Millbrook, 1999. Two girls who are very different are the best of friends.

Lucky Song by Vera B. Williams. Greenwillow, 1997. Family members help Evie make all her wishes come true.

■ READ ALOUD

Little Bear by Elsa Holmelund Minarik. HarperCollins, 1985. These simple stories feature Little Bear and his mother in familiar family situations.

Pablo's Tree by Pat Mora. Simon & Schuster, 1994. Pablo's grandfather decorates his special tree for his birthday.

Shoes from Grandpa by Mem Fox. Orchard, 1992. This cumulative story tells how family members contribute to Jessie's wardrobe once Grandpa has given her a new pair of shoes.

Extraordinary Friends by Fred Rogers. Putnam, 2000. Through photographs and text, friendships between children with physical challenges are explored.

Homework Ideas

Visit *The Learning Site*: www.harcourtschool.com See Resources for Parents and Teachers: Homework Helper

	Literature	Phonics	Language Arts	Theme	Cross-Curricular
WEEK 1	Draw and write about the people in your **family**.	Draw and label a picture of two objects whose names begin with **the /f/ sound**.	Write or dictate sentences **about a trip** you took with your family.	Sort through some family photographs. Write captions for your **favorite pictures**.	Work with a family member to make a list of uncles, aunts, or cousins. **Count** the number in each category.
WEEK 2	Draw and write about your **favorite birthday party**.	Make up a riddle whose answer has **the /i/ sound**. Ask a friend or family member to solve the riddle.	Write a birthday party **invitation**. Decorate the invitation with a picture.	Look at some old photographs of you or members of your family. **Draw and write** about how you and others have changed.	Look at a calendar with a family member and mark the days that are **holidays** or special **family occasions**.
WEEK 3	**Draw a picture** to send to a relative. Write a short message.	Write the name of a friend whose name begins with **the /f/ or /g/ sound**.	**Write a letter** to a friend or family member.	Draw and write about your **favorite relative**.	Look at a **map** with a family member to find places where your relatives live.

Family Ties 11

"Helping Hands" Mural

Materials

- Teacher's Resource Book page 11
- chart paper
- markers
- butcher paper
- paper
- paints
- brushes
- glue sticks

School-Home Connection

Invite family members to visit the classroom to view the mural and to hear children talk about the helpful things they do. Give children time to practice their speeches, rehearsing with them how to speak slowly and clearly, and how to look at the audience as they speak.

Visit *The Learning Site!* at **www.harcourtschool.com**

Introduce

Tell children they are going to make a "Helping Hands" mural. Show children how to trace their hand with a marker, and explain that their hands will be part of the mural. Then ask children how they help family and friends, and list responses on chart paper. Tell children that they will paint a picture of something they do to help others.

Send home the Family Letter to encourage family members to participate in the project.

Prepare

- Children should paint a picture of themselves doing something helpful.

- Put up a sheet of butcher paper, and have children arrange their pictures on it. Children can trace their hands onto the mural paper so it looks as though their hands are holding the pictures. Have children write their names on their hands.

Share

Have each child prepare a short speech to tell how they are helpful at home, in school, and with friends. Children should point out their painting and describe what they are doing in it. Then have children thank visitors for coming to their classroom.

Teacher Notes

Learning Centers

Choose from the following suggestions to enhance your learning centers for the theme Family Ties.
(Additional learning centers for this theme can be found on pages 76 and 122)

SOCIAL STUDIES CENTER

Make a Family Tree

Give children a shape paper with a picture of a bare-limbed tree. Tell them to draw small pictures of each of the people in their family on another piece of paper. Then have children label and cut out the pictures and glue them to the tree as leaves. Children can take turns telling a partner about their family trees.

Materials

- bare-limbed tree pattern (page T22)
- paper
- crayons
- safety scissors
- glue stick
- pencils and markers

WRITING CENTER

Write About a Friend

Tell children to think of something they like to do with a friend. Then give them a piece of paper and tell them to write two sentences telling about their friend and what they like to do together. Have children illustrate their sentences. When finished, children can read their sentences aloud to one another.

Materials

- paper
- pencils
- crayons

MATH CENTER

How Many People Are in Your Family?

Have children work with partners. Give each child a piece of paper. Tell children to list the people in their family on the paper. Then have partners use counters to count how many people are in each of their families. Have partners compare lists to see whether one family is larger than the other.

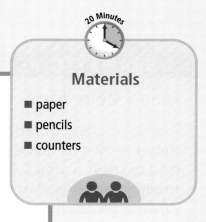

Mom ●   Dad ●
Granma ●   Poppa ●
Cybil ●   Zoe ●
Roger ●   Ralph ●
Me ●

20 Minutes

Materials

- paper
- pencils
- counters

ART CENTER

Family Portrait

Invite children to draw a picture of their whole family doing something together, such as taking a walk, having a picnic, eating dinner, or celebrating a special event. When children finish, have them center and glue their drawing onto a piece of construction paper that is slightly larger than the drawing. The construction paper becomes a frame for the drawing.

20 Minutes

Materials

- paper
- crayons
- construction paper
- glue stick

DRAMATIC PLAY CENTER

May I Help You?

Provide a variety of props that can be used to act out chores or jobs, at home, in school, or at jobs. Call on one child to select a prop to act out a job, such as plastic dishes to set a table or a plastic hammer to do carpentry work. When other children think they know what the chore or job is, they should ask, "May I help you?" Then they should get a related prop from the box and join in acting out the chore. Children should take turns choosing props.

20 Minutes

Materials

- plastic tool belt and toy tools, such as hammers and wrenches
- toy rolling pin, mixing bowl, mixer, measuring cups
- dust mops, dust cloths, small plastic bucket, sponges
- plastic dishes, cups, cutlery, napkins

MANIPULATIVE CENTER

Friends and Helpers

Shuffle the following *Picture Cards* and place them face down in the Manipulative Center: *baby, boy, bus, car, cat, cow, doctor, dog, firefighter, fork, girl, helicopter, nurse, umbrella, watch.* Tell children they are going to work together to sort the cards into three piles: *Friends, Helpers,* and *Helpful Things.* Have children take turns choosing a card and telling which pile they think it belongs in and why.

Materials

- *Picture Cards bah by, boy, bus, car, cat, cow, doctor, dog, firefighter, fork, girl, helicopter, nurse, umbrella, watch*

Teacher Notes

Teacher Notes

Day 1

Day 2

 15-30 Minutes

ORAL LANGUAGE

- **Phonemic Awareness**

- **Sharing Literature**

Phonemic Awareness, 23
Phoneme Isolation and Matching: Initial

Sharing Literature, 24
 Read

Big Book: *Off We Go!*

 Literature Focus, 25
Rhyming Words

Phonemic Awareness, 39
Phoneme Isolation: Initial

Sharing Literature, 40
Library Book: *A Birthday Basket for Tía*

(Skill) **Literature Focus, 41**
Character Traits

 45 Minutes

LEARNING TO READ

- **Phonics**

- **Vocabulary**

 **, 34 T**
Introduce: Consonant *Gg*
Identify/Write **T**

 **, 42 T**
Relating /g/ to *g* **T**

High-Frequency Word, 44 T
Introduce: *on*

Words to Remember, 45

Daily Routines
- **Morning Message**
- **Calendar Language**
- **Writing Prompt**

 15-30 Minutes

LANGUAGE ARTS

- **Writing**
 Daily Writing Prompt

 Shared Writing, 36
Write Naming Words

Writing Prompt, 36
Draw and write about family members.

Share Time, 37
Share a favorite part of *Off We Go!*

 Interactive Writing, 46
Read
Write Sentences

Writing Prompt, 46
Draw and write about a special birthday gift.

Share Time, 47
Share a favorite part of *A Birthday Basket for Tía.*

T = tested skill

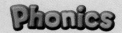 **Phonics**

Consonants *Gg, Ff*

Focus of the Week:
- **HIGH-FREQUENCY WORDS:** *on, to*
- **PHONEMIC AWARENESS**
- **SHARING LITERATURE**
- **WRITING: Naming Words, Lists**

Day 3

Phonemic Awareness, 49
Phoneme Isolation and Matching: Initial

Sharing Literature, 50
Read-Aloud Anthology:
"Let's Go, Froggy!" p. 36

 (Skill) **Literature Focus, 51**
Problem-Solution

Phonics, 52 T
Introduce: Consonant *Ff*
Identify/Write **T**

High-Frequency Word, 54 T
Introduce: *to*

Words to Remember, 55

✎ **Shared Writing, 56**
Write a List

Writing Prompt, 56
Draw and write about a place to visit.

Share Time, 57
Read
Share drawings of things Froggy found
in "Let's Go, Froggy!"

Day 4

Phonemic Awareness, 59
Phoneme Isolation: Initial

Sharing Literature, 60
Big Book of Rhymes and
Songs: "Winter Birds,"
p. 14

 (Skill) **Literature Focus, 61**
Long and Short Words

Phonics, 62 T
Relating /f/ to *f* **T**

High-Frequency Words, 64 T
Review: *on, to*

Read
**PRE-DECODABLE
BOOK 12**
The Park

✎ **Writing, 66**
Write Captions

Writing Prompt, 66
Draw and write about self-selected topics.

Share Time, 67
Discuss the Pre-decodable Book *The Park*.

Day 5

Phonemic Awareness, 69
Phoneme Matching

Sharing Literature, 70
Library Book: *A Birthday
Basket for Tia*

 (Skill) **Literature
Focus, 71**
Retelling the Story

Phonics, 72 T
Review: Consonants /g/*g*, /f/*f*

✎ **Interactive Writing, 74**
Read
Write a Birthday Message

Writing Prompt, 74
Draw and write about a special birthday.

Share Time, 75
Discuss birthday parties.

Phonemic Awareness

Phoneme Isolation and Matching: Initial

Sharing Literature

Big Book:
Off We Go!

Develop Listening Comprehension

Respond to Literature

Literature Focus: Rhyming Words

Phonics

Consonant *Gg*

Writing

Shared Writing: Naming Words

ORAL LANGUAGE

MORNING MESSAGE

Kindergarten News

(Child's name) is going to _____

with _____.

Write Kindergarten News   Talk with children about what they like to do with their families.

Use prompts such as the following to guide children as you write the news:

- **What are some things you do with your family?**
- **Who can show me where to begin writing?**
- **What letter will I write first in the word *going*?**
- **Let's count the letters in (child's name). How many letters are there?**

As you write the message, invite children to contribute by writing letters, words, or names they have previously learned. Remind them to use proper spacing, capitalization, and punctuation.

Calendar Language

Point to and read aloud the names of the months of the year. Tell children there are 12 months in a year. Point to and name the month. Ask: *What month is it now?*

Sunday	Monday	Tuesday	Wednesday	Thursday	Friday	Saturday
		1	2	3	4	5
6	7	8	9	10	11	12
13	14	15	16	17	18	19
20	21	22	23	24	25	26
27	28	29	30	31		

Phonemic Awareness

PHONEME ISOLATION: INITIAL

Listen for Initial /g/   Show children the *Picture Cards gorilla* and *goat*.

MODEL   *Gorilla*. **What sound do you hear at the beginning of** *gorilla*? (/g/)

Goat. **What sound do you hear at the beginning of** *goat*? (/g/)

Say the words with me: *gorilla*, *goat*, *gorilla*, *goat*.

What sound do you hear at the beginning of *gorilla* **and** *goat*? (/g/) **The words** *gorilla* **and** *goat* **begin with /g/.**

Tell children that you are going to say other words that begin with /g/. As you say each word, emphasize the /g/ sound and have children repeat the word and say the initial phoneme /g/.

gallop	**game**	**gate**
girl	**gift**	**garage**

PHONEME MATCHING: INITIAL

Identify Words with the Same Beginning Sound   For each of the following pairs of words, have children identify words that begin with the same sound.

MODEL   *Girl*, *guest*. **The word** *girl* **begins with /g/. The word** *guest* **begins with /g/. The words** *girl* **and** *guest* **begin with the same sound. Say the words** *girl*, *guest*.

Continue with word pairs and ask children to raise their hands if the words begin with the same sound:

gum, **gobble**	**girl**, **gift**	**sun**, **soap**
dish, **rest**	**red**, **rabbit**	**duck**, **mop**
porch, **pack**	**fox**, **hat**	**geese**, **gate**

Repeat word pairs that are the same and have children tell the beginning sound.

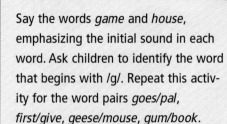

▲ **Big Book**

OBJECTIVES

- *To identify the front cover and back cover of a book*

- *To recognize high-frequency word* go

- *To recognize that a book cover offers information*

- *To listen and respond to a story*

- *To listen for text patterns, including rhyme and repetition*

Materials

■ *Big Book:*
  Off We go!

Sharing Literature

Read Off We Go!

> **READ ALOUD**

Before Reading   Display *Off We Go!* Have a child come up and point to the front cover and the back cover of the book. Point to the title and ask children if they see a word they know. (Go) Ask a child to point to where you should begin reading the title. Read aloud the title as you track the print. After reviewing what the author and the illustrator do, read their names aloud.

Use these prompts to help children set a purpose for reading:

- **What do you see on the front cover?** (frog, ducks, mice)

- **What are the animals doing?** (Possible responses: running, going quickly)

  MODEL   The title of this book is *Off We Go!* On the front cover, I see animals who seem to be running off somewhere. I'll read the story to find out where they might be going.

During Reading   Read the story aloud. As you do,

- read the text in a slow, rhythmic pace. Emphasize the alliteration by elongating the initial sounds. Tell children to listen for words that rhyme.

- reread the text, inviting children to look at the pictures to name each animal that will go next to Grandma's house.

DEVELOP LISTENING COMPREHENSION

After Reading   Have children answer these questions about the story:

- **What animals are in the story?** (mouse, frog, mole, snake, duck, spider)
- **Where are the animals going?** (to their grandma's houses)
- **Why does the author say that "Grandma's house is always best"?** (Possible responses: because a grandma loves you, takes good care of you, bakes good things, or plays with you)

RESPOND TO LITERATURE

Pantomime Action Words   Have children repeat and pantomime the actions of the animals: mouse: *tip-toe, tippety toe;* frog: *hip-hop, hippety hop;* mole: *dig-deep, diggety deep;* snake: *slither-slee, slithery slee;* duck: *scritch-scratch, scritchety scratch;* spider: *creep-crawl, creepity crawl.*

Page through the story to share an example of rhyming words used by the writer.

Literature Focus

RHYMING WORDS

MODEL On the first page I read the words *toe, below,* and *go* at the end of the lines. These words all have the same ending sounds: *toe, below, go.* They are rhyming words. Say the words with me: *toe, below, go.*

Read several pages of the story and ask children to say the rhyming words after you.

BELOW-LEVEL

Show *Picture Cards mouse* and *duck.* Ask children to say the animal names. Then say a rhyming word for each, such as *house, luck.* Have children repeat the picture name and rhyming word and add another word they can think of.

ADVANCED

Brainstorm with children pairs of rhyming words, such as *mouse/house, cat/hat, dog/frog, mole/hole.* Have them illustrate their favorite pair and write or dictate labels for their pictures.

ONGOING ASSESSMENT

As you share *Off We Go!*, note whether children

- **recognize parts of a book.**
- **can read high-frequency word *go.***
- **listen for a period of time.**
- **anticipate rhyming words and repetitive phrases.**

▲ **Practice Book p. 6**

To Maddison Jane, who inspired this book
—J. Y.

To Jack Andrew and Peter with much love
and to Ginger and Maria
— L. M.

Off We Go!

by Jane Yolen
Illustrated by Laurel Molk

Harcourt
Orlando   Boston   Dallas   Chicago   San Diego

Visit *The Learning Site!*
www.harcourtschool.com

Tip-toe, tippity toe,
Over the leaves and down below,
Off to Grandma's house we go,
Sings Little Mouse.

6

7

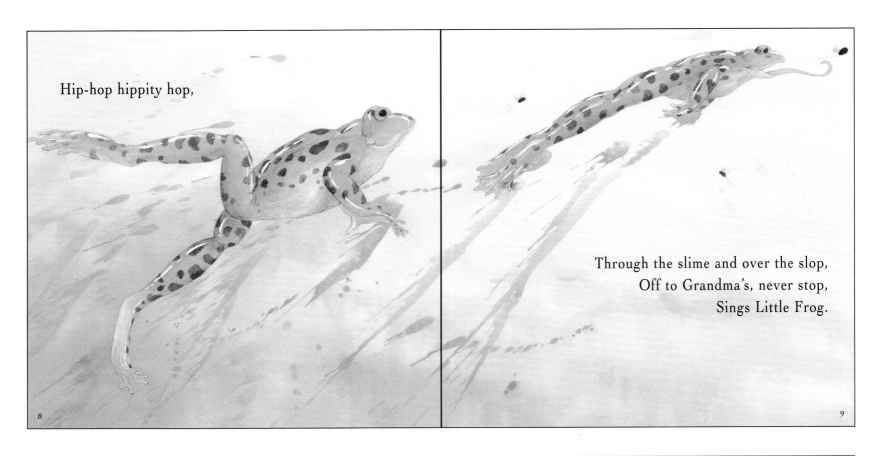

Hip-hop hippity hop,

Through the slime and over the slop,
Off to Grandma's, never stop,
Sings Little Frog.

8

9

Dig-deep, diggity deep
Down where day is dark as sleep,
Off to Grandma's house I creep,
Sings Little Mole.

10

11

Slither-slee, slithery slee,
Down the branch and round the tree,
Off to Grandma's house goes me,
Sings Little Snake.

Scritch-scratch, scritchity scratch,
Directly from the egg I hatch,
Then off to Grandma's
house I dash,
Sings Little Duck.

Creep-crawl, creepity crawl,
From the web and down the wall,
Off to Grandma's house free-fall,
Sings Little Spider.

Tip-toe, tippity toe

Tip-toe, tippity toe
Hip-hop, hippity hop

Tip-toe, tippity toe
Hip-hop, hippity hop
Dig-deep, diggity deep

20

21

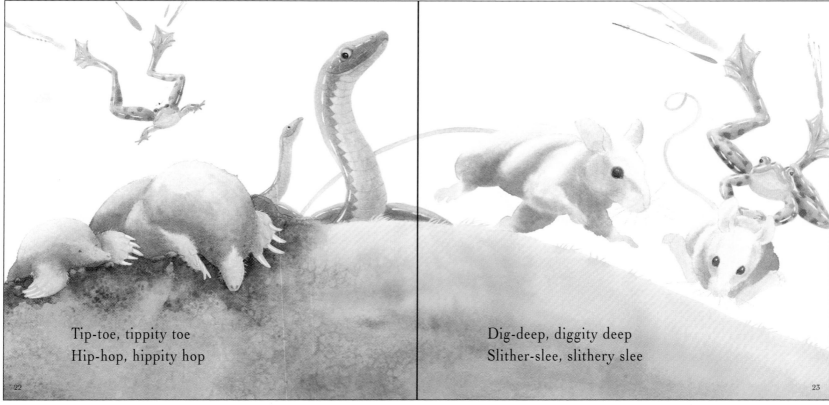

Tip-toe, tippity toe
Hip-hop, hippity hop

22

Dig-deep, diggity deep
Slither-slee, slithery slee

23

Tip-toe, tippity toe
Hip-hop, hippity hop
Dig-deep, diggity deep

24

Slither-slee, slithery slee
Scritch-scratch, scritchity scratch

25

Tip-toe, tippity toe
Hip-hop, hippity hop
Dig-deep, diggity deep
Slither-slee, slithery slee

26

Scritch-scratch, scritchity scratch
Creep-crawl, creepity crawl

27

Wherever Grandma's house is found —
In hole, in tree, or underground,
In web, or bog, or in a nest —
Why, Grandma's house is *always* best.

OBJECTIVES

- *To recognize G and g*

- *To write uppercase and lowercase Gg independently*

Materials

- *Big Book of Rhymes and Songs,* pp. 2–3

- *Music CD*

- *Big Alphabet Card Gg*

- *Big Book: Off We Go!*

- *Write-On/Wipe-Off Boards*

- drawing paper

- crayons

Phonics

Consonant *Gg* ✓Introduce

ACTIVE BEGINNING

Sing "The Alphabet Song" Display "The Alphabet Song" in *the Big Book of Rhymes and Songs.* Point to each letter as you sing the song with children. The song is available on the *Music CD.*

▲ **Big Book of Rhymes and Songs, pages 2-3**

TEACH/MODEL

Introduce the Letter Name Hold up *Big Alphabet Card Gg.*

The name of this letter is *G.* Say the name with me.

Point to the uppercase G. **This is the uppercase *G.***

Point to the lowercase g. **This is the lowercase *g.***

Point to the *Big Alphabet Card* again. **What is the name of this letter?**

Point to the *G* in "The Alphabet Song." **What is the name of this letter?**

Display the front cover of *Off We Go!*

Follow along as I read the title.

Point to the letter *G.* **What is the name of this letter?**

Handwriting

Writing *G* and *g* Write uppercase *G* and lowercase *g* on the board.

Point to the uppercase *G*. **What letter is this?**

Point to the lowercase *g*. **What letter is this?**

MODEL **Watch as I write the letter *G* so that everyone can read it.**

As you give the Letter Talk, trace the uppercase *G*. Use the same modeling procedure for lowercase *g*.

Letter Talk for *G*

Circle left. Stop at the dotted line. Straight line across.

Letter Talk for *g*

Circle left. Straight line down. Curve to the left.

D'Nealian handwriting models are on pages R10–11.

PRACTICE/APPLY

Guided Practice Help children find *Gg* on their *Write-On/Wipe-Off Boards*. Have them trace the uppercase *G* with a finger and then write the letter several times. Then have them do the same for lowercase *g*. Tell children to circle their best *Gg*.

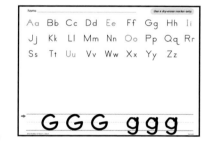

Independent Practice Distribute drawing paper and have children fill their paper with *Gg*'s. Then have them circle their best *Gg*.

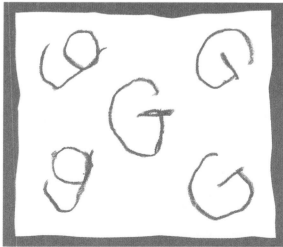

BELOW-LEVEL

Guide each child in writing the letter. Put your hand over the child's hand and write the letter with him or her. Then have the child try it alone.

ADVANCED

Encourage children to use pencils to write *G* and *g* on lined paper. They can paste their paper onto drawing paper and decorate the border using green crayons.

Phonics Resources

Phonics Express™ CD-ROM, **Level A,** Sparkle/Route 3/ Building Site

Phonics Practice Book pages 47–48

▲ **Practice Book page 7**

OBJECTIVES

- *To write naming words*
- *To write a word web*

Materials

- chart paper
- marker

Shared Writing

Write Naming Words

CREATE A WORD WEB

Talk About Family   Ask children to recall where all the animals are going in the story *Off We Go!* (to Grandma's). Explain that *Grandma* is a word that names a person in a family. Have children name people in their family.

Write a Word Web   Tell children that together they are going to make a word web of naming words for the members of a family. Tell them that naming words are words that name people, places, or things. The words they will use for their word web will name people. Draw an oval on chart paper and write the word *Family*. Ask children to suggest naming words for family members and write their suggestions in other ovals, such as mother, father, grandma, grandpa, sister, brother, aunt, uncle, cousin.

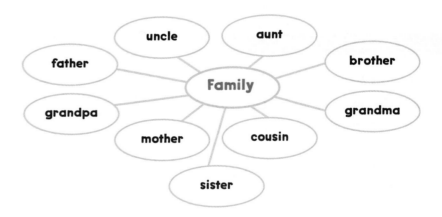

Journal Writing   Have children draw and write about family members in their journal.

WRAP UP Share Time

Reflect on the Lesson Encourage children to tell what they liked best about *Off We Go!* Ask them to take turns choosing a word from the word web that names a family member and telling something about that person in their own family.

S.S.R. *Sustained Silent Reading* Have children read silently from a book of their choice.

 Centers **MANIPULATIVE**

Family Puzzles

Beforehand, make family puzzles by gluing large magazine pictures of a family on sheets of cardboard. Cut the cardboard into six puzzle pieces and store in resealable plastic bags in the center. Children can put together the puzzles and tell stories about the people who are pictured.

Materials

- magazine pictures of people
- glue
- cardboard
- scissors
- resealable plastic bags

Day at a Glance
Day 2

WARM UP

MORNING MESSAGE

Kindergarten News

This is the month of _____.

(Child's name) has a birthday in

(name of month).

Phonemic Awareness

Phoneme Isolation: Initial

Sharing Literature

Library Book:
A Birthday Basket for Tía

by Pat Mora ▾ illustrated by Cecily Lang

Develop Listening Comprehension

Respond to Literature

Literature Focus: Character Traits

Phonics

Relating /g/ to *g*

High-Frequency Word

on

Writing ✏

Interactive Writing: Sentences

Write Kindergarten News Talk with children about what they like best about their birthday.

Use prompts such as the following to guide children as you write the news:

- **Who can name their birthday month?**
- **What are some things you do to celebrate birthdays?**
- **Who can show me the top and the bottom of the page?**

As you write the message, invite children to contribute by writing letters, words, or names they have previously learned. Remind them to use proper spacing, capitalization, and punctuation.

Calendar Language

Point to and read aloud the months of the year. Tell children there are 12 months in a year. Point to and name the month. Ask: *What month is it? Who has a birthday in (name of month)?*

Sunday	Monday	Tuesday	Wednesday	Thursday	Friday	Saturday
		1	2	3	4	5
6	7	8	9	10	11	12
13	14	15	16	17	18	19
20	21	22	23	24	25	26
27	28	29	30	31		

Phonemic Awareness

PHONEME ISOLATION: INITIAL

Listen for /g/ Tell children you will say some words and they will listen for the beginning sound in the words. Say the following tongue twister:

Gus Goat gobbles gooey gumdrops.

> **MODEL** *Gus* begins with /g/. **What sound does *Goat* begin with?** (/g/)

What sound does *gobbles* begin with? (/g/)

What sound does *gooey* begin with? (/g/)

What sound does *gumdrops* begin with? (/g/)

Let's say the tongue twister together.

What sound do you hear at the beginning of each word? (/g/)

Repeat the rhyme several times with children. Replace the word *gumdrops* with another word that begins with /g/, such as *garbage, garlic, gourds, goggles, gum*. Have each child choose one version of the tongue twister to say quickly two times.

BELOW-LEVEL

Tell children to listen as you slowly say each word in the tongue twister elongating the /g/ sound. Have children do the same. Then have them say the word and name the sound they hear at the beginning.

Sharing Literature

Read A Birthday Basket for Tía

READ ALOUD

Before Reading Display *A Birthday Basket for Tía*. Read the title aloud as you track the print. Point to and read aloud the names of the author and the illustrator. Use the cover illustration and the title to build background and to make predictions:

- Point to Cecilia (the young girl). **This is Cecilia.**

- Point to Tía. **This is Cecilia's Tía.** *Tía* **means "aunt."**

- **How do you think these characters feel about each other?** (Possible response: They are hugging each other. They love each other.)

Read the title again and model for children how to predict what the story is about:

MODEL **The title of this book is** *A Birthday Basket for Tía*. **It seems as though Cecilia and Tía care about each other. I think Cecilia gives her tía a special birthday present.**

During Reading Read the story aloud. As you do,

- read with expression as Cecilia describes the things she does with her aunt.

- read slowly as you repeat and add to the list of items that are put into the basket.

- emphasize the use of first-person narrative by pausing after the first few pages to say:

MODEL **Cecilia is telling this story. I know that because the author uses the word** *I* **again and again.** *I curl my cat…, I say…, I smell…., I draw…, I walk…, I put a book in the basket.* **The** *I* **stands for Cecilia. She is telling the story.**

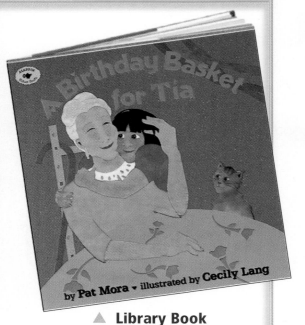

▲ **Library Book**

OBJECTIVES

- *To use pictures and context to make predictions*

- *To identify the beginning, middle, and ending of a story*

- *To connect life experiences to text*

- *To use illustrations and text to understand characters*

Materials

- *Library Book: A Birthday Basket for Tía*

- chart paper

- marker

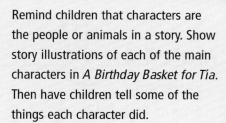

DEVELOP LISTENING COMPREHENSION

After Reading Remind children that stories have a beginning, a middle, and an ending. Ask them:

- **What happens in the beginning of the story?** (Cecilia thinks about a birthday present for Tía.)
- **What happens in the middle of the story?** (Cecilia puts objects in a birthday basket for Tía.)
- **What happens at the end of the story?** (Possible responses: Tía is surprised; Tía dances with Cecilia.)
- **Does Tía like her birthday basket from Cecilia? How do you know?** (She likes it; she takes everything out of the basket and smiles and laughs.)

RESPOND TO LITERATURE

Talk About Family Celebrations Have children tell about birthdays or other family celebrations. Ask them to tell about special presents the person received. Help them speak in complete sentences.

Literature Focus

CHARACTER TRAITS

Tell children that story characters say and do different things. Explain that you can tell what a character is like by what the character says and does. Display the cover of *A Birthday Basket for Tía*. As you name each character, ask a child to point to the character on the cover. Then say these sentences and have children tell which character each riddle describes.

I play with Cecilia. I read to her. I bring her tea when she is sick. I am kind. Who am I? (Tía)

I think about what Tía does for me. I am caring. Who am I? (Cecilia)

I jump into the birthday basket. I am funny. I am curious. Who am I? (Chica)

BELOW-LEVEL

Remind children that characters are the people or animals in a story. Show story illustrations of each of the main characters in *A Birthday Basket for Tía*. Then have children tell some of the things each character did.

ONGOING ASSESSMENT

As you share *A Birthday Basket for Tía*, note whether children

- listen for a period of time.
- use pictures and context to make predictions.

OBJECTIVES

To match consonant Gg to its sound

Materials

- Letter and Sound Chart 23
- Tactile Letter Cards g
- Picture/Word Cards goat, dog
- pocket chart
- Gate Pattern (page T13)
- crayons
- scissors
- tape

Phonics
Relating /g/ to g

ACTIVE BEGINNING

Recite "Goose! Goose!" Have children listen for /g/ as they learn the rhyme. Then have groups of children take turns acting out the rhyme as they recite it again.

Goose! Goose!

Goose! Goose!
Get out of the garden!
Go! Go away!
Gather up your goslings.
Go somewhere else to play.

TEACH/MODEL

Introduce Letter and Sound Display Letter and Sound Chart 23.

Touch the letter G. **What is the name of the letter?**

This letter stands for the /g/ sound. When you say /g/, you can feel it in your throat. Say /gg/.

Read aloud the rhyme on the Letter and Sound Chart, tracking the print.

Read the Gg words in the rhyme aloud. Then point to each g and have children say the /g/ sound. Ask: **What letter stands for the /g/ sound?**

Have children join in as you read the rhyme again. Encourage them to feel the sounds in their throats as they say the /g/g words.

G g

Wiggle, giggle,
Geese in the sun.
Waggle, gaggle,
Oh, what fun!

▲ **Letter and Sound Chart 23**

PRACTICE/APPLY

Guided Practice Distribute *Tactile Letter Cards g* to children. Place *Picture/Word Cards goat* and *dog* in a pocket chart. Say the names of the pictures as you point to the *g* in each. Have children repeat the words.

Tell children: **Some words begin with g and some words end with g.**

Point to the *g* in *goat*. **The /g/ sound is at the beginning of** *goat*.

I'll say some words. If the word begins with the /g/ sound, hold up your g card. If the word doesn't begin with the /g/ sound, don't hold up your g card.

garbage   silly   gold   gas   more   get   gum

Follow the same procedure for the ending sound in *dog*.

rag   but   big   tug   hop   flag   jog

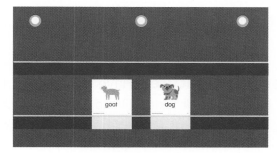

Independent Practice Distribute copies of the Gate Pattern (page T13). Have children draw and label a picture on the gate of something whose name begins with or ends with the /g/ sound.

Ask children to whisper their words to you before they draw them. Children can cut out the patterns and tape them to a wall to create a long fence. Encourage them to take turns coming up to name pictures they see on the gates, animals, objects in the classroom, or people's names that begin or end with *g*.

Display *Picture/Word Cards girl, goat, gorilla,* and *gate*. Point to a card and ask children to identify it. Say the name and identify the beginning sound as /g/. Ask children to identify the beginning letter *g* in the picture name. Continue by having children name each *Picture/Word Card*, identify the beginning sound, and the letter that makes the /g/ sound. Follow the same procedure with *Picture/Word Cards dog, king, pig, ring* to focus on words that end with /g/.

Phonics Resources

Phonics Express™ **CD-ROM, Level A,** Sparkle/Route 3/Train Station, Park, Market

Phonics Practice Book pages 49–50

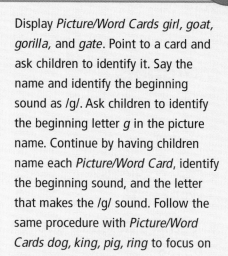

▲ **Practice Book page 8**

OBJECTIVE

To read the high-frequency word on

Materials

■ chart paper

■ marker

■ *High-Frequency Word Card*

on

■ *Teacher's Resource Book,* p. 138

■ *High-Frequency Word Card* files

High-Frequency Word *on*

TEACH/MODEL

On chart paper, write the following sentence from *A Birthday Basket for Tía*. Track the print as you read the sentence aloud.

I put Tía's favorite mixing bowl on the book in the basket.

Point to the word *on* and say: **This is the word** *on*. Have children say the word. Display *High-Frequency Word Card* on. Ask: **What word is this?** Have children repeat the sentence after you. Have a child match the *High-Frequency Word Card* on to the on in the sentence.

PRACTICE/APPLY

Guided Practice   Make copies of the *High-Frequency Word Card* on in the *Teacher's Resource Book*. Give each child a card and tell him or her to point to the word *on* and say it. Then ask children to point to their *High-Frequency Word Card* on each time they say the word *on* and complete the sentence.

The _____ is on the _____.

Independent Practice   Have children use the *High-Frequency Word Cards* in their word file to identify each of the words as you say it. Use the words to tell about something they do at home. Have children listen to the sentence, find the word card and hold it up. Use the words *on, a, my, the, I, like, go,* and *we*.

Words to Remember
Word Wall

Reading Words Hold up the *High-Frequency Word Card on* and have children read it aloud. Then place the word card under the letter *O* of the classroom word chart.

Find Similarities Have children look at their new word *on*. Encourage them to find similarities to other words posted on the chart.

Say the following to guide them appropriately:

• *On* has two letters. Do any of our other words have two letters? Let's read the other words that have two letters. (*my, go, we*)

ADVANCED

Children can extend their knowledge by using the word *on* in a sentence. Have children write the sentence on paper and illustrate it. Then have children read their sentence to a partner.

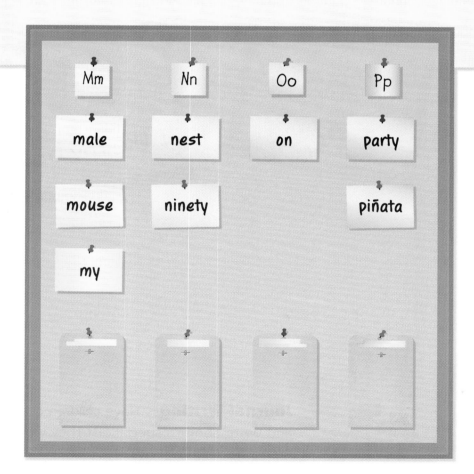

Name _____

Can we go `on` a bike?
color 😊 😕
yes   no

Can we go `on` a fish?
😊 😕 color
yes   no

Can we go `on` a train?
color 😊 😕
yes   no

I can go `on` a

Box for children to draw their own pictures.

High-Frequency Word: on
Have children trace the word on in the first three questions, read the questions, and color the faces to show the answers. Have children write on in the last sentence and complete it by drawing themselves on some form of transportation. Ask children to read their sentence.

Family Ties **9**

▲ **Practice Book page 9**

OBJECTIVES

- *To write sentences*

- *To recognize an uppercase letter and a period*

Materials

- *Library Book: A Birthday Basket for Tía*

- chart paper

- marker

- drawing paper

- crayons or markers

Interactive Writing

Write Sentences

SHARE THE PEN

Talk About Birthday Gifts   Display *A Birthday Basket for Tía* and page through the book. Pause and invite children to point out and name objects in Cecilia's surprise birthday basket.

Write About Birthday Gifts   Tell children that together they will write sentences about birthday gifts they have received. Remind them that some sentences tell about something. On chart paper, write *I like my* _____. Read the words to children. Have a child point to the uppercase letter at the beginning of the sentence and the period at the end. Ask each child to recall a special gift that he or she liked very much. Have each child come to the chart, write the sentence frame, and draw and label a picture of the gift.

Journal Writing   Have children draw and write about a special gift they would like to get.

WRAP UP · Share Time

Reflect on the Lesson Have children tell what they liked best about the story *A Birthday Basket for Tía*. Ask children to take turns reading their sentences about special gifts they have received. Then ask them to name the letter they learned today and say the sound. (/g/) Mention that the word *gift* begins with *g*.

Centers ABC WORDS AND LETTERS

Letter Match

Place the uppercase *Magnetic Letters P, A, M, R, S, C, T, N, D,* and *G* in one container and the matching lowercase letters in another container. Have children work in pairs. One partner chooses one uppercase letter and puts it on the cookie sheet. The other partner finds the matching lowercase letter and puts it next to the uppercase letter on the cookie sheet. Partners continue putting letters side by side until they have matched all ten pairs.

Materials

- *Magnetic Letters P, A, M, R, S, C, T, N, D, G* (uppercase and lowercase)

- two cups, boxes, or other containers

- cookie sheet

Day at a Glance
Day 3

Phonemic Awareness
Phoneme Isolation and Matching: Initial

Sharing Literature
Read-Aloud Anthology:
"Let's Go, Froggy"

Read

Develop Concept Vocabulary

Respond to Literature

Literature Focus: Problem-Solution

Phonics
Consonant *Ff*

High-Frequency Word
to

Writing
Shared Writing: List

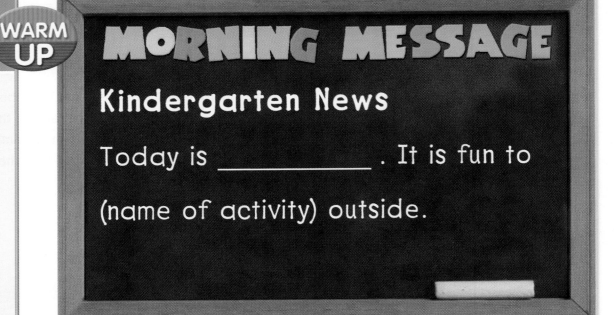

MORNING MESSAGE
Kindergarten News
Today is _____. It is fun to (name of activity) outside.

Write Kindergarten News   Talk with children about what they like to do outside.

Use prompts such as the following to guide children as you write the news:

- **Who can tell about something fun you do outside?**
- **Let's clap the syllables for the word *Today*. Say the first part. Say the second part.**
- **Who can show me a letter?**
- **Who can show me a word?**

As you write the message, invite children to contribute by writing letters, words, or names they have previously learned. Remind them to use proper spacing, capitalization, and punctuation.

Calendar Language

Name the seasons of the year. Have children repeat the seasons of the year with you. Tell them: *It is (season).* Ask: *What season is it?*

Sunday	Monday	Tuesday	Wednesday	Thursday	Friday	Saturday
		1	2	3	4	5
6	7	8	9	10	11	12
13	14	15	16	17	18	19
20	21	22	23	24	25	26
27	28	29	30	31		

Phonemic Awareness

PHONEME ISOLATION: INITIAL

Listen for Initial Sounds Tell children you will say some words and they will listen for the beginning sound in the words. Say the following words, emphasizing the sound at the beginning of each word.

MODEL *Fox.* **I say the word slowly. /ff/ /oo/ /ks/.**

Fox **begins with /f/. Say the word with me.** *Fox.*

What sound does *fox* **begin with?** (/f/)

What sound does *mop* **begin with?** (/m/)

What sound does *dance* **begin with?** (/d/)

What sound does *farmer* **begin with?** (/f/)

What sound does *rose* **begin with?** (/r/)

PHONEME MATCHING: INITIAL

Tell children to listen for the beginning sounds in the words you say to identify words with the same beginning sound.

MODEL fan   pot   fish

The beginning sound in *fan* **is /f/.**

The beginning sound in *pot* **is /p/.**

The beginning sound in *fish* **is /f/.**

Fan **and** *fish* **have the same beginning sounds. Say the words with me:** *fan, fish.*

Say the following words. Ask children to name the words that have the same beginning sound.

fat	fine	door	mouse	man	fix	cat	top	ten
doll	dime	field	pan	four	pipe	lion	four	fin
mouse	meet	sun	red	sand	rain	fox	fish	mop

Sharing Literature

Read "Let's Go, Froggy"

READ ALOUD

Before Reading   Turn to page 36 of the *Read-Aloud Anthology* and read aloud the title "Let's Go, Froggy." Use these prompts to build background.

- **What animal do you think this story is about?** (a frog)
- **Where do you think Froggy might be going?** (Possible responses: to a pond, a field, a river)

During Reading   Read the story aloud. As you read,

- change your voice to represent the two characters.
- ask children to listen for words that sound like a noise.
- emphasize the words *FRRROOGGYY!* and *"I'm re-e-a-d-y!"* each time the words are repeated.
- invite children to join in by pantomiming the actions of Froggy.

▲ **Read-Aloud Anthology**

OBJECTIVES

- *To listen and respond to a story*
- *To identify story events*
- *To understand sound words*
- *To understand that a story has a problem and solution*

Materials

- *Read-Aloud Anthology, pp. 36–39*
- drawing paper
- crayons

DEVELOP CONCEPT VOCABULARY

After Reading   Tell children to listen to the following words you say them. Say: *zap, zip, zoop, zup, zut.* Ask: **Are these real words?**

The words *zap, zip, zoop, zup, zut* are words the author uses to stand for the sounds Froggy makes as he gets dressed.

Have children pantomime the actions of getting dressed as you repeat the words together. Say, and have children repeat, other sound words from the story as they perform Froggy's actions.

RESPOND TO LITERATURE

Draw Story Events   Ask children to recall the things Froggy collects for his bike trip. Have children draw a picture of one thing in the place where Froggy finds it. Have children write or dictate a sentence about their picture.

PROBLEM-SOLUTION

Literature Focus

Tell children that many stories have a problem that the character must work out. Ask children what the problem is in "Let's Go, Froggy." (Froggy cannot find the things he needs for his bike trip.) Explain how a story also has a solution.

MODEL   **You are right. In "Let's Go, Froggy!" Froggy cannot find things. That is the problem. Froggy's father tells Froggy to stop and think where he left each item. Froggy's father helps him solve his problem. Froggy finds his butterfly net, ball, and trading cards.**

Ask children to describe the second problem in the story and how this problem is fixed. (Daddy loses his backpack. Froggy helps him find it.)

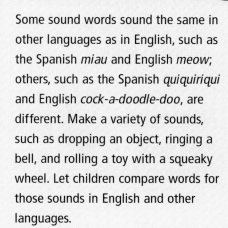

Some sound words sound the same in other languages as in English, such as the Spanish *miau* and English *meow*; others, such as the Spanish *quiquiriqui* and English *cock-a-doodle-doo*, are different. Make a variety of sounds, such as dropping an object, ringing a bell, and rolling a toy with a squeaky wheel. Let children compare words for those sounds in English and other languages.

ONGOING ASSESSMENT

As you share "Let's Go, Froggy," note whether children,

- listen for a period of time.
- can pantomime story actions.

OBJECTIVES

- *To recognize F and f*
- *To write uppercase and lowercase Ff independently*

Materials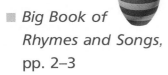

- *Big Book of Rhymes and Songs,* pp. 2–3
- *Music CD*
- *Big Alphabet Card Ff*
- *Big Book: I Read Signs*
- *Write-On/Wipe-Off Boards*
- drawing paper
- crayons

Phonics

Consonant *Ff*  Introduce

ACTIVE BEGINNING

Sing "The Alphabet Song"   Display "The Alphabet Song" in the *Big Book of Rhymes and Songs*. Point to each letter as you sing the song with children. The song is available on the *Music CD*.

▲ **Big Book of Rhymes and Songs, pages 2-3**

TEACH/MODEL

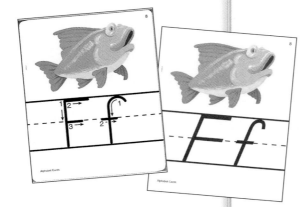

Introduce the Letter Name   Hold up *Big Alphabet Card Ff*.

The name of this letter is *F*. Say the name with me.

Point to the uppercase *F*. **This is the uppercase *F*.**

Point to the lowercase *f*. **This is the lowercase *f*.**

Point to the *Big Alphabet Card* again. **What is the name of this letter?**

Point to the *F* in "The Alphabet Song." **What is the name of this letter?**

Display the sign "Fire Hose" in *I Read Signs*.

Follow along as I read this sign.

Point to the letter *F*. **What is the name of this letter?**

Handwriting

Writing *F* and *f* Write uppercase *F* and lowercase *f* on the board.

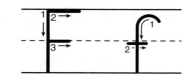

Point to the uppercase *F*. **What letter is this?**

Point to the lowercase *f*. **What letter is this?**

MODEL **Watch as I write the letter *F* so that everyone can read it.**

As you give the Letter Talk, trace the uppercase *F*. Use the same modeling procedure for lowercase *f*.

Letter Talk for *F*

Straight line down. Go to the top. Straight line across. Go to the middle. Straight line across.

Letter Talk for *f*

Curve left and down. Go to the middle. Straight line across.

D'Nealian handwriting models are on pages R10–11.

PRACTICE/APPLY

Guided Practice Help children find *Ff* on their *Write-On/Wipe-Off Boards.* Have them trace the uppercase *F* with a finger and then write the letter several times. Then have them do the same for lowercase *f*. Tell children to circle their best *Ff*.

Independent Practice Distribute drawing paper and have children practice printing *Ff*. Then have them circle their best *Ff*.

As you introduce children to *Ff* letter formation, model each step of the Letter Talk to make sure children understand the ideas of *straight line, curve, left, top, middle, curve down.*

Phonics Resources

***Phonics Express*™ CD-ROM, Level A,** Speedy/Route 2/Building Site

Phonics Practice Book pages 51–52

▲ **Practice Book page 10**

High-Frequency Word *to*

OBJECTIVE

To read the high-frequency word to

Materials

- *Big Book: Off We Go!*

- *High-Frequency Word Card* | to |

- index cards

- *Teacher's Resource Book,* p. 139

TEACH/MODEL

Display the first page in *Off We Go!* Read the lines that tell what Little Mouse sings. Frame the line: *Off to Grandma's house we go.* Say the line and have children repeat it as you track the print.

Point to the word *to* and say: **This is the word *to*.** Have children say the word. Display *High-Frequency Word Card to.* Ask: **What word is this?** Have children repeat the sentence from the *Big Book* with you. Ask a child to match the *High-Frequency Word Card to* to the word *to* in the text.

PRACTICE/APPLY

Guided Practice   Make copies of the *High-Frequency Word Card to* in the *Teacher's Resource Book*. Give each child a card and tell children to point to the word *to* and say it. Then ask children the question below and tell them to point to their word card as they say the word *to* and finish the response.

Where do you like to go?   **I like to go to (place).**

Independent Practice   Have children write and complete the following sentence frame to tell where they might go. Ask children to share their sentence with a partner.

I go to _____.

Word Wall

Reading Words Hold up the *High-Frequency Word Card to* and have children read it aloud. Then ask a child to place the word card under the letter *Tt* of the classroom word chart.

Find Similarities Have children look closely at their new word *to*. Encourage them to find similarities to other words posted on the chart. Ask the following question to guide them appropriately:

• *To* has two letters. Do any of our other words have two let- ters? Let's read the other words that have two letters. (my, go, we, on)

Diagnostic Check: High-Frequency Word

If... children cannot identify the high-frequency word *to* in context,

Then... repeat the Teach/Model les-son, focusing on the isolated word on the word card before presenting the word in text.

ADDITIONAL SUPPORT ACTIVITIES

BELOW-LEVEL	Reteach, p. S2
ADVANCED	Extend, p. S3
ENGLISH-LANGUAGE LEARNERS	Reteach, p. S3

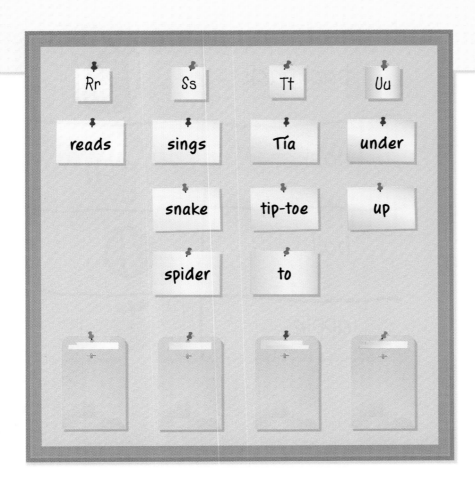

▲ **Practice Book page 11**

OBJECTIVES

- *To understand the purpose of a list*
- *To write a list*
- *To understand that words are made up of letters*

Materials

- chart paper
- marker
- drawing paper
- crayons
- tape

Shared Writing

Write a List

DRAW AND WRITE

Talk About Lists Ask children to recall the story "Let's Go, Froggy!" and name the things Froggy wanted to bring on a bike trip. (bike helmet, butterfly net, ball, peaches, trading cards, backpack)

Write a List Have children pretend they are going on a trip. Tell children that together they will write a list of things to take. Ask each child to name a favorite thing to take. Write the word on chart paper and read the word for the child. Have the child draw a picture of the item. Tape the child's picture next to the word.

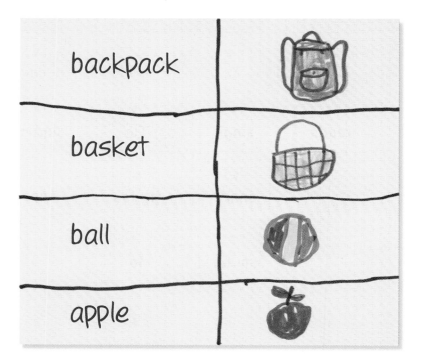

Journal Writing Have children draw and write about a place they would like to visit.

Share Time

Reflect on the Lesson   Have children share their drawings of the things Froggy found in the story, "Let's Go, Froggy!" Have them tell about a trip they would like to take. Ask them to name the letter they learned to write. (*Ff*)

S.S.R.   Have children read silently from a book of their choice.

Four and Five

Provide a variety of countable objects, such as blocks, pegs, or disks, along with several index cards, each marked with a 4, a 5, or a set of four or five dots. Tell children to turn the number cards face down. Then have them turn over a card, say the number aloud, and count out the appropriate number of objects. Have children work with a partner to check each other's work.

Materials

- variety of small objects
- index cards

Day at a Glance
Day 4

WARM UP

Phonemic Awareness
Phoneme Isolation: Initial

Sharing Literature
Big Book of Rhymes and Songs: "Winter Birds"

Read
Big Book of Rhymes and Songs

Respond to Literature

Literature Focus: Long and Short Words

Phonics
Relating /f/ to *f*

Reading
Pre-decodable Book 12: *The Park*

Writing 🖉
Writing: Write a Caption

MORNING MESSAGE
Kindergarten News

(Child's name) goes to

_____ by _____.

Write Kindergarten News Talk with children about how they get from one place to another.

Use prompts such as the following to guide children as you write the news:

• **Who can name some ways you go from one place to another?**

• **Who can show me a word?**

• **Who can show me a space between words?**

As you write the message, invite children to contribute by writing letters, words, or names they have previously learned. Remind them to use proper spacing, capitalization, and punctuation.

Calendar Language

Point to and read aloud the names of the days of the week. Point to and name the day. Say: *Today is _____.* Ask: *What day is today?* Point to the day that came before today. Say: *Yesterday was _____.* Ask: *What day was yesterday?*

Sunday	Monday	Tuesday	Wednesday	Thursday	Friday	Saturday
		1	2	3	4	5
6	7	8	9	10	11	12
13	14	15	16	17	18	19
20	21	22	23	24	25	26
27	28	29	30	31		

Phonemic Awareness

PHONEME ISOLATION: INITIAL

Listen for /f/ Tell children you will say some words and they will listen for the beginning sound in the words. Say the following tongue twister:

Five funny frogs found fat fish!

The beginning sound in *five* is /f/. What sound does *five* begin with? (/f/)

What sound does *funny* begin with? (/f/)

What sound does *found* begin with? (/f/)

What sound does *fat* begin with? (/f/)

What sound does *fish* begin with? (/f/)

Let's say the tongue twister together.

Now let's say it again, but let's change the words *fat fish* to another word that begins with /f/.

Supply new words that begin with /f/ to replace *fat fish*, such as *foxes, fans, fawns, fireflies, forks.* Have children say each new tongue twister with you.

Ask each child to say his or her favorite version of the tongue twister.

▲ **"His Four Fur Feet,"** *Oo-pples and Boo-noo-noos: Songs and Activities for Phonemic Awareness*, pages 83–84.

REACHING ALL LEARNERS

Diagnostic Check: Phonemic Awareness

If... children cannot isolate and identify beginning sound /f/ in words,

Then... help children hear the initial sound by segmenting words by onset and rime: /f/-*ound*, /f/-*ive*, /f/-*ish*, /f/-*at*, /f/-*ox*, /f/-*an* and asking children to repeat and then say the words naturally.

ADDITIONAL SUPPORT ACTIVITIES

BELOW-LEVEL Reteach, p. S4

ADVANCED Extend, p. S5

ENGLISH-LANGUAGE LEARNERS Reteach, p. S5

Sharing Literature

Read "Winter Birds"

READ ALOUD

Before Reading Turn to page 14 of the *Big Book of Rhymes and Songs* and track the print as you read aloud the title, "Winter Birds." Ask a child to come up to point to the top of the page. Remind children that this is where you begin reading. Ask another child to point to the bottom of the page. Remind children that this is where you stop reading. Ask children questions to build background.

- **During what season of the year do you see most birds?**
- **What happens to some birds when winter comes?**
- **What kinds of problems do you think birds have in winter?**

Have children make predictions about the poem by telling what they think the title "Winter Birds" means.

During Reading Read the poem aloud. As you read,

- track the print from left to right and top to bottom.
- read with expression to emphasize the feeling of the poem.
- emphasize the rhyming words.

Read the poem once more, asking children to suggest actions to go with each line. As you read the poem, have one child track the print while the others pantomime the actions.

Winter Birds

When the grass is covered up with snow
And birds are wondering where to go
To find some food that they can munch—
My mother feeds them seeds for lunch.

Ben Kenny

▲ **Big Book of Rhymes and Songs, Page 14**

▲ **Big Book of Rhymes and Songs**

OBJECTIVES

- *To follow words from left to right and from top to bottom on a page*
- *To make predictions*
- *To listen and respond to a poem through movement and art*
- *To identify long and short words*

Materials

- *Big Book of Rhymes and Songs*, p. 14
- drawing paper
- crayons

RESPOND TO LITERATURE

Draw and Write About Birds   Have children draw a picture showing something they can do for the birds during winter. Have them write about the picture and then share it with classmates.

LONG AND SHORT WORDS

Display the poem "Winter Birds." Use words from the poem to help children understand word length.

MODEL   **Some words are short because they have just a few letters. Who can find the word _go_ in the poem? How many letters do you see in the word?** (two) **_Go_ is a short word. Look at the word _covered_. How many letters in this word?** (seven) **_Covered_ is a long word.**

Have children point to other long and short words in the poem. Read the words for children and count the letters together. Write some of the longest words on the board, such as _wondering_ and _mother_, and have children compare the number of letters in these words with those in the shortest words, such as _to_ and _can_.

wondering

mother

to

up

ONGOING ASSESSMENT

As you share "Winter Birds," note whether children

- can track print from left to right and from top to bottom.
- can make predictions.
- listen and respond to a poem.

Phonics
Relating /f/ to f

OBJECTIVE

To match consonant f to its sound

Materials

- ■ Letter and Sound Chart 2
- ■ Tactile Letter Cards f
- ■ Picture Word Cards fish, fox
- ■ Fish Pattern (page TI4)
- ■ scissors
- ■ glue
- ■ blue construction paper
- ■ crayons

ACTIVE BEGINNING

Sing "A Few Fine Fish"   Teach children "A Few Fine Fish." Sing the rhyme to the tune of "Mary Had a Little Lamb," repeating phrases to go with the tune. Have children listen for /f/ as they learn the rhyme. Then have them act out the words as they sing it again.

A Few Fine Fish

Our family has fishing poles
We find fishing fun.
Sometimes we catch a few fine fish.
And sometimes we find none.

TEACH/MODEL

Introduce Letter and Sound   Display *Letter and Sound Chart 2.*

Touch the letter *F.* **What is the name of the letter?**

This letter stands for the /f/ sound. Say /ff/.

Read aloud the rhyme on the *Letter and Sound Chart*, tracking the print. Read the *Ff* words in the rhyme aloud. Then point to each *f* and have children say the /f/ sound. Ask: **What letter stands for the /f/ sound?**

Have children join in as you read the rhyme again. Ask them to feel the air they blow out as they say the words that begin with /f/.

F f

Fancy fish go to the fair.
Fancy fish have fun.
They ride the fabulous Ferris wheel
Until the day is done.

▲ **Letter and Sound Chart 2**

PRACTICE/APPLY

Guided Practice   Distribute *Tactile Letter Cards f* to children. Place *Picture/Word Cards fish* and *fox* in a pocket chart. Say the names of the pictures as you point to the *f* in each. Have children repeat the words.

Tell children: **These words begin with *f*.**

Point to the *f* in *fish*. **The /f/ sound is at the beginning of *fish*.**

Point to the *f* in *fox*. **The /f/ sound is at the beginning of *fox*.**

I'm going to say some words. If the word begins with the /f/ sound, hold up your *f* card. If the word doesn't begin with the /f/ sound, don't hold up your *f* card.

fit	fire	dish	face	mind	funny

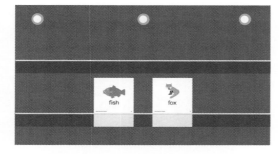

Independent Practice   Pass out copies of the Fish Pattern (page TI4). Have children draw and label a picture on the fish of something whose name begins with the /f/ sound. Ask children to whisper their words to you before they draw them. Children can cut out the patterns and glue their fish to a sheet of blue construction paper. Encourage them to write *Ff* on the paper and add drawings of other animals or objects with names that begin with the /f/ sound.

BELOW-LEVEL

Display the *Letter and Sound Chart Sentence Strips* for Chart 2 in a pocket chart. Focus on one strip at a time. Read the words, and have a child repeat the words and frame each word that begins with *Ff*. Then have the child point to each letter *Ff*, say /f/ and repeat the word after you. Repeat the procedure with another child, using the next sentence strip.

ADVANCED

Have children work with partners. Children can take turns saying words that begin with the sound /f/ while tracing *Tactile Letter Card f* each time a word is said.

Phonics Resources

Phonics Express™ **CD-ROM, Level A** Speedy/Route 2/Train Station, Park, Market

Phonics Practice Book pages 53–54

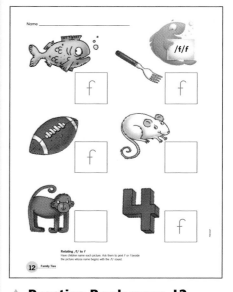

▲ **Practice Book page I2**

OBJECTIVE

To read high-frequency words on and to

Materials

- *Pre-decodable Book 12: The Park*

- *High-Frequency Word Cards We, on, a, the, go, to, like*

- *index card*

- *Picture/Word Cards bus, jeep, van*

Read the Pre-decodable Book

TEACH/MODEL

Review High-Frequency Words   Use the *High-Frequency Word Cards We, go, on, a, to, Picture/Word Card bus* and a period on an index card to build this sentence in the pocket chart: *We go on a [Picture/Word Card bus] to _____.* Point to each word as you read the sentence. Ask children to name a word to complete the sentence. Then point to each word slowly, and have children read the sentence. Invite children to replace *bus* with the *Picture/Word Cards jeep* and *van* in the sentence and follow the same procedure.

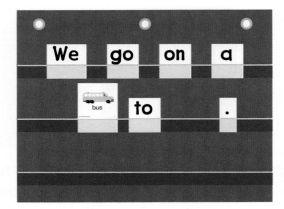

PRACTICE/APPLY

Read the Book   Distribute copies of *The Park*. Read the title to children. Point to each word as you say it. Have children read the book, pointing to each word as they read.

RESPOND

Have children draw a picture of a park. Ask them to draw themselves doing something they like to do at the park.

Pre-decodable Book 12: *The Park*

We go to the park.

2

We go on a bus.

3

We go to the park.

4

We go on a bike.

5

We go to the park.

6

We go on a train.

7

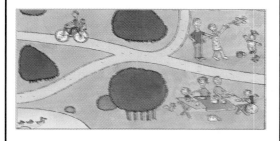

We like to go!

8

■ High-Frequency Words

we, the, go, on, to, like, a

ENGLISH-LANGUAGE LEARNERS

Point to the rebus picture on each page and say the word. Ask children to repeat the word. Then have children read the sentence. Continue this procedure through the book.

School-Home Connection

Take-Home Book Version

◄ Pre-decodable Book "The Park"

▲ **Pop-Pop Independent Reader 12**

OBJECTIVES

- *To understand the purpose of a caption*

- *To write a caption*

Materials

- *Big Book of Rhymes and Songs*, p. 14

- index cards

- marker

Writing

Write a Caption

DRAW AND WRITE

Talk About Winter Display the poem, "Winter Birds" on page 14 of the *Big Book of Rhymes and Songs.* Ask children to recall what winter is like for the birds. (There is snow on the ground. The birds don't know where to go for food. People feed seeds to the birds.) Ask children to think of other ways winter is special for them.

Write a Caption Tell children that they are going to draw pictures to show something special they do during the winter season. Then they will write a caption for their picture. Tell them that a caption is one or more words that tell about a picture. They can write a word that names the picture or they can write a sentence about the picture.

Self-Selected Writing Have children draw and write about self-selected topics in their journal.

Share Time

Reflect on the Lesson Have children tell what the *Pre-decodable Book: The Park* was about. Invite each child to sit in the Author's Chair to share the drawing and read the caption that was written during today's Writing activity.

 S.S.R. Have children read silently from a book of their choice.

 **Centers**  **MANIPULATIVE**

Long and Short

Prepare eight to ten picture/word cards by gluing on index cards pictures or photos of objects or animals whose names begin with /f/f. Label each picture. Use pictures and words such as *fox, fan, fig, fin, fly, family, farmhouse, feather, flamingo, flagpole.*

Have children sort the cards into two groups of four or five pictures: one group with short words and one group with long words.

Materials

- drawings or magazine photographs
- glue
- index cards
- marker

fan

flamingo

WARM UP

Phonemic Awareness
Phoneme Matching

Sharing Literature
Library Book:
A Birthday Basket for Tía

Read

by Pat Mora • illustrated by Cecily Lang

Develop Concept Vocabulary

Respond to Literature

Literature Focus: Retelling the Story

Phonics

Consonants /g/g, /f/f

Writing

Interactive Writing: Birthday Message

MORNING MESSAGE

Kindergarten News

(Child's name) has a _____.

(Child's name) wants to have a

_____.

Write Kindergarten News Talk with children about pets they have or would like to have.

Use prompts such as the following to guide children as you write the news:

- **Who can name their pet?**
- **Who can show me where (child's name) begins and ends?**
- **Who can name a pet they want to have?**

As you write the message, invite children to contribute by writing letters, words, or names they have previously learned. Remind them to use proper spacing, capitalization, and punctuation.

Calendar Language

Point to and read aloud the months of the year. Ask children to raise their hand if that is their birthday month. If they do not know, provide them with the name of the month.

Sunday	Monday	Tuesday	Wednesday	Thursday	Friday	Saturday
		1	2	3	4	5
6	7	8	9	10	11	12
13	14	15	16	17	18	19
20	21	22	23	24	25	26
27	28	29	30	31		

Phonemic Awareness

PHONEME MATCHING

Matching Sounds   Tell children to listen as you sing the following song to the tune of "Row, Row, Row Your Boat." Then have children sing with you and respond by answering the question.

Sing:

Say, say, say the word,

Say the word right now.

Say the word that starts like *girl*.

Say the word right now.

Say: **Is the word *hat* or *goat*?** (*goat*)

Repeat the song replacing the word **girl** with **goose**, **fish**, and **fox**. Replace the words **hat or goat** with **gate or dog**, **pot or fish**, **farm or sun**. Sing the song again and replace the third line with: **Say the word that ends like *pig*. Is the word *dig* or *fun*?** Continue with similar verses.

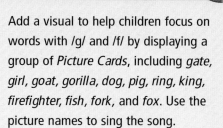

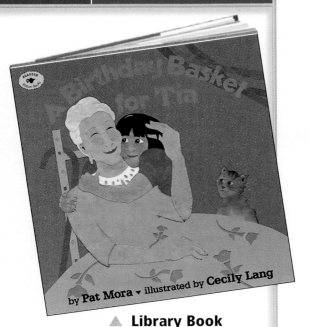

▲ **Library Book**

OBJECTIVES

- *To connect text to life experiences*

- *To recall story details*

- *To describe and categorize common objects*

- *To retell a familiar story*

Materials

- *Library Book: A Birthday Basket for Tía*

- drawing paper

- crayons or markers

Sharing Literature

Read A Birthday Basket for Tía

READ ALOUD

Before Reading   Ask children how they feel on their birthday or when they go to a birthday celebration. (happy, excited, surprised) Display *A Birthday Basket for Tía*. Read the title as you track the print. Ask children what they recall about the story. If children cannot remember all of the gifts Cecilia gave to Tía, use this prompt to help children set a purpose for rereading:

> **MODEL** **I remember this story is about Tía's birthday surprise. Cecilia gives Tía some special gifts. I'll read the story again to see what the gifts are and why they are special.**

During Reading   Reread the story aloud. As you read,

- pause to have children tell why each gift is special. Show children how by modeling your thinking about the first gift named in the story.

> **MODEL** **I see Cecilia puts a book in the birthday basket. Cecilia wants to thank Tía for the many books she read.**

- recall the story events. After reading about the gift of a teacup, have children recall the other gifts that are already in the basket. (book, bowl, flowerpot). Ask children if they recall what Cecilia puts in the basket next. (ball) Then read on.

DEVELOP CONCEPT VOCABULARY

Ask children to tell what Cecilia puts in the basket. Refer to story illustrations if necessary. Write the words on the board and read them aloud: *book, bowl, flowerpot, teacup, ball.* Then ask the following questions. Ask children to read the words with you.

- **Who can point to the longest word?** (*flowerpot*)
- **Which words name objects you use when you eat?** (*bowl, teacup*)
- **Which word names an object you play with?** (*ball*)

RESPOND TO LITERATURE

Draw a Story Event Have children draw and label one thing Cecilia and Tía do together. Ask them to tell about their pictures.

★
Literature Focus

RETELLING THE STORY

Use the following prompts to help children recall story events and retell the story:

Who is in this story? (Cecilia, Tía, and Chica)

What does Cecilia do? (She thinks about special gifts she could put in a birthday basket. She puts a book, a bowl, a flowerpot, a teacup, and a ball in the basket.)

How does Tía feel about the gifts? (She is surprised and happy.)

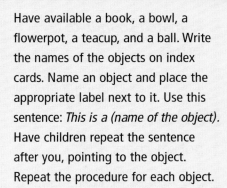

ENGLISH-LANGUAGE LEARNERS

Have available a book, a bowl, a flowerpot, a teacup, and a ball. Write the names of the objects on index cards. Name an object and place the appropriate label next to it. Use this sentence: *This is a (name of the object).* Have children repeat the sentence after you, pointing to the object. Repeat the procedure for each object.

ADVANCED

Provide five sentence strips with the sentence frame *Cecilia puts a _____ in the basket.* Read the sentence frame to children, tracking the print. Have them complete each sentence by drawing a picture of one thing she put in the basket. Read the sentences to children. Have them put the sentences in story order.

ONGOING ASSESSMENT

As you share *A Birthday Basket for Tía*, note whether children,

- **connect text to personal experiences.**
- **recall story details.**

OBJECTIVES

- *To recognize uppercase and lowercase Gg and Ff*

- *To match sounds to letters*

Materials

- pocket chart
- *Big Alphabet Cards Gg, Ff*
- *Alphabet Cards G, F*
- *Picture Word Cards girl, fork, firefighter, gate, fish, gorilla, fox, goat*
- *Tactile Letter Cards G, F*

Phonics

Consonants /g/ g, /f/ f ✔ *Review*

ACTIVE BEGINNING

Recite the G and F Rhymes   Display *Big Alphabet Cards Gg and Ff*. Ask children to name each letter and to "write" the letter in the palm of their hands. Then have children recite or sing "Goose! Goose!" (page 42) and recite "A Few Fine Fish" (page 62).

TEACH/MODEL

Discriminate F and G

Hold up *Big Alphabet Card F* and ask for the letter name.

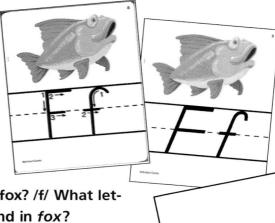

Point to the picture and say its name. Have children repeat it. (*fox*)

What sound do you hear at the beginning of fox? /f/ What letter stands for the /f/ sound in *fox*?

Follow the same procedure for *Big Alphabet Card Gg*.

In the pocket chart place *Alphabet Cards G* and *F* and *Picture Cards fork* and *girl*. Say each picture name and tell children you need to decide where to place each *Picture Card*.

> **MODEL**   I'll start with the fork. *F—ork* begins with the /f/ sound. So I'll put the picture of the fork below *F*.

Model the same process with *Picture Card girl*.

PRACTICE/APPLY

Guided Practice Place these *Picture/Word Cards* on the chalk-ledge:

firefighter, gate, fish, gorilla, fox, goat. Tell children that they will now sort some pictures.

Say the picture name. If the beginning sound is /f/, let's put the card below the *F*. If the beginning sound is /g/, let's put the card below the *G*.

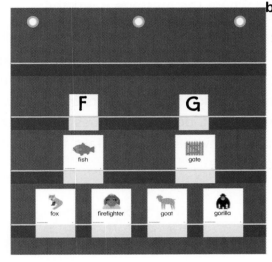

Independent Practice Give each child *Tactile Letter Cards G and F*.

I'm going to say some words. Listen carefully to the sound you hear at the beginning of each word. Think about the letter that stands for that sound, then hold up the letter card that stands for that sound.

gas	fiddle	finger	garden	go	fish
four	give	fine	geese	fancy	ghost

Interactive Writing

Write a Birthday Message

OBJECTIVES

- To identify the front, inside, and back of a card

- To write a birthday message

Materials

- birthday cards
- chart paper
- marker

WRITE TO A CHARACTER

Talk About Birthdays   Show children several birthday cards. Ask them to point to the front, inside, and back of the cards. Demonstrate how the card opens left to right. Ask children to point to where the message is written.

Write a Birthday Message   Tell children that together they are going to write a birthday message to Tía. Explain that you will begin by writing the words *Dear Tía* on chart paper. Say the words aloud and invite a child to write letters they know, such as *D* and *T*. As children suggest ideas for the message, write the words on the chart paper. Invite children to take turns writing letters and words they know.

Dear Tía,

Happy Birthday to you. Today you are ninety years old. We hope you make lots of wishes. Blow out all the candles on your cake.

Your friends,

The Kindergarten Class

Journal Writing   Have children draw and write about a special birthday or other celebration they have had.

 **Share Time**

Reflect on the Lesson Ask children to share experiences about birthday parties they have had or have attended. Tell them to name the foods they ate and the games they played. Have children name ways their parties were the same or different from Tía's party. Read to children the birthday message they wrote for the Interactive Writing activity.

 Have children read silently from a book of their choice.

 **Centers** DRAMATIC PLAY

A Birthday Party

Children can work in small groups to plan and attend a birthday party. Party hosts can decorate with balloons and streamers, set the table, decorate invitations to deliver to guests, put candles on the "cake," and greet the guests. Party guests can wrap presents (toys in boxes) to give to the "birthday child," make cards, "eat" cake, and sing "Happy Birthday."

Materials

- paper plates, cups, napkins, plastic forks
- inflated balloons, crepe paper streamers
- party hats
- a pretend Styrofoam cake and candles
- toys
- boxes, bows, wrapping paper, and tape
- stationery

Learning Centers

Choose from the following suggestions to enhance your learning centers for the theme Family Ties.
(Additional learning centers for this theme can be found on pages 14–16 and 122)

(Additional learning centers for this theme can be found on pages 14–16 and 122)

WRITING CENTER

Helping Others

Tell children to think about a time they helped someone in their family or a friend. Then have them write a few sentences telling whom they helped and what they did. Invite children to illustrate their sentences. When everyone has finished, children can read their sentences to one another and share their illustrations.

I hilpt my frend Ina.
I tid her sho.

20 Minutes

Materials

- paper
- pencils
- crayons

BLOCK CENTER

Building Together

Tell children they are going to play a building game. Shuffle a set of number cards and place them face down in the block center. Have one child begin the game by choosing a number card, taking the same number of blocks, and stacking the blocks one atop the other. The game continues, with children taking turns choosing a card and stacking blocks until the blocks tumble down. Then a new game can begin.

20 Minutes

Materials

- blocks
- number cards (multiple copies of each number): 1, 2, 3, 4, 5

Teacher Notes

Teacher Notes

15-30 Minutes

ORAL LANGUAGE

- **Phonemic Awareness**

- **Sharing Literature**

45 Minutes

LEARNING TO READ

- **Phonics**

- **Vocabulary**

Daily Routines
- Morning Message
- Calendar Language
- Writing Prompt

15-30 Minutes

LANGUAGE ARTS

- **Writing**
  Daily Writing Prompt

Day 1

Phonemic Awareness, 83
Phoneme Isolation: Initial

Sharing Literature, 84
 Read

Big Book: *Off We Go!*
 **Literature Focus, 85**
Compare/Contrast

 **Phonics, 86 T**
Introduce: Short Vowel *Ii*
Identify/Write **T**

 Shared Writing, 88
Write About Animals

Writing Prompt, 88
Draw and write self selected topics.

Share Time, 89
Share sentences from the class book.

Day 2

Phonemic Awareness, 91
Phoneme Isolation

Sharing Literature, 92
Library Book: *Dear Juno*

 **Literature Focus, 93**
Character's Feelings

Phonics, 94 T
Relating /i/ to *i* **T**

 Shared Writing, 96
Write a Letter

Writing Prompt, 96
Draw and write about a friend.

Share Time, 97
Read

Read the letter and point out the greeting and closing.

T = tested skill

 **Phonics**

Ii; Blending
/i/ - /t/

Focus of the Week:
- **PHONEMIC AWARENESS**
- **SHARING LITERATURE**
- **WRITING: Sentences, Letter, List, Story**

Day 3

Phonemic Awareness, 99
Phoneme Blending

Sharing Literature, 100
 Read

Read-Aloud Anthology:
"The Three Bears," p. 58

(Skill) **Literature Focus, 101**
Sequence

 **Phonics**, 102 **T**
Blending /i/ - /t/

 Interactive Writing, 104
Write Opposites

Writing Prompt, 104
Draw and write about big and little things.

Share Time, 105
Retell the story "The Three Bears."

Day 4

Phonemic Awareness, 107
Syllable Segmentation

Sharing Literature, 108
Big Book of Rhymes and Songs: "The Very Nicest Place," p. 22

(Skill) **Literature Focus, 109**
Questions for Research

 **Phonics**, 110 **T**
Review: Short Vowel /i/*i*

 Read

PRE-DECODABLE BOOK 13
Sit on My Chair

 Writing, 112
Write a Sentence

Writing Prompt, 112
Draw and write about homes.

Share Time, 113
Discuss animal homes and Pre-decodable Book 13, *Sit on My Chair*.

Day 5

Phonemic Awareness, 115
Phoneme Isolation and Matching: Medial

Sharing Literature, 116
Big Book: *Off We Go!*

(Skill) **Literature Focus, 117**
Picture Details

 Phonics, 118 **T**
Words with /i/ - /t/

 Interactive Writing, 120
Write a Story

Writing Prompt, 120
Draw and write about visits with friends.

Share Time, 121
Read

Read the class story, "Little Mole's Visit to Grandma's."

Day at a Glance
Day I

WARM UP

Phonemic Awareness
Phoneme Isolation: Initial

Sharing Literature
Big Book:
Off We Go!

Read

Develop Concept Vocabulary

Respond to Literature

Literature Focus:
Compare/Contrast

Phonics

Short Vowel *Ii*

Writing
Animals

MORNING MESSAGE

Kindergarten News

Today is _____.

On (name of day) we have

(name of activity) after school.

Write Kindergarten News Talk with children about activities or special routines they have after school.

Use prompts such as the following to guide children as you write the news:

- **Name some activities you do after school.**
- **Who can show me the beginning of a word?**
- **Who can show me a space between words?**

As you write the message, invite children to contribute by writing letters, words, or names they have previously learned. Remind them to use proper spacing, capitalization, and punctuation.

Calendar Language

Point to and read aloud the days of the week. Name the days of the week again and invite children to join in and clap the syllables for each sentence. Say: *Hooray! It is (name of day).*

Sunday	Monday	Tuesday	Wednesday	Thursday	Friday	Saturday
		1	2	3	4	5
6	7	8	9	10	11	12
13	14	15	16	17	18	19
20	21	22	23	24	25	26
27	28	29	30	31		

Phonemic Awareness

PHONEME ISOLATION: INITIAL

Listen for /i/ Say aloud the following finger rhyme, bending your index finger to show how inchworms move. Say each line of the rhyme again, having children repeat the words after you.

Iggy is an inchworm.

It makes Isabelle itch!

It crawls up her arm

Inch by inch by inch.

Have children listen for and say words with /i/.

Say *Iggy*. The sound I hear at the beginning of *Iggy* is /i/.

Say the sound you hear at the beginning of *Iggy*. (/i/)

Say *inchworm*. What sound do you hear at the beginning of *inchworm*? (/i/)

Say *Isabelle*. What sound do you hear at the beginning of *Isabelle*? (/i/)

Say *itch*. What sound do you hear at the beginning of *itch*? (/i/)

Say *inch*. What sound do you hear at the beginning of *inch*? (/i/)

Repeat the rhyme and have children make inchworm movements with a finger each time they hear a word that begins with /i/. As you say the following words, have children raise their hands when they hear a word that begins with /i/.

insect	alligator	is	itch
kitten	into	ink	baby
imp	puppy	igloo	it

ENGLISH-LANGUAGE LEARNERS

Have children use disks and Side B of the *Write-On/Wipe-Off Board.* Ask children to point to the star and to place a disk in the first box when they hear /i/. Say the words *it, is, if, in, to, at, on.*

▲ **Big Book**

Sharing Literature

Read Off We Go!

READ ALOUD

Before Reading Display the cover of *Off We Go!* Point to the title and track the print as you read it aloud. Page through the story and ask the following questions:

- **What animal families are in this story?** (mice, frogs, moles, snakes, ducks, and spiders)

- **Where do the mice live?** (Possible responses: meadow, field, forest) **How do mice move?** (Possible responses: runs, jumps)

- **Where do frogs live?** (Possible responses: bog, pond) **How do frogs move?** (Possible responses: hops, leaps)

- **Where is each animal going?** (to its Grandma's house)

MODEL I remember that in this story each animal is going to its Grandma's. I know the animals live in different places and move in different ways. Thinking about what I know about animals helps me understand the story.

During Reading Read the story aloud. As you read,

- pause to allow children to examine the pictures of the animals, to see where they live, and to note how they move.

- have children repeat the words that tell how each animal moves.

OBJECTIVES

- *To use prior knowledge to understand characters and settings*

- *To use general and specific language*

- *To categorize words*

- *To compare and contrast*

Materials

- *Big Book: Off We Go!*

- index cards

- marker

- paper bag

DEVELOP CONCEPT VOCABULARY

After Reading Have children name the animals in the *Big Book: Off We Go.* (mouse, frog, mole, snake, duck, spider) Write the animal names on the board. Track the letters as you say each name. Then ask the following questions.

- **Which name begins with /d/?** (duck)
- **Which names begin with /m/?** (mouse, mole)
- **Which animal has eight legs?** (spider)
- **Which animal lives underground?** (mole)

RESPOND TO LITERATURE

Discuss Story Characters Draw and label a simple sketch of a mouse, frog, mole, snake, duck, and spider on separate index cards and place the cards in a paper bag. Have children take out an animal card, say the name, and tell something about the animal. Encourage children to speak in complete sentences.

COMPARE/CONTRAST

Literature Focus

Tell children that the animals in the story are alike in some ways and different in some ways. Display *Off We Go!* and show the first few pages as you talk about the mouse and the frog.

MODEL **I know something that is the same about the mouse and the frog. They are both animals and that they are both going to Grandma's house. Something different is the mouse is gray and pink, lives in the grass, and tip-toes to Grandma's. The frog is green with spots, lives in the mud, and hops to Grandma's.**

Select two other animals from the story and have children tell how they are alike and different.

BELOW-LEVEL

Have children look through the *Big Book* and name each animal. Have them point to the illustration as they describe what the animal looks like. They can describe the animal's color, its size, the number of legs, and how it moves.

ONGOING ASSESSMENT

As you share *Off We Go!,* note whether children

- **can identify characters and settings.**
- **can use general and specific language.**
- **can categorize words.**

Day at a Glance

Day 2

WARM UP

Phonemic Awareness
Phoneme Isolation

Sharing Literature
Library Book:
Dear Juno

Read

dear juno
BY Soyung Pak
ILLUSTRATED BY
Susan Kathleen Hartung

Develop Listening Comprehension

Respond to Literature

Literature Focus: Character's Feelings

Phonics
Relating /i/ to *i*

Shared Writing
Letter

MORNING MESSAGE

Kindergarten News

Now (Child's name) can

_____ .

Write Kindergarten News   Talk with children about new activities they have tried and new things they can do.

Use prompts such as the following to guide children as you write the news:

• **What are some new things you have learned to do this year?**

• **Who can show me the beginning of the sentence?**

• **Who can show me the end of the sentence?**

• **How many words are in the sentence?**

As you write the message, invite children to contribute by writing letters, words, or names they have previously learned. Remind them to use proper spacing, capitalization, and punctuation.

Calendar Language

Tell children that the days of each month are numbered and the numbers tell the date. Point to and read aloud the month and the date. Ask: *What month is it? What is the date?*

Sunday	Monday	Tuesday	Wednesday	Thursday	Friday	Saturday
		1	2	3	4	5
6	7	8	9	10	11	12
13	14	15	16	17	18	19
20	21	22	23	24	25	26
27	28	29	30	31		

Phonemic Awareness

PHONEME ISOLATION

Identify the Position of /i/ in Words   Have children point to the heart shape on Side B of their *Write-On/Wipe-Off Board*. Give each child a disk to use with the board. Explain that they will be working with the three boxes next to the heart. Have them put the disk under the boxes. As you say a word, emphasizing the /i/ sound, have children move the disk into the box to show if they hear the sound at the beginning or in the middle of the word.

MODEL *In.* /i//n/, /i//n/. I hear the /i/ sound at the beginning of *in*. I'll push my disk into the first box because /i/ is the first sound in the word *in*. Say the word with me. *In.* Now move your disk.

Pin. /p/ /i/ /n/, /p/ /i/ /n/. I hear the /i/ sound in the middle of *pin*. I'll push my disk in the middle box, because I hear /i/ in the middle of *pin*. Say the word with me. *Pin.*

Say the following words. Have children push the disk in the first box or the middle box to show where they hear the /i/ sound.

big	in	give
if	lid	win
rib	it	inch
itch	sit	fin

▲ "Kitty Alone," *Oo-pples and Boo-noo-noos: Songs and Activities for Phonemic Awareness,* pages 100–101.

BELOW-LEVEL

Repeat the activity. As you say each word, elongate the /i/ sound: /iinn/ /ppiinn/. Have children repeat the sounds in the word and then move the disk in the corresponding box.

LEARNING TO READ

▲ **Library Book**

OBJECTIVES

- *To use pictures and context to make predictions about story content*

- *To identify setting*

- *To understand the beginning, middle, and ending of a story*

- *To understand characters' feelings*

Materials

- *Library Book: Dear Juno*

- *drawing paper*

- *crayons*

LEARNING TO READ

Sharing Literature

Read Dear Juno

READ ALOUD

Before Reading Display *Dear Juno* and track the print as you read the title. Use these prompts to build background and to help children make predictions:

- **If a family member or friend lives far away, how can you let them know what happened to you in school today?** (Possible responses: e-mail, telephone, letters) **When you write a letter, you begin with the word** *Dear.*

- **Who do you see on the front cover?** (a boy and a dog) **The boy's name is Juno.**

- **What is the boy doing?** (opening a letter)

- **Who do you see on the back cover?** (a woman and a cat)

- **What is the woman doing?** (reading a letter)

Have children tell what they think the story will be about.

During Reading Read the story aloud. As you read,

- pause to identify the setting after reading the first page.

  Where is the boy? (The boy is sitting on a swing in his yard.)

  What time of day is it? (It is night.)

- pause to discuss unfamiliar words.

  MODEL **A persimmon is a kind of fruit that grows on trees. It is usually orange and has lots of seeds.**

DEVELOP LISTENING COMPREHENSION

After Reading   Have children answer these questions:

- **In the beginning of the story, who sends Juno a letter?** (his grandmother)

- **In the middle of the story, who helps Juno read the letter?** (Mom and Dad)

- **What does Juno do with the letter?** (He takes the letter to school.)

- **What happens at the end of the story?** (Grandmother sends another letter with colored pencils, a photograph, and a toy plane.)

- **How does Juno know that his grandmother is coming to visit?** (He guesses because she sends him a toy airplane.)

RESPOND TO LITERATURE

Draw Pictures   Distribute drawing paper folded in half to children. On one half of the paper, have children draw a picture that shows something they would like to send to someone in the mail. Then on the other half, have children draw something they would like to get in the mail.

CHARACTER'S FEELINGS

Tell children that you find out about a character's feelings by thinking about what the character says and does.

MODEL   I know that Juno cares about his grandmother. When he gets her letter, he opens it carefully. He acts as though this letter is special. He looks at the photograph and flower in the letter. He thinks about how they tell him about his grandmother.

Ask children to tell what else they know about Juno by what he says and does. Ask what they know about his grandmother.

BELOW-LEVEL

Look at the pictures in *Dear Juno* with children. Have children describe what they see on each page. Focus children's attention on the characters' expressions, the setting, and the action in each picture to help them follow the sequence of events throughout the story.

ONGOING ASSESSMENT

As you share *Dear Juno*, note whether children

- can identify the front cover and back cover.
- use pictures and context to make predictions.
- can identify the setting.

OBJECTIVE

To match short vowel Ii to its sound

Materials

- ■ *Letter and Sound Chart 17*
- ■ *Tactile Letter Cards Ii*
- ■ *Picture/Word Cards inchworm, pig*
- ■ pocket chart
- ■ *Igloo Pattern (page T15)*
- ■ scissors
- ■ crayons
- ■ tape

Phonics Resources

Phonics Express™ CD-ROM, Level A, Roamer/Route 2/Fire Station, Train Station

▲ Letter and Sound Chart 17

Phonics
Relating /i/ to *i*

ACTIVE BEGINNING

Recite the Rhyme   Teach children the rhyme "Itty Bitty Inchworm." Tell children to listen for the sound /i/ as they recite the rhyme. Then have them curl and straighten their index finger to resemble an inchworm as they recite the rhyme again.

Itty Bitty Inchworm
by Susan Little

Can you imitate an inchworm,

An itty bitty itty one,

That measures inches on a twig,

Inch by inch until it's done?

TEACH/MODEL

Introduce Letter and Sound   Display *Letter and Sound Chart 17.*

Touch the letter *I.* **What is the name of this letter?**

This letter stands for the /i/ sound. Say /ii/.

Read aloud the rhyme on the *Letter and Sound Chart,* tracking the print. Read the *Ii* words in the rhyme aloud. Then point to each *i* and have children say the /i/ sound.

Have children join in as you read the rhyme again.

Guided Practice Distribute a *Tactile Letter Card i* and a *Write-On/Wip-Off Board* to each child. Have children point to the heart shape on side B of their *Write-On/Wipe-Off Board*. Explain that they will be working with the three boxes next to the heart. Then place *Picture/Word Cards inchworm* and *pig* in a pocket chart. Say each word as you point to the *i* in each. Have children repeat the words.

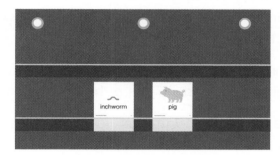

Tell children: **Some words begin with *i* and some words have *i* in the middle.**

Point to the *i* in *inchworm*. **The /i/ sound is at the beginning of the word *inchworm*.**

Point to the *i* in *pig*. **The /i/ sound is in the middle of the word *pig*.**

Tell children: **I'll say some words. If the /i/ sound is at the beginning of the word, put your letter *i* in the beginning box. If the /i/ sound is in the middle of the word, put your letter *i* in the middle box.**

Model the procedure, using the words *inchworm* and *pig*. Then say these words:

ill	igloo	hill	in
pin	big	itch	dip

Independent Practice Pass out copies of the Igloo Pattern (page T15). Have children draw and label on the igloo a picture of something whose name begins with the /i/ sound. Ask children to whisper the name to you before they draw. Children can cut out the patterns and post them on a bulletin board or tape their igloos along a wall to create a village. Encourage them to take turns naming objects on the igloos as well as animals, objects in the classroom, and people's names that begin with /i/.

REACHING ALL LEARNERS

Diagnostic Check: Phonics

If... children cannot relate /i/ to *i*,
Then... use *Letter and Sound Chart 17* again with the plastic overlay in place. As you share the rhyme, have children name the letter *Ii*, track the letter, and underline the letter. Then repeat the Guided Practice.

ADDITIONAL SUPPORT ACTIVITIES

BELOW-LEVEL	Reteach, p. S8
ADVANCED	Extend, p. S9
ENGLISH-LANGUAGE LEARNERS	Reteach, p. S9

Phonics Practice Book pages 57–58

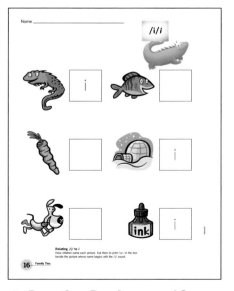

▲ **Practice Book page 16**

Shared Writing

Write a Letter

AN INVITATION

Talk About Writing Letters Remind children that Juno and his grandmother write letters to each other. Ask children why people write letters. (to share news, to send an invitation, to say thank you)

Tell children that, as a class, they are going to write a letter to the school principal, asking him or her to come to the class to read.

Write a Letter Write the word *Dear* at the top of the chart paper and ask children to supply the principal's name. Write the name after *Dear*. Ask children to offer suggestions for the body of the letter, and compose their ideas in a few simple sentences. Then write (*your name*)'s Class as the closing.

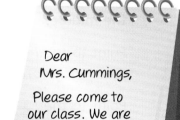

Dear
Mrs. Cummings,

Please come to
our class. We are
reading <u>Dear Juno.</u>
You can read with us.

Mr. Salvi's Class

OBJECTIVES

- *To write a class letter*
- *To recognize the greeting and closing in a letter*
- *To recognize that words make up sentences*

Materials

- chart paper
- marker
- drawing paper
- crayons or markers

Journal Writing Have children draw or write about a friend.

WRAP UP ## Share Time

Reflect on the Lesson   Have children read with you the letter they composed inviting the principal to join them in reading a book. Have them point out the greeting and closing in the letter. Ask them to tell about the letter Juno wrote to his grandmother.

S.S.R. *Sustained Silent Reading*   Have children read silently from a book of their choice.

 **Centers**   ✏️ **LETTERS AND WORDS**

Dotted Ii's

Have children write large letters *I* and *i* on drawing paper. Then they can glue construction paper dots over the letters they have written. When the glue is dry, encourage children to trace the letters with a finger and to write additional *Ii*'s around the edges of the paper.

Materials

- 1-inch construction-paper dots
- drawing paper
- crayons
- glue

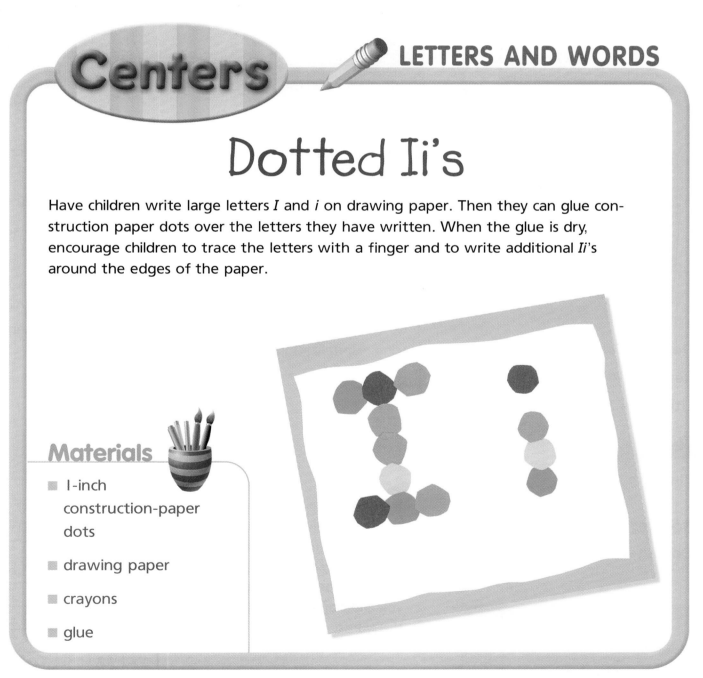

Day at a Glance
Day 3

WARM UP

Phonemic Awareness
Phoneme Blending

Sharing Literature
Read-Aloud Anthology
"The Three Bears"

Read

Develop Concept Vocabulary

Respond to Literature

Literature Focus: Sequence

Phonics
Blending /i/- /t/

Interactive Writing
Opposites

MORNING MESSAGE

Kindergarten News

In the morning (child's name)

_____ , _____ ,

and _____ .

Write Kindergarten News Talk with children about what they do in the morning before coming to school.

Use prompts such as the following to guide children as you write the news:

- **Who can name what you did to get ready to come to school?**
- **Who can point to where to begin reading?**
- **Who can show me the name of (child's name)?**

As you write the message, invite children to contribute by writing letters, words, or names they have previously learned. Remind them to use proper spacing, capitalization, and punctuation.

Calendar Language

Point to and read aloud the names of the days of the week. Say: An activity the class will do on each day. Tuesday we will _____. Have children repeat the sentence with you and clap for each syllables in the words.

Sunday	Monday	Tuesday	Wednesday	Thursday	Friday	Saturday
		1	2	3	4	5
6	7	8	9	10	11	12
13	14	15	16	17	18	19
20	21	22	23	24	25	26
27	28	29	30	31		

Phonemic Awareness

PHONEME BLENDING

Blending   Use the rabbit puppet for this blending activity. Tell children they can listen to the sounds the rabbit says, blend the sounds, and say the words.

MODEL   **/p/ /i/ /t/. Say the sounds with the rabbit: /p/ /i/ /t/.**

If I put the sounds together, I can say the word: /p/ /i/ /t/ *pit*.

Say the sounds with the rabbit and name the word: *pit*.

Use the rabbit puppet to say the following sounds:

/m/ /i/ /t/ (*mitt*)   **/f/ /i/ /t/** (*fit*)

/f/ /a/ /n/ (*fan*)   **/r/ /i/ /m/** (*rim*)

/d/ /i/ /g/ (*dig*)   **/f/ /i/ /g/** (*fig*)

/f/ /i/ /n/ (*fin*)   **/f/ /a/ /t/** (*fat*)

REACHING ALL LEARNERS

Diagnostic Check: Phonemic Awareness

If... children cannot blend sounds and say words,

Then... have them blend onset and rime before blending each phoneme, such as /p/ *it*, /m/ *it*, /d/ *ig*.

ADDITIONAL SUPPORT ACTIVITIES

BELOW-LEVEL   Reteach, p. S10

ADVANCED   Extend, p. S11

ENGLISH-LANGUAGE LEARNERS   Reteach, p. S11

Sharing Literature

Read "The Three Bears"

READ ALOUD

Before Reading Turn to page 58 of the *Read-Aloud Anthology* and read the title aloud. Use these prompts to build background for the story:

- **What do you know about this story?** (Possible responses: There are three bears, big, middle-sized, and little; a girl named Goldilocks visits them.)

Explain that this retelling is written by Anne Rockwell. Have children use what they know about the story to make predictions.

During Reading Read the story aloud. As you read,

- change your voice to represent the different characters.
- have children join in on the repetitive text.

   "Somebody has been eating my porridge."

   "Somebody has been sitting in my chair."

   "Somebody has been lying in my bed."

- pause periodically to recall what has happened so far.

   MODEL **The bears make some porridge. They go for a walk in the woods while the porridge cools. Goldilocks walks into the house. So far she has tasted the porridge and has eaten the little wee bear's porridge.**

▲ **Read-Aloud Anthology**

OBJECTIVES

- *To listen and respond to a story*

- *To identify characters and settings*

- *To name story events*

- *To retell a familiar story*

Materials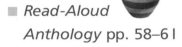

- *Read-Aloud Anthology* pp. 58–61

- drawing paper

- crayons or markers

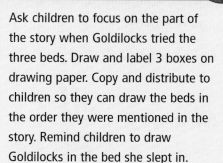

DEVELOP CONCEPT VOCABULARY

Discuss the following words and ask children to answer the questions:

The word *tidy* means "to be neat and clean."

Who is tidy? (the three bears)

The word *porridge* means "a cooked cereal."

Who makes porridge? (the bears)

A latch is a hook or catch that holds a door closed.

Who lifts the latch on the door? (Goldilocks)

RESPOND TO LITERATURE

Favorite Characters Have children draw a favorite character in the story. Ask them to share their picture and use a complete sentence to tell why they like that character.

SEQUENCE

Literature Focus

Tell children that in stories, things happen in a special order. Model how to use order words to retell the story.

MODEL **In "The Three Bears," first, the bears make porridge. Then, they go for a walk. Next, Goldilocks goes into the house. She eats the porridge, sits in the chairs, and sleeps in a bed. Then, the bears come home. Finally, Goldilocks runs away.**

Have children take turns retelling the story. Encourage them to use the Dramatic Play Center and to make puppets to retell the story.

BELOW-LEVEL

Ask children to focus on the part of the story when Goldilocks tried the three beds. Draw and label 3 boxes on drawing paper. Copy and distribute to children so they can draw the beds in the order they were mentioned in the story. Remind children to draw Goldilocks in the bed she slept in.

ONGOING ASSESSMENT

As you share "The Three Bears," note whether children

- listen for a period of time.
- can identify characters and setting.
- use prior knowledge to understand the story.

OBJECTIVES

- *To identify and recognize the initial sound of a spoken word*

- *To blend /i/ and /t/*

Materials

- *Big Alphabet Cards Ii and Tt*

- *Alphabet Cards i, t, s*

- *pocket chart*

- *sentence strips*

Phonics
Blending /i/ - /t/

ACTIVE BEGINNING

Word Hunt   Have children sit in a circle. As you read the following verse, have the children echo. Establish a beat and keep it going throughout the verse.

> **Going on a word hunt.**
>
> **What's this word?**
>
> **/s/ /i/ /t/**
>
> **Together. Sit!**

Continue with the words /p/ /i/ /t/ (*pit*), /f/ /i/ /t/ (*fit*), /t/ /i/ /n/ (*tin*).

TEACH/MODEL

Recognize *i* and *t*
Display *Big Alphabet Card Ii* on the chalk ledge or in a pocket chart.

What letter is this?

What sound does this letter stand for? (/i/)

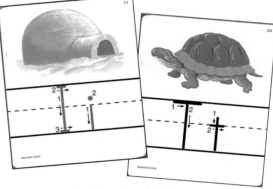

Have children say /i/ with you as you point to the letter.

Do the same procedure for *Big Alphabet Card Tt*.

Word Blending   Explain to children that they are going to blend letters together to read words such as *sit* and *tip*.

- Place the letters *i* and *t* in the pocket chart, separate from each other.

- Point to *i*. Say **/ii/**. Have children repeat the sound after you.
- Point to *t*. Say **/tt/**. Have children repeat the sound after you.

- Slide the *t* next to the *i*. Move your hand under the letters and blend the sounds, elongating them: **/iitt/**. Have children repeat after you.

- Then have children blend read *it* with you.

PRACTICE/APPLY

Guided Practice   Place the letters *s, i,* and *t* in the pocket chart.

- Point to *s* and say **/ss/**. Point to the letter *i* and say **/ii/**. Slide the *i* next to *s*. Move your hand under the letters and blend the sounds, elongating them: **/ssii/**. Have children blend the sounds after you.
- Point to *t*. Say **/tt/**. Have children say the sound.
- Slide the *t* next to the *si*. Slide your hand under *sit* and blend the sounds. Have children blend the sounds as you slide your hand under the word.
- Then have children read the word *sit* along with you.

Follow the same procedure to build and blend *pit, fit,* and *tip* with children.

Independent Practice   Write on sentence strips the sentence frame *It is a _____.* Place one strip in the pocket chart and have children read the sentence frame. Then distribute the sentence strips to children. Have them draw a picture of an animal to complete the sentence. When they have finished, ask them to read their sentence.

▲ **Practice Book page 17**

Family Ties   103

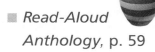

Interactive Writing

Write Opposites

BRAINSTORM AND WRITE

Talk About Opposites On page 59 in the *Read-Aloud Anthology*, read the paragraph describing Goldilocks tasting the porridge. Ask children to recall why Goldilocks does not eat the porridge of the great big bear (too hot) and the middle-sized bear. (too cold) Write the words *hot* and *cold* in two columns on chart paper. Read the words aloud and explain to children that the words *hot* and *cold* are opposites.

Write a List of Opposites Tell children that together they are going to write a list of words that are opposites. Use details from "The Three Bears" to generate more word pairs. Write the story words *big, hard,* and *high* in one column, and have children name the opposites. (little, wee; soft, low) Then have children suggest other possible opposites. Focus on letters and sounds as words are added to the list. Have children take turns coming to the chart to write letters they know. To complete the list, have children add drawings to show the meanings of the words. Then have volunteers stand and share a drawing as you point to and read the corresponding words from the chart.

OBJECTIVES

- *To write opposites*
- *To use letter knowledge to write letters in words*

Materials

- *Read-Aloud Anthology,* p. 59
- chart paper
- marker

Hot

Cold

big, little

Writing Every Day

My Journal

Journal Writing Have children draw or write about things that are big and things that are little.

WRAP UP Share Time

Author's Chair   Have children use the Author's Chair to retell the story "The Three Bears." Ask them to tell their favorite part of the story. Point out words from the story that are also on the opposites chart they wrote during the Interactive Writing activity.

Sustained Silent Reading S.S.R.   Have children read silently from a book of their choice.

Centers  DRAMATIC PLAY

Puppet Play

Have children make stick puppets of Goldilocks and the three bears. Place in the center models made from construction paper character cutouts of the three bears and Goldilocks. Have children use paper, scissors, and glue to create each character. Have children attach the characters to craft sticks. Children can use their puppets to retell the story. Tell them to take their puppets home and use them to tell the story to family members.

Materials

- crayons
- scissors
- craft sticks
- glue
- construction paper

Day at a Glance
Day 4

WARM UP

Phonemic Awareness
Syllable Segmentation

Sharing Literature
Big Book of Rhymes and Songs:
"The Very Nicest Place"

Read
Big Book of Rhymes and Songs

Harcourt

Respond to Literature

Literature Focus: Questions for Research

Reading
Pre-decodable Book 13: Sit on My Chair

Shared Writing
Sentences

MORNING MESSAGE
Kindergarten News

(Child's name) likes to play in the

_____ .

Write Kindergarten News Talk with children about where they like to play.

Use prompts such as the following to guide children as you write the news:

- **Name places where you like to play.**
- **What letter did I write first in (child's name)?**
- **Let's count the letters in (child's name)? How many letters are there?**

As you write the message, invite children to contribute by writing letters, words, or names they have previously learned. Remind them to use proper spacing, capitalization, and punctuation.

Calendar Language

Point to and read aloud the names of the days of the week. Name the days of the week again, inviting children to join in and clap for each day. Say: *Today is _____.* Ask: *What day is today?*

Sunday	Monday	Tuesday	Wednesday	Thursday	Friday	Saturday
		1	2	3	4	5
6	7	8	9	10	11	12
13	14	15	16	17	18	19
20	21	22	23	24	25	26
27	28	29	30	31		

Phonemic Awareness

SYLLABLE SEGMENTATION

Track Syllables in a Word   Ask: **What is a syllable?** (A syllable is a word part.) Tell children to listen as you clap the word parts in the word *rabbit*.

Say *rabbit.* Clap once for each syllable: ***rab-bit.***

Let's say *rabbit* together.

Let's say *rabbit* and clap the syllables: *rab-bit.*

Say the following words and ask children to repeat them and clap for each syllable. Have children tell how many syllables they hear in each word.

bear (bear, 1)

tiger (ti-ger, 2)

butterfly (but-ter-fly, 3)

turtle (tur-tle, 2)

squirrel (squir-rel, 2)

raccoon (rac-coon, 2)

rattlesnake (rat-tle-snake, 3)

monkey (mon-key, 2)

parakeet (par-a-keet, 3)

elephant (el-e-phant, 3)

deer (deer, 1)

porcupine (por-cu-pine, 3)

lizard (liz-ard, 2)

toad (toad, 1)

camel (cam-el, 2)

grasshopper (grass-hop-per, 3)

mon-key

BELOW-LEVEL

Model the process by clapping out one-syllable words and asking children how many claps they hear. Then proceed to two-syllable words.

ADVANCED

Have children work with a partner. Tell them to take turns saying the name of a person, object, or place. Their partner can clap for the syllables and tell how many syllables they hear.

▲ **Big Book of Rhymes and Songs**

OBJECTIVES

- *To listen and respond to a poem*
- *To recite a poem*
- *To share feelings about a poem*
- *To understand that you use a variety of print materials to locate information*
- *To ask questions about text*

Materials

- *Big Book of Rhymes and Songs,* p. 22
- chart paper
- marker
- research materials

Sharing Literature

Read "The Very Nicest Place"

READ ALOUD

Before Reading Display page 22 of the *Big Book of Rhymes and Songs,* and read the title of the poem aloud as you track the print. Help children make a prediction about the poem by asking:

- **What are the names of places where you like to go?**
- **What do you think "the very nicest place" might be?**

During Reading Read the poem aloud. As you read,

- track the print.
- emphasize rhyming words.
- discuss the feelings the poem evokes.

Read the poem again, asking children to join in by repeating each line after you and pantomiming an action to show a fish (put hands together and move back and forth), a bird (flap arms), and a little child (point to self).

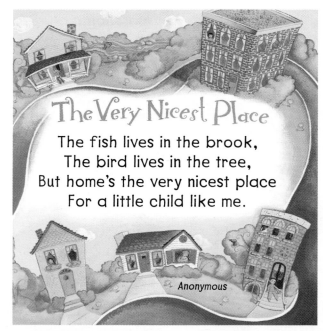

The Very Nicest Place

The fish lives in the brook,
The bird lives in the tree,
But home's the very nicest place
For a little child like me.

Anonymous

▲ **Big Book of Rhymes and Songs, page 22**

RESPOND TO LITERATURE

Discuss Feelings   Have children use describing words to talk about how the words of the poem make them feel.

MODEL The words *But home's the very nicest place For a little child like me* make me think about how cozy and warm a home can be. The poem makes me feel happy and safe.

Encourage children to tell how the poem makes them feel.

QUESTIONS FOR RESEARCH

Reread the first two sentences in the poem: *The fish lives in the brook/The bird lives a in the tree.* Tell children that when you read you sometimes wonder about something and want to find out more information.

MODEL In the poem "The Very Nicest Place," I read about where a fish lives and where a bird lives. I want to find out more about the places where animals live.

Have children suggest questions about animal homes they want to find out more about. Write their ideas on chart paper.

Have available an encyclopedia, a magazine about animals, and books about animal homes. Share the books with children as you explain that you read many kinds of print materials to find out information.

Where does a fish live? Does a fish have a home?

Where does a bird live? How does a bird make its nest?

REACHING ALL LEARNERS

Diagnostic Check: Comprehension

If... children have difficulty asking questions that relate to a text,

Then... pose questions to them such as *Would you like to know more about . . . ? Do you wonder about ...?* Then continue by showing children how to find out answers.

ADDITIONAL SUPPORT ACTIVITIES

BELOW-LEVEL   Reteach, p. S12

ADVANCED   Extend, p. S13

ENGLISH-LANGUAGE LEARNERS   Reteach, p. S13

ONGOING ASSESSMENT

As you share "The Very Nicest Place," note whether children

• listen and respond to a poem.

• can recite the poem.

• share feelings about a poem.

OBJECTIVE

To decode short vowel /i/i words

Materials

- *Alphabet Cards i, s, t*
- pocket chart
- *Pre-decodable Book 13: Sit on My Chair*
- drawing paper
- crayons or markers

Phonics

Short Vowel /i/i ✔ *Review*

TEACH/MODEL

Review Blending Place *Alphabet Cards i* and *t* next to each other in a pocket chart. Move your hand under the letters, blend them, and say: **/iitt/** *it.* Have children blend the sounds with you.

Place *Alphabet Card s* in front of *i* and *t*. Slide your hand under the letters, blend them, and say the word: **/ssiitt/—sit.** Have children blend the sounds and say the word.

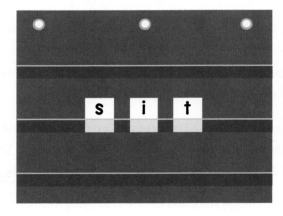

Write this sentence frame on the board: *I sit on my* _____. Have children read the sentence frame aloud as you track the print. Then have children read the sentence and suggest words to finish the sentence, such as *chair, bed, stool,* or *blanket.*

PRACTICE/APPLY

Read the Book Distribute copies of *Sit on My Chair*. Read the title aloud to children. Have children read the book, pointing to each word as they read.

Respond Have children draw a picture of themselves sitting in a chair and color it their favorite color.

Pre-decodable Book 13: *Sit on My Chair*

Sit on my brown chair.

2

Sit on my red chair.

3

Sit on my blue chair.

4

Sit on my white chair.

5

Sit on my purple chair.

6

Sit on my pink chair.

7

I fit on my chair.

8

■ High-Frequency Words

I, on, my

■ Decodable Words

See list on T19.

School-Home Connection

Take-Home Book Version

◀ Pre-decodable Book 13: *Sit on My Chair*

ENGLISH-LANGUAGE LEARNERS

Point to the rebus pictures for a color name and chair on each page and say the words. Then have children read the sentence. Continue this procedure through the book.

▲ **Independent Reader 13: Play Cake**

OBJECTIVES

- *To write a sentence*

- *To recognize that a sentence begins with an uppercase letter and ends with a period*

Materials

- ■ chart paper
- ■ marker
- ■ books about animals and their homes

teaching tip

Be sure children understand that they write the name of the animal in the first blank and the name of the animal's home in the second blank to complete the sentence.

Shared Writing

Write Sentences

BRAINSTORM AND WRITE

Talk About Animal Homes Remind children that in the poem, "The Very Nicest Place," every person and animal has a place to live. List these animal names on chart paper: *bird, frog, bear, dog, spider, mole.* Ask children to tell about the homes they live in. (a nest or tree, a pond or a bog, a cave, a house, a web, a hole in the ground) As they name the animal homes, write the words next to the name of the animal.

Write a Sentence Tell children that together they will write sentences that tell about animal homes. On chart paper, write the sentence frame *A _____ lives in a _____ .* Read the sentence frame to children. Ask children to help you finish the sentence by saying an animal name for you to write on the first line and the name of the place where it lives for you to write on the second line. Read the sentence aloud after you write. Continue by having children choose another animal name from the chart and suggest a home for the animal. Later, children can add drawings to the chart.

Journal Writing Have children draw or write about their homes.

WRAP UP Share Time

Reflect on the Lesson   Invite children to share what they know about animals and their homes. Recall examples of animal homes from the poem "The Very Nicest Place" and the sentences they wrote during Shared Writing. Talk about the *Pre-decodable Book 13: Sit in My Chair.* Ask children to name a special place they like to sit in their homes.

S.S.R. *Sustained Silent Reading*   Have children read silently from a book of their choice.

Centers   BLOCK

My Dream Home

Have children work alone or with a partner, using blocks to build a model of a home they would like to live in. When children are finished, invite them to show you the parts of their home and tell you why they are important. Have children write their name on an index card as a label for their home.

Materials

■ blocks

■ crayons

■ index cards

WARM UP

MORNING MESSAGE

Kindergarten News

(Child's name) likes to read

_____

Phonemic Awareness

Phoneme Isolation and Phoneme Matching: Medial

Sharing Literature

Big Book:
Off We Go!

Read

Respond to Literature

Literature Focus: Picture Details

Phonics

Words with /i/ and /t/

Interactive Writing

Story

Write Kindergarten News Talk with children about some of their favorite stories.

Use prompts such as the following to guide children as you write the news:

- **Name some favorite stories.**
- **Who can show me a letter?**
- **Who can show me a word?**
- **How many words are there in the first line?**
- **Who can point to an uppercase letter?**

As you write the message, invite children to contribute by writing letters, words, or names they have previously learned. Remind them to use proper spacing, capitalization, and punctuation.

Calendar Language

Point to and read aloud the days of the week. Identify the name of the day and invite children to repeat it. Ask: *What is the weather today?* Ask children to draw a sun if it is a sunny day, a cloud if it is cloudy, and raindrops if it is rainy.

Sunday	Monday	Tuesday	Wednesday	Thursday	Friday	Saturday
		1	2	3	4	5
6	7	8	9	10	11	12
13	14	15	16	17	18	19
20	21	22	23	24	25	26
27	28	29	30	31		

Phonemic Awareness

PHONEME ISOLATION: MEDIAL

Listen for Medial /i/ Tell children to listen for the sound in the middle of the word you say.

> **MODEL** *Pit.* **What sound do you hear in the middle of *pit*?** (/i/) **/i/ is the sound you hear in the middle of the word *pit*.**

Follow the same procedure, using the following words. Have children repeat each word and name the sound they hear in the middle.

lip (/i/)	**live** (/i/)	**big** (/i/)	**ship** (/i/)
miss (/i/)	**map** (/a/)	**let** (/e/)	**sad** (/a/)
hat (/a/)	**pet** (/e/)	**lid** (/i/)	**pig** (/i/)

PHONEME MATCHING: MEDIAL

Match Words with /i/ Tell children to listen for the sound in the middle of the two words you say. Have them tell you if the words have the same middle sound.

> **MODEL** *Pit, six.* **I hear /i/ in the middle of *pit*. I hear /i/ in the middle of *six*. *Pit* and *six* have the same middle sound. Say the words with me. *Pit, six.***

Say the following words. Have children repeat the words and say if the words have the same middle sound.

miss, mitt (same)	**gift, gas** (not same)
pill, pal (not same)	**pig, tin** (same)
fix, fit (same)	**pan, pit** (not same)
mat, mix (not same)	**hill, pick** (same)

▲ **Big Book**

OBJECTIVES

- *To use pictures and context to understand story content*

- *To note picture details*

- *To use general and specific language to describe story illustrations*

- *To use prior knowledge*

Materials

- *Big Book: Off We Go!*

- drawing paper

- crayons or markers

Sharing Literature

Read Off We Go!

READ ALOUD/READ ALONG

Before Reading Display *Off We Go!* and read the title aloud. Ask a child to frame the word *Go*. Ask children to recall the characters and events. Use this model to prompt children:

> **MODEL** I remember that the animals in this story all go to visit their Grandmas. Each animal sings a song as it moves along.

Then ask children to tell what else they remember about the story.

During Reading Read the story aloud. As you read,

- emphasize the rhythm of the words and actions.

- pause periodically to point out how pictures, context, and prior knowledge help readers understand the story. Model for children how to share what they know or have learned about each picture:

> **MODEL** The picture shows Little Mole digging. The words tell me that he digs down where it is dark and he creeps to Grandma's house. I know that moles burrow tunnels in the ground. That must be what the mole is doing.

RESPOND TO LITERATURE

Describe Story Illustrations   Have children take turns choosing their favorite story scene. Have them turn to the illustration in the *Big Book*. Tell them to point to the animal as they name it. Tell them to describe how the animal looks: its color, its size, and how it moves. Ask them to describe where the animal lives.

PICTURE DETAILS

Display the first two pages of *Off We Go!* and read the text aloud. Then frame the words *Tip-toe, tippity toe* and say:

MODEL **I read the words tip-toe, tippity toe, but I'm not sure what they mean. Sometimes pictures help readers understand the words. I see that the mice in the picture are using their toes to hold on to the grass. They seem to be balancing carefully on those leaves. I know that when I walk on my tiptoes, I balance carefully.**

Page through the *Big Book* and ask children to tell how the pictures help them understand these words: *Hip-hop, hippity hop; slither-slee, slithery slee;* and *creep-crawl, creepity crawl.*

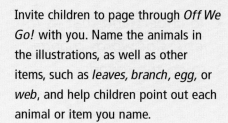

ENGLISH-LANGUAGE LEARNERS

Invite children to page through *Off We Go!* with you. Name the animals in the illustrations, as well as other items, such as *leaves, branch, egg,* or *web,* and help children point out each animal or item you name.

ONGOING ASSESSMENT

As you share *Off We Go!,* note whether children

• recall characters and story events.

• use pictures, context, and prior knowledge to understand the story.

OBJECTIVES

- *To build and read simple one-syllable words*

- *To understand that as the letters of words change, so do the sounds*

Materials

- *Alphabet Cards i, f, n, p, s, t*

- *Word Builders*

- *Word Builder Cards i, f, n, p, s, t*

- pocket chart

- *Magnetic Letters*

- cookie sheet

Phonics
Words with /i/ and /t/

ACTIVE BEGINNING

Chair Game   Place three chairs in the front of the room. Tell children they can play a game using the words *fit* and *sit*. Say each line shown below as you perform the actions. Tell children to repeat each line after you.

I sit, I fit!
(Sit on the middle chair.)

(Child's name) sits, (child's name) fits!
(Point to the chair on your left. Name a child to sit in that chair.)

(Child's name) sits, (child's name) fits!
(Point to the chair on your right. Name a child to sit in that chair.)

We all sit. We all fit!

Have children take turns sitting in the middle chair and calling out names of children to sit next to them.

TEACH/MODEL

Blending Words   Distribute *Word Builders* and *Word Builder Cards i, f, n, p, s, t* to children. As you place *Alphabet Cards* in a pocket chart, tell children to place the same *Word Builder Cards* in their *Word Builders.*

- Place *Alphabet Cards s, i,* and *t* in the pocket chart. Have children do the same.

- Point to *s.* Say /**ss**/. Point to *i.* Say /**ii**/.

- Slide the *i* next to the *s*. Then move your hand under the letters and blend the sounds, elongating them: **/ssii/.** Have children do the same.

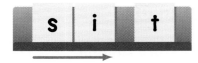

- Point to the letter *t*. Say **/tt/.** Have children do the same.
- Slide the *t* next to the *si*. Slide your hand under *sit* and blend by elongating the sounds: **/ssiitt/.** Have children do the same.
- Then have children blend and read the word *sit* along with you.

PRACTICE/APPLY

Guided Practice   Have children place *Word Builder Cards i* and *t* in their *Word Builders.*

- **Add *p* to *it*. What word did you make?**

- **Change *p* to *f*. What word did you make?**

- **Change *t* to *n*. What word did you make?**

- **Change *f* to *t*. What word did you make?**

Independent Practice   Have children use *Magnetic Letters f, i, n, p, s, t and a cookie sheet* in the Letters and Words Center to build and read *sit, pit, fit, fin, tin.*

▲ **Practice Book page 18**

Family Ties   119

Interactive Writing

Write a Story

BUILD BACKGROUND

Talk About a Story Animal   Ask children to name the animal in the *Big Book Off We Go!* that digs holes in the ground. (Little Mole) Ask them to tell what Little Mole looks like and how he gets to Grandma's.

Write a Story   Tell children that together they will write a story about Little Mole's visit to Grandma's. Help them sequence story events by asking these questions:

How does Little Mole get to Grandma's?

How does Grandma feel when she sees Little Mole?

What happens at the end of the story?

Help children state their ideas in complete sentences. Invite children to write letters and words they know. Point out that you write sentences from left-to-right and top-to-bottom on the paper. Ask children to think of a title for their story and write it on the chart paper.

A Visit to Grandma's

Little Mole dug a tunnel to Grandma's. Grandma was glad to see him. She made a special cake. Little Mole gave Grandma a big kiss. Little Mole went home.

OBJECTIVES

* *To write a story in logical sequence*
* *To write moving left-to-right and top-to-bottom*
* *To use phonetically spelled words to write about experiences*

Materials

* *Big Book: Off We Go!*
* chart paper
* marker

teaching tip

Remind children that sentences need periods at the end.

Journal Writing   Have children draw or write about visits with friends.

WRAP UP **Share Time**

Reflect on the Lesson Have children tell what story they wrote today. (Little Mole's visit to Grandma's.) Gather around the Author's Chair to read the story. Track the print as you read. Ask children to point to uppercase letters at the beginning of sentences and to periods at the end.

S.S.R. Sustained Silent Reading Have children read silently from a book of their choice.

Centers · LISTENING

Off We Go!

Play *Audiotext: Off We Go!* Have children listen and join in to say the rhyming words and repetitive refrains.

Off We Go!
by Jane Yolen
Illustrated by Laurel Molk

Materials

■ *Audiotext: Off We Go!*

■ tape recorder

Learning Centers

Choose from the following suggestions to enhance your learning centers for the theme Family Ties.
(Additional learning centers for this theme can be found on pages 14–16 and 76)

SOCIAL STUDIES CENTER

"Helpers" Collage

Tell children they are going to work with a partner to make a collage of families and friends helping one another. Have children look through old magazines to find and cut out pictures of people helping one another with various tasks, including having fun! Partners can work together to glue their pictures onto paper.

Materials
- old magazines
- safety scissors
- construction paper
- glue sticks

WRITING CENTER

Something I Learned To Do

Tell children to think about a time someone taught them how to do something, such as tie their shoes, ride a bike, feed a pet, bake cookies, use a computer, or play a game. Give children a piece of paper, and have them write about what they learned to do. Children can draw a picture to illustrate their personal narratives. Invite children to read their stories aloud.

My Grampa tot me
how to rid a bik.

Materials
- paper
- pencils
- crayons

Teacher Notes

Teacher Notes

THEME 5

Week 3

Family Ties

⏰ 15-30 Minutes ORAL LANGUAGE

- **Phonemic Awareness**

- **Sharing Literature**

⏰ 45 Minutes LEARNING TO READ

- **Phonics**

- **Vocabulary**

Daily Routines
- **Morning Message**
- **Calendar Language**
- **Writing Prompt**

⏰ 15-30 Minutes LANGUAGE ARTS

- **Writing**
  Daily Writing Prompt

Day 1

Phonemic Awareness, 129
Phoneme Isolation: Final

Sharing Literature, 130

Library Book:
Dear Juno

(Skill) **Literature Focus, 131**
Problem-Solution

**Phonics, 132 T**
Review: Consonant /g/*g*, Short Vowel /i/*i*

 Shared Writing, 134
Writing Process: Prewrite

Writing Prompt, 134
Draw and write about favorite places to play.

Share Time, 135
Discuss favorite parts of *Dear Juno*.

Day 2

Phonemic Awareness, 137
Phoneme Blending

Sharing Literature, 138

Read-Aloud Anthology:
"Jamaica's Find," p. 90

(Skill) **Literature Focus, 139**
Character's Actions

Phonics, 140 T
Introduce: Blending /i/ - /g/

 Shared Writing, 142
Writing Process: Draft

Writing Prompt, 142
Draw and write about jobs you do at home.

Share Time, 143
Retell the story "Jamaica's Find."

T = tested skill

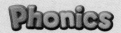 **Phonics**

Focus of the Week:
- **PHONEMIC AWARENESS**
- **SHARING LITERATURE**
- **WRITING: a Story (Writing Process)**

Consonant *Gg;*
Short Vowel *Ii;*
Blending /i/ - /g/

Day 3

Phonemic Awareness, 145
Phoneme Isolation and Matching: Medial

Sharing Literature, 146
Big Book: *Off We Go!*

 (Skill) **Literature Focus, 147**
Retelling

 Phonics, 148 **T**
Words with /i/ - /g/

 Shared Writing, 150
Read
Writing Process: Respond and Revise

Writing Prompt, 150
Draw and write about self-selected topics.

Share Time, 151
Act out the story *Off We Go!*

Day 4

Phonemic Awareness, 153
Phoneme Counting

Sharing Literature, 154
Read-Aloud Anthology: "Grandfather and I," p. 99

 (Skill) **Literature Focus, 155**
Visualizing

 Phonics, 156
Review: Short Vowel /i/*i*

Read

PRE-DECODABLE BOOK 14
My Pig

 Shared Writing, 158
Writing Process: Proofread

Writing Prompt, 158
Draw and write about self-selected topics.

Share Time, 159
Describe a place to take a walk.

Day 5

Phonemic Awareness, 161
Phoneme Counting

Sharing Literature, 162
Read-Aloud Anthology: "The Three Little Pigs," p. 101

 (Skill) **Literature Focus, 163**
Comparing Texts

 Phonics, 164 **T**
Review: /i/ - /g/

 Shared Writing, 166
Writing Process: Publish

Writing Prompt, 166
Draw and write about a surprise for a family member.

Share Time, 167
Read
Author's Chair

Phonemic Awareness
Phoneme Isolation: Final

Sharing Literature
Library Book:
Dear Juno

Develop Concept Vocabulary

Respond to Literature

Literature Focus: Problem-Solution

Phonics
Consonant /g/g,
Short Vowel /i/i

Shared Writing
Writing Process: Prewrite

WARM UP

MORNING MESSAGE

Kindergarten News

_____ and _____ are weekend days. (Child's name) likes to
_____ on the weekend.

Write Kindergarten News Talk with children about their weekend activities.

Use prompts such as the following to guide children as you write the news:

- **Let's name the weekend days:** *Saturday* **and** *Sunday*.
- **Name something you like to do on the weekend.**
- **Who can say the sound at the beginning of** *Saturday*?
- **What letter should I write?**

As you write the message, invite children to contribute by writing letters, words, or names they have previously learned. Remind them to use proper spacing, capitalization, and punctuation.

Calendar Language

Point to and read aloud the days of the week. Point out that Saturday is the last day of the week and Sunday is the first day of the week. Say: *Saturday and Sunday are weekend days.*

Sunday	Monday	Tuesday	Wednesday	Thursday	Friday	Saturday
		1	2	3	4	5
6	7	8	9	10	11	12
13	14	15	16	17	18	19
20	21	22	23	24	25	26
27	28	29	30	31		

Phonemic Awareness

PHONEME ISOLATION: FINAL

Listen for Final /g/   Tell children you will say some words and they will listen for the ending sound in the words. Say the following silly sentence.

MODEL   **Pig put his wig on the dog**

Pig. **Say the word with me.** *Pig.*

Pig **ends with /g/. What sound does** *pig* **end with?**

Wig. **Say the word with me.** *Wig.*

What sound does *wig* **end with?**

Dog. **Say the word with me.** *Dog.*

What sound does *dog* **end with?**

Say the sentence with me.

Say each word and isolate the ending /g/ sound. Have children do the same.

jug	**flag**	**plug**	**beg**	**snug**

Say the following words. Ask children to repeat each word and clap when they hear the /g/ sound at the end of a word.

wig	**peg**	**jam**	**frog**	**plan**
snug	**twig**	**flat**	**mug**	**jog**
hug	**bus**	**rag**	**dig**	**dip**

REACHING ALL LEARNERS

Diagnostic Check: Phonemic Awareness

If… children cannot identify final sounds in words,

Then… say one word at a time, segment the sounds in the word, and have the children repeat them and name the final sound.

ADDITIONAL SUPPORT ACTIVITIES

BELOW-LEVEL   Reteach, p. S14

ADVANCED   Extend, p. S15

ENGLISH-LANGUAGE LEARNERS   Reteach, p. S15

▲ **Library Book**

OBJECTIVES

- *To recall a story*

- *To connect text to life experiences*

- *To describe objects in general and specific language*

- *To identify the problem and solution*

Materials

- *Library Book: Dear Juno*

Sharing Literature

Read Dear Juno

READ ALOUD

Before Reading   Display *Dear Juno*. Model recalling story events for children:

> **MODEL** **I remember that Juno receives a letter from his grandmother. Dried flowers and a photograph come with the letter. Juno knows that Grandmother has a new cat and that flowers grow in her garden. Then Juno writes a letter by himself.**

Ask children to tell what they recall about the story.

During Reading   Read the story aloud. As you read,

- provide opportunities for children to relate to story characters and events. For example, after reading the first few pages of the story, pause to ask children: **Have you ever received a letter in the mail? Who was it from? How did you feel as you waited for someone to help you read it?**

- pause to react to a problem in the story and how the problem is solved.

> **MODEL** **Juno cannot read his grandmother's letter, but he can use the photograph and the flowers she sends as clues to guess what she is writing.**

DEVELOP CONCEPT VOCABULARY

Read the first sentence in *Dear Juno*. Then ask children these questions:

- **What happens when lights blink?** (They go off and on.)
- **Do airplanes have blinking lights?** (Yes)
- **The word *soar* means "to fly high and fast." What does *soared* mean?** (It means the airplane was flying high and fast.)
- **What do you see in the sky at night?** (stars)
- **What do you think a shooting star looks like?** (a light moving across the sky)

RESPOND TO LITERATURE

Share Ideas   Remind children that Juno's grandmother sends a photograph of herself with a cat and some dried red and yellow flowers to share with Juno something about her life. Ask children to tell what they might share with someone such as a favorite toy, a special time, a pet, a book, or a photograph of themselves.

Literature Focus

PROBLEM-SOLUTION

Tell children that in the beginning of the story, Juno receives a special letter from his grandmother. Explain that stories usually have problems that the characters work out. Ask these questions:

What is Juno's problem? (He can't read the letter.)

How does Juno solve the problem? (He looks at the photograph and dried flowers and figures out that his grandmother has a new cat and flowers in her garden.)

Tell children that good readers think about the problem in the story and predict ways a character might work it out.

ADVANCED

Have children draw a picture of something they like to do at school. Ask them to write *Dear* _____ at the top of the picture and sign their name at the bottom of the picture.

ONGOING ASSESSMENT

As you share *Dear Juno,* note whether children

- can recall a story.
- connect text to life experiences.

Phonics

Consonant /g/*g*, Short Vowel /i/*i* ✓Review

OBJECTIVES

- *To recognize uppercase and lowercase Ii and Gg*
- *To match sounds to letters*

Materials

- pocket chart
- *Big Alphabet Cards Ii, Gg*
- *Picture Cards inchworm, goat*
- *Tactile Letter Cards i, g*

ACTIVE BEGINNING

Recite the *I* and *G* Rhymes   Display *Big Alphabet Cards Ii* and *Gg*. Ask children to identify each letter. Have children form a circle. Ask a child to stand in the middle of the circle and hold up *Big Alphabet Card Ii*. Have the children walk around the circle as they recite "Itty Bitty Inchworm." (See page 94.) Follow the same procedure for "Goose! Goose!" (See page 42.)

TEACH/MODEL

Review Letters and Sounds   Display *Big Alphabet Card Ii* in a pocket chart and ask what letter this is.

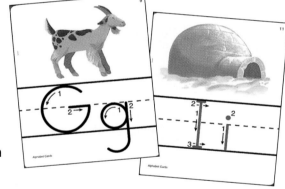

Point to the picture and say its name. Have children repeat it. *(igloo)*

What sound do you hear at the beginning of *igloo*? (/i/)

What letter stands for the /i/ sound in *igloo*? *(Ii)*

Touch the letter and say /i/. Touch the letter again and have children say /i/.

Follow the same procedure for *Big Alphabet Card Gg*.

Place on the chalkledge *Picture Cards* *inchworm* and *goat*. Say each picture name and tell children you need to decide where to place each *Picture Card.*

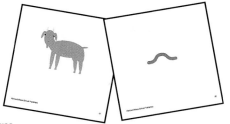

MODEL **I'll start with the inchworm.** **I—nchworm begins with the /i/ sound. So I'll put the picture of the inchworm below *Ii*.**

Model the same process with *Picture Card goat*.

PRACTICE/APPLY

Guided Practice Distribute *Tactile Letter Cards i* and *g* to each child.

I will say some words that begin with /i/ and some that don't. Hold up your *i* card if the word begins with the /i/ sound.

Confirm the answer for each word by holding up the appropriate letter card.

| insect | desk | ink | ill | wall |

I will say some words that begin with /g/ and some that don't. Hold up your *g* card if the word begins with the /g/ sound.

| goal | baby | garden | get | next |

Independent Practice Have children continue to work with their *Tactile Letter Cards i* and *g*.

I'm going to say some words. Listen carefully to the sound you hear at the beginning of each word. Think about the letter that stands for that sound, and then hold up the letter card that stands for that sound.

| itch | India | gone | gain | is |
| inside | game | imp | guard | imagine |

Phonics Resources

Phonics Express™ **CD-ROM, Level A,** Sparkle/Route 3/Harbor, Sparkle/Route 4/Market, Sparkle/ Route 5/Building Site, Roamer/Route 2/Train Station, Roamer/Route 3/Harbor, Roamer/ Route 4/Park

▲ **Practice Book page 19**

OBJECTIVES

- *To list ideas of characters for a story*

- *To understand that names of people, places, and things begin with an uppercase letter*

Day 1: Prewrite
Work together to write a list of animal names and actions.

Day 2: Draft
Have children work together to write additional verses for the story *Off We Go!*

Day 3: Respond and Revise
Have children decide if they want to add or change anything in their story.

Day 4: Proofread
Help children check for capital letters and periods.

Day 5: Publish
Provide each child with a little-book version of their story to illustrate.

Writing Process

Writing a Story

PREWRITE

Reread the Story   Reread the *Big Book: Off We Go!* Invite children to participate by pantomiming the actions of each animal as it goes to Grandma's house. After reading, draw attention to the words that name each animal and name the actions of the animal by framing the words and reading them aloud, such as *tip-toe, tippity toe* for the Little Mouse, *hip-hop, hippity hop* for Little Frog, *dig-deep, diggety deep* for Little Mole, and so on.

Make a List of Ideas   Ask children to imagine other animals that might also be going to Grandma's house for the day. As children brainstorm names of various animals, list the names on chart paper. Next to each animal name, record words that tell how the animal moves.

Animal	How the Animal Moves
Little Bee	bizz-buzz, bizzity buzz
Little Robin	flip-flap, flippity flap
Little Fish	splish-splash, splishity splash

Journal Writing Have children draw and write about places they like to play.

WRAP UP Share Time

Reflect on the Lesson Ask children to tell what they liked best about the story *Dear Juno.* Invite children to say words that have the sound /i/ or /g/.

S.S.R. Have children read silently from a book of their choice.

Centers SCIENCE

Call Me on My Phone

Beforehand, punch a hole in the bottom of several pairs of cups and insert string from the outside to the inside. In both cups, tie the end of the string around the toothpick and then pull it taut so that the toothpick anchors the string inside the cup. Place the cups in the center for pairs of children to use. Children must stand far enough apart so that the string is tight between the two cups. One child speaks and the other listens, just as with a real telephone. Note: If the string is touched while a child is speaking, it will disrupt the vibrations that carry the sound.

Materials

- plastic foam cups
- hole punch
- string
- toothpicks

Day at a Glance

Day 2

(WARM UP)

Phonemic Awareness

Blending Phonemes

Sharing Literature

Read-Aloud Anthology: "Jamaica's Find"

Read

Develop Listening Comprehension

Respond to Literature

Literature Focus: Character's Actions

Phonics

Blending /i/-/g/

Shared Writing ✏

Writing Process: Draft

MORNING MESSAGE

Kindergarten News

(Child's name)'s job is _____.

Write Kindergarten News Talk with children about jobs they can do at home. Ask them to tell why helping is important.

Use prompts such as the following to guide children as you write the news:

- **Who can name jobs you do at home?**
- **Who can show me a word?**
- **Who can show me the beginning of the sentence?**
- **Who can show me the end of the sentence?**

As you write the message, invite children to contribute by writing letters, words, or names they have previously learned. Remind them to use proper spacing, capitalization, and punctuation.

Calendar Language

Point to and read aloud the names of the days of the week. Say: *Today is _____.* **Point to the name of the next day. Say:** *Tomorrow will be _____.*

Sunday	Monday	Tuesday	Wednesday	Thursday	Friday	Saturday
		1	2	3	4	5
6	7	8	9	10	11	12
13	14	15	16	17	18	19
20	21	22	23	24	25	26
27	28	29	30	31		

Phonemic Awareness

BLENDING PHONEMES

Blend Phonemes to Say Words   Use the rabbit puppet to say sounds and have children say the word.

MODEL   The rabbit likes to say words in parts. Listen as the rabbit says this word: /s/ /i/ /t/. What is this word: /s/ /i/ /t/? Say the parts with the rabbit: /s/ /i/ /t/. The word is *sit*. Say the word. *Sit.*

Tell children that the rabbit is going to say some more words in parts. Have them listen to figure out the word the rabbit is saying. Then have children say the word.

/g/ /a/ /s/ (gas)　　　　　　/b/ /a/ /d/ (bad)

/f/ /i/ /n/ (fin)　　　　　　/d/ /i/ /d/ (did)

/b/ /i/ /t/ (bit)　　　　　　/t/ /i/ /n/ (tin)

/f/ /a/ /n/ (fan)　　　　　　/p/ /a/ /t/ (pat)

Family Ties   137

▲ Read-Aloud
Anthology

OBJECTIVES

• *To listen and respond to
a story*

• *To identify the setting of
a story*

• *To understand the beginning, middle, and ending
of a story*

• *To understand a
character's actions*

Materials

■ *Read-Aloud
Anthology, pp. 90–93*

■ drawing paper

■ crayons

Shared Reading

Read "Jamaica's Find"

READ ALOUD

Before Reading Turn to page 90 in the *Read-Aloud Anthology*.
Tell children they are going to hear a story called "Jamaica's Find."
Explain that Jamaica is the name of the girl in the story. Ask children
what they think the title means. Model setting a purpose for
reading:

MODEL **The title of this story is "Jamaica's Find." I see a young
girl in the picture. She is looking at a stuffed puppy dog. I think
that Jamaica finds this dog. I wonder what she does with it. I'll
read the story to find out.**

During Reading Read the story aloud. As you read,

• pause after reading the first sentence to ask children to tell where
the story takes place. As you read on, point out how the setting
changes.

• pause from time to time for children to make predictions about
what Jamaica will do next.

• pause just before the ending, and have children tell how they
think the story will end.

DEVELOP LISTENING COMPREHENSION

After Reading Have children answer these questions:

- **What does Jamaica find in the beginning of the story?** (a red hat and a stuffed dog)

- **What does Jamaica do with the things she finds?** (She brings the red hat to the Lost and Found. She brings the dog home.)

- **What happens at the end of the story?** (Possible response: Jamaica goes back to the park and brings the puppy dog to the Lost and Found. She meets the girl who had lost the dog. They become friends.)

RESPOND TO LITERATURE

Draw Story Events Distribute drawing paper. Have children choose one story event to draw. Have children share their drawings with the class. Ask children to tell if the story event happens at the beginning, middle, or end of the story.

CHARACTER'S ACTIONS

Tell children they can learn about a character by what that character says and does. Use the following questions to discuss Jamaica's actions.

- **What does Jamaica's mother say about the dog?** (It probably belongs to a girl just like her.)

- **Why doesn't Jamaica want to dry the dishes?** (She is upset about taking the dog.)

- **Why do you think she takes the dog back to the park?** (She knows it does not belong to her and she should bring it to the Lost and Found.)

- **How does this story show that Jamaica is a kind, thoughtful, and responsible girl?** (She returns things that don't belong to her.)

ADVANCED

Have children retell the story using their own words. They can use props such as a hat and stuffed dog. If several children are involved, have them take the roles of the various characters to act out what happens.

ONGOING ASSESSMENT

As you share "Jamaica's Find," note whether children

- listen for a period of time.
- can identify the setting of a story.
- can make predictions.

Writing Process

Writing a Story

DRAFT

OBJECTIVES

- *To write sentences*

- *To write*

Materials

- Chart paper

- marker

Splish–splash, splishity splash,
Not too fast and not too slow,
Off to Grandma's house we go,
Sings Little Fish.

Bizz–buzz, bizzity buzz,
Passing flowers down below,
Off to Grandma's house we go,
Sings Little Bee.

Choose an Idea for a Story   Tell children that together they will continue the story *Off We Go!* by writing about more animals who are on their way to Grandma's house. Read the list of writing ideas children suggested during prewriting. (See page 134.) Have children decide which animals they want to include in their story and if they want to use the action words they have listed. Model how to begin.

MODEL   You have decided to write about two of the animals from your list. You also want to keep the action words we listed. Now we must think about putting the words into sentences. Let's look again at the *Big Book*, *Off We Go!* We can use some of the words that the author uses.

Help children orally compose the content of the first sentence; when you are ready to write it, ask questions like these:

- **Where should I start writing on the chart paper?**

- **What animal should we write about first? How shall we begin our story?**

- **Look at the words on our class word chart. Who can tell me how to spell the word to? Who can tell me how to spell the word go?**

- **Listen to the beginning sound in the word fish. What letter stands for the beginning sound?**

- **Can you think of some words that rhyme with go?**

- **What animal should we write about next?**

Say each word aloud as you write. Reread the printed sentences often to help children recall the story line. Encourage several different children to take turns telling their ideas about what to write next.

Writing Every Day

Journal Writing   Have children draw or write about jobs they do at home.

WRAP UP # Share Time

Reflect on the Lesson   Have children take turns sitting in the Author's Chair to retell parts of the story "Jamaica's Find." Ask them to say a silly rhyme using words such as *pig, dig, wig,* and *jig.*

S.S.R. Sustained Silent Reading   Have children read silently from a book of their choice.

Centers   **SOCIAL STUDIES**

"I Like You" Bracelets

Have children make bracelets for family members or friends. Children can use different-colored beads to string a bracelet with string or yarn. Remind children they are not making bracelets for themselves; they are making them for a special family member or friend. Help children knot the string or yarn when their bracelet is completed.

 **Materials**

■ wooden or plastic beads

■ string or yarn

Day 3

WARM UP

Phonemic Awareness

Phoneme Matching and Isolation: Medial

Sharing Literature

Big Book:
Off We Go!

Respond to Literature

Literature Focus: Retelling

Words with /i/ and /g/

Shared Writing

Writing Process: Respond and Revise

ORAL LANGUAGE

MORNING MESSAGE

Kindergarten News

Today is _____.

(Child's name) likes to

wear _____.

Write Kindergarten News Ask children to tell about some of their favorite things to wear. Encourage them to tell why these things are favorites.

Use prompts such as the following to guide children as you write the news:

- **Who can tell about a favorite thing to wear?**
- **Who can point to where to begin reading?**
- **Who can show me where (child's name) begins and ends?**

As you write the message, invite children to contribute by writing letters, words, or names they have previously learned. Remind them to use proper spacing, capitalization, and punctuation.

Calendar Language

Point to and read aloud the seasons of the year. Have children repeat the season names. Name the season it is now. Ask: *What season is it?*

Sunday	Monday	Tuesday	Wednesday	Thursday	Friday	Saturday
		1	2	3	4	5
6	7	8	9	10	11	12
13	14	15	16	17	18	19
20	21	22	23	24	25	26
27	28	29	30	31		

Phonemic Awareness

PHONEME MATCHING: MEDIAL

Listen for Medial Sounds that Match Tell children you will say three words, and they are to listen for two words that have the same sound.

MODEL *Pig, can, sit.* Say the words: *pig can sit.*

I hear the /i/ sound in the middle of *pig*.

I hear the /a/ sound in the middle of *can*.

I hear the /i/ sound in the middle of *sit*.

The words *pig* and *sit* both have the /i/ sound.

Pig and *sit* have the same middle sound. Say the words: *pig, sit.*

Continue with the following sets of words. Have children tell which two words have the same sound in the middle of the word.

win, rip, sand	**tip, skid, ran**	**mitt, pat, tin**
spill, hat, fill	**fix, tip, sad**	**sad, mat, tip**
wilt, flip, slab	**chick, rack, thin**	**hat, trip, slid**

PHONEME ISOLATION: MEDIAL

Listen for /i/ Tell children you will say some words and they will listen for the middle sound in the words.

MODEL *Tim.* Say the word. *Tim.* What sound do you hear in the middle of *Tim*? (/i/) *With.* Say the word. *With.* What sound do you hear in the middle of *with*? (/i/)

Continue by having children say the sound they hear in the middle of each word you say.

fig	cat	lid	dip	pig
ham	sit	rip	sand	chick

▲ "I Make Myself Welcome," *Oo-pples and Boo-noo-noos: Songs and Activities for Phonemic Awareness,* pages 89–90.

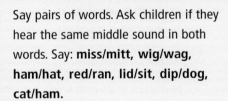

BELOW-LEVEL

Say pairs of words. Ask children if they hear the same middle sound in both words. Say: **miss/mitt, wig/wag, ham/hat, red/ran, lid/sit, dip/dog, cat/ham.**

Off We Go!

by Jane Yolen
Illustrated by Laurel Molk

▲ **Big Book**

OBJECTIVES

- *To listen and respond to a story*

- *To pantomime story action*

- *To make predictions*

- *To describe an event in specific and general language*

- *To tell story events in order*

Materials

- *Big Book: Off We Go!*

- paper

- crayons or markers

- scissors

- glue

- craft sticks

Shared Reading

Read Off We Go!

READ ALOUD

Before Reading   Display *Off We Go!* and ask a child to track the print as you read the title aloud. Ask another child to frame and read the word *Go*. Use these prompts to set a purpose for rereading the story:

MODEL   I remember that this story is about animals going to Grandma's house. I think the animals are very happy to go to Grandma's house. I'll read the story again to see if I am right.

During Reading   Read the story aloud. As you read,

- pause to allow children to say each animal name.

- react to rhythm and action words.

  Let's clap the rhythm of the words on this page.

  Say these words after me: dig-deep diggity deep. Use your hands to show me the action of the mole.

- pause to predict which animal comes next.

  The mouse starts to Grandma's house.

  What animal is next? (frog)

RESPOND TO LITERATURE

Discuss Story Concepts   Ask children to tell what makes a visit to Grandma's special. Encourage children to speak in complete sentences.

Literature Focus

RETELLING

Model for children how to retell the story.

MODEL   To retell this story, I would ask myself, Who are the characters in the story? What do the characters do?

In this story, Little Mouse tippy-toes to Grandma's house. Little Frog hip-hops to Grandma's house. Little Mole digs deep to go to Grandma's house. Little Snake slithers to Grandma's house. Little Duck scritch scratches to Grandma's house. Little Spider creeps and crawls to Grandma's house. The animals all think that Grandma's house is best.

Have children work together in small groups to make stick puppets of the characters in the story *Off We Go!* They can draw each animal, cut it out, and glue it to a craft stick. Have them use their puppets to retell the story.

ADVANCED

Have children pretend each animal is leaving Grandma's to return home. Ask them to think of a song they can sing on the way home. Have children tell the story of each animal's trip back to its home. Have them record their story and place the cassette in the Listening Center.

ONGOING ASSESSMENT

As you share *Off We Go!* note whether children

- listen and respond to the story.
- can pantomime story action.
- can make predictions.

OBJECTIVES

- *To build and read simple one-syllable words*

- *To understand that as letters of words change, so do the sounds*

Materials

- *Word Builders*

- *Word Builder Cards i, f, g, n, p, t*

- *Alphabet Cards i, f, g, n, p, t*

- pocket chart

- *Magnetic Letters*

- cookie sheet

REVIEW LETTERS

Phonics

Words with /i/ and /g/ ✔Introduce

ACTIVE BEGINNING

Action Sentences Teach children the words and actions shown below:

"Dig, dig, dig," said the first little pig. (Use hands to pretend to dig. Then hold up one finger to indicate first little pig.)

"Dig, dig, dig," said the second little pig. (Use hands to pretend to dig. Then hold up two fingers to indicate second little pig.)

"Dig, dig, dig," said the third little pig. (Use hands to pretend to dig. Then hold up three fingers to indicate the third little pig.)

"We all dig," said the three little pigs.

TEACH/MODEL

Blending Words Distribute *Word Builders* and *Word Builder Cards i, f, g, n, p, t* to children. As you place *Alphabet Cards* in a pocket chart, tell children to place the same *Word Builder Cards* in their *Word Builders.*

- Place *Alphabet Cards p, i,* and *g* in the pocket chart. Have children do the same.

- Point to *p.* Say **/pp/**. Point to *i.* Say **/ii/**.
- Slide the *i* next to the *p.* Then move your hand under the letters and blend the sounds, elongating them—**/ppii/**. Have children do the same.

- Point to the letter *g*. Say **/gg/**. Have children do the same.
- Slide the *g* next to the *pi*. Slide your hand under *pig* and blend by elongating the sounds—**/ppiigg/**. Have children do the same.
- Then have children blend and read the word *pig* along with you.

PRACTICE/APPLY

Guided Practice   Have children place *Word Builder Cards i* and *g* in their *Word Builders*.

- **Add *p* to *ig*. What word did you make?**

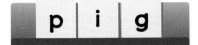

- **Change *p* to *f*. What word did you make?**

- **Change *g* to *n*. What word did you make?**

- **Change *f* to *t*. What word did you make?**

- **Change *n* to *p*. What word did you make?**

Independent Practice   Have children use *Magnetic Letters i, f, g, n, p,* and *t* in the Letters and Words Center to build and read *pig, fig, fin, tin,* and *tip*.

Diagnostic Check: Phonics

If... children have difficulty blending and building words,

Then... have them name the letters as they place them in their *Word Builders*. Say the sound and have them repeat the sound. Have them move their hands under the letters in the *Word Builders* as they blend the sounds with you.

ADDITIONAL SUPPORT ACTIVITIES

BELOW-LEVEL	Reteach, p. S16
ADVANCED	Extend, p. S17
ENGLISH-LANGUAGE LEARNERS	Reteach, p. S17

▲ **Practice Book page 21**

OBJECTIVES

- *To share ideas speaking in complete sentences*
- *To respond to and revise story*
- *To add a title to the story*

Materials

- chart paper
- red marker

Writing Process

Writing a Story

RESPOND AND REVISE

Make Changes Reread the story, tracking the words. Ask questions like these:

- **Is there anything else we need to add to our story?**
- **Do the animals and action words sound like the words in *Off We Go!*? Remember that we are adding to that story, so our words should sound like the words in the story.**
- **Would you like to change any of the words we used?**
- **Our story needs a title. Should we use the same title as the Big Book? Who has an idea for one?**

Make changes as they are suggested by children. You may want to use a red marker to show the changes on the chart paper. Add a title suggested by the children.

Off We Go Too!
Splish-splash, splishity splash,
Not too fast and not too slow,
Off to Grandma's house we go,
Sings Little Fish.

Bizz-buzz, bizzity buzz,
Passing flowers down below,
Off to Grandma's house we go,
Sings Little Bee.

Flip-flap, flippity flap,
Flying high, flying low,
Off to grandma's house we go,
Sings Little Bird

Self-Selected Writing Have children write and draw about anything they'd like. If they have difficulty thinking of a topic, have them ask two friends what they're going to write

WRAP UP # Share Time

Reflect on the Lesson   Have children take turns imitating the animal character they liked best from the story *Off We Go!* Then invite children to sit in the Author's Chair to share what was written in their journal.

S.S.R. *Sustained Silent Reading*   Have children read silently from a book of their choice.

Centers   MATH

A House for Me

Place in the center several felt houses and animals with a flannel board. Have children count as they put houses in a row on the board and count the same number as they place an animal next to each house. Then invite children to point to each animal and house as they count again.

Materials

- flannel board
- felt houses
- felt animals

Day at a Glance
Day 4

WARM UP

Phonemic Awareness
Phoneme Counting

Sharing Literature
Read-Aloud Anthology:
"Grandfather and I"

Read

KINDERGARTEN
READ-ALOUD
Anthology
Harcourt

Respond to Literature

Literature Focus: Visualizing

Phonics

Reading

Pre-decodable Book 14: *My Pig*

Shared Writing

Writing Process: Proofread

MORNING MESSAGE

Kindergarten News

(Child's name) likes to walk in

the _____. He/She likes to

look for _____.

Write Kindergarten News   Talk with children about places they like to walk.

Use prompts such as the following to guide children as you write the news:

- **What are some places you like to go when you take a walk?**
- **What do you like to look at when you take a walk?**
- **What letter did I write first in (child's name)?**
- **What words do you know?**

As you write the message, invite children to contribute by writing letters, words, or names they have previously learned. Remind them to use proper spacing, capitalization, and punctuation.

Calendar Language

Point to the numbers on the calendar. Tell children that the days of each month are numbered and the numbers tell the date. Point to and read aloud the date. Ask: *What is the month? What is the date?*

Sunday	Monday	Tuesday	Wednesday	Thursday	Friday	Saturday
			1	2	3	4	5
6	7	8	9	10	11	12
13	14	15	16	17	18	19
20	21	22	23	24	25	26
27	28	29	30	31		

Phonemic Awareness

PHONEME COUNTING

Count Sounds in Words Tell children to listen to the word you say and to tell how many sounds they hear.

MODEL *Bin.* I hear the /b/ sound, the /i/ sound, and the /n/ sound.

I hear three sounds in the word *bin*.

Let's say the word together: *bin.*

Let's say the sounds together: /b/ /i/ /n/.

How many sounds do you hear in *bin*? (3)

Tell children to repeat the words you say and then to say each sound they hear. Have them tell how many sounds they hear in each word.

Tim	/t/ /i/ /m/	(3)		if	/i/ /f/	(2)
big	/b/ /i/ /g/	(3)		wig	/w/ /i/ /g/	(3)
pat	/p/ /a/ /t/	(3)		had	/h/ /a/ /d/	(3)
pit	/p/ /i/ /t/	(3)		in	/i/ /n/	(2)
tip	/t/ /i/ /p/	(3)		get	/g/ /e/ /t/	(3)
bag	/b/ /a/ /g/	(3)		wag	/w/ /a/ /g/	(3)
cap	/k/ /a/ /p/	(3)		it	/i/ /t/	(2)

BELOW-LEVEL

Tell children to listen to the word you say. Say: **it**. Have children repeat the word. Tell them you will say the sounds in the word. Say: **/i/ /t/**. Have children do the same. Have them say the word again and clap for each sound they hear. Follow this procedure for these words: *sit, in, tin.*

...with a /b/ /a/ /g/
and a /k/ /a/ /p/

▲ **Read-Aloud Anthology**

OBJECTIVES

- *To listen and respond to a story*

- *To relate personal experiences*

- *To visualize story scenes*

Materials

■ *Read-Aloud Anthology, pp. 99–100*

Sharing Literature

Read "Grandfather and I"

READ ALOUD

Before Reading   Turn to page 99 of the *Read-Aloud Anthology*. Read aloud the title "Grandfather and I." Tell children that this is a story about a child and a grandfather taking a walk. Invite children to tell about their grandparents. Use these prompts to build background:

- **The word *hurry* means "to do something quickly or very fast."**

- **When you go on a walk, do you hurry or do you take your time?**

- **When you are late for lunch, do you hurry? Name other times when you must hurry.**

During Reading   Read the story aloud. As you read,

- emphasize the repetitive text by reading expressively and very slowly.

- increase your reading pace as you read the verses that describe hurrying.

RESPOND TO LITERATURE

Take a Walk   Model for children a slow pace of walking, and invite them to try. Tell children that together you are going to take a walk around the room, just the way the characters in the story do. Tell them to walk slowly, to stop and look at things, and to listen for sounds they hear. Have children line up by calling small groups at a time and inviting them to walk in a slow pace.

Literature Focus

VISUALIZING

Tell children that you can make pictures in your mind to help you understand and recall information in a story.

MODEL **The author tells how brothers and sisters hurry. I make a picture in my mind that shows a boy and a girl running this way and that and bumping into each other. I picture going for a walk with a brother or a sister who is in a hurry. I see them racing way ahead of me. I am following far behind them.**

Read the verse about cars and buses that hurry, and ask children:

- **Where do you think these things are?** (Possible response: a city or a town)

- **What do you picture in your mind?** (Possible responses: lots of cars and buses on a city street tooting their horns; a train on a track coming to the city, tooting its whistle; lots of small boats in a harbor)

Read the verse again and have children draw a picture of the scene.

REACHING ALL LEARNERS

Diagnostic Check: Comprehension

If... children cannot visualize parts of the story,

Then... have children close their eyes as you reread one part of the story. After reading, ask children to tell what pictures the words made them think about. Ask children to tell or draw a picture to show what they saw in their mind as you read.

ADDITIONAL SUPPORT ACTIVITIES

BELOW-LEVEL	Reteach, p. S18
ADVANCED	Extend, p. S19
ENGLISH-LANGUAGE LEARNERS	Reteach, p. S19

ONGOING ASSESSMENT

As you share "Grandfather and I," note whether children

- listen for a period of time.
- can relate personal experiences.

OBJECTIVE

To decode words with short vowel /i/i

Materials

- *Alphabet Cards p, i, g, c, a, n*
- *High-Frequency Word Card My*
- index card
- marker
- pocket chart
- *Pre-decodable Book 14: My Pig*

BELOW-LEVEL

Reread the story with children. Have them frame the high-frequency word *my*. Guide them to blend the sounds for *pig* and *can*.

ADVANCED

Invite children to make another page for the book, showing something a pig can do. Children can label the page with this sentence: *My pig can ____.*

Phonics

Short Vowel /i/i ✔Review

TEACH/MODEL

Review Blending Place *Alphabet Cards p, i,* and *g* next to one another in a pocket chart. Move your hand under the letters, blend them, and say: **/ppiigg/—pig.** Have children blend the sounds and say the word.

Place the *High-Frequency Word Card My* in the pocket chart in front of *pig*. Track the print as you read the words: **My pig.** Add *Alphabet Cards c, a, n* to form the word *can* and add a period written on an index card to form the sentence: *My pig can _____.* Track the print as you read the words: **My pig can_____.** Invite children to say a word to finish the sentence.

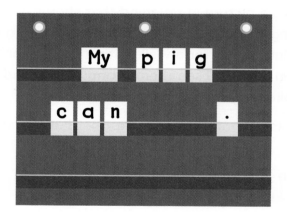

PRACTICE/APPLY

Read the Book Distribute copies of *My Pig*. Have children read the title. Encourage children to point to each word as they say it. Have children read the book, pointing to each word as they read.

Respond Have children draw a picture of something a pet, or an animal they know, can do.

Predecodable Book 14: *My Pig*

My pig can run.

2

My pig can jump.

3

My pig can draw.

4

My pig can dig.

5

My pig can sing.

6

My pig can paint.

7

My pig can hug.

8

■ **High-Frequency Word**

my

■ **Decodable Words**

See the list on page T19.

School-Home Connection

Take-Home Book Version

◄ Pre-decodable Book 14: *My Pig*

▲ ***Too Little***
Independent Reader 14

Writing Process

Writing a Story

PROOFREAD

Make Final Changes Model how to proofread a story by asking questions such as:

- **Who can point to the story title? Did we use uppercase letters in our title?**

- **Who can find a character's name? Did we start each character's name with an uppercase letter?**

- **Who can find the beginning of a sentence? Did we start the sentence with an uppercase letter? Where is the end of the sentence? Is there a period?**

If children answered no to any of the questions, make changes on the chart paper. Talk aloud as you make each change.

OBJECTIVES

- *To understand that a sentence begins with an uppercase letter and ends with a period*

- *To understand that a character's name begins with an uppercase letter.*

Materials

- chart paper

- markers

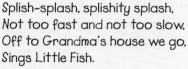

Off We Go Too!
Splish-splash, splishity splash,
Not too fast and not too slow,
Off to Grandma's house we go,
Sings Little Fish.

Bizz-buzz, bizzity buzz,
Passing flowers down below,
Off to Grandma's house we go,
Sings Little Bee.

Flip-flap, flippity flap,
Flying high, flying low,
Off to G̅randma's house we go,
Sings Little Bird.

Self-Selected Writing Have children write and draw about anything they'd like. If they have difficulty thinking of a topic, have them ask two friends what they're going to write about.

WRAP UP Share Time

Reflect on the Lesson Have children tell about a place where they would like to walk and name the person they would walk with. Invite children to tell how they feel about the class story they have written together.

S.S.R. Have children read silently from a book of their choice.

Centers SOCIAL STUDIES

My Family Tree

Explain the expression *family tree*. Place materials in the center for children to make their own family tree by placing their forearm and hand on drawing paper, palm down and fingers spread, while a partner traces the shape. After children color the tree, have them make small drawings to represent the people in their family. Help children label each picture with the family member's name.

Materials

- ■ drawing paper
- ■ pencils
- ■ crayons or markers

Day at a Glance
Day 5

WARM UP

Phonemic Awareness
Phoneme Counting

Sharing Literature
Read-Aloud Anthology:
"The Three Little Pigs"

Read

Develop Concept Vocabulary

Respond to Literature

Literature Focus: Comparing Texts

Phonics
Words with /i/ and /g/

Shared Writing ✏️
Writing Process: Publish

MORNING MESSAGE

Kindergarten News

(Child's name) likes to eat _____.

Write Kindergarten News Talk with children about foods they like to eat. Encourage them to speak clearly.

Use prompts such as the following to guide children as you write the news:

- **Who can name something they like to eat?**
- **Who can show me a letter?**
- **Who can show me a word?**

As you write the message, invite children to contribute by writing words or names they have previously learned. Remind them to use proper spacing, capitalization, and punctuation.

Calendar Language

Point to *Sunday* and tell children that Sunday is the first day of the week. Point to *Monday* and tell children that Monday is the second day, and so on. Ask: *What is the (ordinal number) day of the week?*

Sunday	Monday	Tuesday	Wednesday	Thursday	Friday	Saturday
			1	2	3	4	5
6	7	8	9	10	11	12
13	14	15	16	17	18	19
20	21	22	23	24	25	26
27	28	29	30	31		

Phonemic Awareness

PHONEME COUNTING

Count Sounds   Tell children to listen to the word you say and to tell how many sounds they hear.

MODEL   *Pig.* **I hear the /p/ sound, the /i/ sound, and the /g/ sound.**

I hear three sounds in the word *pig.*

Let's say the word together: *pig.*

Let's say the sounds together: /p/ /i/ /g/.

How many sounds do you hear in *pig*? **(3)**

Tell children to listen to the words you say and then to say each sound they hear. Have them tell how many sounds they hear in each word.

sit	/s/ /i/ /t/	(3)	kit	/k/ /i/ /t/	(3)
fit	/f/ /i/ /t/	(3)	it	/i/ /t/	(2)
fan	/f/ /a/ /n/	(3)	pan	/p/ /a/ /n/	(3)
bag	/b/ /a/ /g/	(3)	wag	/w/ /a/ /g/	(3)
dig	/d/ /i/ /g/	(3)	man	/m/ /a/ /n/	(3)
gas	/g/ /a/ /s/	(3)	as	/a/ /s/	(2)
big	/b/ /i/ /g/	(3)	wig	/w/ /i/ /g/	(3)
rag	/r/ /a/ /g/	(3)	tag	/t/ /a/ /g/	(3)

OBJECTIVES

- *To build and read simple one-syllable words*
- *To understand that as letters of words change, so do the sounds*

Materials

- Word Builders
- Word Builder Cards a, f, g, i, p, t, d
- Alphabet Cards a, f, g, i, p, t, d
- pocket chart

REVIEW LETTERS

Phonics

Words with /i/ and /g/ ✓Review

ACTIVE BEGINNING

Play a Listening Game   Explain to children that they are going to play a game where they will listen to words that have the /g/ sound. Ask them to clap their hands if the word begins with the /g/ sound and stomp their feet if the word ends with the /g/ sound.

go	tag	Gary	get	dog
fig	game	flag	egg	give

TEACH/MODEL

Blending Words   Distribute *Word Builders* and *Word Builder Cards a, f, g, i, p, t, d* to children. As you place *Alphabet Cards* in a pocket chart, tell children to place the same *Word Builder Cards* in their *Word Builders.*

- Place *Alphabet Cards f, i,* and *g* in the pocket chart. Have children do the same.

- Point to *f.* Say **/ff/**. Point to *i.* Say **/ii/**.
- Slide the *i* next to the *f.* Then move your hand under the letters and blend the sounds, elongating them—**/ffii/**. Have children do the same.

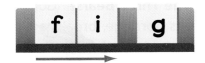

- Point to the letter *g.* Say **/gg/**. Have children do the same.
- Slide the *g* next to the *fi.* Slide your hand under *fig* and blend by elongating the sounds—**/ffiigg/**. Have children do the same.

• Then have children blend and read the word *fig* along with you.

ENGLISH-LANGUAGE LEARNERS

Have children name the letters *d, i, g* as they place them in their *Word Builders.* Say each letter sound and have them repeat the sound. Have them move their hands under the letters in the *Word Builders* as they blend the sounds with you. Continue in the same manner with a new word.

PRACTICE/APPLY

Guided Practice Have children place *Word Builder Cards i* and *g* in their *Word Builders*.

• **Add *d* to *ig*. What word did you make?**

• **Change *g* to *p*. What word did you make?**

• **Change *d* to *t*. What word did you make?**

• **Change *i* to *a*. What word did you make?**

• **Change *t* to *g*. What word did you make?**

Independent Practice   Write the words *pig* and *dig* on cards and place them in a pocket chart. Have children read the words. Then have them fold a sheet of paper in half, write one word on each half of the sheet of paper, and illustrate the word.

ADVANCED

Have children use *Magnetic Letters a, d, f, i, g, p, s* to build words. Tell them to say a sentence using each word they build.

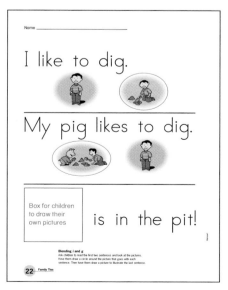

▲ **Practice Book page 22**

Writing Process

Writing a Story

PUBLISH

OBJECTIVES

- *To illustrate a story*

- *To relate story events in logical sequence*

Materials

- drawing paper

- crayons

Make Little Books   Ask children what pictures they could draw to illustrate their addition to the story *Off We Go!* Write each verse on separate sheets of paper, make copies, and staple together with a construction-paper cover, so each child has a copy. Have children listen as you read each verse, using the copy on the chart paper. Then have children draw pictures to illustrate each verse in their little-book version. Children can copy the title on the cover and add their name as one of the authors.

Splish-splash, splishity splash,
Not too fast and not too slow,
Off to Grandma's house we go,
Sings Little Fish.

Splish-splash, splishity splash,

Not too fast and not too slow,

Off to Grandma's house we go,

Sings Little Fish.

Writing Every Day

Journal Writing   Have children draw and write about a surprise they have made for a family member.

WRAP UP # Share Time

Reflect on the Lesson Gather children around the Author's Chair to read aloud to them their addition to the book *Off We Go!*. Ask them what they liked best about the things they did today.

S.S.R. *Sustained Silent Reading* Have children read silently from a book of their choice.

 **Centers**  **LITERACY**

Let's Read

Place the books in the Literacy Center. Tell children to read the books and to choose their favorite one. Ask them to draw and label a picture about their favorite book. Have children write the title of the book on their picture, and then write their name.

 Materials

- *Predecodable Books: The Park, Sit on My Chair, My Pig*

- *Little Shared Book: Off We Go!*

- *Library Books: A Birthday Basket for Tía, Dear Juno*

- *drawing paper*

- *crayons and pencils*

Theme Wrap-Up & Review

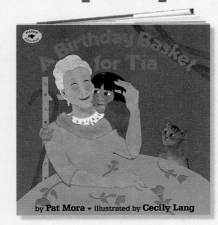

Celebrate *Family Ties*

Show children *Off We Go! A Birthday Basket for Tia* and *Dear Juno*. Help them summarize or retell each story. Invite comments and personal responses; then ask these questions:

- **Which of these books about families is your favorite? Why?**

- **What are some things you can do to show that you care about the members in your family?**

- **What did you learn about sharing ideas through pictures in Dear Juno?**

Teacher Self-Evaluation

As you reflect on the theme *Family Ties*, ask yourself:

- **Which activities best met my goals for this theme? Which ones did not?**

- **Have children become more aware of things they can do to help family members?**

- **Which activities met a variety of children's learning styles?**

THEME PROJECT

"Helping Hands" Mural

Summing Up   As children talk about their paintings, have them speak slowly and clearly.

REVIEW

Phonics

Blend Words Place Alphabet Cards *g, f, i, s p, t* on a table or on the chalk ledge. Tell children they can use these letters to build words. Call out the letters *p-i-g.* Have children choose each letter, say the sound it stands for, and place it in a pocket chart. Help children blend the sounds to say *pig.* Follow the same procedure to build these words: *fig, pit, fit, sit.*

High-Frequency Words

Word Match Make two sets of word cards for *on, to, go, we.* Tell children to turn the cards face down in rows on a table or desk. Have them take turns flipping a card, naming the word, and flipping another card to find a matching word. If the word does not match, children should turn both cards face down and another child takes a turn. If the words match, the child keeps the word set and takes another turn.

Take-Home Book
Theme 5 Practice Book, pp. 23–24

Comprehension

Problem/Solution Display *Dear Juno.* Help children recall Juno's problem. Ask them to tell how Juno solved the problem. Display *A Birthday Basket for Tia.* Ask children what the problem in the story is. Ask them how Cecilia solves the problem.

Writing

Sentences about Family Activities Have children draw a picture about a family activity they enjoy. Ask them to write a sentence about the family activity. Remind them to begin with an uppercase letter and use a period at the end of their sentence.

We mk cks.

ASSESSMENT

• Assessment Handbook

Monitoring of Progress

Diagnostic Checks Use the Diagnostic Checks as a point-of-use assessment of children's understanding.

Theme Skills Assessment Use the Theme Skills Assessment to monitor a child's understanding of letter recognition, word recognition, sound-symbol relationships, and decoding skills taught in this theme.

Animal Families

Children will focus on how baby animals learn about their world from their families. They will discover how real animals play in their natural habitats.

Theme Resources

READING MATERIALS

Big Book

◀ *Does a Kangaroo Have a Mother, Too?*
by Eric Carle

Library Books

◀ *Are you there, Baby Bear?*
by Catherine Walters

◀ *A Time for Playing*
by Ron Hirschi
illustrated by Thomas
D. Mangelsen

Read-Aloud Anthology

◀ *The Three Billy-Goats Gruff*
retold by P. C. Asbjörnsen
◀ *Chicken Forgets* by Miska Miles
◀ *The Town Mouse and the Country Mouse* retold by Lorinda Bryan Cauley
◀ *Five Little Pigs*

Big Book of Rhymes and Songs

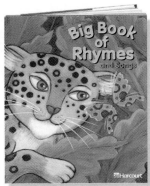

◀ *Five Speckled Frogs*
◀ *Mary Had a Little Lamb*
◀ *The Kitty Ran Up the Tree*

Independent Readers

▲ *Lil's Big Day*

▲ *Where Do Pigs Play?*

▲ *A Dog Has Pups*

PHONICS

Theme 6 Practice Book

Phonics Practice Book

Pre-decodable Books

▲ I Have, You Have

▲ Soup

▲ The Dig

Alphabet Patterns

lion, house
pages TI5-TI6

 Phonics Express™ CD-ROM

Level A

TEACHING TOOLS

Big Alphabet Cards
Ll, Hh

High-Frequency Word Cards
you, have

Picture/Word Cards

English-Language Learners Kit

Letter and Sound Charts
Charts 20 and 7

Teacher's Resource Book
pages 57–70

Intervention Kit

Letter and Sound Chart Sentence Strips
20 and 7

Lamb has a lunch box.

Oo-pples and Boo-noo-noos

Ooples and Boo-noo Noos

MANIPULATIVES

Tactile Letter Cards

Write-On/Wipe-Off Board
Letters and Sounds Place Mat

Word Builder and Word Builder Cards

Magnetic Letters

Aa Bb Cc

ASSESSMENT

Assessment Handbook
Group Inventory
Theme 6 Test

Big Book ▶

Library Book ▶

Week 1

• **Sharing Literature** • **Listening Comprehension**	**Big Book:** 　*Does a Kangaroo Have a Mother, Too?* **Library Book:** *Are you there, Baby Bear?* **Read-Aloud Anthology:** 　"The Three Billy Goats Gruff" **Big Book of Rhymes and Songs:** 　"Five Speckled Frogs"
• **Phonemic Awareness** • **Phonics** • **High-Frequency Words**	**Consonant /l/ l** T **Consonant /h/ h** T **Review Consonants** *Hh, Ll* T **High-Frequency Words** you, have T
• **Reading**	**Pre-decodable Book 15:** *I Have, You Have* **Independent Reader 15:** *Lil's Big Day*
• **Writing**	**Shared Writing** 　Naming Words 　Class Story **Interactive Writing** 　Word Web **Independent Writing** 　Sentences 　Sign
• **Cross-Curricular Centers**	**Art** 　Favorite Animals Posters **Science** 　Bird Feeders **Dramatic Play** 　Play Time **Math** 　Sort the Animals **Manipulatives** 　Animal Puzzles

T = tested skill

Week 2

Big Book: 　*Does a Kangaroo Have a Mother, Too?* **Library Book:** *A Time for Playing* **Read-Aloud Anthology:** "Chicken Forgets" **Big Book of Rhymes and Songs:** 　"Mary Had a Little Lamb"
Review Consonant /p/ p, 　**Short Vowel /i/ i** T **Blending /i/ - /p/** **Words with /i/ and /p/** **Review Blending /i/ - /p/**
Pre-decodable Book 16: *Soup* **Independent Reader 16:** *Where Do Pigs Play?*
Shared Writing 　Chart 　Story **Interactive Writing** 　List **Independent Writing** 　Questions 　Family
Writing 　Write Stamp Stories **Science** 　Animal Habitats   **Cooking** 　Berry Good for You ABC **Letters and Words** 　Word Factory   **Listening** 　Listen to the Big Book

Library Book ▶

Theme Organizer
Half-Day Kindergarten

Use the following chart to help organize your half-day kindergarten schedule. Choose independent activities as time allows during your day.

Week 3

Big Book:
Does a Kangaroo Have a Mother, Too?

Library Book: *A Time for Playing*

Read-Aloud Anthology: "The Town Mouse and the Country Mouse" "Five Little Pigs"

Big Book of Rhymes and Songs:
"The Kitty Ran Up the Tree"

Phonogram -*it*

Phonogram -*ig*

Phonogram -*ip*

Build Sentences

Pre-decodable Book 17: *The Dig*

Independent Reader 17: *A Dog Has Pups*

Shared Writing
Writing Process
Write a Personal Narrative

 Science
Animals at Play

 Block
A House for a Mouse

 Math
Animal Shapes

 Literacy
Favorite Books

 Math
Numbers 1–5

ORAL LANGUAGE

Morning Message
Phonemic Awareness
Sharing Literature
- Big Book: *Does a Kangaroo Have a Mother, Too?*
- Library Book: *Are you there, Baby Bear?*
- Library Book: *A Time for Playing*
- *Read-Aloud Anthology*
- *Big Book of Rhymes and Songs*

LEARNING TO READ

Phonics
Pre-decodable Books 15–17
- *I Have, You Have*
- *Soup*
- *The Dig*

High-Frequency Words

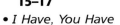
Independent Readers 15–17
- *Lil's Big Day*
- *Where Do Pigs Play?*
- *A Dog Has Pups*

LANGUAGE ARTS

Shared Writing
Interactive Writing
Independent Writing
Writing Every Day

INDEPENDENT ACTIVITIES

Sharing Literature
Respond to Literature
Phonics
Independent Practice
Handwriting
Practice Book pages
High-Frequency Words
Independent Practice
Practice Book pages

About the
Authors and Illustrators

Eric Carle

Author and Illustrator of *Does a Kangaroo Have a Mother, Too?*
Eric Carle is a well-known artist, designer, and author of children's books. He was a designer for the New York Times and the art director for a large advertising agency. He now devotes his time to writing and illustrating children's books. Among Carle's books is *The Very Hungry Caterpillar*, first published in 1969.

Catherine Walters

Author and Illustrator of *Are you there, Baby Bear?*
Catherine Walters has written and illustrated another book about Alfie the little bear cub, *When Will It Be Spring?* She has illustrated several other popular books for children, including *The Brave Little Bunny* and *Never Trust a Squirrel!* Ms. Walters lives in England with her family.

Ron Hirschi

Author of *A Time for Playing*
Ron Hirschi grew up in the Pacific Northwest where he developed a respect for animals and an understanding of what they need to survive in a fast-changing world. Hirschi graduated from the University of Washington with a B.S. in Wildlife Ecology, and has worked as a wildlife biologist. He collaborated with Thomas Mangelsen on two other books in this series, *A Time for Sleeping* and *A Time for Babies*.

Thomas D. Mangelsen

Photographer of *A Time for Playing*
Thomas D. Mangelsen's photographs have been published in *National Geographic*, *Audubon*, and *National Wildlife*. Mangelsen has devoted his career to the appreciation and protection of North American wildlife. He has collaborated with Ron Hirschi on an acclaimed series of books about the seasons.

Theme Assessment

MONITORING OF PROGRESS

After completing the theme, most children should show progress toward mastery of the following skills:

Concepts of Print
- ❏ Understand that printed materials provide information.
- ❏ Recognize that sentences in print are made up of separate words.

Phonemic Awareness
- ❏ Distinguish orally stated one-syllable words and separate into beginning or ending sounds.
- ❏ Count the number of sounds in syllables and syllables in words.

Phonics and Decoding
- ❏ Match all consonant sounds and short-vowel sounds to appropriate letters.
- ❏ Read one-syllable and High-Frequency Words.
- ❏ Understand that as letters of words change, so do the sounds.

Vocabulary and High-Frequency Words
- ❏ Read High-Frequency Words *you* and *have*.
- ❏ Identify and sort words in basic categories.
- ❏ Learn words associated with the calendar.

Comprehension
- ❏ Use pictures and context to make predictions about story contents.
- ❏ Retell familiar stories.

Literary Response
- ❏ Distinguish fantasy from realistic text.
- ❏ Identify types of everyday print materials.

Writing
- ❏ Write consonant-vowel-consonant words.
- ❏ Write sentences using a capital letter at the beginning and a period at the end.
- ❏ Use prephonetic knowledge to spell independently.

Listening and Speaking
- ❏ Recognize and use complete, coherent sentences when speaking.
- ❏ Recite rhymes.

Assessment Options

Assessment Handbook
- Group Inventory, Form B
- Phonemic Awareness Inventory
- Theme Skills Assessment
- Concepts About Print Inventory
- Observational Checklists

Reaching All Learners

Levels of Support

Point-of-use Notes in the Teacher's Edition

pp. 193, 205, 209, 215, 219, 221, 223, 225, 229, 239, 241, 243, 253, 257, 261, 269, 273, 277, 279, 285, 299, 303, 307, 309, 311, 319, 325, 331, 333, 335

Additional Support Activities

High-Frequency Words:
pp. S20-S21

Comprehension:
pp. S30-S31, S36-S37

Phonemic awareness:
pp. S22-S23, S28-S29, S32-S33

Phonics: pp. S24-S25, S26-S27, S34-S35

Intervention Resources Kit

■ ENGLISH-LANGUAGE LEARNERS

Levels of Support

Point-of-use Notes in the Teacher's Edition

pp. 195, 211, 213, 223, 225, 229, 231, 233, 241, 243, 257, 261, 263, 265, 279, 281, 287, 289, 299, 319, 325, 327

Additional Support Activities

High-Frequency Words:
pp. S20-S21

Comprehension:
pp. S30-S31, S36-S37

Phonemic awareness:
pp. S22-S23, S28-S29, S32-S33

Phonics:
pp. S24-S25, S26-S27, S34-S35

 Visit *The Learning Site!* at
www.harcourtschool.com
See Language Support activities

English-Language Learners Resources Kit

■ ADVANCED

Levels of Challenge

Point-of-use Notes in the Teacher's Edition

pp. 193, 205, 209, 215, 219, 221, 225, 229, 231, 243, 253, 255, 257, 261, 265, 271, 273, 279, 285, 289, 299, 301, 303, 307, 311, 315, 317, 319, 323, 325, 331, 335

Additional Support Activities

High-Frequency Words:
pp. S20 - S21

Comprehension and Skills:
pp. S30 - S31, S36 - S37

Phonemic Awareness:
pp. S22 - S23, S28 - S29, S32 - S33

Phonics:
pp. S24 - S25, S26 - S27, S34 - S35

Accelerated Instruction

Use higher-grade-level materials for accelerated instruction.

Theme Project, pp. 182

Combination Classrooms
Partner Research

Pair an advanced researcher and a beginning researcher who have a common interest in a particular animal. Encourage them to work together to gather information from books, magazines, and if available, the Internet. Children can create a simple report on the animal that includes pictures and text and place it in the Literacy Center for others to read.

Lions live in Dens

Students with Special Needs
Remembering Facts and Information

Children with special needs can often use some help when it comes to remembering information. Make learning facts interesting by creating "study cards" that depict facts or information. Children can work with a partner to quiz each other on the facts.

Bear   Cub

Recommended Reading

Below are suggestions for reading materials that will meet kindergarten children's diverse needs. Books that are on a child's level provide support for new skills. Advanced books give children an opportunity to stretch and challenge their reading potential. Read-aloud books are important because they expose children to story language and vocabulary.

■ BELOW-LEVEL

Animal Alphabet by Bert Kitchen. Dial, 1984. Guess the identity of twenty-six unusual animals illustrating the letters of the alphabet in this wordless book.

The Hungry Fox by Claire Llewellyn. Rigby, 2003. A hungry fox sneaks up on the farmer's henhouse and gets a big surprise.

Look! Now Look! by Jan Pritchett. Rigby, 2003. Some animals can almost disappear right before your eyes. This book shows how.

Curly & the Cherries by Tony Mitton. Rigby, 2003. A wordless children's book of a hungry caterpillar searching for something to eat.

■ ON-LEVEL

Have You Seen My Duckling? by Nancy Tafuri. Greenwillow, 1984. A mother duck searches the pond when she finds that one of her ducklings is missing.

Brown Bear, Brown Bear, What Do You See? by Bill Martin Jr.. Henry Holt, 1996. In this classic picture book, vivid illustrations and repetitive, predictable text appeal to beginning readers.

Bear's Busy Family by Stella Blackstone. Barefoot Books, 1999. A young narrator introduces her family and all the special things they do.

Are You My Mother? by P.D.Eastman. Random House, 1960. A newly hatched bird goes on an adventure in search of his mother.

■ ADVANCED

Hiccup by Taylor Jordan. Golden Books, 1998. What does a hippo do when he develops a case of the hiccups? His little sister may just have an answer.

Catch That Cat! by Carl Meister. Children's, 1999. A playful cat leads the way through words that are opposites.

Little Elephant by Miela Ford. Greenwillow, 1994. A baby elephant needs a lot of practice as it learns to play in the water.

City Cats, Country Cats by Barbara Shook Hazen. Golden Books, 1999. This lively book shows city cats and country cats playing in different ways.

■ READ ALOUD

Bashi, Elephant Baby by Theresa Radcliffe. Viking Penguin, 1997. Lifelike illustrations help tell the story of a baby elephant trapped in the mud and saved by his mother and the herd.

Safe, Warm, and Snug by Stephen R. Swinburne. Harcourt, 1999. This rhyming book shows how baby animals are protected by their parents.

Little Lions by Jim Arnosky. Putnam, 1998. A mother mountain lion watches over her two cubs as they play on a rocky ledge.

Koala Lou by Mem Fox. Harcourt, 1991. A young koala tries to win back her parents' attention, which has been sidetracked by their other children.

Homework Ideas

Visit *The Learning Site*: www.harcourtschool.com See Resources for Parents and Teachers: Homework Helper

	Literature	Phonics	Language Arts	Theme	Cross-Curricular
WEEK 1	Draw and write about your favorite mother and baby from *Does a Kangaroo Have a Mother, Too?*	Make a list of words that **begin with h.** Add to the list as you and family members think of new words.	Write instructions for taking care of a **pet.**	Find pictures of baby animals in magazines. Cut out the pictures and make a baby animal **poster.**	**Name an animal** and challenge a family member to give the correct name for the baby animal.
WEEK 2	Draw and write about the baby bear in *Are you there, Baby Bear?*	Draw two objects whose names begin with **the /l/ sound.**	Write three questions about **baby animals.** Ask family members to answer the questions.	Make a list of your **favorite animals.**	Find a magazine picture of an **animal's home.** Cut out the picture and label it.
WEEK 3	**Draw a picture** that shows how animals like to play.	Draw a picture of two things whose names **rhyme with fig.**	Write a list of action words that **describe** how baby animals play.	Find a book about **baby animals** and read it with a family member.	**Sing** the song, "Old Macdonald Had a Farm" for a family member. Use the names of baby animals.

"Animal Family" Posters

Materials

- Teacher's Resource Book page 13
- poster board
- paints
- brushes
- markers
- crayons
- old magazines
- safety scissors
- glue sticks
- paper and pencils

School-Home Connection

Invite family members to visit the classroom to view the "Animal Family" posters. Tell children to be prepared to answer questions about the animals on their posters. Rehearse with them how to listen carefully to questions and how to give specific answers. Invite visitors to share information and stories about the kinds of animal families on the posters.

Visit *The Learning Site!* at **www.harcourtschool.com**

Introduce

Tell children they are going to work together to make "Animal Family" posters. Ask them to name animal parents and babies, and list them on the board. Assign children to groups in charge of making or finding pictures of their animal family.

Send home the Family Letter to encourage family members to participate in the project.

Prepare

- Groups can draw, paint, or cut out and label pictures of their animal parents and babies and glue them to their posters, and add speech balloons with the sounds the animals make.

- Groups can make a list comparing animal parents and animal babies: what they look like, what they eat, and what they can or cannot do.

Share

Display completed posters in the classroom, school library, school halls, or another area of the school. Invite families and other classrooms to join a guided tour of the display. Groups can present their posters and tell the kinds of things animal babies learn to do as they grow up.

Hens	Chicks
Cluck	Peep
Have feathers	Have down
Can fly	Can not fly
Lay eggs	Can not lay eggs
	Need to be warmed by mother

Teacher Notes

Learning Centers

Choose from the following suggestions to enhance your learning centers for the theme Animal Families.
(Additional learning centers for this theme can be found on pages 246 and 292.)

SCIENCE CENTER

Animal Parents and Animal Babies

Give each child a sheet of paper. Tell them to fold the paper in half and, with the fold at the top, to draw and label a picture of an animal baby. Then have children swap pictures with a partner and identify each other's animal babies. Partners should unfold the paper and, on the full-size paper, draw a picture of the parent of the animal baby drawn on the front.

20 Minutes

Materials

- construction paper
- crayons
- pencil

MANIPULATIVE CENTER

Pop-Up Joey

Provide shape papers of a mother kangaroo and her joey for children to trace onto construction paper, color, and cut out. Have children cut a slit to be the mother kangaroo's pouch and slide the joey into it. Partners can have their joeys play "peek-a-boo" with each other, sliding them deep into the pouch to hide and then popping them up while saying "peek-a-boo."

20 Minutes

Materials

- shape patterns: mother kangaroo, joey (page T25)
- construction paper
- pencils
- crayons
- safety scissors

184   **Animal Families**

ART CENTER

Clay Animal Families

Tell children they are going to work with a partner to make an animal family from clay or modeling dough. Provide a variety of materials in the center that children can use to decorate their clay animal families. Then have partners choose an animal they would like to make. Each child can make an animal parent and one or more animal babies.

Materials

- modeling dough or clay
- yarn
- feathers

DRAMATIC PLAY CENTER

Who's Playing?

Place the following *Picture Cards* face down in the dramatic play center: *bear, cat, dog, duck, goat, horse, kangaroo, lamb, pig, rabbit, seal*. Have partners draw a card, look at it, and act out the animal playing. Other children in the group should try to guess the animal being imitated. Have partners taking turns acting out a pair of animals playing.

Materials

- *Picture Cards bear, cat, dog, duck, goat, horse, kangaroo, lamb, pig, rabbit, seal*

[NOTE: Pictures of the animals mentioned in the Library Book *A Time for Playing* can be drawn on index cards and used as part of the activity.]

All About Animals

Have each child work with a partner. Place a set of sentence strips face down in front of each child. Each partner names an animal. Partners can alternate turning over a sentence strip, reading it, and completing it with something their animal character would say if it could speak.

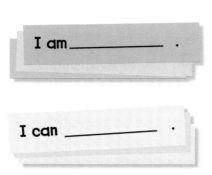

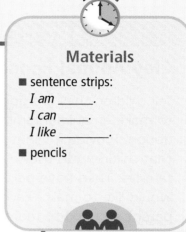

20 Minutes

Materials

■ sentence strips:
  I am _____.
  I can ____.
  I like _____.
■ pencils

Write About an Animal Baby

Give children a sheet of paper and tell them to choose an animal baby they would like to write about. On one side of the paper have children write two things their animal baby can do. Then have children turn the paper over and write two things it cannot do. Have children draw pictures to illustrate their sentences.

A fol can run.

Its leggs ar long.

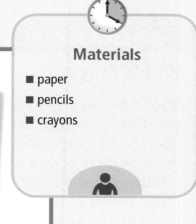

20 Minutes

Materials

■ paper
■ pencils
■ crayons

Teacher Notes

Teacher Notes

THEME 6

Week 1

Animal Families

15-30 Minutes

ORAL LANGUAGE

- **Phonemic Awareness**

- **Sharing Literature**

Day 1

Phonemic Awareness, 193
Phoneme Matching and Isolation: Initial

Sharing Literature, 194
Read
Big Book: *Does a Kangaroo Have a Mother, Too?*
 Skill **Literature Focus, 195**
Using Prior Knowledge

Day 2

Phonemic Awareness, 209
Phoneme Isolation

Sharing Literature, 210
Library Book: *Are You There, Baby Bear?*
Skill **Literature Focus, 211**
Real and Make-Believe

45 Minutes

LEARNING TO READ

- **Phonics**

- **Vocabulary**

Daily Routines
- Morning Message
- Calendar Language
- Writing Prompt

**Phonics, 204 T**
Introduce: Consonant *Ll*
Identify/Write **T**

Phonics, 212 T
Review: Consonant *Ll*
Relating /l/ to *l* **T**

High-Frequency Word, 214 T
Introduce: *you*

Words to Remember, 215

15-30 Minutes

LANGUAGE ARTS

- **Writing**
  Daily Writing Prompt

 Writing, 206
Write a Sentence

Writing Prompt, 206
Draw and write about self-selected topics.

Share Time, 207
Share sentences and drawings from Writing.

 Shared Writing, 216
Write Naming Words

Writing Prompt, 216
Draw and write about something that is lost.

Share Time, 217
Read
Share a favorite part of *Are You There, Baby Bear?*

T = tested skill

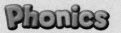 **Phonics**

Consonants *Ll, Hh*

Focus of the Week:
- **HIGH-FREQUENCY WORDS:** *you, have*
- **PHONEMIC AWARENESS**
- **SHARING LITERATURE**
- **WRITING: Signs, Class Story, Word Web**

Day 3

Phonemic Awareness, 219
Phoneme Matching and Isolation: Initial

Sharing Literature, 220
Read-Aloud Anthology: "The Three Billy-Goats Gruff," p. 49

(Skill) **Literature Focus, 221**
Retell the Story

 Phonics, 222 **T**
Introduce: Consonant *Hh*
Identify/Write **T**

High-Frequency Word, 224 T
Introduce: *have*

Words to Remember, 225

 Writing, 226

Read
Write a Sign

Writing Prompt, 226
Draw and write about self-selected topics.

Share Time, 227
Retell "The Three Billy-Goats Gruff."

Day 4

Phonemic Awareness, 229
Phoneme Isolation

Sharing Literature, 230
Big Book of Rhymes and Songs: "Five Speckled Frogs," p. 30

(Skill) **Literature Focus, 231**
Number Words

 Phonics, 232 **T**
Review: Consonant *Hh*
Relating /h/ to *h* **T**

High-Frequency Words, 234 T
Review: *you, have*

Read
PRE-DECODABLE BOOK 15
I Have, You Have

 Shared Writing, 236
Write a Class Story

Writing Prompt, 236
Draw and write about favorite things to do in the water.

Share Time, 237
Brainstorm things that can be counted.

Day 5

Phonemic Awareness, 239
Phoneme Isolation

Sharing Literature, 240
Library Book: "*Are You There, Baby Bear?*"

(Skill) **Literature Focus, 241**
Make Inferences

 Phonics, 242 **T**
Review: Consonants *Ll, Hh*

 Interactive Writing, 244

Read
Write a Word Web

Writing Prompt, 244
Draw and write about bear facts.

Share Time, 245
Share pictures of favorite animals in *Are You There, Baby Bear?*

Animal Families 191

WARM UP

Phonemic Awareness

Phoneme Matching and Phoneme Isolation: Initial

Sharing Literature

Big Book:
Does a Kangaroo Have a Mother, Too?

Read

Develop Listening Comprehension

Respond to Literature

Literature Focus: Using Prior Knowledge

Phonics

Consonant *Ll*

Writing

Sentences

MORNING MESSAGE

Kindergarten News

_____ and _____ make good pets. (Child's name) has a pet _____. (Child's name) wants to get a pet _____.

Write Kindergarten News Talk with children about pets they have or would like to have.

Use prompts such as the following to guide children as you write the news:

• **What kinds of animals make good pets?**

• **Let's count the letters in _____ 's name.**

• **What letter should I write first in (animal name)?**

• **Let's clap the syllables for (animal name).**

As you write the message, invite children to contribute by writing letters, words, or names they have learned previously. Remind them to use proper spacing, capitalization, and punctuation.

Calendar Language

Point to and read aloud the names of the days of the week. Name a day of the week and invite children to name the following day. Continue on until you've named all seven days.

Sunday	Monday	Tuesday	Wednesday	Thursday	Friday	Saturday
		1	2	3	4	5
6	7	8	9	10	11	12
13	14	15	16	17	18	19
20	21	22	23	24	25	26
27	28	29	30	31		

Phonemic Awareness

PHONEME MATCHING: INITIAL

Identify Beginning Sounds   Say these two words, emphasizing the initial sounds, and have children repeat them: *log, light*.

> **MODEL**   *Log* and *light* begin with the same sound. *Log* begins with the /l/ sound. *Light* begins with the /l/ sound. They both have the same beginning sound. Say /l/-og, /l/-ight, /l/ with me.

Tell children that you are going to say other pairs of words. Explain that you will ask them to raise their hand if the words begin with the same sound.

lizard, lake

shoe, lamp

lettuce, lime

lion, nine

loose, lunch

PHONEME ISOLATION: INITIAL

Identify the Initial Sound in Words   Say the following sets of words. Ask: *Which two words begin with the same sound? What is that sound?*

> **MODEL**   Listen as I say three words: *loose, pack, lunch. Loose* and *lunch* have the same beginning sound—/l/. *Pack* does not. Say *loose* and *lunch* with me. What is the beginning sound? (/l/)

- **Which two words begin with the same sound:** *lizard, boat, lake*? (*lizard, lake*) **Say *lizard* and *lake* with me.**
- **What is the first sound you hear in *lizard* and *lake*?** (/l/)
- **Which two words begin with the same sound:** *lamp, lost, shoe*? (*lamp, lost*) **Say *lamp* and *lost* with me.**
- **What is the first sound you hear in *lamp* and *lost*?** (/l/)

Sharing Literature

Read Does a Kangaroo Have a Mother, Too?

▲ **Big Book**

OBJECTIVES

- *To listen and respond to a story*
- *To make and confirm predictions*
- *To use prior knowledge to understand a selection*

Materials

- Big Book: *Does a Kangaroo Have a Mother, Too?*

READ ALOUD

Before Reading   Display the cover of *Does a Kangaroo Have a Mother, Too?* Track the print of the title and the author's name while reading the words aloud. Then use these prompts to help set a purpose for reading:

- **Do you think kangaroos have mothers?** (Possible response: yes)
- **What do you already know that makes you think kangaroos have mothers?** (Possible response: People have mothers. I have seen other animals that have mothers.)
- **Do you think that all animals have mothers?** (Possible response: yes)
- **What do you want to find out when we read this book?** (Possible response: I want to find out if all animals have mothers.)

Page through the book, pausing briefly to allow children to preview the setting on each page.

During Reading   Read the selection aloud. As you read,

- emphasize the language pattern of the questions and answers on each page by using voice fluctuations.
- emphasize the repetitive phrases by tracking the print each time you read them.
- model how to make and confirm predictions.

MODEL The kangaroo has a mother, the lion has a mother, the giraffe has a mother. I think the next animal, the penguin, will have a mother, too.

DEVELOP LISTENING COMPREHENSION

After Reading Have children answer these questions about the selection:

- **What is the answer to the question *Does a kangaroo have a mother, too?*** (Yes, a kangaroo has a mother.)
- **What is your favorite animal in this book?** (Possible response: The monkey is my favorite animal.)
- **In what kinds of places do these animals live?** (in the water, on land, on ice)
- **Which animal builds a home for her babies underground?** (the fox)

RESPOND TO LITERATURE

Extend the Story Invite children to discuss *Does a Kangaroo Have a Mother, Too?* by taking turns asking and answering questions about additional animals. For example, a child might ask, *Does a tiger have a mother, too?* and the class would answer, *Yes! A tiger has a mother. Just like me and you.*

USING PRIOR KNOWLEDGE

Literature Focus

Tell children that readers usually know something about the people or things in the books they read. Then, when they read a book, they can learn more.

MODEL Before I read *Does a Kangaroo Have a Mother, Too?*, I already knew something about the animals in the book. That helps me recognize the animals in the pictures and understand the book better.

Page through the book, stopping to ask questions such as *What do you know about giraffes? Where do penguins live?* and *What do you know about elephants?* As children answer these questions, lead them to see that they already knew about animals and that this knowledge helps them enjoy the book.

ENGLISH-LANGUAGE LEARNERS

Below On-Level Advanced ELL

Reinforce that the phrase *Just like me and you* is used to tell that two things are the same. Point out similarities among children, such as *Justin has two hands* or *Letitia is wearing two shoes*. Have children respond by saying *Just like me and you.*

ONGOING ASSESSMENT

As you share *Does a Kangaroo Have a Mother, Too?* note whether children

- **listen for a period of time.**
- **can make and confirm predictions.**

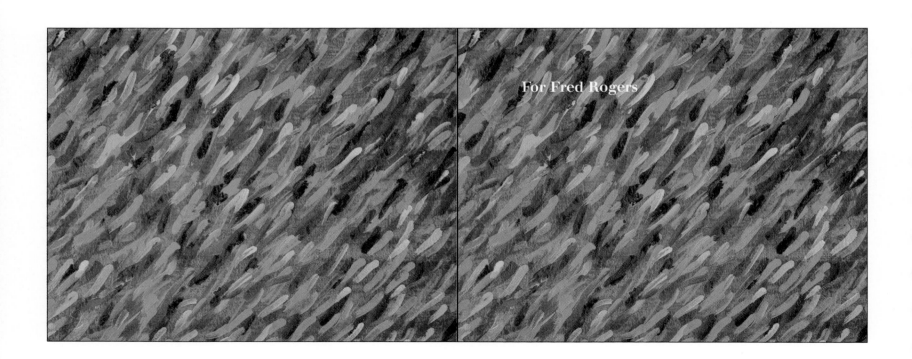

For Fred Rogers

DOES A KANGAROO

HAVE A MOTHER, TOO ?

by Eric Carle

Harcourt

Orlando   Boston   Dallas   Chicago   San Diego

Visit *The Learning Site!*
www.harcourtschool.com

YES !

A **KANGAROO** has a mother.
Just like me and you.

Does a lion have a mother, too?

6

7

Yes!

A **LION** has a mother.
Just like me and you.

Does a giraffe have a mother, too?

8

9

Yes!

A **GIRAFFE** has a mother.
Just like me and you.

Does a penguin have a mother, too?

10

11

Yes!

A **PENGUIN** has a mother.
Just like me and you.

Does a swan have a mother, too?

12

13

Yes!

A **SWAN** has a mother.
Just like me and you.

Does a fox have a mother, too?

14

15

Yes!

A **FOX** has a mother.
Just like me and you.

Does a dolphin have a mother, too?

16

17

Yes!

A **DOLPHIN** has a mother.
Just like me and you.

Does a sheep have a mother, too?

18

19

Yes!

A **SHEEP** has a mother.
Just like me and you.

Does a bear have a mother, too?

Yes!

A **BEAR** has a mother.
Just like me and you.

Does an elephant have a mother, too?

Yes!

An **ELEPHANT** has a mother.
Just like me and you.

Does a monkey have a mother, too?

24

25

Yes!

A **MONKEY** has a mother.
Just like me and you.

And do animal mothers love their babies?

26

27

YES! YES! Of course they do.

Animal mothers love their babies, just as yours loves you.

28

Names of animal babies, parents, and groups in this book

Kangaroo A baby kangaroo is a ***joey***. Its mother is a ***flyer*** and its father is a ***boomer***. A group of kangaroos is a ***troop*** or a ***mob*** or a ***herd***.

Lion A baby lion is a ***cub***. Its mother is a ***lioness*** and its father is a ***lion***. A group of lions is a ***pride***.

Giraffe A baby giraffe is a ***calf***. Its mother is a ***cow*** and its father is a ***bull***. A group of giraffes is a ***tower*** or a ***herd***.

Penguin A baby penguin is a ***chick***. Its mother is a ***dam*** and its father is a ***sire***. A group of penguins is a ***colony*** or a ***parade***.

Swan A baby swan is a ***cygnet***. Its mother is a ***pen*** and its father is a ***cob***. A group of swans is a ***wedge*** or a ***herd***.

Fox A baby fox is a ***cub*** or a ***pup***. Its mother is a ***vixen*** and its father is a ***dog fox***. A group of foxes is a ***pack*** or a ***skulk***.

Dolphin A baby dolphin is a ***calf***. Its mother is a ***cow*** and its father is a ***bull***. A group of dolphins is a ***school*** or a ***pod***.

Sheep A baby sheep is a ***lamb***. Its mother is a ***ewe*** and its father is a ***ram***. A group of sheep is a ***flock***.

Bear A baby bear is a ***cub***. Its mother is a ***sow*** and its father is a ***boar***. A group of bears is a ***pack*** or a ***sloth***.

Elephant A baby elephant is a ***calf***. Its mother is a ***cow*** and its father is a ***bull***. A group of elephants is a ***herd***.

Monkey A baby monkey is an ***infant***. Its mother is a ***mother*** and its father is a ***father***. A group of monkeys is a ***group*** or a ***troop*** or a ***tribe***.

Deer A baby deer is a ***fawn***. Its mother is a ***doe*** and its father is a ***buck***. A group of deer is a ***herd***.

29

YES! YES! Of course they do.

Animal mothers love their babies, just as yours loves you.

28

Phonics

Consonant *Ll*  Introduce

OBJECTIVES

- *To recognize L and l*

- *To write uppercase and lowercase Ll independently*

Materials

- *Big Book of Rhymes and Songs pp. 2–3*

- *Music CD*

- *Big Book: Does a Kangaroo Have a Mother, Too?*

- *Big Alphabet Card Ll*

- *Write-On/Wipe-Off Boards*

- drawing paper

- crayons

ACTIVE BEGINNING

Sing "The Alphabet Song" Display "The Alphabet Song" in the *Big Book of Rhymes and Songs*. Play the Music CD and point to each letter as you sing the song with children.

▲ **Big Book of Rhymes and Songs, pp. 2-3**

TEACH/MODEL

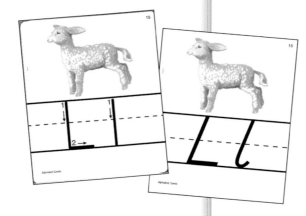

Introduce the Letter Name Hold up *Big Alphabet Card Ll*.

The name of this letter is *l*. Say the name with me.

Point to the uppercase *L*. **This is the uppercase *L*.**

Point to the lowercase *l*. **This is the lowercase *l*.**

Point to the *Big Alphabet Card* again. **What is the name of this letter?**

Point to the *Ll* in "The Alphabet Song." **What is the name of this letter?**

Display page 9 of *Does a Kangaroo Have a Mother, Too?*

Follow along as I read these sentences. Track the print as you read page 9.

Point to the letter *L* in *LION*. **What is the name of this letter?**

Point to the letter *l* in *like*. **What is the name of this letter?**

Handwriting

Writing *L* and *l*   Write uppercase *L* and lowercase *l* on the board.

Point to the uppercase *L*. **What letter is this?**

Point to the lowercase *l*. **What letter is this?**

Model how to write uppercase *L*. **Watch as I write the letter *L* so that everyone can read it.**

Letter Talk for *L*

Straight line down, then straight to the right.

Trace the letter and repeat the Letter Talk. Use the same modeling procedure for lowercase *l*.

D'Nealian handwriting models are on pages R10–R11.

Letter Talk for *l*

Straight line down.

PRACTICE/APPLY

Guided Practice   Help children find *Ll* on their *Write-On/Wipe-Off Boards*. Have them trace uppercase *L* with a finger and write the letter several times. Then have them do the same for the lowercase *l*.

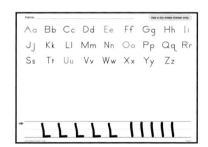

Independent Practice

Distribute drawing paper and have children fill their paper with *Ll*'s. Ask them to draw a line under their best *Ll*.

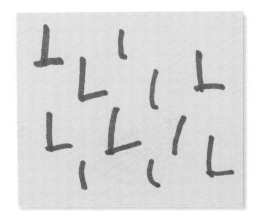

BELOW-LEVEL

Model how to make an *L* with the thumb and forefinger of your left hand. As children do the same, have them trace their forefinger and thumb, while saying the Letter Talk for *L*.

ADVANCED

Tell children to select five crayons of different colors. Have them use them to practice drawing *Ll*'s on lined paper.

Phonics Resources

Phonics Express™ CD-ROM, **Level A,** Roamer/Route 5/ Harbor

Phonics Practice Book pages 61–62

▲ **Practice Book page 7**

OBJECTIVES

- *To understand the elements of sentences*

- *To write sentences*

- *To write by moving left to right*

Materials

- chart paper
- marker
- drawing paper
- crayons

Writing Every Day

Day 1: Write a Sentence
Have children write about animals.

Day 2: Write Naming Words
Work together to graph lost items.

Day 3: Write a Sign
Have children write signs for a play.

Day 4: Write a Class Story
Work together to complete sentence frames about frogs.

Day 5: Write a Word Web
Have children help you write names of story characters.

Writing

Write a Sentence

REVIEW SENTENCES

Talk About Sentences   Review with children that a sentence tells a complete thought. Write this sentence on chart paper: *A kangaroo has a mother*. Read the sentence aloud, tracking the print. Point to the uppercase letter at the beginning of the sentence, and ask: **What does a sentence start with?** (*an uppercase letter*) Then, point to the period at the end of the sentence and ask: **What does this period mean?** (*Possible response: The sentence stops.*)

Write a Sentence   Write and distribute to children copies of the following sentence: *A _____ has a mother.* Have children complete the sentence with an animal name and draw a picture. Suggest that children might like to draw animals other than those in *Does a Kangaroo Have a Mother, Too?*

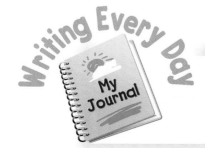

Self-Selected Topics   Ask children to write about self-selected topics in their journals.

WRAP UP

Share Time

Reflect on the Lesson   Invite children to read their sentences and share their drawings from the writing lesson. Ask them to tell something they know about the animals they've selected to write about.

S.S.R. *Sustained Silent Reading*   Have children read silently from a book of their choice.

Centers   ART

Favorite Animals Posters

Have children sort through magazine pictures and select their favorite animals. Then tell them to cut out the pictures and make animal posters by gluing their pictures onto construction paper. Have children write their name on their poster and label the animals.

Materials

- magazine pictures of animals, including some baby animals if possible

- scissors

- glue

- construction paper

- crayons

WARM UP

MORNING MESSAGE

Kindergarten News

The weather today is _____.

It is _____ outside.

Phonemic Awareness

Phoneme Isolation

Sharing Literature

Library Book:
Are You There, Baby Bear?

Read

Catherine Walters

**Develop Listening
Comprehension**

Respond to Literature

Literature Focus: Real and
Make-Believe

Phonics

Relating /l/ to *l*

High-Frequency Word

you

Shared Writing

Naming Words

Write Kindergarten News Talk with children about the day's weather. Help children identify the weather as sunny, cloudy, snowy or rainy, then talk about the temperature outside.

Use prompts such as the following to guide children as you write the news:

- **What is the weather like today?**
- **What letter will I write first in (*cloudy*)?**
- **What letter will I write last in (*cold*)?**
- **Let's clap the syllables in the word *cloudy*. How many parts do you clap?**

As you write the message, invite children to contribute by writing letters or words they have learned previously. Remind them to use proper spacing, capitalization, and punctuation. Ask children to point out spaces between words.

Calendar Language

Point to and read aloud the names of the days of the week. Tell children you will name the school days. Point to and read aloud *Monday* through *Friday*. Ask children to repeat the names of the school days.

Sunday	Monday	Tuesday	Wednesday	Thursday	Friday	Saturday
		1	2	3	4	5
6	7	8	9	10	11	12
13	14	15	16	17	18	19
20	21	22	23	24	25	26
27	28	29	30	31		

Phonemic Awareness

PHONEME ISOLATION

Listen for /l/ Tell children you will say some words and they will listen for the beginning sound in those words.

Say: *lizard*. Have children repeat *lizard*.

Say it again, emphasizing the /l/ sound.

Say: **/l/ is the sound I hear at the beginning of *lizard*—/l/.**

Say *lizard*—/l/ with me.

Then say the following words. Have children repeat each word and make the sound they hear at the beginning of each word.

lucky   lamb   laundry   lettuce

Read the following rhyme to children, emphasizing the sound of /l/ at the beginning of words.

Little Lucy lost her lamb

and her lizard that kept hissing.

Lucky Lucy found her lamb,

but the lizard is still missing!

Reread the rhyme slowly, and direct children to raise their hand each time they hear the /l/ sound.

BELOW-LEVEL

Follow this routine to review the beginning sound /l/. Use individual words from the rhyme: *Lucy* /l/ *Lucy* begins with /l/; *lamb* /l/ *lamb* begins with /l/; *Lucky* /l/ *Lucky* begins with /l/; *lizard* /l/ *lizard* begins with /l/.

ADVANCED

Have children take turns with a partner, saying a word that begins with the /l/ sound.

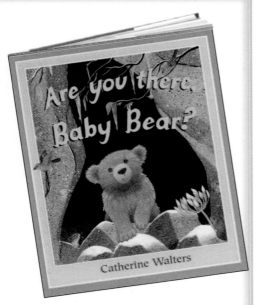

▲ **Library Book**

OBJECTIVES

- *To make and confirm predictions*

- *To identify characters, settings, and important events*

- *To understand characters*

- *To distinguish between real and make-believe*

Materials

- Library Book: Are You There, Baby Bear?

- Library Book: Hold the Anchovies!

- drawing paper

- crayons

Sharing Literature

Read Are You There, Baby Bear?

READ ALOUD

Before Reading   Display the cover of *Are You There, Baby Bear?* Read the title and the author's name aloud. Ask children what animal they see on the cover. Then use these prompts to build background:

- **What do you know about bears?** (Possible response: They are big, brown animals.)

- **Look at the picture. What season is it?** (winter) **How do you know?** (There is snow on the rocks and there is ice hanging on the branches of the tree.)

- **What do bears do in the winter?** (They sleep.)

Page through the book, pausing briefly on each page to allow children to preview the illustrations. Have children tell what they think will happen next before you turn the page.

During Reading   Read the story aloud. As you read,

- use different voices to portray the various animal characters.

- emphasize the questions that Alfie, the little bear, asks each animal.

- pause after reading about the bison to model how to make and confirm predictions.

MODEL **Alfie thinks a beaver and then a bison are his new baby brother or sister. I think when he sees the next animal, he will think it is his baby brother or sister, too.**

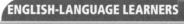

DEVELOP LISTENING COMPREHENSION

After Reading Have children answer these questions about the story:

- **Why does Alfie leave his cave?** (because the baby bear has not arrived and Alfie thinks it might be lost)
- **Does Alfie get a new brother or a new sister?** (He gets a brother and a sister.)
- **How do you think Alfie feels at the end of the story?** (Possible response: happy)

RESPOND TO LITERATURE

Draw a Picture of Alfie and the Baby Bears Have children draw a picture of Alfie and his new baby brother and sister. Tell them to show something that the three young bears might do when they play together, such as climb trees.

Literature Focus

REAL AND MAKE-BELIEVE

Page through the books *Hold the Anchovies!* and *Are You There, Baby Bear?* Model for children how to tell if a book has characters that are real or make-believe.

MODEL As I look through the pages of these books I can tell that what happens in *Hold the Anchovies!* could happen in real life because it shows photographs of real people making pizza. In *Are You There, Baby Bear?*, I can see drawings of animals talking to each other. This story is make-believe because animals don't talk to each other in real life.

ENGLISH-LANGUAGE LEARNERS Below / On-Level / Advanced / ELL

Name the animals in the book and have children repeat the names. Then say the name of an animal on a page and ask children to point to the corresponding picture and repeat the name. When children become familiar with the animal names, encourage them to take turns naming an animal and asking a partner to point to the correct picture in the book.

ONGOING ASSESSMENT

As you share *Are You There, Baby Bear?*, note whether children

- can make and confirm predictions.
- understand characters.

OBJECTIVE

To match consonant l to its sound

Materials

- *Letter and Sound Chart 20*
- *Tactile Letter Cards l*
- *Teacher's Resource Book p. 70*
- *Picture/Word Cards ladder, nail*
- pocket chart
- Lion Pattern (page T15)
- scissors
- crayons
- glue
- drawing paper

Phonics
Relating /l/ to l

ACTIVE BEGINNING

Recite "Lemonade"   Teach children the rhyme, "Lemonade." Then chant the rhyme again, substituting for the words *lawn* and *leafy* for the words, *lake* and *cool*.

Lemonade

Squeeze a lemon, squeeze a lemon.

Make some lemonade.

Let's have lunch on the lawn

In the leafy shade.

by Susan Little

L l

Lamb has a lunch box.
What did she pack?
Lettuce and lemonade
For her lunchtime snack.

▲ **Letter and Sound Chart 20**

TEACH/MODEL

Introduce Letter and Sound   Display *Letter and Sound Chart* 20. Touch the letter *L.* **What is the name of this letter?**

This letter stands for the /l/ sound. When you say this letter, you touch your tongue behind your top front teeth. Say /ll/.

Read aloud the rhyme on the *Letter and Sound Chart*, tracking the print. Reread the *Ll* words in the rhyme. Point to the *L* or *l* in each word.

What letter stands for the /l/ sound?

Have children join in as you read the rhyme again. Tell them to touch their tongue behind their top front teeth as they say the /l/ words.

PRACTICE/APPLY

Guided Practice   Distribute *Tactile Letter Cards l*. Then place *Picture/Word Cards ladder* and *nail* in the pocket chart. Say the names of the pictures as you point to the *l* in each. Have children repeat the words.

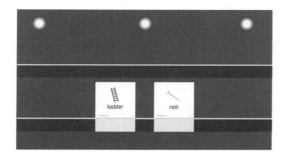

Tell children: **Some words begin with *l* and some words end with *l*.**

Point to the *l* in *ladder*. **The /l/ sound is at the beginning of *ladder*.**

I'll say some words. If the word begins with the /l/ sound, hold up your *l* card. If it doesn't begin with the /l/ sound, don't hold up your card.

| like | pick | look | leaf | dot | land | lips |

Follow the same procedure for the ending sound in *nail*.

| pail | top | wheel | pile | crib | trail | smile |

Independent Practice   Distribute copies of the Lion Pattern (page TI5). Have children cut out the lion and glue it on drawing paper. Have children draw pictures of words whose names begin or end with the /l/ sound. Ask children to whisper their words to you before they draw them. Children can label their pictures and write the letter *Ll*.

ENGLISH-LANGUAGE LEARNERS

Have children point to each *Picture Card*, say the name of the picture, and make the beginning sound they hear.

Phonics Resources

Phonics Express™ CD-ROM, Level A, Roamer/Route 5/ Market, Fire Station, Train Station

Phonics Practice Book pages 63–64

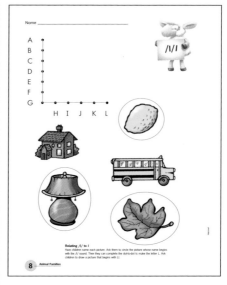

▲ **Practice Book page 8**

Animal Families   213

High-Frequency Word: *you* ✔ *Introduce*

OBJECTIVE

To read high-frequency word you

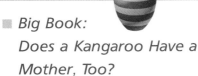

Materials

■ *Big Book:
Does a Kangaroo Have a
Mother, Too?*

■ *High-Frequency Word Card*

 you

■ *Teacher's Resource Book* p. 139

■ rabbit puppet

TEACH/MODEL

High-Frequency Word *you* Read page 6 in *Does a Kangaroo Have a Mother, Too?* Stop and point to the word *you* and say: **This is the word *you*.** Have children say the word. Display the *High-Frequency Word Card you.* Ask: **What word is this?** Ask a child to match the *High-Frequency Word Card you* to the word *you* in the *Big Book*.

PRACTICE/APPLY

Guided Practice Make copies of the *High-Frequency Word Card you* in the *Teacher's Resource Book*. Have children sit in a circle. Give each child a card and tell children to point to the word *you* and say it. Use the rabbit puppet to model how to use the word *you* in a question. Have the rabbit say: **Who are you?** Have a child repeat this question with the rabbit and point to the word card as he or she says the word *you*. Continue modeling with the rabbit puppet in the same way with these sentences: **What do you like? Do you have a bike? Are you hungry?**

Independent Practice Pair children and have them use questions to interview each other. Ask them to point to their *High-Frequency Word Card you* each time they say the word in their questions.

Words to Remember
Word Wall

Reading Words Hold up the *High-Frequency Word Card you* and have children read it aloud. Then place the word card under the letter *Y* of the classroom word chart.

Go on a Word Hunt Have children look at the words on the word chart. As you ask clues such as the following, have children point to and read the words.

- **This word has three letters. It means "the person you are talking to."** (*you*)
- **This word has one letter. It means "myself."** (*I*)
- **This word begins with /m/. It means "something that belongs to me."** (*my*)
- **This word begins with the /l/ sound.** (*like*)
- **This word has three letters. It begins with *t*.** (*the*)

BELOW-LEVEL

Write on chart paper short sentences that include the word *you*. Have children match the *High-Frequency Word Card you* with the word in each sentence.

ADVANCED

Have children spell *you* and other high-frequency words they know, using the *Magnetic Letters* on a cookie sheet.

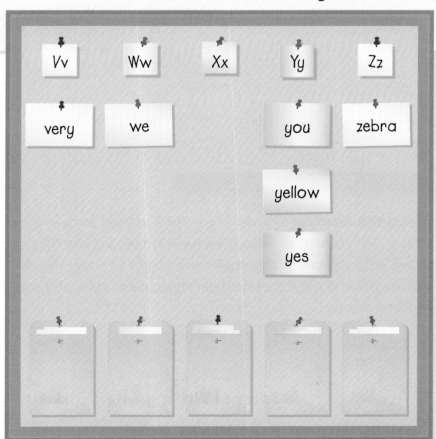

▲ **Practice Book page 9**

Animal Families   215

OBJECTIVES

- *To understand that some words name objects*
- *To write naming words*
- *To share information and ideas*

Materials

- Library Book: *Are You There, Baby Bear?*
- chart paper
- markers

Shared Writing

Write Naming Words

GRAPH LOST ITEMS

Talk About Naming Words Remind children everything has a name, just as people do. Page through the book *Are You There, Baby Bear?* Point to animals, leaves, flowers, and trees in the pictures, and ask children to name them.

Write Naming Words Ask children to name things that they have lost. Remind children that every item that was lost is a naming word. As they name objects, write the words across the bottom of chart paper.

We have lost:		
mittens	crayons	toys

SHARE

Read the Naming Words Point to and read each word on the chart. Ask children to raise their hand if they've lost that object. Have children color a box above the object to show they lost it. When the chart is complete, help children compare and count the naming words.

Writing Every Day

My Journal

Journal Writing Have children draw and write about something they have lost.

WRAP UP # Share Time

Reflect on the Lesson Invite children to talk about their favorite part of the story *Are You There, Baby Bear?* Then ask them to tell what word they learned today. (*you*)

S.S.R. *Sustained Silent Reading* Have children read silently from a book of their choice.

Centers SCIENCE

Bird Feeders

Remind children that in *Are You There, Baby Bear?* the forest is full of animals searching for food in the winter. Tell children that they can help birds by making pine cone feeders to hang outside. Have children spread peanut butter over pine cones, filling in all the hollows. Then pour bird seed into a plastic bag and have children shake their pine cones in the bag to cover them with seed. Tie yarn around the top of each pine cone to make a hanger. Encourage children to hang their feeders outside their homes in a spot where they can observe the birds.

Materials

- large pine cones
- peanut butter
- plastic knives
- bird seed
- plastic bags
- yarn

Day at a Glance
Day 3

WARM UP

Phonemic Awareness
Phoneme Matching and Phoneme Isolation: Initial

Sharing Literature
Read-Aloud Anthology:
  "The Three Billy-Goats Gruff"

Read

Develop Listening Comprehension

Respond to Literature

Literature Focus: Retell the Story

Phonics
Consonant *Hh*

High-Frequency Word
have

Shared Writing
Sign

MORNING MESSAGE

Kindergarten News

This month is _____.

(Child's name) likes to eat _____.

(Child's name) likes to eat _____.

Write Kindergarten News Talk with children about some of their favorite foods. Encourage them to speak clearly.

Use prompts such as the following to guide children as you write the news:

- **Say the name of the month with me. Let's clap the syllables.**
- **Who has a favorite food? What is it?**
- **What letter will I write first in (food name)?**
- **Who can show me a word?**

As you write the message, invite children to contribute by writing letters, words, or names they have learned previously. Remind them to use proper spacing, capitalization, and punctuation.

Calendar Language

Display a calendar for the current month and read the name of the month. Say: *This month is _____ .* Have children repeat the sentence. Then ask several children *What month is this?* and have them answer, *This month is _____ .*

Sunday	Monday	Tuesday	Wednesday	Thursday	Friday	Saturday
		1	2	3	4	5
6	7	8	9	10	11	12
13	14	15	16	17	18	19
20	21	22	23	24	25	26
27	28	29	30	31		

Phonemic Awareness

PHONEME MATCHING: INITIAL

Identify Beginning Sounds   Say these two words, emphasizing the initial sounds, and have children repeat them: *head*, *hand*.

MODEL   *Head* and *hand* begin with the same sound. *Head* begins with the /h/ sound. Say *head* with me. *Hand* begins with the /h/ sound. Say *hand* with me. They both have the same beginning sound /h/.

Tell children that you will say other words. Have them raise their hand if the words begin with the same sound.

heart, team	hippo, hill
hut, hound	hello, beach
helicopter, hood	field, heat

PHONEME ISOLATION: INITIAL

Identify the Initial Sound in Words   Say the following sets of words. Ask: **Which two words begin with the same sound? What is that sound?**

MODEL   Listen for the two words that begin with the same sound: *helicopter, farm*, *hood*. *Helicopter* and *hood* have the same beginning sound—/h/. *Farm* does not. Say *helicopter* and *hood* with me. What is the beginning sound? Let's listen for more beginning sounds.

• **Which two words begin with the same sound:** *team*, *heart*, *hose*? (*heart, hose*) **Say** *heart* **and** *hose* **with me. What is the first sound you hear in** *heart* **and** *hose*? (/h/)

• **Which two words begin with the same sound:** *hippo*, *field*, *hill*? (*hippo, hill*) **Say** *hippo* **and** *hill* **with me. What is the first sound you hear in** *hippo* **and** *hill*? (/h/)

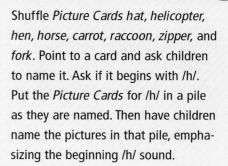

BELOW-LEVEL

Shuffle *Picture Cards hat, helicopter, hen, horse, carrot, raccoon, zipper,* and *fork*. Point to a card and ask children to name it. Ask if it begins with /h/. Put the *Picture Cards* for /h/ in a pile as they are named. Then have children name the pictures in that pile, emphasizing the beginning /h/ sound.

ADVANCED

Have children look through magazines, grocery store flyers, and advertisements to find pictures or words that begin with the /h/ sound. Have them cut out the pictures and glue them on construction paper to make a poster.

▲ **Read-Aloud Anthology**

OBJECTIVES

• *To listen and respond to a story*

• *To understand action words*

• *To retell story events in sequence*

Materials

■ *Read-Aloud Anthology, pp. 49–50*

Sharing Literature

Read "The Three Billy-Goats Gruff"

READ ALOUD

Before Reading Show children page 49 in the *Read-Aloud Anthology* and read the title aloud. Then use these prompts to help children build background:

• **What is a billy-goat?** (a kind of goat)

• **One of the characters in this story is a troll. What do trolls look like?** (Possible response: Trolls are small and have a mean face.)

• **Have you ever seen a troll in real life or are trolls just make-believe characters in stories?** (Trolls are just in stories.)

During Reading Read the story aloud. As you read,

• use different voices to portray the three billy-goats and the troll.

• to help children keep track of story events, stop at the end of page 49 and review events that have happened so far.

MODEL First, the smallest billy-goat went over the bridge. He told the troll that the billy-goat who was coming next was much bigger. Then, the second billy-goat went over the bridge. He told the troll not to eat him but to wait for the big billy-goat who was coming next.

DEVELOP LISTENING COMPREHENSION

After Reading Have children answer these questions about the story:

- **Why do the three billy-goats want to go across the bridge?** (to go up the hillside to make themselves fat)

- **How do the first and second billy-goats cross the bridge without the troll gobbling them up?** (They each tell the troll that the next billy-goat is bigger and he should wait for the next one.)

- **What happens at the end of the story?** (The big billy-goat tosses the troll into the water.)

RESPOND TO LITERATURE

Dramatize Action Words Say various phrases that contain action words from the story such as *"I'm coming to gobble you up," the bridge creaked and groaned, "tripping over my bridge,"* and *tossed him into the water.* Repeat and model each action word to children, and then have them act out the phrases as you say them.

Literature Focus

RETELL THE STORY

Ask children to name the characters in "The Three Billy-Goats Gruff" and retell what happens to each of them in the story. Use this model to demonstrate retelling a story:

> **MODEL** **If I wanted to tell what this story is about, I would think about what happens to each character, starting with the first character at the beginning of the story.**

Help children recall what happens between each billy-goat and the troll. Ask: **Where are the billy-goats at the beginning of the story? Where are they at the end? Many things have to happen to the billy-goats in the middle in order to have a happy ending. Do you remember what happened?**

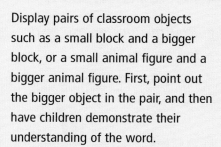

BELOW-LEVEL

Display pairs of classroom objects such as a small block and a bigger block, or a small animal figure and a bigger animal figure. First, point out the bigger object in the pair, and then have children demonstrate their understanding of the word.

ONGOING ASSESSMENT

As you share "The Three Billy-Goats Gruff," note whether children

- **listen for a period of time.**

- **understand action words.**

OBJECTIVES

- *To recognize H and h*
- *To write uppercase and lowercase Hh independently*

Materials

- *Big Book of Rhymes and Songs* pp. 2–3
- *Music CD*
- *Big Book: I Read Signs*
- *Big Alphabet Card Hh*
- *Write-On/Wipe-Off Boards*
- drawing paper
- crayons

Phonics
Consonant Hh  Introduce

ACTIVE BEGINNING

Sing "The Alphabet Song" Display "The Alphabet Song" in the *Big Book of Rhymes and Songs*. Play the Music CD and point to each letter as you sing the song with children.

▲ **Big Book of Rhymes and Songs, pp. 2-3**

TEACH/MODEL

Introduce the Letter Name Hold up *Big Alphabet Card Hh*.

The name of this letter is *h*. **Say the name with me.**

Point to the uppercase *H*. **This is the uppercase *H*.**

Point to the lowercase *h*. **This is the lowercase *h*.**

Point to the *Big Alphabet Card* again. **What is the name of this letter?**

Point to the *Hh* in "The Alphabet Song." **What is the name of this letter?**

Direct children's attention to the signs on pages 11 and 22 in *I Read Signs*.

Point to the letter *H* in *HOSE*. **What is the name of this letter?**

Point to the letter *H* in *HILL*. **What is the name of this letter?**

Handwriting

Writing _H_ and _h_   Write uppercase _H_ and lowercase _h_ on the board.

Trace the letter and repeat the Letter Talk. Use the same modeling procedure for lowercase h.

Point to the uppercase _H_.
What letter is this?

Point to the lowercase _h_.
What letter is this?

Model how to write uppercase _H_.
Watch as I write the letter _H_ so that everyone can read it.

Letter Talk for _H_

Straight line down; straight line down; short line across to connect the lines.

Letter Talk for _h_

Straight line down and halfway up the line again; curve to the right and down.

D'Nealian handwriting models are on pages R10–R11.

PRACTICE/APPLY

Guided Practice   Help children find _Hh_ on their _Write-On/Wipe-Off Boards_. Have them trace uppercase _H_ with their finger and write the letter several times. Then, have them do the same for lowercase _l_.

Independent Practice   Distribute drawing paper and have children fold the paper in half and write uppercase _H_'s on one side of the paper and lowercase _h_'s on the other side. Have children circle their best _H_ and _h_.

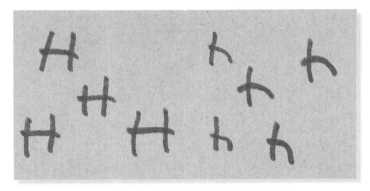

BELOW-LEVEL

Guide each child in writing the letter. Put your hand over the child's hand and write the letter as you repeat the Letter Talk. Then have the child try it alone.

ENGLISH-LANGUAGE LEARNERS

As you introduce children to _Hh_ letter formation, model each step of the Letter Talk to make sure they understand the terms *straight, across, down, halfway,* and *curve.*

Phonics Resources

Phonics Express™ CD-ROM, Level A, Scooter/Route 2/ Building Site

Phonics Practice Book pages 65–66

▲ **Practice Book page 10**

OBJECTIVE

To read high-frequency word have

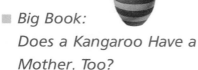

Materials

- *Big Book: Does a Kangaroo Have a Mother, Too?*

- *High-Frequency Word Card*

- *Teacher's Resource Book* p. 139

- a small object for each child

High-Frequency Word: *have* ✓ *Introduce*

TEACH/MODEL

Display the cover of *Does a Kangaroo Have a Mother, Too?* Read the title and point to the word *Have*. Say: **This is the word *Have*.** Have children say the word. Display the *High-Frequency Word Card Have*. Ask: **What word is this?** Have children repeat the title of the *Big Book* with you. Ask a child to match the *High-Frequency Word Card Have* to the word *Have* on the cover.

PRACTICE/APPLY

Guided Practice Make copies of the *High-Frequency Word Card have* in the *Teacher's Resource Book*. Give each child a card and tell children to point to the word *have* and say it. Then hand every child an object, such as a crayon, a book, or a paintbrush. Ask children the question below, and ask children to point to their word card as they respond.

What do you have? Children should respond: *I have a (name of item).*

Independent Practice Have children use the following sentence stem to tell about something they have, such as a pet or a toy. Ask them to point to the *High-Frequency Word Card have* each time they say the word.

I have a _____.

Word Wall

Reading Words Hold up *High-Frequency Word Card* *have* and have children read it aloud. Then place the word card under the letter *H* of the classroom word chart.

Find Similarities Have children look very closely at their new word *have*. Encourage them to find similarities to other words posted on the chart. Ask the following question to guide them appropriately:

- *Have* has four letters. Do any of the other words have four letters? Let's read the other word that has four letters. (*like*)

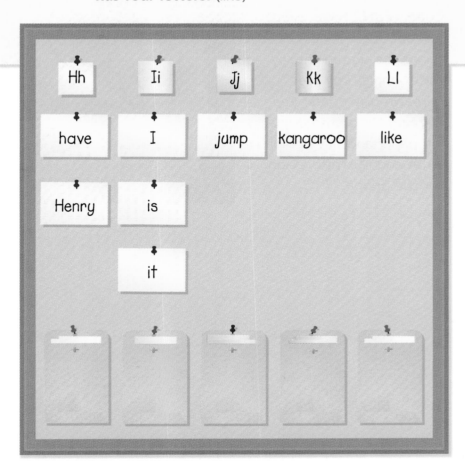

REACHING ALL LEARNERS

Diagnostic Check: High-Frequency Word

If... children have difficulty recognizing the high-frequency word *have*,

Then... have them trace over the word on their individual word card with a finger. Then have them "write" the word with a finger on their desktops.

ADDITIONAL SUPPORT ACTIVITIES

BELOW-LEVEL	Reteach, p. S20
ADVANCED	Extend, p. S21
ENGLISH-LANGUAGE LEARNERS	Reteach, p. S21

▲ **Practice Book page 11**

Animal Families 225

OBJECTIVES

- *To understand the purpose of a sign*

- *To write a sign*

- *To write by moving from left to right*

- *To share information, using complete, coherent sentences*

Materials

- ■ drawing paper

- ■ crayons

Writing

Write a Sign

BUILD BACKGROUND

Talk About Signs   Remind children of the book *I Read Signs* and that signs are used to give information, to help keep people safe, and to name a place. Have them talk about signs they see in the classroom and in the school.

Write a Sign   Tell children that they are going to write a sign for the bridge that the billy-goats cross in the story "The Three Billy-Goats Gruff." Have them talk about the kinds of things the sign might say— for example, *Troll lives here, No billy-goats, Troll warning.* Distribute drawing paper and have children write and illustrate a sign for the bridge.

kep of the brij

Self-Selected Topics   Ask children to write about self-selected topics in their journals.

 **Share Time**

Readers Theatre Invite children to share their signs by acting out the story "The Three Billy-Goats Gruff." Select several children to act out the billy-goats crossing the bridge. Have other children take turns acting out the troll and reading their signs to the goats until everyone has had a turn.

 Have children read silently from a book of their choice.

 **Centers** DRAMATIC PLAY

Play Time

Place copies of the character cutouts from the *Teacher's Resource Book* at the center. Have children color and cut out the characters and tape them to craft sticks. Tell children to draw the setting of "The Three Billy-Goats Gruff" and practice retelling the story with their props.

 **Materials**

- *Teacher's Resource Book*, p. 88
- crayons
- scissors
- tape
- craft sticks
- drawing paper

Day at a Glance

Day 4

WARM UP

Phonemic Awareness
Phoneme Isolation

Sharing Literature

Big Book of Rhymes and Songs:
"Five Speckled Frogs"

Read
Big Book of Rhymes and Songs

Develop Concept Vocabulary

Respond to Literature

Literature Focus: Number Words

Phonics

Relating /h/ to *h*

Reading

Pre-decodable Book 15: *I Have, You Have*

Shared Writing

Class Story

MORNING MESSAGE

Kindergarten News

We like to _____.

On weekends, my family _____.

Write Kindergarten News Talk with children about what they like to do with their families.

Use prompts such as the following to guide children as you write the news:

- **What are some things you like to do with your family?**
- **Who can show me the word *We*?**
- **Let's clap the syllables in the word *weekends*. How many parts do we clap?**
- **What punctuation mark should I put at the end of the sentence?**

As you write the message, invite children to contribute to writing letters or words they have learned previously. Remind them to use proper spacing, capitalization, and punctuation.

Calendar Language

Point to the numbers on the calendar. Tell children the days of each month are numbered and the numbers tell the date. Point to and read aloud the name of the month and the date. Have children name the month and the date with you.

Sunday	Monday	Tuesday	Wednesday	Thursday	Friday	Saturday
		1	2	3	4	5
6	7	8	9	10	11	12
13	14	15	16	17	18	19
20	21	22	23	24	25	26
27	28	29	30	31		

Phonemic Awareness

PHONEME ISOLATION

Listen for /l/ and /h/   Sing the following phrases to the tune of "Old MacDonald":

MODEL   **I know a word that begins with /l/—**
lucky, _light_, and _leaf_.
Who knows a word that begins with /l/?

Have children name three words that begin with /l/ to complete the last line of the song. Then sing the song again, using those words with children. Repeat the song again for the /h/ sound, using the following model:

I know a word that begins with /h/—
hippo, _house_, and _hot_.
Who knows a word that begins with /h/?

Have children name three words that begin with /h/ to complete the last line of the song. Then sing the song again, using those words with the children.

▲ **"A-Hunting We Will Go,"** _Oo-pples and Boo-noo-noos: Songs and Activities for Phonemic Awareness,_ page 54

BELOW-LEVEL

Show children a pair of _Picture Cards_ for the letters _l_ and _h_. Ask children to name both pictures. Say /l/, and then ask children to name the picture that begins with /l/. After children have identified all the /l/ _Picture Cards_, follow the same procedure for the /h/ words.

Animal Families   239

▲ Library Book

OBJECTIVES

- *To identify the front cover, back cover, and title of a book*
- *To recall story events*
- *To understand characters*
- *To make inferences*

Materials

- Library Book: *Are You There, Baby Bear?*
- chart paper
- marker
- drawing paper
- crayons

Sharing Literature

Read Are You There, Baby Bear?

READ ALOUD

Before Reading   Display the cover of *Are You There, Baby Bear?* and read the title aloud. Show the front of the book and the back of the book, using the words *front* and *back*. Hold up the front of the book and point to the title. Ask: **What is this?** (title) Then use these prompts to help children recall the story:

- **What is the name of the little bear in this story?** (Alfie)
- **Why does Alfie leave his cave?** (to look for his baby brother or sister)

Help children set a purpose for listening to the story before you reread it.

MODEL   **I remember that Alfie has different feelings. I want to reread the story to remember what Alfie feels.**

During Reading   Reread the story aloud. As you read,

- stop to point out the various feelings Alfie has throughout the story. Ask questions such as **How is Alfie feeling now? What happens in the story to make him have this feeling?**
- after reading the page where Alfie is sitting in leaves, model how things Alfie does and says help the reader understand him.

MODEL   **Winter is coming and the baby bear still hasn't come. Alfie gets worried and goes out to look for the baby bear. I can tell that Alfie is kind.**

DEVELOP CONCEPT VOCABULARY

After Reading Remind children that Alfie has a lot of different feelings during the story. Draw descriptive faces for these words on chart paper: *bored, worried, excited, discouraged*. Then point to each face as you discuss the words:

- Say *bored*. *Bored* is how you feel when you don't have anything interesting to do. Tell me about a time when you felt bored. Show me what it looks like to be bored.

- Say *worried*. *Worried* is how you feel when you're not sure about things. Tell me about a time when you felt worried. Show me what it looks like to be worried.

- Say *excited*. *Excited* is how you feel when something great is happening. Tell me about a time when you felt excited. Show me what it looks like to be excited.

- Say *discouraged*. *Discouraged* is how you feel when things don't go the way you want them to. Tell me about a time when you felt discouraged. Show me what it looks like to be discouraged.

RESPOND TO LITERATURE

Draw a Picture of Feelings Have children draw and label pictures of Alfie and show how he feels during one part of the story.

Literature Focus

MAKE INFERENCES

Tell children that authors sometimes give clues to help readers understand things about a story. Sometimes readers need to use these clues and be "story detectives."

MODEL The author never says that this story begins in the fall, just before winter, but I can tell from story clues that it does. (Display the first two pages of *Are You There, Baby Bear?*) I see snow in the mountains, but there is no snow on the ground and I see colored leaves on the trees. By being a "story detective," I figured out that it is fall.

BELOW-LEVEL

Use visual clues to help children grasp concepts. Page through the story again, having children tell what is happening. Discuss how the illustrations help them understand the story.

ENGLISH-LANGUAGE LEARNERS

As you read and discuss each illustration, point to an object and tell what color it is. Then ask: *What color is this (bird)?*

ONGOING ASSESSMENT

As you share *Are You There, Baby Bear?*, note whether children

- understand characters.
- can recall story events.

OBJECTIVES

- *To recognize uppercase and lowercase Ll and Hh*
- *To match sounds to letters*

Materials

- *Big Alphabet Cards Ll, Hh*
- pocket chart
- *Picture Cards hat, helicopter, hen, horse, ladder, lamb, lemon, lunch box*
- *Tactile Letter Cards l, h*

Phonics
Consonants *Ll,Hh*

 Review

ACTIVE BEGINNING

Sing the *L* and *H* Songs Display *Big Alphabet Cards Ll* and *Hh*. Ask children to name each letter and to trace the letter in the palm of their hand. Then have children join in singing "Lemonade" (page 212) and "Hiking" (page 232).

TEACH/MODEL

Discriminate *L* and *H*
Display *Big Alphabet Card L* in a pocket chart and ask for the letter name.

Point to the picture and say its name: **lamb.** Have children repeat it. (lamb)

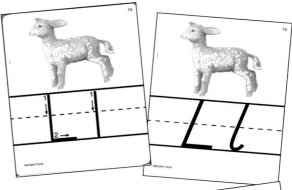

What sound do you hear at the beginning of *lamb*? (/l/) **What letter stands for the /l/ sound in *lamb*?** (*l*)

Follow the same procedure for *Big Alphabet Card Hh.*

Place *Picture Cards lamb* and *hen* on the chalk ledge. Say each picture name and tell children you need to decide which picture name goes with the beginning sound.

MODEL I'll choose *lamb*. **L—amb begins with the /l/ sound. So I'll put the picture of the lamb below *Ll*.**

Model the same process with *Picture Card hen*.

PRACTICE/APPLY

Guided Practice   Place these *Picture Cards* on the chalk ledge: *ladder, hat, lunch box, horse, helicopter, lemon.* Tell children that they will now sort some pictures.

Say the picture name. **If the beginning sound is /l/, let's put the card below the *Ll*. If the beginning sound is /h/, let's put the card below the *Hh*.**

Independent Practice   Give each child *Tactile Letter Cards l* and *h*.

I'm going to say some words. Listen carefully to the sound you hear at the beginning of each word. Think about the letter that stands for that sound, and then hold up the card for that letter.

lock	hot	ham	lips	help	lime
hill	hippo	lake	laugh	hip	loose

REACHING ALL LEARNERS

Diagnostic Check: Phonics

If... children cannot identify or relate sound to letters *Ll* and *Hh*,

Then... have children focus on one letter/sound at a time. Encourage children to look for *Picture Cards* whose names begin with /h/ first. Then have them name the pictures whose names begin with /l/.

ADDITIONAL SUPPORT ACTIVITIES

BELOW-LEVEL	Reteach, p. S24
ADVANCED	Extend, p. S25
ENGLISH-LANGUAGE LEARNERS	Reteach, p. S25

Phonics Resources

Phonics Express™ CD-ROM, **Level A,** Scooter/Route 2/ Market; Scooter/Route 3/Park; Sparkle/Route 2/Fire Station; Sparkle/ Route 1/Train Station

Phonics Practice Book page 69

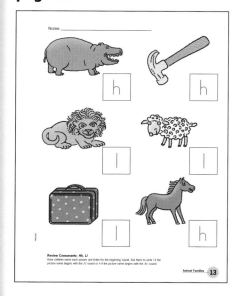

▲ **Practice Book page 13**

Animal Families   243

Interactive Writing

Write a Word Web

BUILD BACKGROUND

Write Names of Characters   Tell children that together they will write a word web for the characters in the story *Are You There, Baby Bear?* Draw a word web on the chart paper and write *Story Characters* in the center circle. Add six spokes and circles to the web. Then ask children to name the story characters. (Alfie, Mother Bear, Father Bear, beaver, bison, mountain lion) Model for children how to listen to the sounds of letters so they know what letter comes next in a name.

MODEL   Let's write the name *Alfie*. Say *Alfie* with me. *Alfie* begins with the /a/ sound. Who would like to write the letter that stands for /a/? Remember this is a name. So I will need to see an uppercase letter.

Slowly say each letter of the name *Alfie* as you write it. Continue to stop in the middle of saying and writing each name on the web, and allow children to listen to the sound and write the next letter.

SHARE

Read the Word Web   After the web is complete, read it to children. Point to *Alfie* and remind children that it begins with an uppercase letter because it is a name. Have children find the other two characters with names and point to the uppercase letters. (Mother Bear, Father Bear)

Journal Writing   Have children draw and write about something they learned about bears from *Are You There, Baby Bear?*

OBJECTIVES

• *To write a word web*

• *To identify story characters*

• *To relate sounds to letters*

Materials

■ chart paper

■ marker

 # Share Time

Reflect on the Lesson   Invite children to share the pictures they drew of Alfie to show their to show how he feels during one part of the story, *Are You There, Baby Bear?*

 S.S.R.   Have children read silently from a book of their choice.

 Centers MANIPULATIVES

Animal Puzzles

Glue pictures onto separate pieces of poster board. Cut each picture into irregularly-shaped pieces. Place each puzzle's pieces into a large envelope. Then have children select an envelope and assemble the puzzle. When children complete their puzzle, ask them to identify the animal they see and to talk about the place where that animal lives.

 Materials

- magazine or calendar pictures of animals in their natural environment

- glue

- scissors

- poster board

- large envelopes

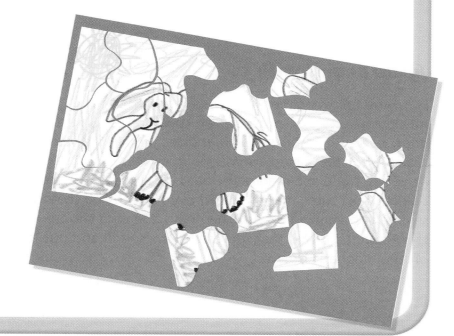

Learning Centers

Choose from the following suggestions to enhance your learning centers for the theme Animal Families.
(Additional learning centers for this theme can be found on pages 184–186 and 292.)

MATH CENTER

Count the Animals

In the math center, provide a variety of counting books featuring animals and pictures of animals cut from magazines. Have partners work together to use counters to count the animals in each illustration. Children should place one counter on each animal in an illustration. Have partners take turns choosing illustrations and counting.

 20 Minutes

Materials

- pictures of animals cut from magazines
- counting books featuring animals
- counters

MANIPULATIVE CENTER

Turtle Begins with *t*

Place the following *Picture Cards* facedown in the manipulative center: *alligator, cat, cow, dog, duck, fish, fox, goat, gorilla, hen, horse, lamb, mouse, pig, rabbit, raccoon, seal,* and *turtle.* Also place *Magnetic Letters a, c, d, f, g, h, l, m, p, r, s, t* and the magnetic board in the center. Have children take turns turning a card over, identifying it, and saying its beginning sound. Then have the child choose the *Magnetic Letter* that represents the sound and put it on the magnetic board.

20 Minutes

Materials

- *Magnetic Letters a, c, d, f, g, h, l, m, p, r, s, t*
- magnetic board
- *Picture Cards alligator, cat, cow, dog, duck, fish, fox, goat, gorilla, hen, horse, lamb, mouse, pig, rabbit, raccoon, seal, turtle*

Teacher Notes

Teacher Notes

Week 2

Animal Families

15-30 Minutes

ORAL LANGUAGE

- **Phonemic Awareness**

- **Sharing Literature**

45 Minutes

LEARNING TO READ

- **Phonics**

- **Vocabulary**

Daily Routines
- Morning Message
- Calendar Language
- Writing Prompt

15-30 Minutes

LANGUAGE ARTS

- **Writing**
  Daily Writing Prompt

Day 1

Phonemic Awareness, 253
Phoneme Matching and Isolation: Final

Sharing Literature, 254

Read

Big Book: *Does
a Kangaroo Have
a Mother, Too?*

 Literature Focus, 255
Illustrations in Picture Books

 Phonics, 256 T
Review: Consonant /p/*p*, Short Vowel /i/*i*

 Writing, 258
Write About Your Family

Writing Prompt, 258
Draw and write about self-selected
topics.

Share Time, 259
Share books about family members.

Day 2

Phonemic Awareness, 261
Phoneme Blending

Sharing Literature, 262

Read

Library Book: *A Time
for Playing*

 Literature Focus, 263
Main Idea/Details

 Phonics, 264 T
Introduce: Blending /i/ - /p/

 Shared Writing, 266
Write a Chart

Writing Prompt, 266
Draw and write about an animal at
play.

Share Time, 267
Share a favorite animal in *A Time for
Playing.*

---

250   **Animal Families**

T = **tested skill**

Focus of the Week:
- PHONEMIC AWARENESS
- SHARING LITERATURE
- WRITING: Charts, Lists, Sentences

Day 3

Phonemic Awareness, 269
Phoneme Isolation: Medial

Sharing Literature, 270
Read-Aloud Anthology:
"Chicken Forgets," p. 51

(Skill) **Literature
Focus, 271**
Making Predictions

Phonics, 272 T
Words with /i/ - /p/

Interactive Writing, 274

Read

Grocery Lists

Writing Prompt, 274
Draw and write about favorite foods.

Share Time, 275
Retell "Chicken Forgets."

Day 4

Phonemic Awareness, 277
Syllable Segmentation

Sharing Literature, 278
Big Book of Rhymes and
Songs: "Mary Had a Little
Lamb," p. 15

(Skill) **Literature
Focus, 279**
Rhyming Words

Phonics, 280 T
Review: Short Vowel /i/*i*

Read
PRE-DECODABLE
BOOK 16
Soup

Shared Writing, 282
Write a Thank-You Note

Writing Prompt, 282
Write a thank-you note to a family member.

Share Time, 283
Discuss the Pre-decodable Book *Soup.*

Day 5

Phonemic Awareness, 285
Phoneme Segmentation

Sharing Literature, 286
Big Book: *Does a Kangaroo
Have a Mother, Too?*

(Skill) **Literature
Focus, 287**
Words in a Sentence

Phonics, 288 T
Review: Blending /i/ - /p/

Writing, 290
Write Questions

Writing Prompt, 290
Draw and write about self-selected topics.

Share Time, 291

Read

Share and answer questions.

Day at a Glance
Day 1

ORAL LANGUAGE

WARM UP

Phonemic Awareness

Phoneme Matching and Phoneme Isolation: Final

Sharing Literature

Big Book:
Does a Kangaroo Have a Mother, Too?

Read

DOES A KANGAROO HAVE A MOTHER, TOO?
by Eric Carle

Develop Concept Vocabulary

Respond to Literature

Literature Focus: Illustrations in Picture Books

Phonics

Consonant /p/p,
Short Vowel /i/i

Writing

Family Book

MORNING MESSAGE

Kindergarten News

(Child's name) _____ over the weekend.

(Child's name) _____ over the weekend.

Write Kindergarten News Talk with children about activities they did or places they went over the weekend.

Use prompts such as the following to guide children as you write the news:

- **Who would like to tell about something you did over the weekend?**
- **What letter will I write first in (child's name)?**
- **Do any of the names we've written begin with the same letter?**
- **Let's count the letters in (child's name). How many letters are there?**

As you write the message, invite children to write letters, words, and names they have learned previously. Remind them to use proper spacing, capitalization, and punctuation.

Calendar Language

Ask what day of the week it is today. Ask what day came before today. Point to that day on the calendar and say: *The day before today was _____* . Have children say the word that means *before today*. (*yesterday*)

Sunday	Monday	Tuesday	Wednesday	Thursday	Friday	Saturday
			1	2	3	4	5
6	7	8	9	10	11	12
13	14	15	16	17	18	19
20	21	22	23	24	25	26
27	28	29	30	31		

Phonemic Awareness

PHONEME MATCHING FINAL

Identify Final Sounds   Say these three words, emphasizing the final sounds, and have children repeat them: *hop*, *mat*, *nap*.

MODEL   *Hop* and *nap* end with the same sound. *Hop* ends with the /p/ sound and *nap* ends with the /p/ sound. They both have the same ending sound.

Tell children that you will say another group of words. Have them raise their hand if the words end with the same sound.

lip, cup   top, win   ram, hum

sit, cat   rag, bell   bug, bag

PHONEME ISOLATION: FINAL

Identify the Final Sound in Words   Say the following sets of words and ask: **Which two words end with the same sound? What is that sound?**

MODEL   Listen for the two words that have the same ending sound: *lip*, *side*, *cup*. *Lip* and *cup* have the same ending sound—/p/. *Side* does not. Say *lip* and *cup* with me. What is the ending sound? Let's listen for more ending sounds.

- Which two words end with the same sound: *rag, bug, bell*? *(rag, bug)* **Say rag and bug with me. What is the last sound you hear in rag and bug?** (/g/)

- Which two words end with the same sound: *top, map, win*? *(top, map)* **Say top and map with me. What is the last sound you hear in top and map?** (/p/)

- Which two words end with the same sound: *lick, ram, hum*? *(ram, hum)* **Say ram and hum with me. What is the last sound you hear in ram and hum?** (/m/)

▲ **Big Book**

OBJECTIVES

- *To use illustrations to gather information*

- *To follow words from left to right and from top to bottom on the printed page*

- *To ask and answer questions about a book*

Materials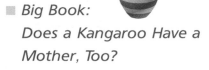

- *Big Book: Does a Kangaroo Have a Mother, Too?*

- drawing paper

- crayons

Sharing Literature

Read **Does a Kangaroo Have a Mother, Too?**

READ ALOUD

Before Reading   Display *Does a Kangaroo Have a Mother, Too?* and read the title aloud. Direct children's attention to the artwork. Then use these prompts to help set a purpose for rereading:

- **What can you learn about kangaroos from this picture?** (Possible response: A kangaroo mother carries her baby in a pouch.)

- **What does the picture teach you about a kangaroo's body?** (Possible response: Kangaroos have a pouch for their babies.)

Page through the book, pausing briefly to allow children to view the art on each page. Have children suggest what they might learn about the bodies of animals and where they live from the pictures.

During Reading   Reread the story aloud. As you read,

- track the print from left to right.

- point to where you begin reading at the top of the page and to where you end at the bottom. After you reread the first few pages, ask children to point to where to begin and end reading on the remaining pages.

- model for children how to gather information from pictures.

MODEL In this picture, both the elephant mother and her baby are gray and have big ears and a trunk. There is something different about them, too. The mother has tusks, or long pointed teeth, and the baby doesn't. I learn from the picture that tusks grow on elephants as they get older.

DEVELOP CONCEPT VOCABULARY

After Reading   Begin a chart on the board by writing the words *Land* and *Water* as column headings. Read the headings to children. Have children name each animal from the book and tell you if it lives on land or in water. Record the animal names in the chart, under the appropriate headings. (Land: kangaroo, lion, giraffe, fox, sheep, bear, elephant, monkey; Water: swan, dolphin. Note that children may want to place penguins in either column.) Then ask the following questions:

• **Which animal has a long, fluffy tail?** (*fox*)

• **Which animal lives in the icy cold all year round?** (*peguin*)

• **Which word names an animal that lives on the land and has a very long neck?** (*giraffe*)

• **Which word names an animal that lives in the water and has only white feathers?** (*swan*)

RESPOND TO LITERATURE

Draw Animal Mothers and Babies   Have children draw pictures of their favorite animal mothers and babies in the story. Tell them to draw a setting that shows where the animals live. Display the pictures in the classroom.

ADVANCED

Share the information on page 29 of the book. Have children label their pictures of mothers and babies, using these terms.

ONGOING ASSESSMENT

As you share *Does a Kangaroo Have a Mother, Too?*, note whether children

• can use illustrations to gather information.

• can follow words from left to right and from top to bottom on the printed page.

• ask and answer questions about a book.

★ **Literature Focus**

ILLUSTRATIONS IN PICTURE BOOKS

Tell children that pictures in books can give them information. Remind them that they have used the pictures in *Does a Kangaroo Have a Mother, Too?* to find out what the animals look like and where they live. Display page 15.

MODEL   **I can get information about swans by looking at this picture. I see that as swans get older, they get black coloring around their eyes. All swans have yellow beaks. Mother swans have more than one baby at a time.**

OBJECTIVES

- To recognize uppercase and lowercase Ii and Pp

- To match sounds to letters

Materials

- pocket chart

- Alphabet Cards Ii, Pp

- Picture Cards inchworm, puzzle

- Tactile Letter Cards i, p

Phonics

Consonant /p/p, ✔Review
Short Vowel /i/i

ACTIVE BEGINNING

Recite the *I* Rhyme and Sing the *P* Song   Display *Alphabet Cards Ii* and *Pp*. Ask children to identify each letter. Have children form a circle. Ask a child to stand in the middle of the circle and hold up *Alphabet Card Ii*. Have the children walk around the circle as they sing "Itty Bitty Inchworm." (p. 94) Follow the same procedure for "Popcorn!" (Vol. 1 p. 356)

TEACH/MODEL

Review Letters and Sounds   Display *Alphabet Card Ii* in a pocket chart and ask what letter this is.

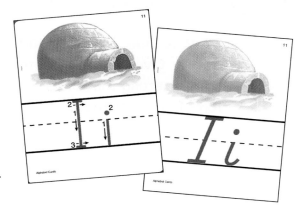

Display *Picture Card inchworm* in the pocket chart. Point to the *Picture Card* and say its name. Have children repeat it. *(inchworm)*

What sound do you hear at the beginning of *inchworm*? (/i/) What letter stands for the /i/ sound in *inchworm*? (*Ii*)

Touch the letter and say /i/. Touch the letter again and have children say /i/.

Follow the same procedure for *Alphabet Card Pp*.

Place *Picture Cards inchworm* and *puzzle* on the chalk ledge. Say each picture name and tell children you need to decide where to put each *Picture Card*.

I'll start with the inchworm. *I—nchworm* begins with the /i/ sound. So I'll put the picture of the inchworm below *Ii*.

Model the same process with *Picture Card puzzle*.

PRACTICE/APPLY

Guided Practice   Distribute *Tactile Letter Cards i* and *p* to each child.

I will say some words that begin with /i/ and some that don't. Hold up your *i* card if the word begins with the /i/ sound.

Confirm the answer for each word by holding up the appropriate *Letter Card*.

ink   book   inch   if   bus   iguana

I will say some words that begin with /p/ and some that don't. Hold up your *p* card if the word begins with the /p/ sound.

pickle   people   turtle   pie   toy   peach

Independent Practice   Have children continue to work with their *Tactile Letter Cards i* and *p*.

I'm going to say some words. Listen carefully to the sound you hear at the beginning of each word. Think about the letter that stands for that sound. Then hold up the *Letter Card* for that letter.

pear   igloo   pot   pumpkin   ill

pineapple   itchy   pig   iguana   pen

Diagnostic Check: Phonics

If... children cannot identify or relate sounds to letters *Ii* and *Pp*,

Then... have children make each letter with clay or string while saying the letter name. Give children *Picture/Word Cards inchworm, peanut*. Have children find each letter on a *Picture/Word Card* and say *This (picture name) begins with _____.*

ADDITIONAL SUPPORT ACTIVITIES

BELOW-LEVEL   Reteach, p. S26

ADVANCED   Extend, p. S27

ENGLISH-LANGUAGE LEARNERS   Reteach, p. S27

Phonics Resources

Phonics Express™ CD-ROM,
Level A, Scooter/Route 3/Park;
Roamer/Route 4/Park

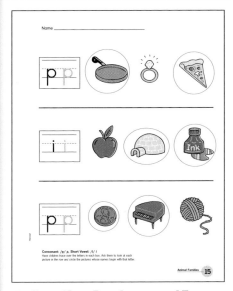

▲ **Practice Book page 15**

Animal Families   257

Writing

Write About Your Family

FAMILY BOOK

Talk About Names   Write *Mom, Dad, Grandma, Grandpa*, and some first names on chart paper, and underline the uppercase letter at the beginning of each. Remind children that people's names usually begin with an uppercase letter.

Label Family Members   Tell children that they are going to write about their family members. Give each child two pieces of drawing paper folded in half like a book. Have children write *My Family* on the cover and draw a picture of where they live. Then ask them to write the name of a family member on each page of the book. Remind children to use an uppercase letter for each name. Children can draw a picture to go with each name.

OBJECTIVES

• *To write sentences*

• *To capitalize names in sentences*

Writing Every Day

Day 1: Family Book
Have children draw and label members of their family.

Day 2: Chart
Create a chart showing animals and their actions in the story *A Time for Playing*.

Day 3: Grocery List
Work together to create a list of foods families would buy at the grocery store.

Day 4: Thank-You Note
Use the story *Soup* to write a note from Pig to Cat.

Day 5: Questions
Have children use a sentence frame to write a question about an animal in the *Big Book*.

Self-Selected Writing   Have children draw and write about self-selected topics in their journals.

WRAP UP Share Time

Author's Chair Have children read their books about their family members to the class. Ask children to point to the uppercase letter in each name they wrote.

 **S.S.R.** Have children read silently from a book of their choice.

Centers  WRITING

Write Stamp Stories

Cut simple shapes of animals, such as giraffes, elephants, and dolphins, from sponges. Provide shallow pans of paint in which children can dip the animal-shaped sponges. Have children write about the animals, using sponge prints in place of animal names in their stories. Display the stories in the classroom.

Materials

■ sponges

■ paint

■ aluminum pie plates

■ drawing paper

■ crayons

The ___ is tal.

WARM UP

Phonemic Awareness
Phoneme Blending

Sharing Literature
Library Book:
A Time for Playing

Read

A Time for
PLAYING
Ron Hirschi
PHOTOGRAPHS BY
Thomas D. Mangelsen

**Develop Listening
Comprehension**

Respond to Literature

Literature Focus: Main Ideas
and Details

Phonics
Blending /i/–/p/

Shared Writing ✏
Chart

MORNING MESSAGE

Kindergarten News

We can _____ and _____

to help in school.

(Child's name) (job description) at

home.

Write Kindergarten News   Talk with children about jobs they can do at school and at home. Begin a discussion about why helping is important.

Use prompts such as the following to guide children as you write the news:

• **Who can name some of our classroom jobs?**

• **Who helps out with jobs at home? What do you do?**

• **Who can show me a word?**

• **Who can show me a letter?**

As you write the message, invite children to write letters, words, and names they have learned previously. Remind them to use proper spacing, capitalization, and punctuation.

Calendar Language

Point to and read aloud the names of the days of the week. Ask what day today is. Ask children what day comes after today. Point to the name of the day and say: *Tomorrow is ___.* **Invite volunteers to name today and tomorrow.**

Sunday	Monday	Tuesday	Wednesday	Thursday	Friday	Saturday
		1	2	3	4	5
6	7	8	9	10	11	12
13	14	15	16	17	18	19
20	21	22	23	24	25	26
27	28	29	30	31		

Phonemic Awareness

PHONEME BLENDING

Blend Sounds Use the rabbit puppet for this blending activity.

MODEL The rabbit likes to say words in parts. Listen as it says this word: /d/ /i/ /p/. What is this word: /d/ /i/ /p/? Say it with the rabbit: /d/ /i/ /p/. Now listen to the rabbit blend the sounds: /ddiipp/. What is this word: /ddiipp/? Say it with the rabbit: /ddiipp/. The word is *dip*. Say the word.

Tell children the rabbit is going to say more words in parts. Have them listen to figure out the word the rabbit is saying. Use the following examples.

/t/ /i/ /p/ *(tip)*   /p/ /i/ /t/ *(pit)*

/s/ /a/ /t/ *(sat)*   /m/ /a/ /p/ *(map)*

/p/ /i/ /n/ *(pin)*   /k/ /u/ /p/ *(cup)*

/s/ /i/ /p/ *(sip)*   /p/ /e/ /n/ *(pen)*

/h/ /a/ /t/ *(hat)*   /r/ /i/ /p/ *(rip)*

▲ **"Chickery Chick,"** *Oo-pples and Boo-noo-noos: Songs and Activities for Phonemic Awareness,* **pages 61–63.**

/d/ /i/ /p/

REACHING ALL LEARNERS

Diagnostic Check: Phonemic Awareness

If... children have difficulty blending sounds to say words,

Then... model blending and saying words from the lesson by writing the words on chart paper and tracking the print under the letters as you elongate the sounds.

ADDITIONAL SUPPORT ACTIVITIES

BELOW-LEVEL Reteach, p. S28

ADVANCED Extend, p. S29

ENGLISH-LANGUAGE LEARNERS Reteach, p. S29

▲ **Library Book**

OBJECTIVES

- *To make and confirm predictions*

- *To ask and answer questions about a text*

- *To identify main idea and details*

Materials

■ *Library Book:
A Time for Playing*

Sharing Literature

Read A Time for Playing

READ ALOUD

Before Reading Display the cover of *A Time for Playing*. Track the print of the title and the names of the author and photographer as you read these aloud. Ask children to tell what a photographer does. Then use these prompts to help children set a purpose for reading:

- **What kind of animals do you see on the cover?** (polar bears)

- **What do you think they are doing?** (playing)

- **Do you think all animals play the same way?** (Possible response: No)

Have children look at the cover and tell what they might learn from the book.

During Reading Read the selection aloud. As you read,

- pause on each page to allow children to comment on the photographs.

- model for children how to confirm predictions.

> **MODEL** When I saw the cover of this book and read the title, I thought the book might be about polar bears. But as I read, I see that the book is about different kinds of animals playing.

WRAP UP Share Time

Reflect on the Lesson Have children talk about their favorite animal in *A Time for Playing*. Encourage them to speak in complete sentences.

S.S.R. Have children read silently from a book of their choice.

 Centers SCIENCE

Animal Habitats

Have children choose an animal from the book and draw a picture of that kind of animal engaged in play. Have children glue their picture to a craft stick and place the stick in a small ball of clay. Demonstrate how to use the trays and natural materials to create habitats for their animals.

 Materials

- *Library Book: A Time for Playing*
- craft sticks
- clay
- plastic meat trays or cardboard box tops
- natural materials such as straw, twigs, stones, moss

Day at a Glance
Day 3

WARM UP

Phonemic Awareness
Phoneme Isolation: Medial

Sharing Literature
Read-Aloud Anthology:
"Chicken Forgets"

Read

Develop Concept Vocabulary

Respond to Literature

Literature Focus: Making Predictions

Phonics

Words with /i/ and /p/

Interactive Writing
List

MORNING MESSAGE

Kindergarten News

(Child's name) has learned to

_____ .

We have all learned to _____ .

Write Kindergarten News Talk with children about things they have learned to do recently.

Use prompts such as the following to guide children as you write the news:

- **What is something new you have just learned to do?**
- **What is something we have all learned to do in our class?**
- **Where should I begin to write?**
- **What letter will I write last in the word** *learned*?

As you write the message, invite children to write letters and words they have learned previously. Remind them to use proper spacing, capitalization, and punctuation.

Calendar Language

Point to and read aloud the months of the year. Tell children there are twelve months in a year. Point to and say the name of the current month. Ask: *What month is it now?*

Sunday	Monday	Tuesday	Wednesday	Thursday	Friday	Saturday
		1	2	3	4	5
6	7	8	9	10	11	12
13	14	15	16	17	18	19
20	21	22	23	24	25	26
27	28	29	30	31		

Phonemic Awareness

PHONEME ISOLATION: MEDIAL

Identify Medial Sounds   Select *Picture Cards pig, cat.* Model for children how to break these words into sounds and how to listen for the middle sound.

MODEL   Hold up *Picture Card pig.* Ask: **What is the name of this picture?** (*pig*) **Let's break the word** *pig* **into sounds: /p/ /i/ /g/. I hear three sounds. Say them with me: /p/ /i/ /g/. Now let's blend the sounds and listen for the middle sound.** Emphasize the middle sound: **/p/ /i/ /g/.** *Pig* **has the /i/ sound in the middle. What is the middle sound?** (/i/) **Say it with me.**

Hold up *Picture Card cat.* Ask: **What is the name of this picture?** (*cat*) **Let's break the word** *cat* **into sounds: /k/ /a/ /t/. I hear three sounds. Say them with me: /k/ /a/ /t/. Now let's blend the sounds and listen for the middle sound.** Emphasize the middle sound: **/k/ /a/ /t/.** *Cat* **has the /a/ sound in the middle. What is the middle sound?** (/a/) **Say it with me.**

Tell children that you will show them more pictures. Ask them to name each picture and break the word into sounds. Ask children to identify the middle sound. Use *Picture Cards fish, hat, lamb, van, yak.*

BELOW-LEVEL

Tell children that you will use the sound they say, /i/ or /a/, in the middle of a word. Have them say one of the sounds. Then hold up an appropriate *Picture Card* for the lesson. Have children repeat the sound and say the picture name that has that medial sound.

Sharing Literature

Read "Chicken Forgets"

READ ALOUD

Before Reading Show children page 51 of the *Read-Aloud Anthology* and read aloud the title. Tell children that this story is about a little chicken who forgets things. Ask these questions:

- **Did you ever forget something? What did you forget?**

- **How do you feel when you forget things?**

- **What do you think the chicken might forget?**

During Reading Read the story aloud. As you read,

- use different voices to portray the various animal characters.

- emphasize the instructions that the little chicken repeats to himself along the way.

- pause when reading about the goat and model for children how to make predictions.

MODEL **I remember that the frog tells the little chicken to get flies. Frogs like to eat flies. I think the goat will tell him to get something the goat likes to eat. What do you think goats like to eat?** (grass/weeds) **Let's see if you are right.**

▲ **Read-Aloud Anthology**

OBJECTIVES

- *To listen and respond to a story*

- *To connect text to life experiences*

- *To describe story events*

- *To make predictions about a story*

Materials

- *Read-Aloud Anthology*, pp. 51–52

- chart paper

- drawing paper

- crayons

DEVELOP CONCEPT VOCABULARY

After Reading Write the words *frog, goat, bee, robin* on chart paper and draw a sketch of each animal beside its name. Point to each word as you read it aloud. Then give children these clues and have them name the correct animal.

- **Which animal wants the little chicken to get big green flies?** (the frog)

- **Which animal wants the little chicken to get green weeds?** (the goat)

- **Which animal wants the little chicken to get clover blossoms?** (the bee)

- **Which animal wants the little chicken to get blackberries?** (the robin)

RESPOND TO LITERATURE

Draw and Write About the Story Have children draw pictures that show what they would want the little chicken to get. Have them label their pictures.

★ Literature Focus

MAKING PREDICTIONS

Tell children that sometimes they can guess what will happen next in a story. Model for children how to make predictions.

MODEL I guessed that the goat would tell the chicken to get something that the goat liked to eat. I thought that would happen because the same thing happened earlier in the story when the chicken met the frog.

Tell children that when they are listening to or reading a story, it is fun to use what they know to guess what might happen next.

ADVANCED

Ask children to draw and write a new page of the story. Tell them to think of other animals that the little chicken could meet along the way. Then have each child draw a picture of an animal, along with the chicken and his basket. Display the sentence stem "Get _____ ." Have children complete the sentence with the word that names the food that the animal would want the chicken to get.

ONGOING ASSESSMENT

As you share "Chicken Forgets," note whether children

- can listen for a period of time.

- can connect text to life experiences.

OBJECTIVES

- *To build and read simple one-syllable words*

- *To understand that as letters of words change, so do the sounds*

Materials

- *Alphabet Cards i, n, p, s, t*

- *Word Builders*

- *Word Builder Cards i, n, p, s, t*

- pocket chart

- *Magnetic Letters*

- cookie sheet

REVIEW LETTERS

Phonics
Words with /i/ and /p/

ACTIVE BEGINNING

Action Rhyme   Teach children this rhyme and the actions that go with it:

Tip toe, **tip toe**, (Walk on tip toes.)

Stretch and bend. (Stretch up high, touch the floor.)

Pick a daisy, **pick a rose**, (Pretend to pick flowers.)

And give them to a friend. (Hold hand out, as if handing flowers to someone.)

TEACH/MODEL

Blending Words   Distribute *Word Builders* and *Word Builder Cards i, n, p, s, t* to children. As you place *Alphabet Cards* in a pocket chart, tell children to place the same *Word Builder Cards* in their *Word Builders*.

- Place *Alphabet Cards t, i,* and *p* in the pocket chart. Have children do the same.

- Point to *t*. Say **/tt/**. Point to *i*. Say **/ii/**.
- Slide the *i* next to the *t*. Then move your hand under the letters and blend the sounds, elongating them—**/ttii/**. Have children do the same.

- Point to the letter *p*. Say **/pp/**. Have children do the same.
- Slide the *p* next to the *ti*. Slide your hand under *tip* and blend by elongating the sounds—**/ttiipp/**. Have children do the same.

• Then have children read the word *tip* along with you.

PRACTICE/APPLY

Guided Practice   Have children place *Word Builder Cards i* and *p* in their *Word Builders*.

• **Add *s* to *ip*. What word did you make?**

• **Change *s* to *t*. What word did you make?**

• **Change *p* to *n*. What word did you make?**

• **Change *t* to *p*. What word did you make?**

Independent Practice   Have children use the *Magnetic Letters i, n, p, s, t* and a cookie sheet in the Letters and Words Center to build and read *tip, sip, tin, pin, pit*.

BELOW-LEVEL

Have children use their *Word Builders* and *Word Builder Cards* to blend /i/ and /p/ with you. Follow the procedure used in the Teach/Model section of the lesson.

ADVANCED

Have children use the *Magnetic Letters d, i, n, p* and *High-Frequency Word Cards I, like, the* to build sentences: *I like the pin. I like the dip.*

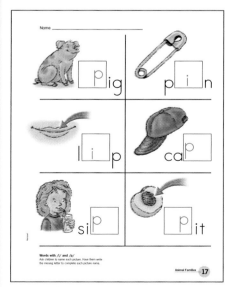

▲ **Practice Book page 17**

OBJECTIVES

- *To understand the purpose of a list*

- *To write a list*

- *To write letters at the beginning and end of words*

Materials

- ◼ chart paper

- ◼ marker

Interactive Writing

Grocery List

BUILD BACKGROUND

Write a List   Tell children that together they will make a list of foods. Ask children to name foods that their families buy at the grocery store. As children suggest them, ask: **What should the title of our list be?** Write a child's suggestion and ask him or her to underline it. Read the title to children. Then invite them to write letters in the words on the list.

Model for children how to listen for and write sounds in a word. Use sounds and letters already taught.

MODEL **My family likes to eat carrots. Say the word *carrot* with me. I hear the /k/ sound at the start of *carrots*. What letter makes the /k/ sound? I know *c* makes the /k/ sound in the word *cat*. It must make the /k/ sound in *carrots*. Who would like to come and write the letter *c* to begin the word *carrots*?**

Write all children's suggestions on the list; however, stop and follow the same procedure for other words that have a sound that was previously taught.

Shopping List
bread
milk
eggs

SHARE

Read the List   Read the list and point out how the words are written one below the other. Ask questions about the words, such as: **Which word has the most letters? Which word begins with the letter _____?**

Writing Every Day

My Journal

Journal Writing   Have children write and draw about their favorite food.

WRAP UP ## Share Time

Reflect on the Lesson Ask children to retell the story "Chicken Forgets." Then ask children to share their drawings of what they would tell the little chicken to get.

S.S.R. *Sustained Silent Reading* Have children read silently from a book of their choice.

 **Centers** COOKING

Berry Good for You

Remind children that the chicken started off to find blackberries for his mother. Tell them that there are many kinds of berries. Display the berries that children are going to taste, and identify each variety. Have children mix berries into a cup of yogurt. After children have tasted each variety, ask them to draw and label their favorite berry. NOTE: Children with food allergies can suffer potentially dangerous reactions. Check with parents before offering children foods to eat in class.

Materials

- varieties of berries, such as blackberries, blueberries, raspberries, strawberries

- plain or vanilla yogurt

- paper cups

- plastic spoons

Animal Families **275**

WARM UP

Phonemic Awareness

Syllable Segmentation

Sharing Literature

Big Book of Rhymes and Songs:
"Mary Had a Little Lamb"

Read
Big Book of Rhymes and songs

Harcourt

Respond to Literature

Literature Focus: Rhyming Words

Phonics

Pre-decodable Book 16: Soup

Shared Writing ✏

Thank-You Note

MORNING MESSAGE

Kindergarten News

_____ is my friend.

We like to _____.

Write Kindergarten News Talk with children about friends they have and what they like to do with their friends.

Use prompts such as the following to guide children as you write the news:

• **What do you like to do with a friend?**

• **What letter will I write first in (child's name)?**

• **Who can write the word *like* for me?**

• **How many words are in the second sentence?**

As you write the message, invite children to write letters, words, or names they have learned previously. Remind them to use proper spacing, capitalization, and punctuation.

Calendar Language

Have children name the days of the week in order. Then ask them to name class activities that occur on each day.

Sunday	Monday	Tuesday	Wednesday	Thursday	Friday	Saturday
		1	2	3	4	5
6	7	8	9	10	11	12
13	14	15	16	17	18	19
20	21	22	23	24	25	26
27	28	29	30	31		

Phonemic Awareness

SYLLABLE SEGMENTATION

Name Syllables   Tell children that you are going to listen for syllables in a word and clap them. Say the word *classroom* and clap the two syllables. Say: **Classroom has two syllables. Class is the first syllable. Room is the second syllable. Say classroom with me and clap the syllables: class—room.**

Have children repeat the word with you and clap the syllables.

Tell children that you will say some words and you want them to tell you how many syllables are in each word.

giraffe (gir-affe; two)   **penguin** (pen-guin; two)   **bear** (bear; one)

lion (li-on; two)   **dolphin** (dol-phin; two)   **kangaroo** (kan-ga-roo; three)

dog (dog; one)   **kitten** (kit-ten; two)   **monkey** (mon-key; two)

lizard (liz-ard; two)   **duck** (duck; one)   **elephant** (el-e-phant; three)

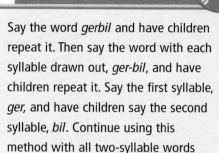

BELOW-LEVEL

Say the word *gerbil* and have children repeat it. Then say the word with each syllable drawn out, *ger-bil*, and have children repeat it. Say the first syllable, *ger,* and have children say the second syllable, *bil*. Continue using this method with all two-syllable words listed in the lesson.

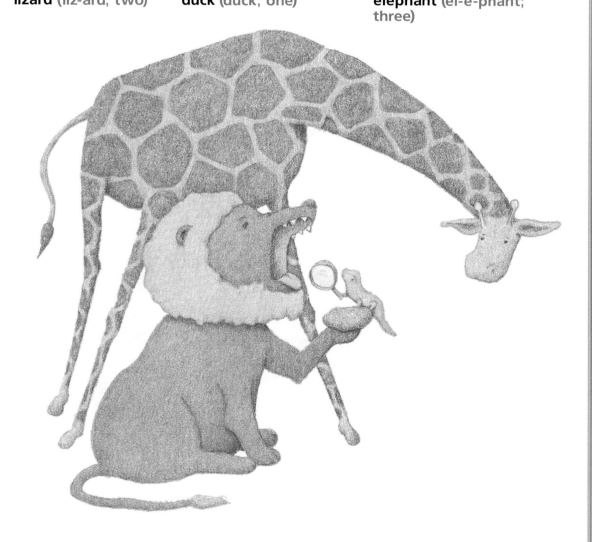

Sharing Literature

Read "Mary Had a Little Lamb"

READ ALOUD

Before Reading Display page 15 of the *Big Book of Rhymes and Songs*. Track the print of the title while reading the words aloud. Then use these prompts to build background:

- **What do you know about lambs?**
- **Would a lamb really go to school?**

During Reading Read the rhyme aloud. As you read,

- track the print.
- emphasize and frame the rhyming words *snow* and *go*.
- react to the picture and the text.

▲ **Big Book of Rhymes and Songs**

OBJECTIVES

- *To listen responsively to a nursery rhyme*
- *To follow words from top to bottom on a page*
- *To listen for rhythm and rhyme in text patterns*

Materials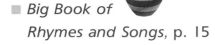

- *Big Book of Rhymes and Songs*, p. 15
- drawing paper
- crayons

Mary Had a Little Lamb

Mary had a little lamb,
Its fleece was white as snow,
And everywhere that Mary went
The lamb was sure to go.

It followed her to school one day,
Which was against the rule.
It made the children laugh and play
To see a lamb at school.

RESPOND TO LITERATURE

Draw a Picture   Remind children that the lamb followed Mary everywhere. Reread the sentence *Everywhere that Mary went her lamb was sure to go.* Copy and distribute the following to each child: *The lamb followed Mary to _____.*

Ask children to finish the sentence with the name of a different place. Then have them illustrate their sentences. Display children's work on a bulletin board titled "Mary's Lamb Went Everywhere!"

REACHING ALL LEARNERS

Diagnostic Check: Comprehension

If... children have difficulty identifying and naming rhyming words,

Then... model for them how to create rhyming sounds for their names. For example, say *Tony* and then change the beginning sound to create a rhyme, *bony, phony.* Encourage children to make up a silly name to rhyme with their own.

ADDITIONAL SUPPORT ACTIVITIES

BELOW-LEVEL	Reteach, p. S30
ADVANCED	Extend, p. S31
ENGLISH-LANGUAGE LEARNERS	Reteach, p. S31

ONGOING ASSESSMENT

As you share "Mary Had a Little Lamb," note whether children

- can listen responsively to a nursery rhyme.
- can follow words from top to bottom on a page.
- can listen for rhythm and rhyme in text patterns.

★ **Literature Focus**

RHYMING WORDS

Point to and read the words *snow* and *go* in "Mary Had a Little Lamb." Have children repeat the words with you. Remind children that rhyming words have the same ending sounds. Read the second verse of the rhyme, pointing out the rhyming words *day* and *play* and *rule* and *school*.

OBJECTIVE

To decode short vowel /i/i words

Materials

- *Alphabet Cards i, d, I*
- *Word Cards have, the, We*
- pocket chart
- *Pre-decodable Book 16: Soup*
- drawing paper
- crayons

Phonics

Short Vowel /i/i  Review

TEACH/MODEL

Review Blending Place the *Alphabet Cards i* and *d* next to one another in a pocket chart. Move your hand under the letters, blend them, and say /iidd/. Have children blend the sounds along with you.

Place the *Alphabet Card I* in front of the *i* and *d*. Slide your hand under the letters, blend them, and say the word /lliidd/ - *lid*. Have children blend the sounds and say the word.

Place the *Word Cards We, have, the* in the pocket chart, in front of *lid*. Track the print as you read the sentence. Have children repeat the sentence as you track it again.

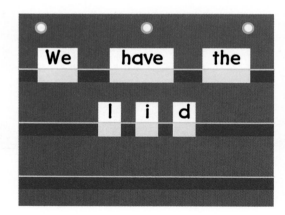

PRACTICE/APPLY

Read the Book Distribute copies of *Soup*. Read the title. Ask children to identify the *S* at the beginning of the word and the *p* at the end.

Have children read the story, pointing to each word as they read.

Respond Have children draw themselves sipping soup from a cup. Ask children to write the word *sip* on their pictures and then read it.

Pre-decodable Book 16: _Soup_

We have a pot.

2

We have onions.

3

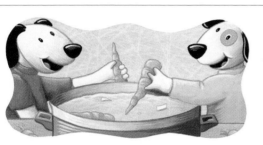

We have carrots.

4

We have the lid.

5

We have cups.

6

Sip, sip, sip.

7

We like soup!

8

■ **High-Frequency Words**

we, have, the, like

■ **Decodable Words**

See word list on T19.

School-Home Connection

Take-Home Book Version

◄ Pre-decodable Book 16: _Soup_

ENGLISH-LANGUAGE LEARNERS   Below   On-Level   Advanced   ELL

Point to the rebus picture on each page and say the word. Ask children to repeat the word. Name other objects in the illustrations and ask children to repeat them as well.

Where Do Pigs Play?

by Chi Winwood

▲ **_Where Do Pigs Play?_ Independent Reader 16**

Shared Writing

Write a Thank-You Note

OBJECTIVES

- *To understand the purpose of a thank-you note*
- *To write a thank-you note*
- *To share information and ideas, speaking in complete, coherent sentences*

Materials

- chart paper
- marker

BUILD BACKGROUND

Talk About Thank-You Notes   Explain that people write notes to thank others for gifts or thoughtful things that they have done. Brainstorm situations in which children might write thank-you notes.

Write a Thank-You Note   Tell children that you are going to work together to write a thank-you note from the puppies to their mom in the book, *Soup*. Write the greeting, *Dear Mom*, on chart paper. Mention that this tells who the note is being written to. Ask children to suggest the sentences the puppies would say to their mom. Write their ideas as sentences. Then write the closing, *Love, Your Puppies*, and explain that this tells who the note is from. Ask children to point out where you will begin writing and call on them to point to letters, words, and periods.

Dear Mom,

Thank you for the soup. It was good.

Love,
Your Puppies

SHARE

Read the Thank-You Note   Read the completed thank-you note aloud. Point to and read the greeting, reminding children that this tells who the note is for. Repeat the procedure with the closing. Then count the words in each sentence with children.

Journal Writing   Have children write a thank-you note to a family member.

Share Time

Share Sentences Ask children to tell about the book they read, *Soup*. Have them tell what the story is about. They can share their pictures of items to add to the soup.

S.S.R. Have children read silently from a book of their choice.

Centers ABC LETTERS AND WORDS

Word Factory

Have children arrange *Magnetic Letters* on the cookie sheet to make three-letter words. Have them record each word they make on paper. Encourage children to create as many words as they can.

Materials

- *Magnetic Letters i, p, g, r, t, d, l, h, m, s, c, a, n, f*
- cookie sheet
- paper
- crayons

WARM UP

Phonemic Awareness
Phoneme Segmentation

Sharing Literature
Big Book:
Does a Kangaroo Have a Mother, Too?

Read

Respond to Literature
Literature Focus: Words in a Sentence

Phonics
Blending /i/–/p/

Writing
Questions

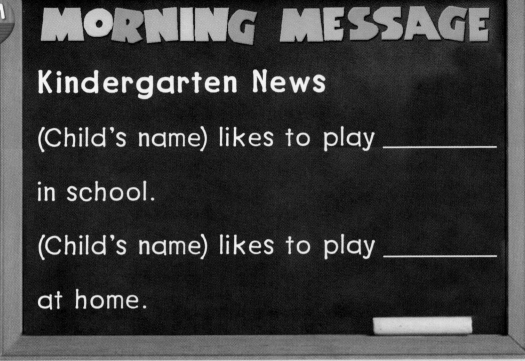

MORNING MESSAGE

Kindergarten News

(Child's name) likes to play _____

in school.

(Child's name) likes to play _____

at home.

Write Kindergarten News Talk with children about the games they like to play at school or at home. Remind them to speak clearly.

Use prompts such as the following to guide children as you write the news:

- **What games do you like to play at school? at home?**
- **Point to the word *likes*.**
- **How many syllables are in the word (name of game)? Clap and say the word with me.**

As you write the message, invite children to write letters, words, or names they have learned previously. Remind them to use proper spacing, capitalization, and punctuation.

Calendar Language

Name the days of the week, inviting children to clap syllables for each day. Tell children to count the days of the week as you point to each one. Ask children how many days there are in a week.

Sunday	Monday	Tuesday	Wednesday	Thursday	Friday	Saturday
		1	2	3	4	5
6	7	8	9	10	11	12
13	14	15	16	17	18	19
20	21	22	23	24	25	26
27	28	29	30	31		

Phonemic Awareness

PHONEME SEGMENTATION

Listen for Sounds Use the rabbit puppet for this blending activity.

MODEL The rabbit likes to count the sounds in words. Listen as it counts the sounds of this word: *fit*. Say it with the rabbit: *fit*. Now listen to the rabbit count the sounds: /f/ /i/ /t/. *Fit* has three sounds. I hear /f/ /i/ /t/. Hold up a finger for each sound and count them as you say them with the rabbit: /f/ /i/ /t/.

Tell children the rabbit will say some words and they will listen to hear the sounds in each word. Then you will ask them to tell you the number of sounds.

pig (/p/ /i/ /g/; three) **cap** (/k/ /a/ /p/; three) **mitt** (/m/ /i/ /t/; three)

in (/i/ /n/; two) **lid** (/l/ /i/ /d/; three) **it** (/i/ /t/; two)

dad (/d/ /a/ /d/; three) **pass** (/p/ /a/ /s/; three) **sip** (/s/ /i/ /p/; three)

fin (/f/ /i/ /n/; three) **at** (/a/ /t/; two) **leg** (/l/ /e/ /g/; three)

▲ **Big Book**

OBJECTIVES

- *To participate actively when predictable and patterned selections are read aloud*

- *To follow print that is read from left to right*

- *To recognize that sentences in print are made up of separate words*

Materials

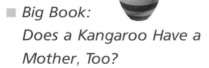

- *Big Book: Does a Kangaroo Have a Mother, Too?*

- chart paper

- drawing paper

- crayons

Sharing Literature

Read Does a Kangaroo Have a Mother, Too?

READ ALOUD

Before Reading Display *Does a Kangaroo Have a Mother, Too?* and ask a child to point to the title. Read it aloud and then model how to set a purpose for rereading:

> **MODEL** I remember that there are pictures of a kangaroo, a giraffe, a penguin, a swan, and a gorilla in this book. I'm sure there are some more animals, but I can't remember what they are. I am also trying to remember if a baby penguin looks like its mother. I'm going to read the book again to find out.

During Reading Reread the selection aloud. As you read,

- point to the words *have* and *a* and to the spaces between words on page 5.

- have children show you where to begin reading on each page.

- encourage children to listen for the repetitive response: *Yes! A _____ has a mother.*

RESPOND TO LITERATURE

Make a Class Book   Reread these parts of the book: *A _____ has a mother. Just like me and you.* Tell children that together they will make a book that shows more mother animals with their babies. Ask children to name other animals. List them on chart paper. Then have children draw a picture of an animal mother and her babies. Encourage children to use the chart for reference. Copy and distribute the parts you read from the book and have children fill in the blank. Combine the children's pages in a class book titled "Mothers Love Their Babies."

WORDS IN A SENTENCE

Turn to the first page in the *Big Book*. Direct children's attention to the sentence *A KANGAROO has a mother.* Point to the word *KANGAROO* and model for children how to find a word. Have children count aloud as you track the words in the sentence. Follow the same procedure for the remaining two sentences on the page.

MODEL **I know this is a word because I see a space before it and a space after it. This is the word *kangaroo*.**

OBJECTIVES

- *To build and read simple one-syllable words*

- *To understand that as letters of words change, so do the sounds*

Materials

- *Alphabet Cards d, g, i, p, r*

- *Word Builders*

- *Word Builder Cards d, g, i, p, r*

- pocket chart

- index cards

- drawing paper

- crayons

Phonics

Blending /i/ - /p/ Review

ACTIVE BEGINNING

Play a Listening Game   Explain to children that they are going to play a game in which they listen to words that have the /p/ sound. Ask them to clap if the word begins with the /p/ sound and snap if the word ends with the /p/ sound.

pick	pencil	chip	strap	pickle
pillow	creep	paint	slip	drip

TEACH/MODEL

Blending Words   Distribute *Word Builders* and *Word Builder Cards d, g, i, p, r* to children. As you place *Alphabet Cards* in a pocket chart, tell children to place the same *Word Builder Cards* in their *Word Builders*.

- Place *Alphabet Cards d, i,* and *p* in the pocket chart. Have children do the same.

- Point to *d*. Say **/dd/**. Point to *i*. Say **/ii/**.

- Slide the *i* next to the *d*. Then move your hand under the letters and blend the sounds, elongating them—**/ddii/**. Have children do the same.

- Point to the letter *p*. Say **/pp/**. Have children do the same.

- Slide the *p* next to the *di*. Slide your hand under *dip* and blend by elongating the sounds—**/ddiipp/**. Have children do the same.

- Then have children read the word *dip* along with you. Follow the same procedure with these words: *rip, dig, pig*.

PRACTICE/APPLY

Guided Practice Have children place *Word Builder Cards i* and *p* in their *Word Builders*.

- **Add *r* to *ip*. What word did you make?**

- **Change *r* to *d*. What word did you make?**

- **Change *p* to *g*. What word did you make?**

- **Change *d* to *p*. What word did you make?**

Independent Practice Write the words *pig*, *dip*, and *rip* on index cards and place them in a pocket chart. Have children read the words. Then have them choose one of the words to write and illustrate on drawing paper.

ENGLISH-LANGUAGE LEARNERS

Below / On-Level / Advanced / ELL

Place the *Alphabet Cards t, i, p* in a pocket chart. Point to each card and say the letter name and sound. Have children do the same. Use the same procedure in the Teach/Model section.

ADVANCED

Have children use the *Magnetic Letters a, c, d, i, n, p, r, s* and *High-Frequency Word Card you* to build these sentences: *Can you dip? Can you sip? Can you rip?*

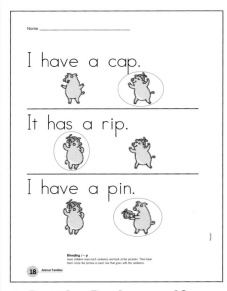

▲ **Practice Book page 18**

OBJECTIVES

- To understand that a question ends with question mark

- To write questions

Materials

- Big Book:
  Does a Kangaroo Have a Mother, Too?

- drawing paper

- chart paper

- crayons

Writing

Write Questions

EXTENDING LITERATURE

Talk About Questions   Read aloud the title of *Does a Kangaroo Have a Mother, Too?* Track the print and point out the question mark. Say: **This is a question mark.** Tell children that all written questions end with a question mark. Page through the book, pausing to have children point to each question mark.

Write Questions   Tell children that they are going to write a question about one of the animals in the book. Distribute drawing paper with this sentence frame: *Does a _____ have _____?* Display page 9 in the *Big Book* and model for children how they might complete the question:

MODEL **I will choose the giraffe from the *Big Book* to complete my question. I see that the giraffe has spots.** Read the question aloud as you write it on chart paper. ***Does a giraffe have spots?*** **Then have children repeat the question and ask a child to trace over the question mark with a crayon.**

Make the *Big Book* available to children as they are completing their questions with words and pictures.

Does a **lion** have **a tal?**

Self-Selected Writing   Have children draw and write about anything they'd like. If they have difficulty thinking of a topic, have them ask two friends what they're going to write about.

WRAP UP Share Time

Author's Chair Provide time for children to read the questions that they wrote in the writing lesson. Each child can call on another student to answer his or her question.

S.S.R. *Sustained Silent Reading* Have children read silently from a book of their choice.

Centers   LISTENING

Listen to the Big Book

Place the *Little Books* and *Audiotext* in the center. As children listen to *Does a Kangaroo Have a Mother, Too?* encourage them to join in with the response to each question as it is read.

Materials

- *Little Books: Does a Kangaroo Have a Mother, Too?*
- *Audiotext*
- tape recorder

Learning Centers

Choose from the following suggestions to enhance your learning centers for the theme Animal Families.
(Additional learning centers for this theme can be found on pages 184–186 and 246.)

SCIENCE CENTER

Materials

- old magazines
- scissors
- index cards
- glue sticks

Matching Game

Have children cut pictures of animal parents and animal babies from magazines. Have them sort the pictures they cut out into two piles: animal babies and animal parents. If children find pictures with an animal parent and an animal baby, have them cut the adult and baby animals apart. Have them glue each picture onto an index card, shuffle the cards, and spread them face down on the table. Children can take turns turning two cards over to match an animal baby with its animal parent.

ART CENTER

Materials

- paper
- crayons
- safety scissors
- glue stick
- craft sticks

Animal Stick Puppets

Tell children they are going to make animal stick puppets. Give children a piece of paper and tell them to draw one picture of an animal baby and another picture of one of its parents. Have children cut out the pictures and glue them to craft sticks to make animal stick puppets. Children can use the puppets to have an animal puppet parade.

Teacher Notes

THEME 6

Week 3

Animal Families

15–30 Minutes

ORAL LANGUAGE

- **Phonemic Awareness**

- **Sharing Literature**

45 Minutes

LEARNING TO READ

- **Phonics**

- **Vocabulary**

Daily Routines
- Morning Message
- Calendar Language
- Writing Prompt

15–30 Minutes

LANGUAGE ARTS

- **Writing**
  Daily Writing Prompt

Day 1

Phonemic Awareness, 299
Phoneme Matching and Isolation: Initial

Sharing Literature, 300
Library Book: *A Time for Playing*

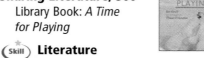

(Skill) **Literature Focus, 301**
Reading to Get Information

**Phonics**, 302 T
Introduce: Phonogram *-it*

Shared Writing, 304
Writing Process: Prewrite

Writing Prompt, 304
Draw and write about self-selected topics.

Share Time, 305
Read
Share sentences and illustrations.

Day 2

Phonemic Awareness, 307
Phoneme Matching and Isolation: Medial

Sharing Literature, 308
Read
Read-Aloud Anthology: "The Town Mouse and the Country Mouse," p. 83

(Skill) **Literature Focus, 309**
Beginning, Middle, Ending

Phonics, 310 T
Introduce: Phonogram *-ig*

Shared Writing, 312
Writing Process: Draft

Writing Prompt, 312
Draw and write about a visit to family members.

Share Time, 313
Act out the story "The Town Mouse and the Country Mouse."

T = tested skill

Phonics

Phonograms *-it*, *-ig*, *-ip*

Focus of the Week:
- • PHONEMIC AWARENESS
- • SHARING LITERATURE
- • WRITING: Personal Narrative (Writing Process)

Day 3

Phonemic Awareness, 315
Phoneme Matching and Isolation: Final

Sharing Literature, 316
Read

Big Book: *Does a Kangaroo Have a Mother, Too?*

(Skill) **Literature Focus, 317**
End Punctuation

Phonics, 318 T
Introduce: Phonogram *-ip*

 Shared Writing, 320
Writing Process: Respond and Revise

Writing Prompt, 320
Draw and write animal facts.

Share Time, 321
Say an action rhyme and name words that rhyme with *skip*.

Day 4

Phonemic Awareness, 323
Phoneme Deletion

Sharing Literature, 324
Big Book of Rhymes and Songs: "The Kitty Ran Up the Tree," p. 11

(Skill) **Literature Focus, 325**
Matching Words

Phonics, 326 T
Phonograms *-it*, *-ig*, *-ip*

Read
PRE-DECODABLE BOOK 17
The Dig

Shared Writing, 328
Writing Process: Proofread

Writing Prompt, 328
Draw and write about animal homes.

Share Time, 329
Discuss the Pre-decodable Book *The Dig*.

Day 5

Phonemic Awareness, 331
Phoneme Segmentation

Sharing Literature, 332
Read-Aloud Anthology: "Five Little Pigs," p. 10

(Skill) **Literature Focus, 332**
Rhyming Words

Phonics, 334 T
Build Sentences

Shared Writing, 336
Writing Process: Publish

Writing Prompt, 336
Draw and write about self-selected topics.

Share Time, 337
Read

Read sentences and share drawings.

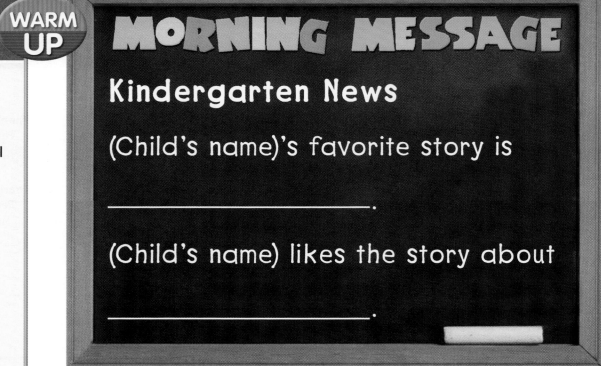

Day at a Glance
Day 1

MORNING MESSAGE

Kindergarten News

(Child's name)'s favorite story is

_____.

(Child's name) likes the story about

_____.

Phonemic Awareness

Phoneme Matching and Phoneme Isolation: Initial

Sharing Literature

Library Book:
A Time for Playing

Read

A Time for PLAYING

Ron Hirschi
PHOTOGRAPHS BY
Thomas D. Mangelsen

Develop Concept Vocabulary

Respond to Literature

Literature Focus: Reading to Get Information

Phonics

Phonogram *-it*

Shared Writing ✏

Writing Process: Prewrite

Write Kindergarten News Talk with children about some of their favorite stories. Ask children to explain why these stories are their favorites.

Use prompts such as the following to guide children as you write the news:

• **What is your favorite story?**

• **Who can show me the beginning of a word?**

• **What letter will I write first in the word *favorite*?**

• **Let's clap the syllables in *story*. How many syllables do you clap?**

As you write the message, invite children to write letters, words, and names they have learned previously. Remind them to use proper spacing, capitalization, and punctuation.

Calendar Language

Point to and read aloud the months of the year. Read them again and have children repeat the names. Point to the current month. Say: *This month is _____. What is the name of this month?*

Sunday	Monday	Tuesday	Wednesday	Thursday	Friday	Saturday
		1	2	3	4	5
6	7	8	9	10	11	12
13	14	15	16	17	18	19
20	21	22	23	24	25	26
27	28	29	30	31		

Phonemic Awareness

PHONEME MATCHING: INITIAL

Matching Initial Sounds   Say these two words, emphasizing the initial sounds, and have children repeat the words with you: *fish, fox.*

MODEL *Fish* and *fox* begin with the same sound. *Fish* begins with the /f/ sound and *fox* begins with the /f/ sound. They both have the same beginning sound—/f/.

Tell children that you will say more groups of words. Have them raise their hand if the words begin with the same sound.

foot, fan	**camp, cane**
hammer, neck	**pool, hedge**
juice, jet	**table, tools**
gate, goose	**mouse, live**

PHONEME ISOLATION: INITIAL

Isolating Initial Sounds   Say the following sets of words and have children repeat them: *love, cake, land.*

MODEL Listen for the two words that have the same beginning sound: *love, cake, land*. *Love* and *land* have the same beginning sound—/l/. *Cake* does not. Say *love* and *land* with me. What is the beginning sound? Let's listen for more beginning sounds.

For each of the following sets of words, have children repeat the word pairs that sound the same, and then ask: **What is the beginning sound?**

love, cake, land (love, land; /l/)	**camp, cane, food** (camp, cane; /k/)
soda, hide, here (hide, here; /h/)	**pool, hand, hedge** (hand, hedge; /h/)
neck, goose, gate (goose, gate; /g/)	**foot, fence, wire** (foot, fence; /f/)
pan, sink, pencil (pan, pencil; /p/)	**rug, doll, dance** (doll, dance; /d/)
hammer, last, hero (hammer, hero; /h/)	**soup, mouse, meal** (mouse, meal; /m/)

REACHING ALL LEARNERS

Diagnostic Check: Phonemic Awareness

If... children have difficulty identifying beginning sounds,

Then... say a sound to children and ask them to think of a classmate whose name begins with that sound. Have them repeat the sound and then the name.

ADDITIONAL SUPPORT ACTIVITIES

BELOW-LEVEL Reteach, p. S32

ADVANCED Extend, p. S33

ENGLISH-LANGUAGE LEARNERS Reteach, p. S33

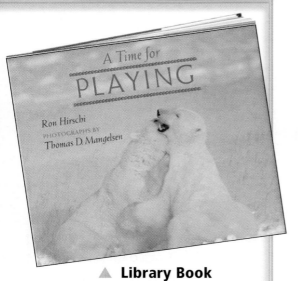

▲ **Library Book**

OBJECTIVES

- *To recall information*

- *To recognize uppercase and lowercase letters*

- *To distinguish between story and information books*

Materials

- *Library Book: A Time for Playing*

- chart paper

- marker

Sharing Literature

Read A Time for Playing

READ ALOUD

Before Reading Display the cover of *A Time for Playing*. Read the title and ask children to identify uppercase and lowercase letters. Then use these prompts to help children recall details about the selection:

- **What animals do you remember in this book?** (polar bears, chipmunks, squirrels, elk, bears, otters, foxes, lions, zebras)

- **What are all the animals doing?** (playing)

- **Why is it important for animals to play?** (Possible response: because they learn things)

Page through the book. Have children look for any animals that they forgot to name.

During Reading Reread the selection aloud. As you read,

- emphasize the text about tree squirrels that describes how play activity prepares them for survival.

- model for children how to get information from the photographs:

MODEL In this picture of the sea otter, I see that it likes to float on its back. I also see that it's holding a starfish. Now I know that sea otters like to eat starfish.

DEVELOP CONCEPT VOCABULARY

After Reading Write these words on chart paper: *danger, safety, shelter, predator,* and *survival*. Point to and read each word. Discuss the following definitions with children.

- *Danger* means some kind of trouble happening.
- *Safety* means staying away from trouble.
- *Shelter* is a place to keep safe.
- A *predator* is an animal that hunts another animal.
- *Survival* means staying alive.

RESPOND TO LITERATURE

Discuss the Book Have children tell one thing they learned from the book.

Literature Focus

READING TO GET INFORMATION

Explain that some books tell stories and other books give information. Display *A Time for Playing* and read the title.

MODEL **This book is an information book. I learned how animals get food. I learned how animals play. Most of all, I learned that when animals play, they learn to do things that help them stay alive.**

LEARNING TO READ

Phonics
Phonogram *-it* ✔Introduce

OBJECTIVES

- *To find letter patterns in words*

- *To blend letter patterns to read words*

- *To write consonant-vowel-consonant words*

Materials

- chart paper

- marker

- *Write-On/Wipe-Off Boards*

- drawing paper

- crayons

ACTIVE BEGINNING

Say a Rhyme   Teach children the following rhyme. Have them clap as they say the words.

Hit, hit, hit the ball.

Catch it in the mitt.

Hit it! Catch it!

TEACH/MODEL

Discriminate Sounds   Say the words *quit* and *sit* and have children repeat them. Ask how the two words are the same. (They both have /it/; they rhyme.) Divide the class into 6 groups. Ask children to stand. Tell them that you are going to say a word to each group and that the group should sit when they hear a word that rhymes with *quit*:

lit	bat	fit	can	mitt	hit

Build *-it* Words   Write the word *pit* on chart paper. Track the print as children read the word. Then write the word *sit*. Again, track the print as children read the word. Ask children to read the two words and have them tell how the words are the same. (They have *i* and *t*; they rhyme.) Continue by writing the word *fit* and having children read the word.

pit
sit
fit

PRACTICE/APPLY

Guided Practice Tell children that you will say some words. If the word rhymes with *mitt*, have them write the word on their *Write-On/Wipe-Off Boards*. Have them use the chart with *-it* words as a reference.

man   sit   ran   pit   bug   dog   fit

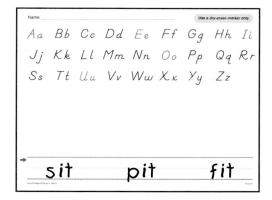

Independent Practice Distribute to children paper with the sentence frame *I _____ on a mat.* Have children complete the sentence, using one of the words written on the chart paper. Then have them illustrate their sentence.

BELOW-LEVEL

Have children use Elkonin boxes to work on sounds they hear in the words. Ask them to move markers into the boxes for *fit*, *hit*, *mitt*, and *lit*.

ADVANCED

Encourage children to write other words that belong in the *-it* family.

early spelling

Have children write one of the *-it* words from their *Write On/Wipe Off Board* in their journal.

▲ **Practice Book page 19**

OBJECTIVES

- *To generate ideas for a class writing project*
- *To recognize a personal narrative*

Writing Process

Personal Narrative

PREWRITE

Explore the Theme   Discuss with children how much fun it is to take care of a pet as if it were a part of a family. If you have a pet in the classroom, remind children that they act as the pet's "family" and they help take care of it. Tell children that this week, they will work together to write a personal narrative about a girl and her pet.

Build Background about Personal Narratives   Tell children that a personal narrative is a story that a person tells about something that happened to him or her. Have children talk to a partner about something they have done with a pet. Explain that their stories are personal narratives.

Reread "Mary Had a Little Lamb" and tell children that together they are going to write about what they think Mary would say about the lamb following her to school.

Writing Every Day

Day 1: Prewrite
Talk about a personal narrative.

Day 2: Draft
Have children compose sentences from a character's point of view.

Day 3: Respond and Revise
Have child check the sequence of events in the personal narrative.

Day 4: Edit
Model how to check word spacing and punctuation.

Day 5: Publish
Have children illustrate the personal narrative.

Self-Selected Topics Ask children to write about self-selected topics in their journals.

DEVELOP LISTENING COMPREHENSION

After Reading Model for children what each mouse learned.

MODEL The Town Mouse is bored in the country and doesn't like the food. The Country Mouse is scared in the town and in the house. Each mouse decides that he likes his own home better.

Have children answer these questions:

- **Where would you like to live? Why?** *(Possible response: I would like the country because it's quiet.)*

- **Where is it more dangerous to live for the mice? Why?** *(Possible response: in the town because there are more people and dogs)*

- **What lesson does each mouse learn?** *(Possible response: Each mouse likes his own home better.)*

RESPOND TO LITERATURE

Make Characters-on-a-String Pictures Have each child draw and cut out pictures of the Country Mouse and the Town Mouse. Help them staple the pictures to pieces of yarn. Then have children fold a piece of drawing paper in half and draw a picture of the Country Mouse's home on one side and a picture of the Town Mouse's home on the other side. Help them staple the yarn to the middle of the page. Have children move the mice from picture to picture, recalling what happens when the mice are in each location.

Literature Focus

BEGINNING, MIDDLE, ENDING

Draw a story map on chart paper. Review with children what happens at the beginning of the story. (The Town Mouse visits his cousin, the Country Mouse.) Write the event in the first box. Repeat the process for the events at the middle and ending of the story. When the story map is complete, have children recall the story events, using the words *At the beginning of the story, in the middle of the story,* and *at the end of the story.*

BELOW-LEVEL

Give story clues such as the following and ask children to tell whether you are talking about the Town Mouse or the Country Mouse: *He lived in a snug little hole in a log.* (Country); *He used a silk handkerchief as a bedspread.* (Town); *He fixed his own food.* (Country); *Dogs lived in his house.* (Town)

ONGOING ASSESSMENT

As you share "The Town Mouse and the Country Mouse," note whether children

- understand the characters.
- recognize the beginning, middle, and ending of a story.

OBJECTIVES

- *To find letter patterns in words*

- *To blend letter patterns to read words*

- *To write consonant-vowel-consonant words*

Materials

- chart paper

- marker

- *Write-On/Wipe-Off Boards*

- drawing paper

- crayons

Phonics
Phonogram -ig ✔Introduce

ACTIVE BEGINNING

Action Rhyme Teach children the following rhyme and the actions that go with it. Have children recite the rhyme several times.

My pet pig loves to dig.

Dig, dig, dig! (Pretend to dig with a shovel.)

The hole she digs gets very big.

Big, big, big! (Spread your arms apart to show *big, bigger, biggest*.)

TEACH/MODEL

Discriminate Sounds Say the words *jig* and *dig* and have children repeat them. Ask: **How are the two words the same?** (They both have /ig/; they rhyme.) Tell children that you are going to say some words and that they should dance a little jig when they hear a word that rhymes with *jig*:

big	bed	wig	mouse	fig	dig

Build -ig Words Write the word *pig* on chart paper. Track the print as children read the word. Then write the word *dig*. Again, track the print as children read the word. Ask children to read the two words and have them tell what letters are the same. (*i* and *g*) Continue by writing the word *fig* and having children read the word.

pig
dig
fig

PRACTICE/APPLY

Guided Practice   Tell children that you will say some words. If the word rhymes with *jig*, have them write the word on their *Write-On/Wipe-Off Boards*. Have them use the chart with *-ig* words as a reference.

pig   **milk**   **fig**   **hop**   **jump**   **dig**

Independent Practice   Distribute paper to children. Ask them to fold it in half. Have children read the words written on chart paper and write and illustrate a word on each side of the fold on their paper.

▲ **Practice Book page 20**

OBJECTIVES

- *To write a group story*

- *To share information and ideas, speaking in complete, coherent sentences*

Materials

- chart paper

- marker

Writing Process

Personal Narrative

DRAFT

Review the Topic   Remind children about the personal narrative, using Mary and her lamb. Tell children to imagine going to school in the morning and sitting down at their desk. All of a sudden, a lamb comes through the doorway! What would Mary say?

Write Sentences   On chart paper, write the sentence *My lamb followed me to school today!* Then help children compose the remainder of the personal narrative based on what they think could have happened to Mary at school that day. Use questions such as the following to guide children:

- **I know it is against the rules to have a lamb at school. How does this make Mary feel?**

- **Pretend you are Mary at a center and the lamb is messing up your magnetic letters. How would you tell about it in a sentence?**

- **The children begin to laugh because lambs aren't supposed to be in school. What do you think Mary would do?**

> My lamb followed me to school today! I was afraid. I thought I might get sent to the principal's office. I went to the Letters and Words Center to try to keep my lamb from getting into Jenny's desk, but he started to eat the letters! Everyone saw my lamb and started to laugh. I began to laugh, too!

Journal Writing   Have children write and draw about a visit to a family member's house.

WRAP UP # Share Time

Reflect on the Lesson Have children take turns acting out the story, "The Town Mouse and the Country Mouse."

S.S.R. *Sustained Silent Reading* Have children read silently from a book of their choice.

Centers   **BLOCK**

A House for a Mouse

Have small groups of children work together to build a house for the Country Mouse and a house for the Town Mouse. When the houses are constructed, have children draw pictures of items that might be found in or around each house. Have them place the pictures in or around each structure. Allow time for groups to share their houses and pictures.

Materials

- building blocks
- blank index cards
- crayons or markers

Day at a Glance
Day 3

WARM UP

Phonemic Awareness

Phoneme Matching and Phoneme Isolation: Final

Sharing Literature

Big Book:
Does a Kangaroo Have a Mother, Too?

Read

Respond to Literature

Literature Focus: Matching Words

Phonics

Phonogram *-ip*

Shared Writing

Writing Process: Respond and Revise

MORNING MESSAGE

Kindergarten News

In (name of season), (child's name)

likes to _____.

In (name of season), (child's name)

likes to _____.

Write Kindergarten News Talk with children about what they like to do in the current season.

Use prompts such as the following to guide children as you write the news:

- **What season is it now? What do you like to do in (name season)?**
- **Will I write an uppercase or lowercase letter in (child's name)?**
- **Who can show me where (child's name) begins and ends?**
- **Who can write the words *likes* and *to*?**

As you write the message, invite children to write letters, words, or names they have learned previously. Remind them to use proper spacing, capitalization, and punctuation.

Calendar Language

Point to and read aloud the seasons of the year. Have children repeat the seasons of the year with you. Ask: *What season is it now? What season will it be next?*

Sunday	Monday	Tuesday	Wednesday	Thursday	Friday	Saturday
		1	2	3	4	5
6	7	8	9	10	11	12
13	14	15	16	17	18	19
20	21	22	23	24	25	26
27	28	29	30	31		

Phonemic Awareness

PHONEME MATCHING: FINAL

Matching Final Sounds Say these two words, emphasizing the final sounds, and have children repeat the words with you: *sit, yet.*

MODEL *Sit* has the /t/ sound at the end: /s/–/i/–/t/. Say *sit* with me. *Yet* has the /t/ sound at the end: /y/–/e/–/t/. Say *yet* with me. *Sit* and *yet* have the same ending sound: /t/.

Tell children that you will say more groups of words. Have them raise their hand if the words have the same ending sound.

buss, hiss	hall, will	tag, bug	neck, stick
hit, dock	sub, web	swim, ham	lid, sad
mop, step	jug, fan		

PHONEME ISOLATION: FINAL

Isolating Final Sounds Say the following set of words and have children repeat them: *bus, cap, hiss.*

MODEL Listen for the two words that have the same ending sound: *bus, cap, hiss. Bus* and *hiss* have the same ending sound: /s/. *Cap* does not. Say *bus* and *hiss* with me. What is the ending sound? Let's listen for more ending sounds.

For each of the following sets of words, have children repeat the word pairs that have the same ending sound, and then ask: **What is the ending sound?**

bus, cap, hiss (*bus, hiss*; /s/)	tag, ox, bug (*tag, bug*; /g/)
pat, hit, dock (*pat, hit*; /t/)	swim, ham, tap (*swim, ham*; /m/)
dug, mop, step (*mop, step*; /p/)	win, neck, stick (*neck, stick*; /k/)
hall, will, jet (*hall, will*; /l/)	sub, bed, web (*sub, web*; /b/)
jug, ten, fan (*ten, fan*; /n/)	pick, lid, sad (*lid, sad*; /d/)

▲ **"The Barnyard Song,"** *Oo-pples and Boo-noo-noos: Songs and Activities for Phonemic Awareness,* page 57.

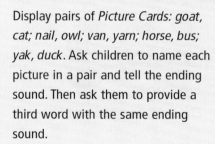

ADVANCED

Display pairs of *Picture Cards: goat, cat; nail, owl; van, yarn; horse, bus; yak, duck.* Ask children to name each picture in a pair and tell the ending sound. Then ask them to provide a third word with the same ending sound.

▲ **Big Book**

OBJECTIVES
- *To listen and respond to a story*
- *To recall story events*
- *To recognize end punctuation*

Materials

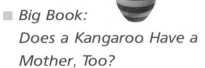

■ *Big Book:*
  Does a Kangaroo Have a Mother, Too?

■ drawing paper

■ crayons

Sharing Literature

Read Does a Kangaroo Have a Mother, Too?

READ ALOUD

Before Reading   Display the cover of *Does a Kangaroo Have a Mother, Too?* Ask children where the title is and read it aloud. Direct children's attention to the question mark in the title and tell them what it is. Then use these prompts to help children recall details:

- **On every page, there is a question that asks whether a certain animal has a mother, too. What is the answer every time?** (Yes!)
- **Which animal is very big and gray?** (the elephant)
- **Which animal lives in a very cold place?** (the penguin)
- **Which animal has curly hair?** (the sheep)

During Reading   Reread the selection aloud. As you read,

- emphasize the language pattern of the questions and point to the question mark each time you read a question.
- emphasize the word *Yes!* on each page.
- have children read the high-frequency words with you throughout the story.

Say: **Here are the words I know:** *a, like, have, you.* **Read them with me when I point to them.**

RESPOND TO LITERATURE

Extend the Story Distribute copies of the following sentence frames to children: *I can _____. Can you _____? Yes!* Have children work with a partner to think of an activity that they both can do. Have children write the name of the activity and illustrate it. Then have children trace over each type of end punctuation and read their sentences.

END PUNCTUATION

Turn to the first page of the *Big Book* and read it. Point to the punctuation at the end of each sentence.

MODEL **When I see this exclamation point, I know I should read with excitement:** *Yes!* (use louder voice) **When I see a period, I know that this is the end of the sentence:** *A kangaroo has a mother.* (voice drops lower at end) **When I see a question mark, it means that this is a question:** *Does a lion have a mother, too?* (voice raises higher at the end)

Read other pages in the book and point to the end punctuation. Have children practice reading exclamations, sentences, and questions by repeating them with you.

ADVANCED

Write the words in the repetitive phrase *Just like me and you* on individual word cards. Ask children to match the words on the cards to the words in the *Big Book*.

ONGOING ASSESSMENT

As you share *Does a Kangaroo Have a Mother, Too?* note whether children

- can listen for a period of time.
- can recall story events.
- can recognize end punctuation.

OBJECTIVES

- *To find letter patterns in words*

- *To blend letter patterns to read words*

- *To write consonant-vowel-consonant words*

Materials

- ◼ chart paper

- ◼ marker

- ◼ Write-On/Wipe-Off Boards

- ◼ Word Builder Cards

- ◼ Word Builders

Phonogram *-ip* ✓ Introduce

ACTIVE BEGINNING

Action Rhyme　Teach children this rhyme and the actions that go with it. Have children recite the rhyme several times.

I can skip, skip, skip. (Skip.)

I can slip, slip, slip. (Move forward as if on skates.)

I can snip, snip, snip. (Make scissor-motions with fingers.)

Skip! Slip! Snip! (Do all three motions.)

TEACH/MODEL

Discriminate Sounds　Say the words *skip* and *lip* and have children repeat them. Ask how the two words are the same. (They both have /ip/; they rhyme.) Tell children that you are going to say some words and that they should clap when they hear a word that rhymes with *lip*:

| hip | cup | dip | cap | rip | sip |

Build *-ip* Words　Write the word *lip* on chart paper. Track the print as children read the word. Then write the word *dip*. Again, track the print as children read the word. Ask children to read the two words and have them tell how they are the same. (They have *i* and *p*; they rhyme.) Continue by writing the word *sip* and having children read the word.

lip
dip
sip

PRACTICE/APPLY

Guided Practice   Tell children that you will say some words. If the word rhymes with *hip*, have them write the word on their *Write-On/Wipe-Off Boards*. Have them use the chart with *-ip* words as a reference.

lip   ham   bed   sip   sick   slim   dip

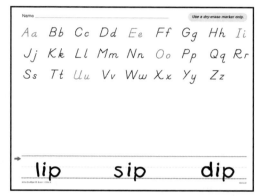

Independent Practice   Have children use their *Word Builder Cards* and *Word Builders* to make the words *lip, hip, dip, sip,* and *rip*. Refer them to the chart with *-ip* words as a starting point.

Diagnostic Check: Phonics

If… children cannot identify letter patterns in words,

Then… write the words from the lesson on index cards and read them to children. Then have children find the words that have matching letters and put those cards in a pile. Read the words again and have children repeat them with you.

ADDITIONAL SUPPORT ACTIVITIES

BELOW-LEVEL	Reteach, p. S34
ADVANCED	Extend, p. S35
ENGLISH-LANGUAGE LEARNERS	Reteach, p. S35

early spelling

Have children write one of the *-ip* words from their *Write On/Wipe Off Board* in their journal.

▲ **Practice Book page 21**

Animal Families   319

OBJECTIVES

- *To improve a group writing piece through rereading and revising*

- *To read high-frequency words*

Materials

- *correction tape*

- *marker*

Writing Process

Personal Narrative

RESPOND AND REVISE

Reread the Sentences   Reread the personal narrative, tracking the print. Pause to allow children to read the words *I, to, the,* and *we.* Ask questions such as the following:

- **Is there anything else we should add to our personal narrative?**
- **Are the events told in the right order?**
- **Would you like to change any of the words we used?**

Make Revisions   Use correction tape and a marker to replace words that children suggest should be changed. After all changes are made, reread the narrative to children.

Journal Writing   Have children write and illustrate an animal fact.

WRAP UP # Share Time

Reflect on the Lesson Have children say the Action Rhyme from the phonics lesson with you and do the actions that go with it. Ask children to name words that rhyme with *skip*.

S.S.R. *Sustained Silent Reading* Have children read silently from a book of their choice.

  **Centers** **MATH**

Animal Shape Pictures

Cut out shapes in a variety of colors. Have children assemble pieces into an animal or an animal family. Encourage them to make animals that they saw in *Does a Kangaroo Have a Mother, Too?* Then have them glue the shapes onto construction paper. Have children label their animals.

Materials

- small and larger sizes of triangles, rectangles, squares, and circles cut from brown, black, gray, white, black, blue, and white construction paper

- construction paper

- glue

- crayons

Day at a Glance
Day 4

Phonemic Awareness

Phoneme Manipulation

Sharing Literature

Big Book of Rhymes and Songs:
"The Kitty Ran Up the Tree"

Read

Big Book of Rhymes and Songs

Respond to Literature

Literature Focus: Matching Words

Phonics

Read the *Pre-decodable Book 17: The Dig*

Shared Writing

Writing Process: Edit

WARM UP

MORNING MESSAGE

Kindergarten News

(Child's name) will _____ today.

After school, (child's name) will go

to _____.

Write Kindergarten News   Talk with children about where they will go and what they will do after school today. Encourage them to speak clearly.

Use prompts such as the following to guide children as you write the news:

- **Where will you go after school today? What will you do?**
- **What letter does the word *today* start with?**
- **How many letters are in (child's name)?**
- **How many sentences are there?**

As you write the message, invite children to write letters, words, or names they have learned previously. Remind them to use proper spacing, capitalization, and punctuation.

Calendar Language

Ask what day today is and say: *Today is _____.* Ask what day came before today. Point to the name of the day and say: *Yesterday was _____.* Invite volunteers to name *yesterday* and *today.*

Sunday	Monday	Tuesday	Wednesday	Thursday	Friday	Saturday
			1	2	3	4
5	6	7	8	9	10	11
12	13	14	15	16	17	18
19	20	21	22	23	24	25
26	27	28	29	30	31	

Phonemic Awareness

PHONEME MANIPULATION

Delete Phonemes   Use the rabbit puppet for this phoneme activity. Have the rabbit say the word *hop* and have children repeat it with the rabbit. Then say:

The rabbit likes to take away sounds from words. Listen as he says *hop* without the /h/. Have rabbit say *op*. **Take away the /h/ from *hop* and say *op* with the rabbit. Listen as the rabbit says *hop* without the /p/.** Have the rabbit say *ho*. **Take away the /p/ from *hop* and say *ho* with the rabbit.**

Tell children the rabbit is going to ask them to take away sounds from words. Use the following examples.

Say *Max*. Now say *Max* without the /m/. (*ax*) **Say *Max* without the /ks/.** (*Ma*)

Say *fish*. Now say *fish* without the /f/. (*ish*) **Say *fish* without the /sh/.** (*fi*)

Say *net*. Now say *net* without the /n/. (*et*) **Say *net* without the /t/.** (*ne*)

Say *sip*. Now say *sip* without the /s/. (*ip*) **Say *sip* without the /p/.** (*si*)

Say *tan*. Now say *tan* without the /t/. (*an*) **Say *tan* without the /n/.** (*ta*)

Say *wig*. Now say *wig* without the /w/. (*ig*) **Say *wig* without the /g/.** (*wi*)

ADVANCED

Have children delete initial sounds from nonsense words, such as *zooch* without the /z/ or *minky* without the /m/.

Sharing Literature

Read "The Kitty Ran Up the Tree"

READ ALOUD/READ ALONG

Before Reading   Display page 11 of the *Big Book of Rhymes and Songs* and track the print of the title while reading the words aloud. Then use these prompts to build background:

• **Which way is up? Point in that direction.**

• **Have you ever seen a cat climbing something?**

Tell children you are going to read a poem about a kitty climbing a tree. Ask: **What do you think made the kitty climb the tree?**

During Reading   Read the rhyme aloud. As you read,

• track the print.

• raise your voice when reading repetitive text.

• react to the word *up* each time you say it by pointing up or looking up.

▲ **Big Book of Rhymes and Songs**

OBJECTIVES

• *To listen responsively to a rhyme*

• *To follow words from top to bottom on a page*

• *To match words in a repetitive text*

Materials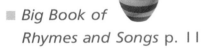

■ *Big Book of Rhymes and Songs* p. 11

■ chart paper

■ drawing paper

■ crayons

■ index cards

■ marker

The Kitty Ran Up the Tree

The kitty ran up the tree,
The kitty ran up the tree,
Her nose went up
And her toes went up
And the kitty ran up the tree.

Dennis Lee

RESPOND TO LITERATURE

Reillustrate the Poem Have children name other animals that could climb a tree. List the names on chart paper. Point to each name and read it aloud. Then reread the poem substituting an animal from the chart for *kitty*. Have children reillustrate the poem, showing their favorite animal.

Animals
bear
snake
bug

bear

bug

snake

Literature Focus

MATCHING WORDS

Write the words *kitty, ran, up, the,* and *tree* on index cards. Then track the print as you read the first line of the rhyme. Hand individuals the word card *kitty* and ask them to find the same word in the second and last lines of the rhyme. Have them hold up the card below the matching words in the rhyme. Follow the same process for the words *ran, up, the,* and *tree*.

ONGOING ASSESSMENT

As you share "The Kitty Ran Up the Tree," note whether children

- listen responsively to a rhyme.
- can follow words from top to bottom on a page.

OBJECTIVE

To decode phonogram -it, -ig, -ip words

Materials

- *Alphabet Cards d, i, g*
- pocket chart
- *Pre-decodable Book 17: The Dig*
- *High-Frequency Word Cards*

- index card
- drawing paper
- crayons

ENGLISH-LANGUAGE LEARNERS

Explain to children that the animals pictured in the book are raccoons and the candy that is pictured is called jelly beans.

Phonics

Phonograms -it, -ig, -ip

TEACH/MODEL

Decode Words Place *Alphabet Cards d, i,* and *g* next to one another on the chalk ledge. Point to the letter *d* and say /d/. Point to the letters *i* and *g* and say sounds /i/ and /g/. Then say *dig*.

Place the *High-Frequency Word Cards We, have,* and *the* and the index card with *map* written on it in the pocket chart. Have children read the words as you point to them. Track the print as you read the sentence. Have children repeat the sentence as you track it again.

Tell children that the word *dig* and the sentence, *We have the map.* are clues to what the story they will read is about. Ask: What do you think the characters will do?

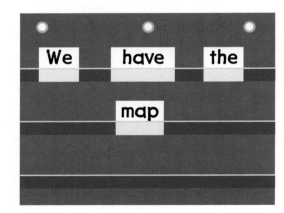

PRACTICE/APPLY

Read the Book Distribute copies of *The Dig*. Read the title together, encouraging children to point to each word as they read it. Have children read the book, pointing to each word as they read.

Respond Have children draw and label pictures of something they would like to find in a treasure chest.

Pre-decodable Book 17: *The Dig*

We have a map.

2

We have a shovel.

3

We dig, dig, dig.

4

We have a box.

5

We have a key.

6

We have the lid.

7

Jellybeans!

8

High-Frequency Words

we, have, the

Decodable Words

See word list T19

School-Home Connection

Take-Home Book Version

◄ Pre-decodable Book 17 *The Dig*

A Dog Has Pups
by Jeffrey Allen

▲ **A Dog Has Pups**
Independent Reader 17

Animal Families **327**

OBJECTIVES

- *To improve a group writing project through proofreading*

- *To apply knowledge of punctuation*

Materials

- correction type

- marker

Writing Process

Personal Narrative

PROOFREAD

Model Proofreading Remind children that this is their chance to make the writing better. Direct children's attention to the beginning uppercase letter and end mark in each sentence. After reading the first sentence, ask: **Should this sentence end with an exclamation point?**

MODEL **I know that this sentence should end with an exclamation point because the writer wants us to use a voice that is surprised when we read it. An exclamation point at the end of a sentence also tells me that I must start the next sentence with an uppercase letter.**

Ask children to look at the spaces between words to be sure the words are far enough apart. Edit any changes that children suggest should be made to make the sentences correct.

Journal Writing Have children write and draw about animal homes.

WRAP UP Share Time

Reflect on the Lesson   Ask children what story they learned to read. (*The Dig*) Have them tell what happens in the story. Ask them to name their favorite part of today's lesson.

S.S.R. Sustained Silent Reading   Have children read silently from a book of their choice.

Centers ABC LITERACY

Favorite Books from Animal Families

Place the books in the Literacy Center. Tell children to read the books and to choose their favorite one. Ask them to draw and label a picture about their favorite book. Have them write the title of the book on their pictures. Remind children to write their names on their pictures.

Materials

- *Pre-decodable Books 15,16,17: I Have, You Have; Soup; The Dig*

- *Little Books: Does a Kangaroo Have a Mother, Too?*

- *Library Books: Are You There, Baby Bear?; A Time for Playing*

Day at a Glance

Day at a Glance
Day 5

WARM UP

Phonemic Awareness
Phoneme Segmentation

Sharing Literature
Read-Aloud Anthology:
"Five Little Pigs"

Read

Respond to Literature

Literature Focus: Rhyming Words

Phonics
Build Sentences

Shared Writing ✏

Writing Process: Publish

MORNING MESSAGE

Kindergarten News

(Child's name) will be celebrating a birthday soon.

(Child's name)'s family will be celebrating (occasion) this week.

Write Kindergarten News Talk with children about special days, such as birthdays or holidays, they may be celebrating soon with family or friends.

Use prompts such as the following to guide children as you write the news:

- **What special day will you be celebrating soon?**
- **Who can show me the top of the page?**
- **Who can write the first letter in the word *soon*?**
- **How many words are in the last sentence?**

As you write the message, invite children to write letters, words, and names they have learned previously. Remind them to use proper spacing, capitalization, and punctuation.

Calendar Language

Ask what day today is. Ask children what day comes after today. Point to the name of the day and say: *Tomorrow is _____.* Invite volunteers to name today and tomorrow.

Sunday	Monday	Tuesday	Wednesday	Thursday	Friday	Saturday
			1	2	3	4
5	6	7	8	9	10	11
12	13	14	15	16	17	18
19	20	21	22	23	24	25
26	27	28	29	30	31	

Phonemic Awareness

PHONEME SEGMENTATION

Identify the Number of Sounds in Words   Tell children that you will say a word and they will listen to hear how many sounds are in it. Say *mop*. Elongate each sound slightly. Have children repeat the word. Then say: **/m/ /o/ /p/**. Hold up one finger for each sound as you say it. **There are three sounds in *mop*. Now you try it. You can count with your fingers.** *Sock*, **/s/ /o/ /k/. How many sounds does *sock* have?** (3) **What are the sounds?** (/s/ /o/ /k/)

Tell children you are going to say some words. Ask them to tell you the sounds in each word and how many sounds there are.

pit (/p/ /i/ /t/; 3)   **dog** (/d/ /o/ /g/; 3)

top (/t/ /o/ /p/; 3)   **on** (/o/ /n/; 2)

at (/a/ /t/; 2)   **cot** (/k/ /o/ /t/; 3)

log (/l/ /o/ /g/; 3)   **if** (/i/ /f/; 2)

met (/m/ /e/ /t/; 3)   **us** (/u/ /s/; 2)

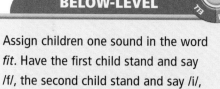

BELOW-LEVEL

Assign children one sound in the word *fit*. Have the first child stand and say /f/, the second child stand and say /i/, and the third child stand and say /t/. With the group, count the number of children standing. Say: Fit *has three sounds.*

ADVANCED

Ask children to count the sounds in longer words, such as *popcorn*.

▲ **Read-Aloud Anthology**

OBJECTIVES

- *To participate in an action rhyme*
- *To identify rhyming words*

Materials

- *Read-Aloud Anthology* p. 10
- *Teacher's Resource Book*, p. 150
- crayons
- scissors
- tape

Sharing Literature

Read "Five Little Pigs"

READ ALOUD

Before Reading   Display page 10 of the *Read-Aloud Anthology*, and track the title as you read it aloud. Ask these questions:

- **Where do pigs live?**
- **What might five little pigs do?**

During Reading   Read the rhyme aloud. As you read,

- emphasize the rhyming words *sound/round; around/ground; tail/pail; care/share.*
- emphasize the repetitive phrase, *This little pig.*
- hold up one finger to indicate each pig and encourage children to do the same.

RESPOND TO LITERATURE

Act Out the Rhyme   Distribute to each child copies of five finger puppets in the *Teacher's Resource Book*. Have children draw a pig on each puppet to represent the characters in the rhyme. Help children cut out and tape each puppet. Then have them retell the poem while wearing them on their fingers.

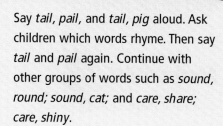

BELOW-LEVEL

Say *tail*, *pail*, and *tail*, *pig* aloud. Ask children which words rhyme. Then say *tail* and *pail* again. Continue with other groups of words such as *sound, round; sound, cat;* and *care, share; care, shiny.*

ONGOING ASSESSMENT

As you share "Five Little Pigs," note whether children

• participate in the action rhyme.

★ Literature Focus

RHYMING WORDS

Remind children that rhyming words have the same ending sound, but different beginning sounds. Name the first pair of rhyming words in "Five Little Pigs": *sound* and *round*. Then reread the rhyme, pausing at the last word of the second, fourth, sixth, and final lines. Ask children to name the rhyming word that completes each sentence.

OBJECTIVE

To use knowledge of letters, words, and sounds to read simple sentences

Materials

- chart paper
- marker
- index cards
- pocket chart
- *Pre-decodable Book 17: The Dig*

Phonics
Build Sentences ✔ *Review*

ACTIVE BEGINNING

Act Out a Nonsense Rhyme   Teach children the following rhyme and actions.

I have a pig who likes to play.

She likes to dig and skip all day!
(Pretend to dig and skip.)

She likes to swim and take a dip,
(Pretend to swim.)

She'd love to skate and slide and slip,
(Pretend to skate.)

But there's one problem that troubles her a bit—(Point to head and frown.)

She's too big and her skates don't fit! (Try to tug on a skate, while shaking head.)

TEACH/MODEL

Review *-it, -ig, -ip*   Copy the chart below onto chart paper.

Read aloud the words and remind children that the words in each column belong to the same word family—the *-it* family, the *-ig* family, and the *-ip* family.

Model reading the word *sit*, first by elongating the sounds, /ssiitt/, and then by reading it naturally. Then have children elongate the sounds and read the word. Continue with the remaining words. Frame the words *sit* and *fit* and ask how the two words are alike. (Possible responses: They rhyme; they both have *i* and *t*.) Do the same for *pig* and *dig*; *dip* and *lip*.

sit	pig	dip
fit	dig	lip

PRACTICE/APPLY

Guided Practice Write the following words on index cards: *The, pig, likes, to, sit, dig, dip, hit, sip*. Display the words in a pocket chart as shown:

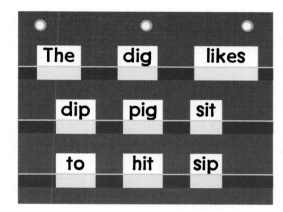

Point to each word and have children read it. Remind them to blend the sounds together to read the word. Then rearrange the cards to make the following sentence:

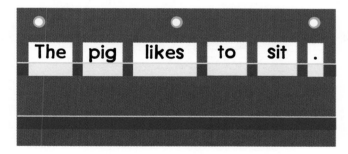

Track the words as you assist children in reading the sentence. Then substitute the word *dig* for *sit*, and have children read the sentence. Continue by changing one of the words to provide many opportunities for children to read the sentence.

Independent Practice Have children reread the *Pre-decodable Book, The Dig*, for more practice reading connected text.

BELOW-LEVEL

Have children use their *Word Builders* and *Word Builder Cards* to build and blend the following words: *sit, hit, pig, dip*.

ADVANCED

Have children read *Independent Reader 17, A Dog Has Pups* for more practice in reading connected text.

early spelling

Have children write one of the words from the Guided Practice sentences in their spelling journal. Ask children to draw a picture to describe that word.

▲ **Practice Book page 22**

Animal Families 335

OBJECTIVES

- *To illustrate a personal narrative*

Materials

- *Drawing paper*
- glue
- cotton balls
- crayons

Writing Process

Personal Narrative

PUBLISH

Illustrate the Personal Narrative   Distribute to each child drawing paper, glue, a cotton ball, and crayons. Reread the narrative while tracking the print. Ask children to draw themselves with the lamb, doing an activity at school. They can glue the cotton to their drawing of the lamb. Display the writing and each child's illustration on a bulletin board titled "A Lamb at School?" Gather children around the bulletin board to view their illustrations and to hear the narrative.

Self-Selected Writing   Have children draw and write about anything they'd like. If they have difficulty thinking of a topic, have them ask two friends what they're going to write about.

WRAP UP **Share Time**

Author's Chair   Remind children that an action word tells what somebody does. Have children read their sentences and share their pictures from the writing lesson. After they've read their sentences, have them repeat the action word.

S.S.R.   Have children read silently from a book of their choice.

 **Centers**  **MATH**

Numbers I to 5

Ask children to draw one, two, three, four, or five pigs on their paper. Allow them to decide how many pigs they want to draw. Have children glue a piece of ribbon on each pig as a tail. Write the numbers *I–5* on squares of paper and place them on a bulletin board. When children are finished with their pictures, help them place the picture under the corresponding number on the bulletin board. If any number does not have pictures under it, ask children to draw additional pictures for the display.

Materials

- construction paper
- crayons
- glue
- short pieces of curling ribbon
- squares of paper
- bulletin-board space

Theme Wrap-Up & Review

Celebrate *Animal Families*

Show children *Does a Kangaroo Have a Mother Too?*, *Are you there, Baby Bear?* and *A Time for Playing*. Help them summarize or retell each story. Invite comments and personal responses; then ask these questions:

• **How do the animals in each book grow and change?**

• **In what ways have you grown and changed?**

• **Which book shows photographs of real animals. What do the photographs show?**

Teacher Self-Evaluation

As you reflect on the theme *Animal Families*, ask yourself:

• **Which activities best met my goals for this theme? Which ones did not?**

• **Have children become more aware of how animals change as they grow?**

• **Do children understand the difference between a story about animals and a book that provides factual information about animals?**

THEME PROJECT

"Animal Family" Posters

Summing Up   During the guided tour of the posters, have children speak clearly using complete sentences as they describe their posters.

Brs have fr. Brs et fsh.
Brs ply in wtr.

REVIEW

Phonics

Build and Blend Words Place *Alphabet Cards i* and *t* in a pocket chart. Help children blend the sounds. Place *Alphabet Card h* in front of *i* and *t*. Help children blend the sounds and say *hit*. Follow the same procedure to blend *fit* and *pit*. Then place *Alphabet Cards i* and *g* in the pocket chart and blend the words *pig, dig, fig*. Follow the same procedure for *i* and *p*, blending the words *lip, dip, rip, tip*.

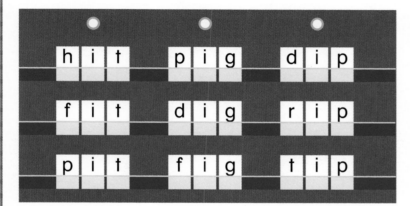

High-Frequency Words

Read Sentences Place *Picture Cards lamb, lemon, lunch box, ladder, hat, helicopter, hen*, and *horse* in a pocket chart. Place *High-Frequency Word Cards I, have, a*, and *you* in the pocket chart. Place *High-Frequency Word Cards I, have, a* in one row. Ask a child to place a *Picture Card* at the end of the sentence and read the sentence. For example: *I have a (Picture Card lamb)*. Have children repeat the activity, replacing *I* with *you*.

Comprehension

Real and Make-Believe Display *Library Books Are you there, Baby Bear?* and *A Time for Playing*. Point to *Are you there, Baby Bear?* and ask children to recall what the story is about. Tell children that the animals in this story talk and act like people. Explain that the story is make-believe because animals do not talk and act like people.

Point to *A Time for Playing*. Page through the book, pointing out the photographs of real animals playing. Read several pages and tell children that this book tells the things real animals do when they play. It gives facts about animals and how they play.

Writing

Write About Animals Have children draw a picture of an animal family they have read about. Have them write a fact sentence about the animal family.

The kngro hs a pch.

Take-Home Book Theme 6 Practice Book, pp. 23–24

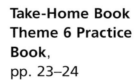
Pip the Pig

ASSESSMENT

• Assessment Handbook

Monitoring of Progress

Diagnostic Checks Use the Diagnostic Checks as a point-of-use assessment of children's understanding.

Theme Skills Assessment Use the Theme Skills Assessment to monitor a child's understanding of letter recognition, word recognition, sound-symbol relationships, and decoding skills taught in this theme.

Summative Assessment

Administer the Group Inventory, Form B, in the Assessment Handbook.

Administer the Phonemic Awareness Inventory in the Assessment Handbook.

Bug Surprises

It's fun to learn about insects. Children will read about insect habitats and learn about insect life cycles. Children will begin to understand the wonder of nature.

Theme Resources

READING MATERIALS

Big Book

◀ **Look Closer**
by Brian and Rebecca Wildsmith

Library Books
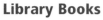
◀ **Butterfly** by Moira Butterfield
illustrated by Paul Johnson

◀ **Wonderful Worms**
by Linda Glaser
illustrated by
Loretta Krupinski

Big Book of Rhymes and Songs

◀ **Fuzzy Wuzzy Creepy Crawly**
◀ **When It Comes to Bugs**
◀ **Eency Weency Spider**

Read-Aloud Anthology
◀ **The Ants and the Grasshopper**
by Aesop
◀ **Anansi and the Biggest, Sweetest Melon**
◀ **The Fearsome Beast**
retold by Judy Sierra
◀ **The Ants Came Marching**

Independent Readers

▲ **Insects and Spiders**   ▲ **A Bug Needs a Home**   ▲ **Amazing Ants**

PHONICS

Theme 7 Practice Book

Phonics Practice Book

Decodable Books

▲ **Kip the Ant**   ▲ **The Big Ram**   ▲ **What Can Hop?**

Alphabet Patterns
bed, kangaroo, octopus
pages T16–T17
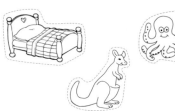

Phonics Express™ CD-ROM
Level A

TEACHING TOOLS

Big Alphabet Cards

Bb, Kk, Oo

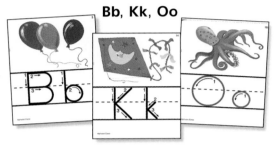

Letter and Sound Charts

Charts 3, 16, and 14

Letter and Sound Chart Sentence Strips

3, 16, and 14

Bear bounced a ball.

High-Frequency Word Cards

do, what

Picture/Word Cards

Teacher's Resource Book

pages 53, 66, 64

Oo-pples and Boo-noo-noos

English-Language Learners Kit

Intervention Kit

MANIPULATIVES

Tactile Letter Cards

Write-On/Wipe-Off Board Letters and Sounds Place Mat

Word Builder and Word Builder Cards

Magnetic Letters

Aa Bb Cc

ASSESSMENT

Assessment Handbook

Group Inventory

Theme 7 Test

Big Book ▶

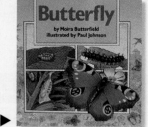

Library Book ▶

	Week 1	Week 2
• **Sharing Literature** • **Listening Comprehension**	**Big Book:** *Look Closer* **Library Book:** *Butterfly* **Read-Aloud Anthology:** "The Ants and the Grasshopper" **Big Book of Rhymes and Songs:** "Fuzzy Wuzzy, Creepy Crawly"	**Big Book:** *Look Closer* **Library Book:** *Wonderful Worms* **Read-Aloud Anthology:** "Anansi and the Biggest, Sweetest, Melon" **Big Book of Rhymes and Songs:** "When It Comes to Bugs"
• **Phonemic Awareness** • **Phonics** • **High-Frequency Words**	Consonant *Bb* **T** Consonant *Kk* **T** Review Consonants *Bb, Kk* **T** High-Frequency Words *do, what* **T**	Short Vowel /o/*o* **T** Blending /o/ - /t/ Words with /o/ and /t/
• **Reading**	**Decodable Book 1:** *Kip the Ant* **Independent Reader 18:** *Insects and Spiders*	**Decodable Book 2:** *The Big Ram* **Independent Reader 19:** *A Bug Needs a Home*
• **Writing**	**Shared Writing** List Story Map **Interactive Writing** Describing Words **Independent Writing** Naming Words Chart	**Shared Writing** Message **Interactive Writing** Questions Action Words **Independent Writing** Sentences Dialogue
• **Cross-Curricular Centers**	🔬 **Science** The Bug Zoo 🖌 **Art** Butterfly Art 🦋 **Dramatic Play** Put on a Play ABC **Letters and Words** Word Factory ✏ **Writing** Bug Greeting Cards	🔵 **Math** Bug Graph 🔬 **Science** Bug Models ♟ **Manipulatives** What's Inside? 🎧 **Listening** Story Time ♟ **Manipulatives** Bug Puzzles

T = tested skill

Library Book ▶

Week 3

Big Book: *Look Closer*

Library Book: *Wonderful Worms*

Read-Aloud Anthology:
"The Fearsome Beast"
"The Ants Came Marching"

Big Book of Rhymes and Songs:
"Eency Weency Spider"

Review Consonant *Pp,*
Short Vowel *Oo* T

Blending /o/ - /p/

Words with /o/ and /p/

Blending /o/ - /p/

Decodable Book 3: *What Can Hop?*

Independent Reader 20: *Amazing Ants*

Interactive Writing
Writing Process

 Math
Take a Guess

 Letters and Words
Letter Games

 Art
Insect Models

 Cooking
Spider Snacks

Literacy
Reading Time

Theme Organizer
Half-Day Kindergarten

Use the following chart to help organize your half-day kindergarten schedule. Choose independent activities as time allows during your day.

ORAL LANGUAGE

Morning Message

Phonemic Awareness

Sharing Literature
- Big Book: *Look Closer*
- Library Book: *Butterfly*
- Library Book: *Wonderful Worms*
- Read-Aloud Anthology
- Big Book of Rhymes and Songs

LEARNING TO READ

Phonics
Decodable Books 1–3
- *Kip the Ant*
- *The Big Ram*
- *What Can Hop?*

High-Frequency Words

**Independent Readers
18–20**
- *Insects and Spiders*
- *A Bug Needs a Home*
- *Amazing Ants*

LANGUAGE ARTS

Shared Writing
Interactive Writing
Independent Writing
Writing Every Day

INDEPENDENT ACTIVITIES

Sharing Literature
Respond to Literature
Phonics
Independent Practice
Handwriting
Practice Book pages
High-Frequency Words
Independent Practice
Practice Book pages

About the
Authors and Illustrators

Brian and Rebecca Wildsmith

Authors and Illustrators of *Look Closer*

Brian Wildsmith grew up in a mining village in England. As a young man he enjoyed playing cricket. Wildsmith won a scholarship to the Slade School of Fine Art in London. He became an art teacher but soon devoted all his time to painting. Wildsmith also does pen-and-ink illustrations. Much of his career has been devoted to creating children's books filled with engaging illustrations. Wildsmith and his daughter Rebecca collaborated on *Look Closer*.

Linda Glaser

Author of *Wonderful Worms*

Linda Glaser has had an organic garden and worm compost pile for over ten years. During that time, she has come to value the amazing work that worms do. Glaser lives in Berkeley, California with her husband and two daughters. She teaches English, Children's Literature, and Creative Writing at Vista Community College. Glaser has also written *Keep Your Socks On, Albert*.

Loretta Krupinski

Illustrator of *Wonderful Worms*

Loretta Krupinski is an avid gardener and lives in Old Lyme, Connecticut. She loves sailing, and is a professional maritime artist. She has also illustrated *Lost in the Fog* and *Sailing to the Sea*.

Theme Assessment

Assessment Options

Assessment Handbook

• Group Inventory

• Phonemic Awareness Inventory

• Theme Skills Assessment

• Concepts About Print Inventory

• Observational Checklists

MONITORING OF PROGRESS

After completing the theme, most children should show progress toward mastery of the following skills:

Concepts of Print
- ❏ Follow words from left to right and from top to bottom on the printed page.
- ❏ Distinguish letters from words.

Phonemic Awareness
- ❏ Track isolated phonemes.
- ❏ Count the number of sounds in syllables and syllables in words.

Phonics and Decoding
- ❏ Match all consonant sounds and short-vowel sounds to appropriate letters.
- ❏ Read one-syllable and High-Frequency Words.

Vocabulary and High-Frequency Words
- ❏ Read High-Frequency Words *do* and *what*.
- ❏ Describe common objects and events in both general and specific language.
- ❏ Understand content words.

Comprehension
- ❏ Ask and answer questions about essential elements of text.
- ❏ Understand the main idea and details.

Literary Response
- ❏ Identify types of everyday print materials.
- ❏ Make inferences based on information provided in text.
- ❏ Identify characters, settings, and important events.

Writing
- ❏ Write by moving from left to right and from top to bottom.
- ❏ Write about self-selected topics.

Listening and Speaking
- ❏ Share information and ideas, speaking audibly in complete, coherent sentences.
- ❏ Recite short poems.

Reaching All Learners

■ **BELOW-LEVEL**

Levels of Support

Point-of-use Notes in the Teacher's Edition

pp. 363, 365, 375, 377, 385, 387, 391, 393, 401, 403, 421, 425, 429, 433, 437, 441, 445, 447, 448, 455, 457, 467, 471, 479, 483, 485, 487, 493

Additional Support Activities

High-frequency Words:
  pp. S38–S39

Comprehension and Skills:
pp. S48–S49, S54–S55

Phonemic Awareness:
pp. S40–S41, S46–S47, S50–S51

Phonics:
pp. S42–S43, S44–S45, S52–S53

Intervention Resource Kit

■ **ENGLISH-LANGUAGE LEARNERS**

Levels of Support

Point-of-use Notes in the Teacher's Edition

pp. 365, 371, 383, 387, 391, 393, 396, 405, 431, 433, 437, 439, 441, 447, 448, 453, 467, 475, 487, 493, 494, 501, 503

Additional Support Activities

High-frequency Words:
  pp. S38–S39

Comprehension and Skills:
pp. S48–S49, S54–S55

Phonemic Awareness:
pp. S40–S41, S46–S47, S50–S51

Phonics:
pp. S42–S43, S44–S45, S52–S53

Visit *The Learning Site!* at
www.harcourtschool.com
See Language Support activities

English-Language Learners Resource Kit

■ ADVANCED

Levels of Challenge

Point-of-use Notes in the Teacher's Edition

pp. 363, 373, 375, 377, 381, 383, 387, 391, 395, 396, 405, 421, 423, 425, 429, 433, 437, 439, 441, 445, 447, 453, 457, 467, 469, 471, 477, 479, 485, 487, 491, 493, 503

Additional Support Activities

High-frequency Words:
pp. S38–S39

Comprehension and Skills:
pp. S48–S49, S54–S55

Phonemic Awareness:
pp. S40–S41, S46–S47, S50–S51

Phonics:
pp. S42–S43, S44–S45, S52–S53

Accelerated Instruction

Use higher-grade-level materials for accelerated instruction.

Theme Project, pp. 353

Combination Classrooms
Writing Together

Pair children to write and draw about their favorite bug from the theme. Try to include an advanced writer and a beginning writer in each pair. Encourage children to collaborate on drawing the bug in a natural setting and writing information they know about the bug. The advanced writer may act as the scribe for the beginning writer.

Students with Special Needs
Focusing Attention

While sharing literature, such as the *Big Book Look Closer*, seat children who are easily distracted right in front of you. These children will be better able to stay focused when situated where the relevant stimulus is the only thing in their line of sight.

Recommended Reading

Below are suggestions for reading materials that will meet kindergarten children's diverse needs. Books that are on a child's level provide support for new skills. Advanced books give children an opportunity to stretch and challenge their reading potential. Read-aloud books are important because they expose children to story language and vocabulary.

■ BELOW-LEVEL

Curly Finds a Home by Tony Mitton. Rigby, 2003. Everyone Curly meets has a home. Will Curly find one?

The Ants Came Marching in by Martin Kelly. Handprint, 2000. Introduces a classic children's song most everyone already knows.

Clementina's Cactus by Ezra Jack Keats. Viking, 1999. A wordless book of a girl and her father that notice a lone cactus in the desert, all shriveled and prickly. Yet, there is something beautiful hiding in its thick skin.

Flower in the Garden by Lucy Cousins. Candlewick, 1992. A wordless book of what is found in a garden.

■ ON-LEVEL

I Like Bugs by Margaret Wise Brown. Golden Books, 1999. Bright, bold art and rhymingtext covers all sorts of interesting insects.

Old Black Fly by Jim Aylesworthy. Henry Holt, 1995. A busy fly bothers everyone in the house, but meets his end when a cake is dropped on him.

Dr. Seuss's A B C by Dr. Seuss. Random House, 1963. Humorous illustrations and rhymes help children learn letters and sounds.

The Frog and the Fly by Leslie Wood. Oxford, 1985. A frog catches a fly, but the fly is able to escape.

■ ADVANCED

Buggy Riddles by Katy Hall. Puffin, 1993. Illustrated collection of riddles about insects.

The Icky Bug Alphabet Book by Jerry Pullotta. Charlesbridge, 1990. This alphabetical exploration of bugs and insects is informative and entertaining.

Bugs! Bugs! Bugs! by Bob Barner. Chronicle Books 1999. All kinds of bugs are pictured in this brightly illustrated book.

In the Tall, Tall Grass by Denise Fleming. Henry Holt, 1995. A small boy discovers many insects in the tall grass near his home.

■ READ ALOUD

It's a Good Thing There Are Insects by Allan Fowler. Children's Press, 1991. These facts about insects include descriptions of how they look, what they do, and what they produce.

Those Amazing Ants by Patricia Brennan Demuth. Simon & Schuster, 1994. This engaging picture book presents facts about how ants hunt, eat, breed, and build homes.

The Very Hungry Caterpillar by Eric Carle. Putnam, 1994. A caterpillar eats his way through this modern classic tale of metamorphosis.

Why Mosquitoes Buzz in People's Ears by Verna Aardema. Econo-Clad Books, 1999. This is a vividly illustrated retelling of an African folktale.

Homework Ideas

Visit The Learning Site: www.harcourtschool.com See Resources for Parents and Teachers: Homework Helper

	Literature	Phonics	Language Arts	Theme	Cross-Curricular
WEEK 1	Draw and write about what you see when you **look closer** at a leaf or a blade of grass.	Look through magazines and find pictures whose names begin with **the /b/ sound**. Cut out the pictures and label them.	Make a list of **insects that fly.**	Draw and label a picture of **bugs that crawl.**	Use clay to make models of **insects.**
WEEK 2	Write a sentence about your **favorite bug**.	Draw two objects whose names have **the /o/ sound.**	Draw and label a picture about **bugs** you can find near your house.	Draw and write about how caterpillars become **butterflies.**	If possible, observe insects outdoors. **Draw and label** pictures of what you see.
WEEK 3	Draw and label a picture about **worms.**	Work with a family member to think of words that **rhyme** with mop.	**Write** or dictate a story about a bug you have read about so far in this theme.	**Sing** a song about an insect, such as "The Itsy Bitsy Spider."	**Imitate** the movements of an insect. Challenge a family member to name the insect.

Give a Bug Talk!

Materials

- Teacher's Resource Book page 15
- poster board
- paper
- crayons
- markers
- pencils
- books about bugs and insects
- old magazines
- safety scissors
- glue stick

Introduce

Tell children they are going to work together to give a talk about bugs. Ask them to name insects and bugs and list them on the board. Assign children to groups responsible for making diagrams, drawing or finding pictures, and writing surprising facts about their bug.

Send home the Family Letter to encourage family members to participate in the project.

Prepare

- Groups can draw or cut out pictures and make labeled diagrams of their assigned bug. Children can add a sentence to tell about the bugs.

- Have children practice giving their talk. Make sure each team member has a chance to speak.

Share

Rehearse with children how to listen politely while others are speaking, how to speak loudly and clearly, and how to point to parts of a diagram to share information.

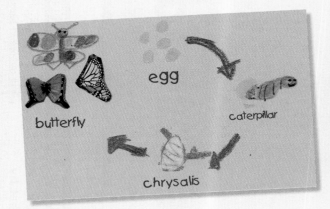

School-Home Connection

Invite family members to visit the classroom to hear the bug talks. Allow time for visitors to share their knowledge about bugs.

Visit *The Learning Site!* at **www.harcourtschool.com**

Teacher Notes

Learning Centers

Choose from the following suggestions to enhance your learning centers for the theme Bug Surprises.
(Additional learning centers for this theme can be found on pages 414 and 460)

ART CENTER

Surprising Bugs

Provide a variety of materials in the art center that children can use to make surprising bugs. Remind children that some bugs have six legs and others have more, and that some bugs fly but others crawl. Challenge children to use their imaginations as they use surprising materials to create their bugs. Then have children tell about their bugs and what they can do.

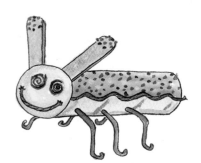

20 Minutes

Materials

- recyclable objects: cartons, paper tubes, small cups
- construction paper
- craft sticks
- yarn
- safety scissors
- glue sticks and pipe cleaners
- sequins and glitter

DRAMATIC PLAY CENTER

Ant March

Play "The Ants Came Marching" on the *Music CD*. Have children listen to the song twice. Then have them act it out as they sing along with the tape, marching one by one and pointing to their thumb in the first verse; marching two by two and pretending stooping to tie their shoe in the second verse, and so on.

20 Minutes

Materials

- Music CD

WRITING CENTER

Write About a Bug

Tell children to choose a kind of bug they would like to write about. Have children write a sentence that tells what kind of bug they are writing about, and a sentence or two that tell something surprising the bug does. Have children draw a picture to illustrate their sentences.

Bes are surprizng bgs.
Did you no this?
Bes can mak huny!

Materials

■ paper
■ pencils
■ crayons

SCIENCE CENTER

Bug Collage

Have children look through magazines to find and cut out pictures of flying, creeping, crawling, and even swimming bugs. Then have children paste their pictures on a piece of paper to make a collage about bugs. Children can write labels for the bugs they can identify.

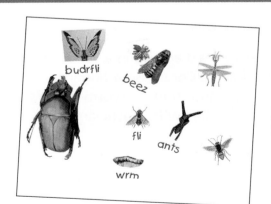

budrfli
beez
fli   ants
wrm

Materials

■ old magazines
■ safety scissors
■ glue sticks
■ paper
■ pencils

LITERACY CENTER

Bug Guessing Game

Tell children they are going to play a bug guessing game. Give each child a sheet of paper and two sentence strips. At the top of the paper, have children glue the sentence strip *What is it?* Have children draw a picture of a bug below the question. Then have children write the name of the bug to complete the sentence strip *It is a _____*, and paste that sentence strip on the back of their paper. Have children look at one another's drawings, read the sentence at the top of the page, and try to identify the bug.

What is it?

Materials

- sentence strips: *What is it? It is a _____.*
- paper
- glue stick
- crayons

SAND AND WATER CENTER

Anthills and Worm Tunnels

Have children work together to build anthills in a sand tray or classroom sandbox. Then have children use a finger to trace a pattern of paths in the sand to make worm tunnels. Children can decorate their structures with plastic ants and plastic worms.

Materials

- sand tray or classroom sandbox
- plastic ants
- plastic worms

Teacher Notes

Teacher Notes

THEME 7

Week 1

Bug Surprises

⏱ 15-30 Minutes

ORAL LANGUAGE

- **Phonemic Awareness**

- **Sharing Literature**

 ⏱ 45 Minutes

LEARNING TO READ

- **Phonics**

- **Vocabulary**

Daily Routines
- Morning Message
- Calendar Language
- Writing Prompt

⏱ 15-30 Minutes

LANGUAGE ARTS

- **Writing**
  Daily Writing Prompt

Day 1

Phonemic Awareness, 363
Phoneme Segmentation

Sharing Literature, 364
 Read

Big Book: *Look Closer*

(Skill) **Literature Focus, 365**
Making Predictions

 Phonics, 372 T
Introduce: Consonant *Bb*
Identify/Write T

 **Shared Writing, 374**
Write a List

Writing Prompt, 374
Draw and write about a favorite place to take a walk.

Share Time, 375
Share a favorite insect in *Look Closer*.

Day 2

Phonemic Awareness, 377
Phoneme Isolation

Sharing Literature, 378
 **Read**

Library Book: *Butterfly*

(Skill) **Literature Focus, 379**
Main Idea/Details

 Phonics, 380 T
Relating /b/ to *b*

High-Frequency Word, 382 T
Introduce: *do*

Words to Remember, 383

Writing, 384
Write Naming Words

Writing Prompt, 384
Draw and write about self-selected topics.

Share Time, 385
Recall the four stages of a butterfly's life.

T = tested skill

Phonics

Consonants *Bb, Kk*

Focus of the Week:
- **HIGH-FREQUENCY WORDS:** *do, what*
- **PHONEMIC AWARENESS**
- **SHARING LITERATURE**
- **WRITING:** Lists, Naming Words, Charts, Story Map

Day 3

Phonemic Awareness, 387
Phoneme Isolation and Matching: Initial

Sharing Literature, 388
Read

Read-Aloud Anthology: "The Ants and the Grasshopper," p. 110

 Literature Focus, 389
Drawing Conclusions

Phonics, 390 **T**
Introduce: Consonant *Kk*
Identify/Write **T**

High-Frequency Word, 392 T
Introduce: *what*

Words to Remember, 393

 Shared Writing, 394
Write a Story Map

Writing Prompt, 394
Draw and write about winter activities.

Share Time, 395
Retell the story "The Ants and the Grasshopper."

Day 4

Phonemic Awareness, 397
Phoneme Isolation and Matching: Initial

Sharing Literature, 398
Big Book of Rhymes and Songs: "Fuzzy Wuzzy, Creepy Crawly," p. 18

 Literature Focus, 399
Syllables in Words

Phonics, 400 **T**
Relating /k/ to *k* **T**

High-Frequency Words, 402 T
Review: *do, what*

Read

DECODABLE BOOK 1
Kip the Ant

 Interactive Writing, 404
Write Describing Words

Writing Prompt, 404
Draw pictures and write caterpillar or butterfly descriptions.

Share Time, 405
Discuss new words from "Fuzzy Wuzzy, Creepy Crawly."

Day 5

Phonemic Awareness, 407
Phoneme Deletion

Sharing Literature, 408
Read

Library Book: *Butterfly*

 Literature Focus, 409
Understanding Content Words

Phonics, 410 **T**
Review: Consonants *Bb, Kk*

Shared Writing, 412
Write a Chart

Writing Prompt, 412
Draw and write about self-selected topics.

Share Time, 413
Discuss surprising parts of *Butterfly*.

Day at a Glance
Day 1

WARM UP

Phonemic Awareness
Phoneme Segmentation

Sharing Literature
Big Book:
Look Closer

Read

Brian and Rebecca Wildsmith
Look Closer

Develop Listening Comprehension

Respond to Literature

Literature Focus: Making Predictions

Phonics
Consonant *Bb*

Shared Writing
List of Insects

MORNING MESSAGE

Kindergarten News

Today is _____.

The weather is _____.

Write Kindergarten News   Talk with children about today's weather.

Use prompts such as the following to guide children as you write the news:

- **What is the weather today?**
- **Who can show me where to begin writing?**
- **Let's clap the syllables for (day of the week). How many parts does it have?**
- **What letter will I write first in (day of the week)?**

As you write the message, invite children to write letters, names, or words they have previously learned. Remind them to use proper spacing, capitalization, and punctuation.

Calendar Language

Point to and read aloud the days of the week. Tell children you will name the school days. Point to and read aloud *Monday* through *Friday*. Ask children to repeat the names of the school days.

Sunday	Monday	Tuesday	Wednesday	Thursday	Friday	Saturday
		1	2	3	4	5
6	7	8	9	10	11	12
13	14	15	16	17	18	19
20	21	22	23	24	25	26
27	28	29	30	31		

Phonemic Awareness

PHONEME SEGMENTATION

Identify the Number of Sounds in Words   Say the word *bug* and have children repeat it. Then say:

Bug. **Watch while I hold up one finger for each sound in the word: /b/ /u/ /g/. Say the sounds with me: /b/ /u/ /g/. The word *bug* has three sounds. Now you try it. Say the word *not.* Hold up one finger for each sound you hear as you say the sounds slowly: /n/ /o/ /t/. How many sounds did you hear? Count your fingers.** (three)

As you provide the following words, ask children, *How many sounds do you hear in ___?* Encourage children to slowly repeat the sounds and count with their fingers.

big /b/ /i/ /g/	**in** /i/ /n/	**fill** /f/ /i/ /l/
top /t/ /o/ /p/	**bet** /b/ /e/ /t/	**on** /o/ /n/
jam /j/ /a/ /m/	**bag** /b/ /a/ /g/	**buzz** /b/ /u/ /z/
bat /b/ /a/ /t/	**box** /b/ /o/ /ks/	**rib** /r/ /i/ /b/
cub /k/ /u/ /b/	**tub** /t/ /u/ /b/	**belt** /b/ /e/ /l/ /t/

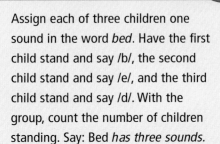

▲ **Big Book**

OBJECTIVES

- *To listen and respond to a selection*
- *To connect text to life experiences*
- *To make predictions*

Materials

- *Big Book: Look Closer*
- chart paper
- marker

Sharing Literature

Read Look Closer

READ ALOUD

Before Reading Display the cover of *Look Closer*, and ask a volunteer to point to the title. Track the print as you read it aloud. Read aloud the authors' names. Use the following prompts to build background:

- **What do you see on the cover?** (a bug, water, and a plant)
- **What other bugs do you know about?**

Page through the book, pausing briefly on each page to allow children to preview the illustrations. Have children tell what they think the selection will be about.

During Reading Read the story aloud. As you read,

- emphasize the repetitive text.
- encourage children to look closer at each picture to try to identify the bugs.
- pause for predictions after the question *What could it be?*

> **MODEL** I can see some little bugs on the fence. I think they are snails. I'll turn the page and see if I am right. On the next page, I see bigger pictures of the bugs. They *are* snails.

Read the story once more, inviting children to join in and repeat the question *What could it be?* with you.

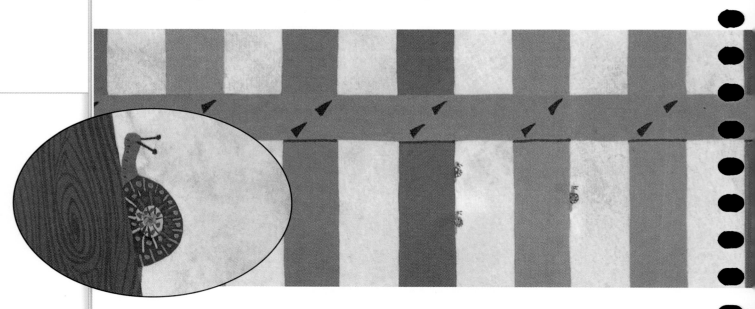

DEVELOP LISTENING COMPREHENSION

After Reading   Have children answer these questions:

- **What is the story about?** (looking at different kinds of bugs)
- **What are some of the bugs you see in this selection?** (Possible responses include: ants, bees, ladybugs, spider)
- **Which of these bugs have you seen before?**

RESPOND TO LITERATURE

Make a Word Web   Write the word *insect* in a circle on chart paper. Tell children that the word *insect* means "a kind of bug." Have children name the kinds of insects that are in the story. Find each insect name in the text and ask a child to frame the word. Say the word aloud and have children repeat. Then add the word to the word web. Invite children to draw a picture to go with each word.

MAKING PREDICTIONS

Show children how they can use picture clues in *Look Closer* to make predictions about what insects they will see. Have children study the picture of the stone wall on page 7. Ask a child to point out the picture clue that shows a bug is there. Turn the page and display the close-up picture of the same insect. Next, display page 17, and have children describe the tiny picture clue they see in the grass. Ask children what the picture clue looks like, and have them predict what they will see on the next page. (spider) Turn the page to confirm their predictions.

BELOW-LEVEL

Page through *Look Closer* with children and help them recall the names of the insects.

ENGLISH-LANGUAGE LEARNERS

Page through *Look Closer* with children and invite them to name the insects using their first languages. Then say the names of the insects in English, and have children repeat them.

ONGOING ASSESSMENT

As you share *Look Closer,* note whether children

- **listen for a period of time.**
- **can connect text to their experiences.**
- **can make predictions.**

▲ **Practice Book pages 5–6**

Brian and Rebecca Wildsmith

Look Closer

For Ornella

Look Closer

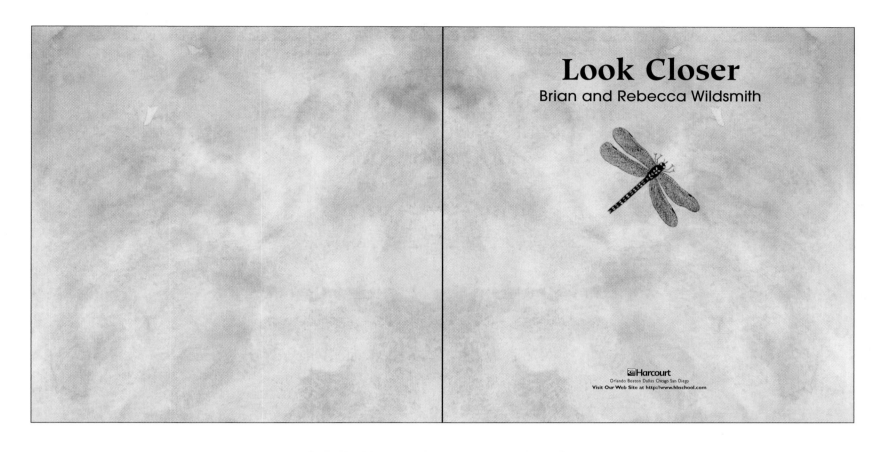

Look Closer
Brian and Rebecca Wildsmith

Harcourt
Orlando Boston Dallas Chicago San Diego
Visit Our Web Site at http://www.hbschool.com

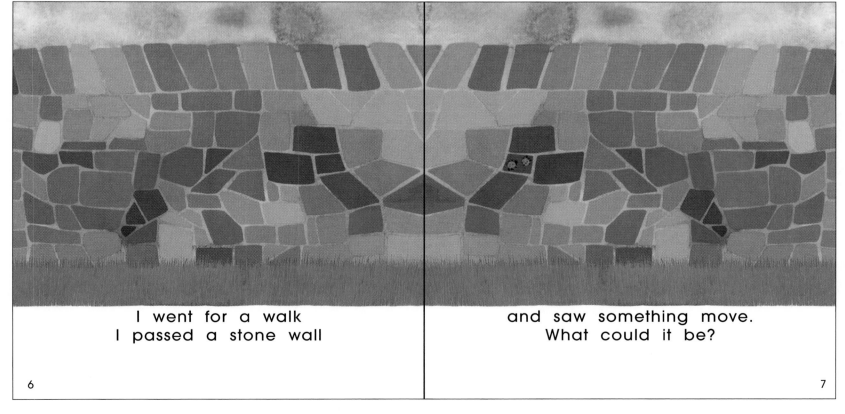

I went for a walk
I passed a stone wall

and saw something move.
What could it be?

6

7

Ladybugs.

8

I passed a wood fence
and saw something move.
What could it be?

9

Snails.

10

I passed wild roses
and saw something move.
What could it be?

11

Caterpillars.

12

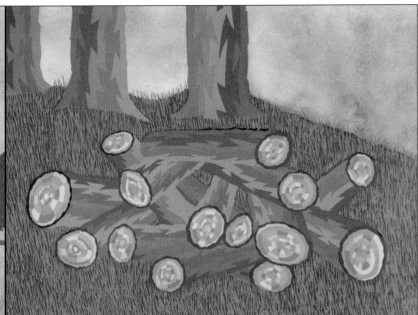

I passed a wood pile
and saw something move.
What could it be?

13

Ants.

14

I passed some purple thistles
and saw something move.
What could it be?

15

A bee.

16

I passed some tall grass
and saw something move.
What could it be?

17

A spider.

18

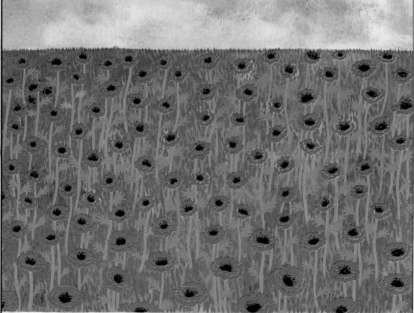

I passed a poppy field
and saw something move.
What could it be?

19

Butterflies.

20

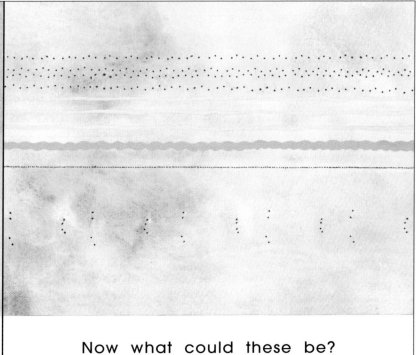

Now what could these be?

21

Ah! They are all going home —

22

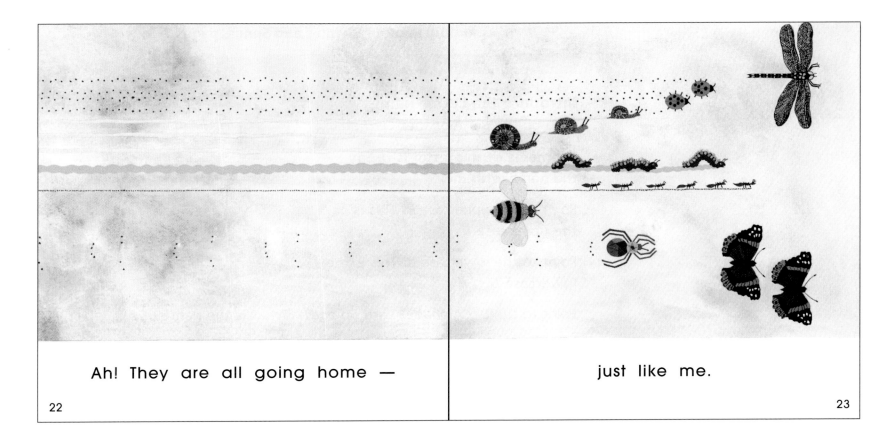

just like me.

23

Consonant *Bb* ✔ *Introduce*

OBJECTIVES

- *To recognize B and b*
- *To write uppercase and lowercase Bb independently*

Materials

- ■ *Big Book of Rhymes and Songs, pp. 2–3*
- ■ *Music CD*
- ■ *Big Book: From Anne to Zach*
- ■ *Big Alphabet Card Bb*
- ■ *Write-On/Wipe-Off Boards*
- ■ chart paper
- ■ drawing paper
- ■ crayons

ACTIVE BEGINNING

Sing "The Alphabet Song" Display "The Alphabet Song" in the *Big Book of Rhymes and Songs*. Point to each letter as you sing the song with children.

THE ALPHABET SONG

A B C D E F G,
H I J K L M N O P,
Q R S, T U V,
W X Y and Z.

Now I've sung my ABC's.
Next time won't you
sing with me?

▲ **Big Book of Rhymes and Songs, pages 2–3**

TEACH/MODEL

Introduce the Letter Name
Hold up the *Big Alphabet Card Bb*.

The name of this letter is *b*. Say the name with me.

Point to the uppercase *B*. **This is the uppercase *B*.**

Point to the lowercase *b*. **This is the lowercase *b*.**

Point to the *Big Alphabet Card Bb* again. **What is the name of this letter?**

Point to the *B* in "The Alphabet Song." **What is the name of this letter?**

Display page 5 in *From Anne to Zach*.

Follow along as I read the page.

Point to the letter *B*. **What is the name of this letter?**

Handwriting

Writing *B* and *b* Write uppercase *B* and lowercase *b* on the board.

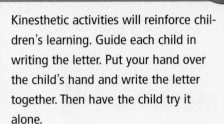

Point to the uppercase *B*. **What letter is this?**

Point to the lowercase *b*. **What letter is this?**

Model how to write uppercase *B*. **Watch as I write the letter *b* so that everyone can read it.**

As you give the Letter Talk, trace the uppercase *B*. Use the same modeling procedure for lowercase *b*.

Letter Talk for B

Straight line down. Go to the top of this line. Curved line out, down, and around. Touch the middle of the straight line. Curved line out, down, and around. Touch the bottom line.

Letter Talk for b

Straight line down. Circle around and touch the bottom line.

D'Nealian handwriting models are on pages R10–11.

PRACTICE/APPLY

Guided Practice Help children find *Bb* on their *Write-On/Wipe-Off Boards*. Have them trace the uppercase *B* with a finger and then write the letter several times. Then have them do the same for lowercase *b*. Tell children to circle their best *B*.

Independent Practice Have children fold their paper in half. Have them write uppercase *B*s on one side of the paper and lowercase *b*s on the other side.

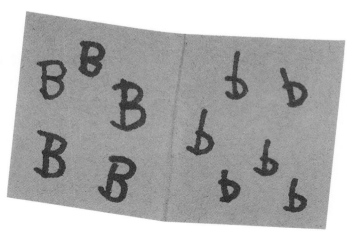

Day 1

BELOW-LEVEL

Kinesthetic activities will reinforce children's learning. Guide each child in writing the letter. Put your hand over the child's hand and write the letter together. Then have the child try it alone.

ENGLISH-LANGUAGE LEARNERS

Providing a model will help children understand the movements involved in letter formation. As you introduce children to *Bb*, model each step of the letter talk to make sure children understand the ideas of straight line, middle, and circle.

Phonics Resources

Phonics Express™ CD-ROM, Level A, Speedy/ Route 3/Train Station

Phonics Practice Book pages 71–72

▲ **Practice Book page 7**

OBJECTIVES

- *To understand the purpose of a list*
- *To write a list*

Materials

- Big Book: *Look Closer*
- chart paper
- marker

Shared Writing

Write a List

SUMMARIZE WITH A LIST

Talk About Lists Remind children that a list is a group of words. Discuss how lists can help people remember things. Page through *Look Closer* and have children recall each of the insects in the book.

Write a List Write the title *Insects* on chart paper. Tell children that together they are going to make a list of insect names so it will be easier to remember them. Record the insect names from *Look Closer* as children repeat them. Then ask children to name other insects they know, and add their suggestions to the list.

Insects
ladybug
bee
ant
mosquito

Journal Writing Have children write and draw about their favorite place to take a walk.

WRAP UP Share Time

Reflect on the Lesson Gather children around the Author's Chair.
Read the list of insects from Shared Writing as children repeat the names.
Ask children to tell about their favorite insect in the list. Ask them to
name the letter they learned today. (Bb)

S.S.R. Have children read silently from a book of their choice.

Centers SCIENCE

The Bug Zoo

If possible, take children outdoors to collect insects, or collect a variety of insects
yourself and place them in clear, unbreakable jars along with leaves and grass or
other materials from the insects' natural habitat. Encourage children to use hand
lenses to look at the insects and observe how they are alike and different. Children
can draw and label pictures of the insects. Release the insects back into their natural
habitat after a few days.

Materials

- clean, unbreakable jars with lids

- grass, leaves, other natural materials

- paper

- crayons

- hand lenses

Day at a Glance
Day 2

WARM UP

Phonemic Awareness
Phoneme Isolation

Sharing Literature
Library Book:
Butterfly

Read

Butterfly
by Moira Butterfield
illustrated by Paul Johnson

Develop Listening Comprehension

Respond to Literature

Literature Focus:
Main Idea/Details

Relating /b/ to *b*

High-Frequency Word
do

Writing
Naming Words

MORNING MESSAGE

Kindergarten News

(Child's name) likes to _____

in school.

Today we will _____.

Write Kindergarten News Talk with children about their favorite school activities.

Use prompts such as the following to guide children as you write the news:

- **Tell me what you like to do in school.**
- **Who can show me the top of the page?**
- **Who can show me a word?**
- **Who can name the beginning sound in the word *today*?**

As you write the message, invite children to write letters or words they have previously learned. Remind them to use proper spacing, capitalization, and punctuation.

Calendar Language

Point to the numbers on the calendar. Tell children that the days of each month are numbered and the numbers tell the dates. Point to and read aloud today's date. Name the month and the date.

Sunday	Monday	Tuesday	Wednesday	Thursday	Friday	Saturday
			1	2	3	4	5
6	7	8	9	10	11	12
13	14	15	16	17	18	19
20	21	22	23	24	25	26
27	28	29	30	31		

Words to Remember

Word Wall

Reading Words Hold up the *High-Frequency Word Card do* and have children read it aloud. Place the word card under the letter *d* of the classroom word chart.

Find Similarities Have children look closely at their new word *do*. Ask them to name the letters in the word. Then have them read the other high-frequency words on the chart that have the letter *o*. (*go, on, to, you*) Ask children to count the letters in the word *do*. Have them read the words on the chart that also have two letters. (*my, go, we, on, to*)

BELOW-LEVEL

Have children trace over the letters of their individual word cards with their fingers. Then have them write the word in the air with their fingers.

ADVANCED

Have children look in books, magazines, or newspapers to find the word *do*.

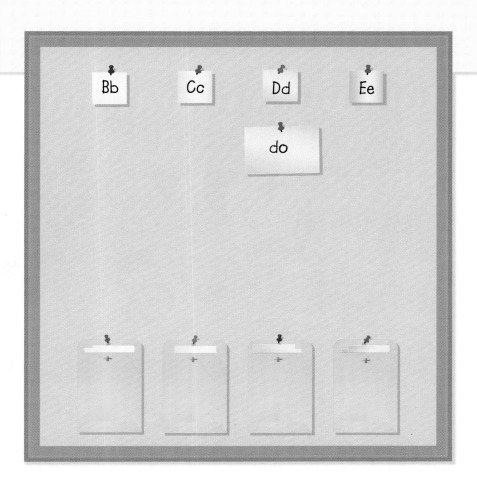

▲ **Practice Book page 9**

Bug Surprises 383

OBJECTIVES

- *To write naming words*
- *To label pictures for a book*

Materials

- *Library Book: Butterfly*
- construction paper
- crayons

Writing

Write Naming Words

DRAW AND WRITE

Talk About Naming Words Remind children that naming words are words that name a person, place, or thing. Page through *Butterfly*. Point out some words that name things, such as *butterfly, caterpillar, leaf, twig*. Write the words on the board.

Write Naming Words Have children make a butterfly book. Tell them to fold a piece of construction paper in half. On the front "cover" have them draw a picture of a caterpillar. On the inside of the "book" have them draw what the caterpillar changes into—a butterfly. Encourage children to draw and label details in their books, such as *leaf, flower*, and *branch*.

Self-Selected Topics Ask children to write about self-selected topics in their journals.

WRAP UP # Share Time

Reflect on the Lesson Gather children around the classroom Author's Chair. Have children recall the four stages of the butterfly's life. Then invite each child to sit in the chair to share the pictures and words in the butterfly book written today.

S.S.R. *Sustained Silent Reading* Have children read silently from a book of their choice.

Centers **ART**

Butterfly Art

Place butterfly patterns, scissors, paints, and brushes in the center. Have children cut along the black line of the folded construction paper and unfold the paper to reveal a butterfly shape. Next, ask children to put two or three dabs of paint on one side of the butterfly shape, fold the paper and press firmly. Then direct children to open the butterfly and let the paint dry. Children can display the butterflies by attaching them to a horizontal string with clothespins.

Materials

- patterns
  (paper folded in half, with outline of one butterfly wing drawn)

- scissors

- tempera paint

- brushes

- string

- clothespins

WARM UP

Phonemic Awareness
Phoneme Isolation and Matching: Initial

Sharing Literature
Read-Aloud Anthology: *The Ants and the Grasshopper*

Develop Listening Comprehension

Respond to Literature

Literature Focus: Drawing Conclusions

Phonics

Consonant *Kk*

High-Frequency Word
what

Shared Writing
Writing: Story Map

MORNING MESSAGE

Kindergarten News

(Child's name) likes to play

_____ at home.

(Child's name) likes to play

_____ at school.

Write Kindergarten News Talk with children about what they like to do during playtime at home and at school.

Use prompts such as the following to guide children as you write the news:

- **What games do you like to play at home? at school?**
- **Who can show me where to begin writing?**
- **Let's clap the syllables in _____'s name. How many parts does it have?**
- **How many letters in _____'s name?**

As you write the message, invite children to write letters, names, or words, they have previously learned. Remind them to use proper spacing, capitalization, and punctuation.

Calendar Language

Point to and read aloud the names of the days of the week. Have children identify the first day of the week. (Sunday) Have children identify the last day of the week. (Saturday)

Sunday	Monday	Tuesday	Wednesday	Thursday	Friday	Saturday
		1	2	3	4	5
6	7	8	9	10	11	12
13	14	15	16	17	18	19
20	21	22	23	24	25	26
27	28	29	30	31		

Phonemic Awareness

PHONEME ISOLATION: INITIAL

Isolate Initial Sounds   Say the words *horse* and *hello* slowly several times, emphasizing the initial sound. Have children repeat the words. Say:

MODEL   *Horse, hello*. I listen for the first sound in each word. *Horse* begins with the /h/ sound. *Hello* begins with the /h/ sound. *Horse, hello*. I hear the /h/ sound in *horse* and *hello*. *Horse* and *hello* have the same beginning sound. Say *horse* and *hello* with me.

For each of the following word pairs, ask: **Do the two words begin with the same sound?**

sing, sun (yes)

garden, gate (yes)

puddle, music (no)

vegetable, violin (yes)

fiddle, cotton (no)

ants, food (no)

winter, work (yes)

dance, day (yes)

PHONEME MATCHING: INITIAL

Match Initial Sounds   Say the words *dance*, *beautiful*, and *day* several times, emphasizing the initial sounds. Have children repeat the words. Say:

MODEL   *Dance, beautiful, day*. I listen for the first sound in each word. *Dance* begins with the /d/ sound. *Beautiful* begins with the /b/ sound. *Day* begins with the /d/ sound. *Dance, day*. I hear the /d/ sound in *dance* and *day*. The words *dance* and *day* have the same beginning sound. Say *dance* and *day* with me.

For each of the following words, ask: **Which two words begin with the same sound? What is the sound?**

summer, fall, sing (summer, sing; /s/)

garden, sun, seeds (sun, seeds; /s/)

lazy, moon, music (moon, music; /m/)

rain, plant, row (rain, row; /r/)

weak, cold, cover (cold, cover; /k/)

dance, work, dig (dance, dig; /d/)

kick, long, kitchen (kick, kitchen; /k/)

ADVANCED

Challenge children to extend the skill. Say word pairs such as *wind/wait*, *north/noon*, *seeds/safe*, and have children name a third word that begins with the same sound.

▲ **Read-Aloud Anthology**

OBJECTIVES

- *To listen and respond to a story*

- *To connect text to life experiences*

- *To identify a story lesson*

- *To understand characters*

- *To draw conclusions*

Materials

- *Read-Aloud Anthology, pp. 110–111*

- drawing paper

- crayons

Sharing Literature

Read "The Ants and the Grasshopper"

READ ALOUD

Before Reading Tell children that they are going to listen to a fable about some ants and about a grasshopper who learns a lesson. Read aloud the title "The Ants and the Grasshopper." Use these prompts to build background:

- **When would you rather be playing than working?**
- **When is it important to work?**

During Reading Read the story aloud. As you read,

- pause periodically for children to recall what has happened so far in the story.
- change your voice to read the parts of the grasshopper and the ants.
- pause after reading the part about Grasshopper knocking on the door of the ants' house to ask for help. Invite children to predict whether or not the ants will help him solve his problem.

DEVELOP LISTENING COMPREHENSION

After Reading   Have children answer these questions about the story:

- **What does Grasshopper do all spring, summer, and fall?** (He plays the fiddle.)
- **What do the ants do all spring, summer, and fall?** (They plant and harvest a garden so that they will have food for the winter.)
- **What lesson does Grasshopper learn?** (It's best to work first and play when the work is done.)

RESPOND TO LITERATURE

Write a New Ending   Have children draw and label pictures that show a new ending for the story.

Literature Focus

DRAWING CONCLUSIONS

Remind children that they can use story clues to figure out information.

MODEL The ants warn Grasshopper to get ready for winter, but he doesn't listen. When Grasshopper knocks at their door in the winter, the ants let him in and feed him. I think the ants are kind because they share their food with Grasshopper.

Invite children to draw conclusions about the grasshopper, who kept his promise to the ants by helping them in the spring. Ask what they think about him.

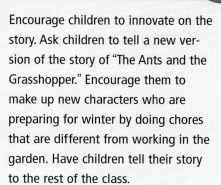

ADVANCED

Encourage children to innovate on the story. Ask children to tell a new version of the story of "The Ants and the Grasshopper." Encourage them to make up new characters who are preparing for winter by doing chores that are different from working in the garden. Have children tell their story to the rest of the class.

ENGLISH-LANGUAGE LEARNERS

Physical activities can reinforce children's understanding of vocabulary. Read passages from the fable and call on children to act out action words such as *dancing, hoeing, laughed, twirled, watered, raked, shivering,* and *knocked.*

ONGOING ASSESSMENT

As you share "The Ants and the Grasshopper," note whether children

- listen and respond to the story.
- can recall story details.
- can make predictions.

OBJECTIVES

- *To recognize K and k*
- *To write uppercase and lowercase Kk independently*

Materials

- *Big Book: I Read Signs*
- *Big Alphabet Cards Ff, Gg, Hh, Ii, Ll, Kk*
- *Write-On/Wipe-Off Boards*
- drawing paper
- crayons

Phonics

Consonant *Kk*  *Introduce*

ACTIVE BEGINNING

Review the Letters Stand *Big Alphabet Cards Ff, Gg, Hh, Ii,* and *Ll* on the chalk ledge. Call on a child to point to each letter as you name it. Ask: **Can you tell me a word that begins with that letter?**

TEACH/MODEL

Introduce the Letter Name Hold up the *Big Alphabet Card Kk.*

The name of this letter is *k*. Say the name with me.

Point to the uppercase *K*. **This is the uppercase *K*.**

Point to the lowercase *k*. **This is the lowercase *k*.**

Point to the *Big Alphabet Card* again. **What is the name of this letter?**

Display each of these signs from *I Read Signs*: WALK, DON'T WALK, KEEP RIGHT. As you display them, say:

Repeat the words after me.

Point to the letter *K*. **What is the name of this letter?**

Handwriting

Writing *K* and *k*   Write uppercase *K* and lowercase *k* on the board.

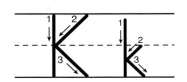

Point to the uppercase *K*. **What letter is this?**

Point to the lowercase *k*. **What letter is this?**

Model how to write uppercase *K*. **Watch as I write the letter *k* so that everyone can read it.**

As you give the Letter Talk, trace the uppercase *K*. Use the same modeling procedure for lowercase *k*.

Letter Talk for *K*

Straight line down. Slant left and down. Slant right and down.

Letter Talk for *k*

Straight line down. Slant left and down. Slant right and down.

D'Nealian handwriting models are on pages R10–11.

PRACTICE/APPLY

Guided Practice   Help children find *Kk* on their *Write-On/Wipe-Off Boards*. Have them trace the uppercase *K* with a finger and then write the letter several times. Then have them do the same for lowercase *k*. Tell children to circle their best *Kk*.

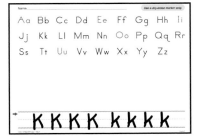

Independent Practice   Distribute drawing paper and show children how to draw the outline shape of a kite. Have children fill the kite shape with *Kk*s. Then have them circle their best *Kk*.

Phonics Resources

Phonics Express™ CD-ROM, Level A, Roamer/Route 1/Fire Station

Phonics Practice Book pages 75–76

▲ **Practice Book page 10**

High-Frequency Word *what* ✓Introduce

OBJECTIVE

To read high-frequency word what

Materials

- *Big Book: Look Closer*
- *Picture Word Cards*
- *High-Frequency Word Card*
- sentence strip
- *Teacher's Resource Book,* p. 139

TEACH/MODEL

Display pages 6–7 of *Look Closer*. Track the print as you read aloud the pages.

Frame the print as you reread the question *What could it be?* Point to the word *What* and say: **This is the word *What*.** Have children say the word.

Display *High-Frequency Word Card what.* Ask: **What word is this?** Point out that the word *What* in the *Big Book* begins with an uppercase letter and the word on the word card begins with a lowercase letter. Have children repeat the question with you. Ask a child to match the *High-Frequency Word Card what* to the word *What* in the Big Book.

PRACTICE/APPLY

Guided Practice   Make copies of the *High-Frequency Word Card what* in the *Teacher's Resource Book*, and give each child a card. Write *What could it be?* on a sentence strip and place it in a pocket chart. Read the question, tracking each word. Ask a child to match the word on the card to the word *What* on the strip. Have children repeat the question. Display several *Picture Word Cards*. Have a child choose a *Picture Word Card*, read the question again, and give the answer. Repeat the activity with the other *Picture Word Cards*.

> **What could it be?**

Independent Practice   Have children add the *High-Frequency Word Card What* to their word files. Then have them use the cards with the words *what, like, you,* and *do* to form the sentence *What do you like?* Children can work with a partner to ask one another this question and respond.

Words to Remember
Word Wall

Reading Words Hold up the *High-Frequency Word Card what* and have children read it aloud. Place the word card under the letter *w* of the classroom word chart.

Find Similarities Have children look closely at their new word *what*. Encourage them to find similarities to other words posted on the chart. Ask the following questions to guide them appropriately:

- **The word *what* has four letters. Do any of our other words have four letters? Let's read the words.** (*like, have*)
- **The word *what* has the letter *a*. Which other words have the letter *a*?** (*a, have*)
- **The word *what* has the letter *t*. Which other words have the letter *t*?** (*the, to*)

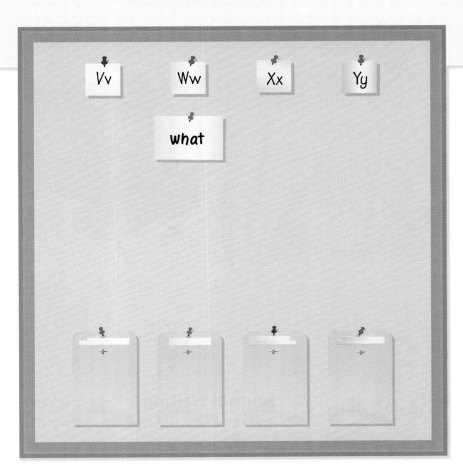

Diagnostic Check: High-Frequency Word

If... children cannot recognize the word *what* and read it in context,

Then... have children spend time looking at the *High-Frequency Word Card what*, saying the word after you, naming the letters in the word, and matching the word on the card to the word in print.

ADDITIONAL SUPPORT ACTIVITIES

BELOW-LEVEL	Reteach, p. S38
ADVANCED	Extend, p. S39
ENGLISH-LANGUAGE LEARNERS	Reteach, p. S39

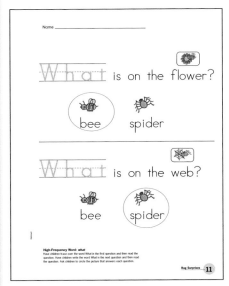

▲ **Practice Book page 11**

Bug Surprises **393**

OBJECTIVES

• *To understand the purpose of a story map*

• *To write a story map*

Materials

■ chart paper

■ marker

Shared Writing

Write a Story Map

BUILD BACKGROUND

Talk About Story Maps   Remind children that a story map tells what happens at the beginning, middle, and ending of a story. Discuss the sequence of story events in "The Ants and the Grasshopper."

Write a Story Map   Draw a story map on chart paper. Ask children to name the events that happened at the beginning, middle, and ending of the "The Ants and the Grasshopper." Record their responses on the chart. Invite children to illustrate the story map.

BEGINNING	MIDDLE	ENDING
Grasshopper played while the ants worked.	When the winter came, Grasshopper had no food.	The ants shared their food with Grasshopper.

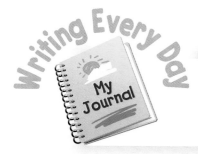

Journal Writing   Have children write and draw about something they do in the winter.

WRAP UP Share Time

Reflect on the Lesson Display the story map children created during Shared Writing for "The Ants and the Grasshopper." Have them use the map to take turns retelling the story. Retell the story more than once so that each child has a chance to participate. Ask children to name the letter they learned. (*Kk*)

S.S.R. *Sustained Silent Reading* Have children read silently from a book of their choice.

Centers — DRAMATIC PLAY

Put on a Play

Have children use the props in the center to act out the story of "The Ants and the Grasshopper." Encourage them to make up dialogue that the characters will say. After some children act out the story, have them switch roles and act it out again.

 Materials

- garden tool props (brooms, shovels)
- watering can
- baskets or paper sacks
- sunglasses
- cardboard fiddle
- winter scarves

Day at a Glance
Day 4

WARM UP

Phonemic Awareness
Phoneme Isolation and Matching

Sharing Literature
Big Book of Rhymes and Songs: *"Fuzzy Wuzzy, Creepy Crawly"*

Read

Big Book of Rhymes and Songs

Harcourt

Develop Concept Vocabulary

Respond to Literature

Literature Focus: Syllables in Words

Phonics
Relating /k/ to *k*

Reading
Decodable Book 1: *Kip the Ant*

Interactive Writing
Describing Words

MORNING MESSAGE
Kindergarten News
(Child's name) just learned how to
_____. (Child's name)
knows how to _____.

Write Kindergarten News   Talk with children about new things they can do and how they learned to do them.

Use prompts such as the following to guide children as you write the news:

- **Tell about something you just learned to do.**
- **Who can show me a word?**
- **How many words are in the first line? in the second line?**

As you write the message, invite children to write letters, names, or words they have previously learned. Remind them to use proper spacing, capitalization, and punctuation.

Calendar Language

Point to and read aloud the names of the seasons of the year. Have children repeat the names with you. Ask: *What season is it now?*

Sunday	Monday	Tuesday	Wednesday	Thursday	Friday	Saturday
		1	2	3	4	5
6	7	8	9	10	11	12
13	14	15	16	17	18	19
20	21	22	23	24	25	26
27	28	29	30	31		

Phonemic Awareness

PHONEME ISOLATION: INITIAL

Listen for /k/ Have children repeat the following sentence after you:

The king is going to Kentucky, and he'll bring a kettle.

King begins with /k/. Say the word *king*. Say the beginning sound in *king*. /k/

Say the word *Kentucky*. What sound does *Kentucky* begin with?

Say the word *kettle*. What sound does *kettle* begin with?

Now say the tongue twister again.

PHONEME MATCHING: INITIAL

Tell children that the king can only bring things to Kentucky whose names begin with the /k/ sound. Say:

Key. The king can bring a key because *key* begins with the /k/ sound. Say the word *key*. Say the tongue twister: The king is going to Kentucky, and he'll bring a key.

Then say the following words. Have children repeat each word and tell whether the king can bring what it names to Kentucky. If he can, have children repeat the tongue twister, inserting the word.

kite (yes)	**kitten** (yes)	**salt** (no)	**kangaroo** (yes)
kit (yes)	**pen** (no)	**kerchief** (yes)	**bat** (no)
Kate (yes)	**Bob** (no)	**Ken** (yes)	**Pete** (no)

▲ "Kicklety Kacklety," *Oo-pples and Boo-noo-noos: Songs and Activities for Phonemic Awareness*, pages 98–99.

REACHING ALL LEARNERS

Diagnostic Check: Phonemic Awareness

If... children cannot isolate and match initial phonemes in words,

Then... focus only on phoneme isolation by saying a word, and having children identify the beginning sound: **What is the beginning sound in** *king*? /k/

ADDITIONAL SUPPORT ACTIVITIES

BELOW-LEVEL	Reteach, p. S40
ADVANCED	Extend, p. S41
ENGLISH-LANGUAGE LEARNERS	Reteach, p. S41

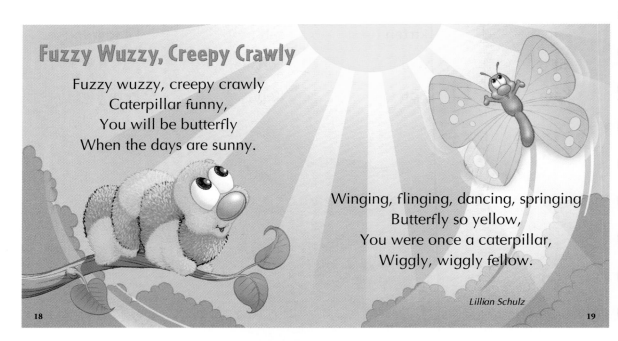

▲ **Big Book of Rhymes and Songs**

OBJECTIVES

- *To "echo read" a short poem*
- *To describe things*
- *To respond to a poem through movement*
- *To recognize syllables in words*

Materials

- *Big Book of Rhymes and Songs* pp. 18–19
- drawing paper
- crayons

Sharing Literature

Read "Fuzzy Wuzzy, Creepy Crawly"

READ ALOUD

Before Reading   Read aloud the title of the poem, "Fuzzy Wuzzy, Creepy Crawly," without displaying the *Big Book of Rhymes and Songs*. Ask children to speculate what the poem might be about. Ask these questions to guide children's thinking:

- **What creeps? What crawls?**
- **Do you know anything that is fuzzy?**

Then display pages 18–19 of the book and tell children that the poem is about a caterpillar turning into a butterfly.

During Reading   Read the poem aloud. As you read,

- track the print.
- emphasize the rhyming words.

Point out that the poem has two parts. Invite one group of children to be the caterpillars and a second group to be the butterflies. Read the poem once more, inviting children in each group to "echo read" each of the lines in their part of the poem. Have the groups switch roles and "echo read" again.

Fuzzy Wuzzy, Creepy Crawly

Fuzzy wuzzy, creepy crawly
Caterpillar funny,
You will be butterfly
When the days are sunny.

Winging, flinging, dancing, springing
Butterfly so yellow,
You were once a caterpillar,
Wiggly, wiggly fellow.

Lillian Schulz

18   19

▲ **Big Book of Rhymes and Songs, pages 18–19**

DEVELOP CONCEPT VOCABULARY

After Reading   Have children listen as you read the poem again. Tell them that the poet used describing words to tell what the caterpillar and the butterfly are like. Write *caterpillar* and *butterfly* side by side on the board. As you say each of the following describing words, ask children to tell whether it describes the caterpillar or the butterfly: *wiggly, fuzzy, yellow, creepy, crawly*. Record the words under the names of the appropriate creatures.

RESPOND TO LITERATURE

Pantomime the Poem   Have children "echo read" the poem again. This time, while one group repeats each line after you, have the other group pantomime the actions of the caterpillar or butterfly, as described in the poem.

Literature Focus

SYLLABLES IN WORDS

Say the word *fuzzy* and ask a child to frame the word in the *Big Book*. Then say it again slowly and clap once for each part in the word. Tell children that the word *fuzzy* has two word parts, or syllables. Repeat the procedure with the words *funny, butterfly, caterpillar*, and *fellow*. Say each word. Have a child frame the word. Repeat the word slowly, emphasizing the syllables, and have children clap once for each of the word parts.

BELOW-LEVEL

Simplify the task so children can grasp the concept. Say one-syllable words, such as *tree, leaf, wing*, and *clap* once. Have children repeat the words and clap the syllables with you. Then continue with two-syllable words.

ENGLISH-LANGUAGE LEARNERS

Show children objects that illustrate the meanings of *fuzzy* and *yellow*; demonstrate actions to show *wiggly, creepy*, and *crawly*. Visit *The Learning Site:* **www.harcourtschool.com**

See LANGUAGE SUPPORT

ONGOING ASSESSMENT

As you share "Fuzzy Wuzzy, Creepy Crawly," note whether children

• can "echo read" short poems.

• respond to a poem through movement.

Day 4

OBJECTIVES
To match consonant k to its sound

Materials

- *Letter and Sound Chart 16*
- *Tactile Letter Card k*
- *Picture Word Cards king, key*
- Kangaroo Pattern, page T17
- scissors
- crayons
- craft stick

Phonics
Relating /k/ to *k*

ACTIVE BEGINNING

Recite "Wait, Kitty Kitty" Teach children the rhyme "Wait, Kitty Kitty." Have them listen for words with /k/ as they repeat the rhyme after you. Then have groups take turns acting out the rhyme and reciting the rhyme.

Wait, Kitty Kitty

Wait, Kitty Kitty.

I need to find my key.

I'll put it in the keyhole.

Now you're in the kitchen. See?

by Susan Little

TEACH/MODEL

Introduce Letter and Sound Display *Letter and Sound Chart 16*.

Touch the letter *K*. **What is the name of this letter?**

This letter stands for the /k/ sound. Say /kk/.

Read the rhyme on the *Letter and Sound Chart* aloud, tracking the print.

Read the *Kk* words in the rhyme aloud. Then point to each *k* and have children say the /k/ sound. Ask: **What letter stands for the /k/ sound?**

Have children join in as you read the rhyme again.

K k

Koala went to see the king.
She met a kangaroo.
He kissed Koala in the kitchen.
The king kissed her, too!

▲ **Letter and Sound Chart 16**

PRACTICE/APPLY

Guided Practice   Distribute *Tactile Letter Card k* to each child. Then place *Picture Word Cards king* and *key* in a pocket chart. Say the names of the pictures as you point to the *k* in each word. Have children repeat the words.

Tell children: **These words begin with *k*.**

Point to the *k* in *king*. **The /k/ sound is at the beginning of *king*.**

Point to the *k* in *key*. **The /k/ sound is at the beginning of *key*.**

I'm going to say some words. If the word begins with the /k/ sound, hold up your *k* card. If the word doesn't begin with the /k/ sound, don't hold up your card.

jump   kind   kit   dig   keep   kid   kitchen

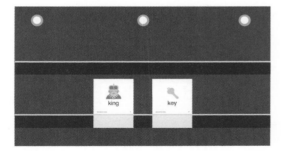

Independent Practice   Distribute copies of the Kangaroo Pattern (page T27). Have children draw and label on the kangaroo a picture of something whose name begins with the /k/ sound. Ask children to whisper their words to you before they draw them. Children can cut out the patterns and tape the kangaroo to a craft stick. Encourage them to take turns naming animals, objects in the classroom, and people's names that begin with *k*.

BELOW-LEVEL

As you introduce the *Letter and Sound Chart*, have children identify each of the characters. (kangaroo, koala, king) After children name each character, have them say the /k/ sound.

ADVANCED

Challenge children to extend their letter-sound knowledge. Ask them to make their own set of picture cards that show things whose names begin with *k*.

Phonics Resources

Phonics Express™ CD-ROM, **Level A,** Roamer/Route 1/Train Station

Phonics Practice Book pages 77–78

▲ **Practice Book page 12**

High-Frequency Words: do, what ✔Review

Read the Decodable Book

OBJECTIVE

To read high-frequency words do, what

Materials

- *Decodable Book 1: Kip the Ant*

- *High-Frequency Word Cards*

- sentence strip

Below • On-Level • Advanced • ELL

BELOW-LEVEL

Reread the sentence strip, *What can Kip do?* with children. Point to the words *do* and *what*. Then reread *Kip the Ant* with children. Have them frame the words *do* and *what*.

ADVANCED

Have children use the frame *What can _____ do?* to write questions with *do* and *what*. Have them use their own names or friends' names to complete the question. Ask children to read their questions to a partner.

TEACH/MODEL

Review High-Frequency Words   Place the *High-Frequency Word Cards do* and *what* in a pocket chart. Point to each word, read it aloud, and have children repeat it after you. Then write *What can Kip do?* on a sentence strip and put it in the pocket chart. Read the question, pointing to each word. Point to each word again, and have children read the question. Ask a volunteer to choose a *High-Frequency Word Card* and match it to the same word in the question.

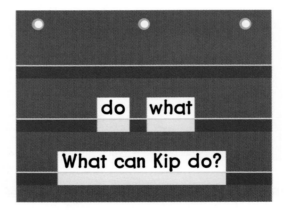

PRACTICE/APPLY

Read the Book   Distribute copies of *Kip the Ant*. Read the title with the children, encouraging them to point to each word as they say it. Have children read the book, pointing to each word as they read.

Respond   Have children draw a picture of something that Kip can do. Ask them to label their pictures.

Decodable Book 1: *Kip the Ant*

What can Kip do?

2

Kip can go.

3

Kip can hit.

4

Kip can dig.

5

Kip can pat.

6

Kip can tap.

7

Kip can nap!

8

■ **High-Frequency Words**

the, do, what, go

■ **Decodable Words**

See Decodable Word List T19.

School–Home Connection

Take-Home Book Version

◄ Decodable Book "Kip the Ant"

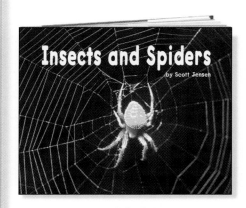

▲ **Insects and Spiders Independent Reader 18**

OBJECTIVES

- *To understand the use of describing words*

- *To write describing words*

Materials

- *Big Book: Look Closer*

- chart paper

- marker

Interactive Writing

Write Describing Words

DISCUSS AND WRITE

Talk About Describing Words   Remind children that describing words can tell how something looks and feels. Recall with children the words that were used in "Fuzzy Wuzzy, Creepy Crawly" to describe the caterpillar (*fuzzy wuzzy, creepy crawly*) and the words that were used to describe the butterfly (*yellow, wiggly*).

Write Describing Words   Tell children that together they will write sentences using describing words to tell about insects.

Allow each child to look through the illustrations in *Look Closer* and to choose a favorite insect to write about. Have children come up to the chart paper to write a sentence using the frame *It is _____*. As each child names an insect, write the name on chart paper. Next to the name, the child can write the words *It is _____*. Then write the word the child has chosen to tell how the insect looks or feels. Talk about letters and sounds in the word as you write. Have the child write his or her name next to the sentence. Read the sentence with the chiildren.

bee
It is yellow and black. Lin

caterpillar
It is fuzzy. Jon

ant
It is black and shiny. Paul.

Writing Every Day

My Journal

Journal Writing   Have children write and draw to describe a caterpillar or butterfly.

WRAP UP Share Time

Reflect on the Lesson Invite children to sit around the Author's Chair. Have children share the new words they learned in the poem "Fuzzy Wuzzy, Creepy Crawly." Display the chart they have written for the Interactive Writing activity. Invite each child to track the sentence he or she has contributed as you read it aloud.

 S.S.R. Have children read silently from a book of their choice.

Centers ABC LETTER AND WORD

Word Factory

Place the *High-Frequency Word Cards* in a box in the center. Children can pull a card from the box, name the word, and count the letters. Then they can use the *Magnetic Letters* to make the word on the cookie sheet. Children can also practice writing the word on drawing paper.

Materials

- box
- *High-Frequency Word Cards my, the, like, you, have, do, what, go, we, on, to*
- *Magnetic Letters*
- cookie sheet
- drawing paper
- crayons

Day at a Glance
Day 5

WARM UP

Phonemic Awareness
Phoneme Deletion

Sharing Literature
Library Book:
Butterfly

Read

Butterfly
by Moira Butterfield
illustrated by Paul Johnson

Respond to Literature

Literature Focus:
Understanding Content
Words

Phonics
Consonants *Bb, Kk*

Writing
Chart

MORNING MESSAGE

Kindergarten News

(Child's name) is my friend.

We like to _____.

Write Kindergarten News Talk with children about their friends. Have them tell about things they like to do with their friends.

Use prompts such as the following to guide children as you write the news:

- **What is your favorite thing to do with your friend?**
- **Where is (child's name) on the page?**
- **Let's listen for the beginning sound in** *my*. **What is it?**
- **Who can show me a space between words?**

As you write the message, invite children to write letters, names, or words they have previously learned. Remind them to use proper spacing, capitalization, and punctuation.

Calendar Language

Point to and read aloud the names of the months of the year. Tell children there are twelve months in a year. Point to and name the month on the calendar. Ask: *What month is it now?*

Sunday	Monday	Tuesday	Wednesday	Thursday	Friday	Saturday
		1	2	3	4	5
6	7	8	9	10	11	12
13	14	15	16	17	18	19
20	21	22	23	24	25	26
27	28	29	30	31		

Phonemic Awareness

PHONEME DELETION

Delete Initial Sounds Tell children to listen as you say the word and then take away the beginning sound. Say:

Big. **Say the word:** *big.* **What would we have if we left the /b/ off the beginning of** *big***? /ig/** *Big* **without the /b/ is** *ig.* **Now you say** *big* **without the /b/.**

Continue with these words:

Say *kit* **without the /k/.** (it)   **Say** *top* **without the /t/.** (op)

Say *bat* **without the /b/.** (at)   **Say** *Kip* **without the /k/.** (ip)

Say *kite* **without the /k/.** (ite)   **Say** *cat* **without the /k/.** (at)

Say *boy* **without the /b/.** (oy)   **Say** *sun* **without the /s/.** (un)

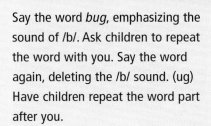

BELOW-LEVEL

Say the word *bug*, emphasizing the sound of /b/. Ask children to repeat the word with you. Say the word again, deleting the /b/ sound. (ug) Have children repeat the word part after you.

▲ **Library Book**

OBJECTIVES

- *To identify the front cover, back cover, and title page of a book*

- *To recall information*

- *To react to details in pictures*

- *To tell the order of events*

- *To understand content words*

Materials

- *Library Book: Butterfly*

Sharing Literature

Read Butterfly

READ ALOUD

Before Reading   Display the cover of *Butterfly* and read aloud the title with children. Ask children to show you the front cover, back cover, and title page of the book. Use these prompts to recall the selection:

- **What is this book about?** (how a butterfly grows and changes)

- **What does a butterfly look like when it hatches from its egg?** (It is a caterpillar.)

Then help children set a purpose for rereading.

MODEL   There are many things that happen to the caterpillar before it becomes a butterfly. Let's read the book again to see all the things that must happen.

During Reading   Reread the selection aloud. As you read,

- point to the picture details that illustrate content vocabulary.

- react to the pictures. Model your thinking.

MODEL   The book says that when the caterpillar grows, its skin gets too tight. I wonder what happens to the old skin. I look at the picture, and I see that the caterpillar gets out of its old skin. It leaves the old skin behind.

- pause to let children talk about what they see in the pictures.

RESPONDING TO LITERATURE

Review the Butterfly Life Cycle Display the cover of *Butterfly*, and use the four pictures to guide children in a discussion of the butterfly life cycle.

★ **Literature Focus**

UNDERSTANDING CONTENT WORDS

Tell children that books that give information, like *Butterfly*, often have special words about the subject. Use these examples:

MODEL When I read about the butterfly eggs, I find out they are laid in a *clump*. In the picture, I see that the tiny eggs are stuck together in a group.

I find out that the caterpillar's body has *segments*. The author tells me what segments are—*lots of little sections in a row*. I can also see from the picture that segments are little parts of the caterpillar.

Follow the same procedure to discuss other content words in the book, such as *sticky silk* and *chrysalis*.

BELOW-LEVEL

Write the words *caterpillar, segments, chrysalis,* and *butterfly* on index cards. As you name each word, help children match each word with a picture in the book *Butterfly* that illustrates its meaning. Then have children match the word cards to pictures independently.

ONGOING ASSESSMENT

As you reread *Butterfly,* note whether children

- can identify the front cover, back cover, and title page of the book.
- recall information.
- react to details in pictures.

Phonics
Consonants
Bb, Kk ✔Review

OBJECTIVES

- *To recognize uppercase and lowercase Bb and Kk*
- *To match sounds to letters*

Materials

- pocket chart

- *Big Alphabet Cards Bb, Kk*

- *Picture Cards baby, bear, boy, bus, kangaroo, key, king, kite*

- *Tactile Letter Cards b, k*

ACTIVE BEGINNING

Share the Rhymes for *B* and *K* Display *Big Alphabet Cards Bb* and *Kk*. Ask children to name each letter and to "write" the letter in the palm of their hands. Then have children sing "Barry Was the Batter," (page 380) and recite "Wait, Kitty Kitty." (page 400)

TEACH/MODEL

Discriminate *B* and *K*
Display *Big Alphabet Card B* in a pocket chart and ask for the letter name.

Point to the picture and say its name. Have children repeat it. (*boy*) **What sound do you hear at the beginning of *boy*? /b/**
What letter stands for the /b/ sound in *boy*? (*b*)

Follow the same procedure for *Big Alphabet Card Kk*.

Place *Picture Cards boy* and *kite* on the chalk ledge. Say each picture name and tell children you need to decide where to put each *Picture Card*.

MODEL **I'll start with the boy. *B—oy* begins with the /b/ sound. So I'll put the picture of the boy below *Bb*.**

Model the same process with the *Picture Card kite*.

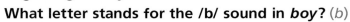

PRACTICE/APPLY

Guided Practice   Place these *Picture Cards* on the chalk ledge: *baby, key, bus, kangaroo, king, bear.* Tell children that they will now sort the pictures.

Say the picture name. **If the beginning sound is /b/, let's put the card below the *Bb*. If the beginning sound is /k/, let's put the card below the *Kk*.**

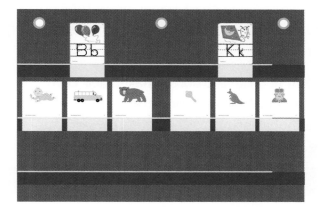

Independent Practice   Have children form two groups. Give each child in one group the *Tactile Letter Card b* and each child in the second group the *Tactile Letter Card k.*

I'm going to say some words. Listen carefully to the sound you hear at the beginning of the word. Think about the letter that stands for that sound. If you are holding that letter, stand up and show me your letter card.

| bird | kiss | boot | barn | koala | best |
| kick | boat | keep | bed | kind | beach |

Diagnostic Check: Phonics

If... children cannot recognize and apply letter/sounds /b/*b* and /k/*k*,

Then... have children focus on one letter/sound at a time. Encourage children to look for pictures whose names begin with /b/ first. Then do the same for the /k/ sound.

ADDITIONAL SUPPORT ACTIVITIES

BELOW-LEVEL	Reteach, p. S42
ADVANCED	Extend, p. S43
ENGLISH-LANGUAGE LEARNERS	Reteach, p. S43

Phonics Resources

Phonics Express™ CD-ROM, **Level A,** Speedy/Route 3/ Market; Speedy/Route 4/Park; Speedy/Route 5/Train Station; Roamer/Route 1/Park; Roamer/Route 2/Train Station; Roamer/Route 3/Harbor

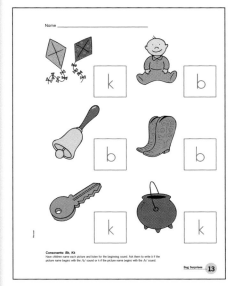

▲ **Practice Book page 13**

OBJECTIVES

- *To understand the purpose of a chart*
- *To write a chart*
- *To sequence events in a chart*

Materials

- *Library Book: Butterfly*
- chart paper
- drawing paper folded in fourths
- crayons

Writing

Write a Chart

DISCUSS BUTTERFLIES

Talk About the Life Cycle of a Butterfly   Page through *Butterfly* and review the four stages of a butterfly's life cycle: *egg, caterpillar, chrysalis, butterfly*. Tell children that a good way to remember information like this is to make a chart.

Display *Butterfly*. On chart paper, draw four boxes and number them *1–4*. Add labels that describe each stage: *egg, caterpillar, chrysalis,* and *butterfly*.

Write Charts   Have children make their own charts. Distribute the paper folded in fourths. Using the book cover as a model, children should number each box *1–4* and draw each stage of the butterfly's life cycle. Have them add labels to their chart.

Journal Writing   Have children write about self-selected topics in their journals.

WRAP UP Share Time

Reflect on the Lesson   Ask children to look at the charts they made during the Writing activity and to talk about the part of *Butterfly* that surprised them most. What did they learn that they didn't know before?

S.S.R.   Have children read silently from a book of their choice.

Centers 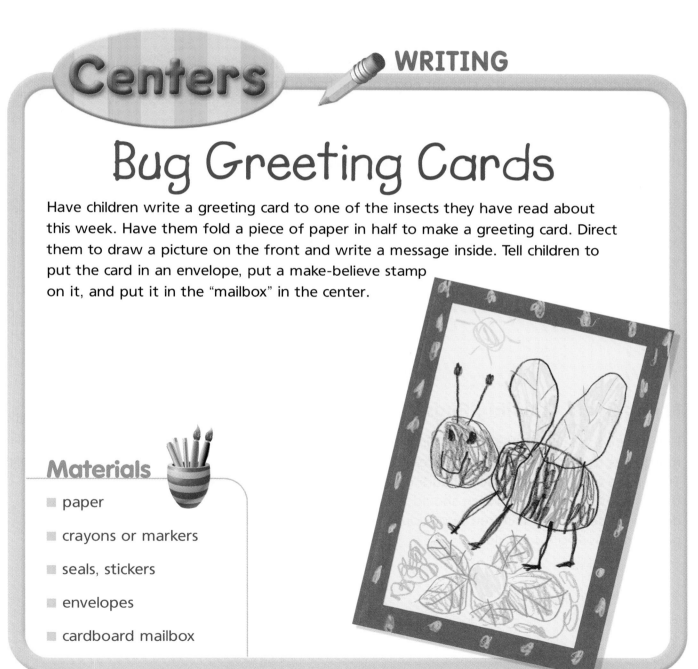 WRITING

Bug Greeting Cards

Have children write a greeting card to one of the insects they have read about this week. Have them fold a piece of paper in half to make a greeting card. Direct them to draw a picture on the front and write a message inside. Tell children to put the card in an envelope, put a make-believe stamp on it, and put it in the "mailbox" in the center.

Materials

■ paper

■ crayons or markers

■ seals, stickers

■ envelopes

■ cardboard mailbox

Learning Centers

Choose from the following suggestions to enhance your learning centers for the theme Bug Surprises.
(Additional learning centers for this theme can be found on pages 354–356 and 460)

ART CENTER

Make a Butterfly

Give each child a sheet of paper and have them fold it in half. Then have children place the straight edge of the half-butterfly shape paper along the fold of their paper. Have children trace everything except the straight edge and cut along the trace marks. Then have children unfold their paper to reveal a butterfly. Children can decorate their butterflies with colorful patterns.

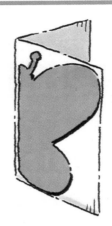

20 Minutes

Materials

- paper
- shape paper of half a butterfly (page T27)
- safety scissors
- crayons or markers

SCIENCE CENTER

Flying Bugs, Crawling Bugs

Have children play a sorting game. First, have children look through magazines to find and cut out pictures of different kinds of bugs. Then have children paste each picture on an index card and combine the cards into one pile. Children should take turns choosing a card and deciding whether the pictured bug should be placed in a "flying bugs" pile or a "crawling bugs" pile.

20 Minutes

Materials

- old magazines
- safety scissors
- index cards

Teacher Notes

Week 2

Bug Surprises

Day 1

 ORAL LANGUAGE — 15-30 Minutes

- **Phonemic Awareness**

Phonemic Awareness, 421
Phoneme Isolation and Matching: Medial

- **Sharing Literature**

Sharing Literature, 422
 Read

Big Book: *Look Closer*

(Skill) **Literature Focus, 423**
Text Patterns

 LEARNING TO READ — 45 Minutes

- **Phonics**

, **424** T
Introduce: Short Vowel *Oo*
Identify/Write T

- **Vocabulary**

Daily Routines
- **Morning Message**
- **Calendar Language**
- **Writing Prompt**

LANGUAGE ARTS — 15-30 Minutes

- **Writing**
  Daily Writing Prompt

 Writing, 426
Write Sentences

Writing Prompt, 426
Draw and write about self-selected topics.

Share Time, 427
Share sentences.

Day 2

Phonemic Awareness, 429
Phoneme Segmentation

Sharing Literature, 430
Library Book: *Wonderful Worms*

(Skill) **Literature Focus, 431**
Main Idea/Details

, **432** T
Relating /o/ to *o* T

 Interactive Writing, 434
Write Questions

Writing Prompt, 434
Draw and write about things that grow in a garden.

Share Time, 435
 Read

Share and answer questions about worms.

T = **tested skill**

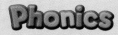

Phonics

Short Vowel *Oo*;
Blending /o/ - /t/

Focus of the Week:
- **PHONEMIC AWARENESS**
- **SHARING LITERATURE**
- **WRITING: Sentences, Questions, Messages, Dialogue**

Day 3

Phonemic Awareness, 437
Phoneme Blending

Sharing Literature, 438

Read

Read-Aloud Anthology:
"Anansi and the Biggest,
Sweetest Melon," p. 104

(Skill) **Literature Focus, 439**
Retelling the Story

 Phonics, 440 T
Blending /o/ - /t/

 **Shared Writing, 442**
Write a Message

Writing Prompt, 442
Draw and write about favorite fruits.

Share Time, 443
Share favorite parts of "Anansi and the Biggest, Sweetest Melon."

Day 4

Phonemic Awareness, 445
Phoneme Isolation: Final

Sharing Literature, 446
Big Book of Rhymes and
Songs: "When It Comes
to Bugs," p. 17

(Skill) **Literature Focus, 447**
Making Inferences

Phonics, 448 T
Review: Short Vowel /o/*o*

Read
DECODABLE BOOK 2
The Big Ram

Interactive Writing, 450
Write Action Words

Writing Prompt, 450
Draw and write about pets.

Share Time, 451
Discuss *The Big Ram*.

Day 5

Phonemic Awareness, 453
Phoneme Segmentation

Sharing Literature, 454

Read

Big Book: *Look Closer*

(Skill) **Literature Focus, 455**
End Punctuation

Phonics, 456 T
Words with /o/ and /t/

 Writing, 458
Write Dialogue

Writing Prompt, 458
Draw and write about self-selected topics.

Share Time, 459
Share a favorite part of the lesson.

WARM UP

Phonemic Awareness

Phoneme Isolation and Matching: Medial

Sharing Literature

Big Book:
Look Closer

Read

Brian and Rebecca Wildsmith
Look Closer

Develop Concept Vocabulary

Respond to Literature

Literature Focus: Text Patterns

Phonics

Short Vowel *Oo*

Writing

Sentences

ORAL LANGUAGE

MORNING MESSAGE

Kindergarten News

Today is _____.

After school (Child's name) will

go _____.

Write Kindergarten News Talk with children about where they will go and what they will do after school today.

Use prompts such as the following to guide children as you write the news:

- **Where do you go after school?**
- **What letter did I write first in _____'s name?**
- **Who can show me a word?**
- **Let's clap for each syllable in the word** *after*. **How many parts do you clap?**

As you write the message, invite children to write letters, names, or words they have previously learned. Remind them to use proper spacing, capitalization, and punctuation.

Calendar Language

Point to and read aloud the names of the days of the week. Ask what day today is. Ask children what day comes before today. Point to the name of the day and say: *Yesterday was _____.* **Call on children to name yesterday and today.**

Sunday	Monday	Tuesday	Wednesday	Thursday	Friday	Saturday
		1	2	3	4	5
6	7	8	9	10	11	12
13	14	15	16	17	18	19
20	21	22	23	24	25	26
27	28	29	30	31		

Phonemic Awareness

PHONEME ISOLATION: MEDIAL

Isolate Medial Sounds   Say the following words and have children repeat them: *top, fox, lot*. Then say:

Top, fox, lot. I listen for the middle sound in each word. *Top* has the /o/ sound in the middle. *Fox* has the /o/ sound in the middle. *Lot* has the /o/ sound in the middle. *Top, fox, lot.* I hear the /o/ sound in the middle of *top, fox,* and *lot. Top, fox,* and *lot* have the same middle sound. Say *top, fox,* and *lot* with me.

For each of the following sets of words, have children repeat the words and isolate and say the middle sound.

pan, cap, hat (/a/)   mud, cub, drum (/u/)   lid, pig, win (/i/)

dot, shop, job (/o/)   stop, cob, not (/o/)   top, fox, hot (/o/)

▲ **"Apples and Bananas,"** *Oo-pples and Boo-noo-noos: Songs and Activities for Phonemic Awareness,* page 55–56.

PHONEME MATCHING: MEDIAL

Match Medial Sounds   Say the following words and have children repeat them: *fox, cap, hot*. Then say:

Fox, cap, hot. I listen for the middle sound in each word. *Fox* has the /o/ sound in the middle. *Cap* has the /a/ sound in the middle. *Hot* has the /o/ sound in the middle. *Fox, cap, hot.* I hear the the /o/ sound in the middle of *fox* and *hot*. The words *fox* and *hot* have the same middle sound. Say *fox, hot* with me.

For each of the following sets of words, ask: **Which two words have the same middle sound? What is that sound?**

box, got, red (box, got; /o/)   wet, rock, hot (rock, hot; /o/)

hop, sat, shop (hop, shop; /o/)   wag, dot, lock (dot, lock; /o/)

BELOW-LEVEL

Focus on isolating and identifying only the medial sound. As you say two words, elongate the medial sound, /p/ /oo/ /t/, /s/ /oo/ /k/. Have children repeat the sounds, identify the middle sound, /o/, and then say the words *pot* and *sock* naturally.

ADVANCED

Challenge children to extend the skill. Have them think of more words with the middle sound /o/.

Sharing Literature

Read *Wonderful Worms*

READ ALOUD

Before Reading Display the cover of *Wonderful Worms* and read aloud the title as you track the print. Frame and read the word *Wonderful.* Ask children if they know what this word means. (great, super, terrific) After children respond to the title, ask them how the author feels about worms. Page through the book, sharing the illustrations with children. Invite them to comment on what they see. Use the following prompts to set a purpose for reading the book.

- **Have you ever seen a worm? Where did you see it?**
- **What do you want to learn about worms?**

During Reading Read the selection aloud. As you read,

- pause periodically to point out picture details.

MODEL The words give me information about worms from the words. But I can get information from the pictures, too. I find out that moles like to eat worms. I know that because I see a mole with a worm in its mouth.

- mention that the boy in the story is giving the information.

▲ **Library Book**

OBJECTIVES

- *To listen and respond to a nonfiction selection*
- *To ask and answer questions about a text*
- *To recall facts*
- *To understand main idea and details*

Materials

- *Library Book: Wonderful Worms*
- drawing paper
- crayons

WRAP UP # Share Time

Reflect on the Lesson Post and read aloud children's written questions about worms, from Interactive Writing. Use the additional information at the back of *Wonderful Worms* to provide answers.

S.S.R. *Sustained Silent Reading* Have children read silently from a book of their choice.

Centers SCIENCE

Bug Models

Have children use recyclable materials to make models of different bugs. Children can make bugs they have read about so far in this theme, or they can make other bugs they know about. Have children write the name of their bug and display the model and its label in the Science Center.

Materials

- fabric scraps
- straws
- chenille sticks
- clay
- markers
- glue
- egg cartons
- clothespins

Day at a Glance
Day 3

WARM UP

Phonemic Awareness
Phoneme Blending

Sharing Literature
Read-Aloud Anthology:
"Anansi and the Biggest,
Sweetest Melon"

Read

Develop Listening Comprehension

Respond to Literature

Literature Focus:
Retelling the Story

Phonics
Blending *o–t*

Shared Writing
Message

MORNING MESSAGE

Kindergarten News

In our class we should _____.

In our class we should not

_____.

Write Kindergarten News Talk with children about classroom rules, such as taking turns, sharing, helping others.

Use prompts such as the following to guide children as you write the news:

- **What are some of the rules in our classroom?**
- **Who can show me the word *we*?**
- **How many words are in the first line?**

As you write the message, invite children to write letters, names, or words they have previously learned. Remind them to use proper spacing, capitalization, and punctuation.

Calendar Language

Have children identify the day of the week. Then ask them to name class activities for the day.

Sunday	Monday	Tuesday	Wednesday	Thursday	Friday	Saturday
		1	2	3	4	5
6	7	8	9	10	11	12
13	14	15	16	17	18	19
20	21	22	23	24	25	26
27	28	29	30	31		

Phonemic Awareness

PHONEME SEGMENTATION

Segment Words into Phonemes   Use the rabbit puppet for this segmenting activity.

MODEL   The rabbit likes to take words apart and say them sound by sound. Say the word *dot*. Listen to the rabbit say it: /d/ /o/ /t/. Now say the word again by repeating the sounds the rabbit says: /d/ /o/ /t/. *Dot.* Now the rabbit wants to say a word and have you say the word sound by sound.

Say the following words. Have children repeat each word, sound by sound. Then have the rabbit segment the sounds so children will know if they are correct.

got (/g/ /o/ /t/)	**pot** (/p/ /o/ /t/)	**box** (/b/ /o/ /ks/)
hop (/h/ /o/ /p/)	**hot** (/h/ /o/ /t/)	**not** (/n/ /o/ /t/)
ox (/o/ /ks/)	**mop** (/m/ /o/ /p/)	**fox** (/f/ /o/ /ks/)
on (/o/ /n/)	**lot** (/l/ /o/ /t/)	**cot** (/k/ /o/ /t/)

Day at a Glance
Day I

WARM UP

Phonemic Awareness
Phoneme Counting

Sharing Literature
Library Book: Wonderful Worms

Read

WONDERFUL WORMS
BY LINDA GLASER
PICTURES BY LORETTA KRUPINSKI

Develop Concept Vocabulary

Respond to Literature

Literature Focus: Summarize

Phonics

Consonant /p/*p*,
   Short Vowel /o/*o*

Interactive Writing ✏

Writing Process: Prewrite

MORNING MESSAGE

Kindergarten News

(Child's name) likes to _____

outside. (Child's name) likes

to _____ outside.

Write Kindergarten News Talk with children about what they like to do outdoors. Ask why the things they suggest are so much fun to do.

Use prompts such as the following to guide children as you write the news:

• **Tell about something you like to do outdoors.**

• **Who can show me the letters in (child's name)?**

• **Let's clap syllables for the word *outside*. How many word parts do you clap?**

• **Who can show me the word *to*?**

As you write the message, invite children to contribute by writing letters, names, or words they have previously learned. Remind them to use proper spacing, capitalization, and punctuation.

Calendar Language

Point to and read aloud the days of the week. Tell children you will name the weekend days. Point to and read aloud *Saturday* and *Sunday*. Ask children to repeat the weekend days.

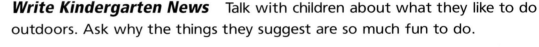

Sunday	Monday	Tuesday	Wednesday	Thursday	Friday	Saturday
		1	2	3	4	5
6	7	8	9	10	11	12
13	14	15	16	17	18	19
20	21	22	23	24	25	26
27	28	29	30	31		

DEVELOP CONCEPT VOCABULARY

After Reading   Read the words that Caterpillar shouts:

I am a great warrior, son of the long one! I crush the rhinoceros to the earth, and I make dust of the elephant. I am invincible!

Use the following procedure to discuss some of the words:

Say *warrior*. A warrior is a fighter. What is a warrior? Have children answer the question in a complete sentence.

Say *invincible*. *Invincible* means "cannot be beaten." What does *invincible* mean? Have children answer the question in a complete sentence.

RESPOND TO LITERATURE

Act Out the Story   Have children take turns playing each character. Put a blanket over a chair to serve as the log. The child who plays Caterpillar should hide under the blanket and use a cardboard tube to say the words in a loud voice.

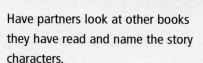

ADVANCED

Have partners look at other books they have read and name the story characters.

ONGOING ASSESSMENT

As you share "The Fearsome Beast," note whether children

• make predictions.

• listen and respond to the story.

Literature Focus

CHARACTERS

Remind children that characters are the people or animals in a story. As children recall the names of the characters in "The Fearsome Beast," record the character names on chart paper. Then give the following clues and have children name each character you are describing.

• **He has a house in a hollow log.** (Rabbit)

• **He says "Borooommm! Borooommm!"** (Frog)

• **He crawls into the hollow log.** (Caterpillar)

• **He growls at the beast in the log.** (Leopard)

• **He leaves fast so he will not be crushed by the beast in the log.** (Rhinoceros)

• **He stomps away from the log so he will not be trampled.** (Elephant)

OBJECTIVES

- *To identify and recognize the initial sound of a spoken word*

- *To blend /o/ and /p/*

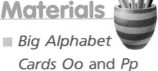

Materials

- *Big Alphabet Cards Oo and Pp*

- *Alphabet Cards o, p, m*

- pocket chart

- index cards

Phonics

Blending /o/ – /p/  Review

ACTIVE BEGINNING

Word Hunt   Have children sit in a circle. As you read the following verse, have the children echo. Establish a beat and keep it going throughout the verse.

Going on a word hunt.

What is this word?

/m/ /o/ /p/

Together: Mop!

Continue with the words /h/ /o/ /p/ (*hop*), /t/ /o/ /p/ (*top*), /p/ /o/ /t/ (*pot*).

TEACH/MODEL

Recognize *o* and *p*   Display *Big Alphabet Card Oo* on the chalk ledge or in a pocket chart.

What letter is this? (*o*)

What sound does this letter stand for? (/o/)

Have children say /o/ with you as you point to the letter.

Do the same procedure for *Big Alphabet Card Pp*.

Word Blending   Explain to children that they are going to blend the two letters together to read words, such as *mop*.

- Place the *Alphabet Cards m, o, p* in the pocket chart, separate from each other.

- Point to *m.* Say **/mm/.** Have children repeat the sound after you.
- Point to *o.* Say **/oo/.** Have children repeat the sound after you.
- Point to *p.* Say **/pp/.** Have children repeat the sound after you.

- Slide the *o* next to *m*. Move your hand under the letters and blend the sounds, elongating them: **/mmoo/**. Have children blend the sounds after you.

- Slide the *p* next to the *mo*. Move your hand under the letters and blend the sounds, elongating them: **/mmoopp/**. Have children repeat after you. Then have children read *mop* with you.

PRACTICE/APPLY

Guided Practice Place the letters *h*, *o*, and *p* in the pocket chart.

- Point to *h* and say **/hh/**. Point to the letter *o* and say **/oo/**. Slide the *o* next to *h*. Move your hand under the letters and blend the sounds, elongating them: **/hhoo/**. Have children blend the sounds after you.
- Point to *p*. Say **/pp/**. Have children say the sound.
- Slide the *p* next to the *ho*. Slide your hand under *hop* and blend the sounds. Have children blend the sounds as you slide your hand under the word.
- Then have children read the word *hop* along with you.

Follow the same procedure to build and blend *top* and *pot* with children.

Independent Practice Write the words *mop, hop, top,* and *pop* on index cards and place them in a pocket chart in the Letters and Words Center. Ask children to point to each letter and blend the sounds to read the words.

▲ **Practice Book page 20**

OBJECTIVES

- *To write the first draft of a class book*

- *To apply concepts of print to a writing activity*

Materials

■ chart paper

■ marker

Writing Process

Write a Wall Book

DRAFT

Review the Topic   Tell children that they are going to write a class book like *Look Closer.* Read aloud children's ideas in the idea web. Then help them choose one to write about first. Model how to make a page for the book.

> **MODEL**   Let's look at the first page in *Look Closer*. The ladybug is the first insect in the story. In which place from our idea web would we find a ladybug? We would find a ladybug on a tree. Now we can replace the words *stone wall* with the word *tree*. Let's write the words together.

Write Sentences   On chart paper, write the sentence frame: *I pass a _____ and I see something move. What can it be?* Invite children to contribute by writing letters and words they have previously learned. Ask questions such as these:

- **On the first page of our book, what should the words be? Where should I start writing?**

- **Which word is always an uppercase letter?**

- **In which place from our web would we find the next insect?**

- **What question will we always ask on each page? Who would like to frame it in the *Big Book*?**

- **What end mark do we put at the end of a question? Who can write it?**

Continue using separate pieces of chart paper to have children help you write and complete the sentence frame with a place from the web for each insect in the book.

I pass a porch
and I see
something move.

What can it be?

Journal Writing   Have children write and draw about a scary day.

WRAP UP # Share Time

Reflect on the Lesson Ask children to talk about their favorite part of the story "The Fearsome Beast." Have them think of how they would have reacted to the "fearsome beast" in the log.

S.S.R. *Sustained Silent Reading* Have children read silently from a book of their choice.

Centers ABC LETTERS AND WORDS

Letter Games

Have children sort the *Picture Cards* by the letter sound they hear at the beginning of each picture name. After they sort the pictures, have children write the letters *b, h, k, l* on index cards and place them on the appropriate pile of picture cards.

Materials

■ *Picture Cards*
baby, bear, boy, bus,
hat, helicopter, hen,
horse, kangaroo, key,
king, kite, ladder, lamb,
lemon, lunch box

■ index cards

■ markers

Day at a Glance
Day 3

WARM UP

Phonemic Awareness
Phoneme Substitution

Sharing Literature
Big Book:
Look Closer

Read

Brian and Rebecca Wildsmith
Look Closer

Respond to Literature

Literature Focus:
Naming Words

Phonics
Words with /o/ and /p/

Interactive Writing
Writing Process: Respond and Revise

MORNING MESSAGE

Kindergarten News

(Child's name) went to _____.

(Child's name) went to _____.

Write Kindergarten News Talk with children about trips they have taken. Ask how they traveled and what they did on their trips.

Use prompts such as the following to guide children as you write the news:

- **Where did you go on your trip?**
- **Who can name the beginning sound in (child's name)?**
- **Who can show me a letter?**
- **Who can show me a word?**

As you write the message, invite children to contribute by writing letters, words, or names they have learned previously. Remind them to use proper spacing, capitalization, and punctuation.

Calendar Language

Point to and read aloud the names of the months of the year. Have children say the first month of the year. (January) **Have them say the last month of the year.** (December)

Sunday	Monday	Tuesday	Wednesday	Thursday	Friday	Saturday
		1	2	3	4	5
6	7	8	9	10	11	12
13	14	15	16	17	18	19
20	21	22	23	24	25	26
27	28	29	30	31		

Phonemic Awareness

PHONEME SUBSTITUTION

Substitute Initial Sounds Tell children that you are going to play a word game. Show them how the game is played. Say:

Hop. **Say the word with me:** *hop.* **What word would we have if we changed the /h/ in** *hop* **to /m/?** *Mop.* **The new word is** *mop.* **Say it with me:** *mop.*

Use the following examples and ask children to say the new words.

Say *cat.* **Change the /k/ to /s/.** (*sat*)

Say *fig.* **Change the /f/ to /b/.** (*big*)

Say *sock.* **Change the /s/ to /r/.** (*rock*)

Say *got.* **Change the /g/ to /h/.** (*hot*)

Say *pin.* **Change the /p/ to /w/.** (*win*)

Say *top.* **Change the /t/ to /p/.** (*pop*)

Say *job.* **Change the /j/ to /k/.** (*cob*)

Say *wet.* **Change the /w/ to /g/.** (*get*)

Say *pack.* **Change the /p/ to /t/.** (*tack*)

▲ "Fooba-Wooba John," *Oo-pples and Boo-noo-noos: Songs and Activities for Phonemic Awareness*, pages 72–73.

BELOW-LEVEL

Assign each of four children the sounds /n/, /d/, /o/, and /t/. Have the children with the sounds /n/, /o/, /t/ stand in a row and say the sounds in sequence to produce the word *not*. Then have the "/n/ child" step aside and let the "/d/ child" stand in. Have children say their sounds again, this time producing the word *dot*.

▲ **Big Book**

OBJECTIVES

- *To understand that sentences are made up of words*

- *To distinguish real and make-believe*

- *To understand naming words*

Materials

- *Big Book: Look Closer*

- drawing paper

- crayons

- chart paper

- marker

Sharing Literature

Read Look Closer

READ ALOUD

Before Reading Display *Look Closer* and track the print as you read the title aloud. Tell children that the insect on the cover is a dragonfly and the flower is a pond lily. Then use these prompts to set a purpose for rereading the selection:

- **What are some of the plants and flowers named in this selection?** (thistles, wild roses, poppies, grass)

- **Where are all the insects going at the end of the book?** (home)

During Reading Reread the story aloud. As you read,

- track the print of the repetitive text on each page.

- frame the words that make up sentences.

- talk about the real events in the book. Pause periodically to talk about how you know the story tells about real things. Begin by modeling the thought process for children after reading pages 6–8:

MODEL I want to know if this story is about something real, so I ask myself: Could a person take a walk past a wall? Could a person see a ladybug on the wall? Would real ladybugs crawl on a wall? The answer to all of these questions is yes. So I know this story is about something real, not make-believe.

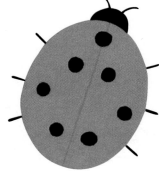

RESPOND TO LITERATURE

Look Closer Game   Use color words and describing words to describe something in the classroom. Then ask **What could it be?** Invite the child who guesses correctly to provide the next set of clues and to ask the question.

NAMING WORDS

Display page 8 of *Look Closer*. Point to the word *Ladybugs* and read it. Tell children that this word names a kind of insect. Remind them that words that name a person, animal, place, or thing are called naming words. Tell children an insect is an animal. Page through the *Big Book* and help children identify other words that name animals and things. Create a word web on chart paper. As children name an animal, add it to the word web. Read each naming word you write and have children repeat it.

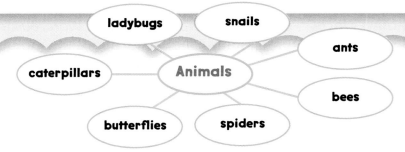

BELOW-LEVEL

Gather some classroom objects on a table. Hold up an object, such as a pencil, and have children name it. Write the word *pencil* and tell children that it is a naming word. Repeat the procedure with the other objects on the table.

ADVANCED

Provide children with self-stick notes. Have them work in pairs to write labels for naming words in the classroom and to attach the labels to the objects.

ONGOING ASSESSMENT

As you share *Look Closer,* note whether children

- understand that sentences are made up of words.
- can distinguish real and make-believe.

OBJECTIVES

- *To build and read simple one-syllable words*
- *To understand that as the letters of words change, so do the sounds*

Materials

- ■ *Alphabet Cards h, m, o, p, t*
- ■ *Word Builders*
- ■ *Word Builder Cards h, m, o, p, t*
- ■ *pocket chart*
- ■ *Magnetic Letters*
- ■ *cookie sheet*

REVIEW LETTERS

Phonics
Words with /o/ and /p/

ACTIVE BEGINNING

Action Rhyme Teach children this rhyme and the actions that go with it:

> **Hop, hop, hop.**
> (Hop up and down.)
>
> **Put your hand on top.**
> (Put hand on head.)
>
> **Mop, mop, mop.**
> (Pretend to clean with a mop.)
>
> **Now you can stop!**
> (Sit down in place.)

TEACH/MODEL

Blending Words Distribute *Word Builders* and *Word Builder Cards h, m, o, p, t* to children. As you place *Alphabet Cards* in a pocket chart, tell children to place the same *Word Builder Cards* in their *Word Builders*.

- Place *Alphabet Cards t, o,* and *p* in the pocket chart. Have children do the same.

- Point to *t*. Say **/tt/**. Point to *o*. Say **/oo/**.
- Slide the *o* next to the *t*. Then move your hand under the letters and blend the sounds, elongating them: **/ttoo/**. Have children do the same.

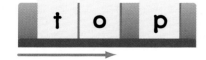

- Point to the letter *p*. Say **/pp/**. Have children do the same.
- Slide the *p* next to the *to*. Slide your hands under *top* and blend by elongating the sounds: **/ttoopp/**. Have children do the same.
- Then have children read the word *top* along with you.

PRACTICE/APPLY

Guided Practice Have children continue to build and read new words. Have them place *Word Builder Cards* o and p in their *Word Builders*.

- **Add *m* to *op*. What word did you make?**

- **Change *m* to *h*. What word did you make?**

- **Change *p* to *t*. What word did you make?**

- **Change *h* to *p*. What word did you make?**

Independent Practice Have children use the *Magnetic Letters h, m, o, p, t* in the Letters and Words Center to build and read *top, hop, mop, hot, pot*.

 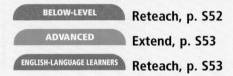

▲ **Practice Book page 21**

OBJECTIVES

- *To improve a group writing piece through rereading and revising*

Writing Process

Write a Wall Book

RESPOND AND REVISE

Reread the Pages   Reread the sentences on each page, tracking the print. Ask questions such as the following:

- **I've read the sentence and questions in our book. What is missing?** (Possible responses: the answers; the insects) **Let's add those on separate pieces of paper.** Have children help you revise the book by helping you write the missing answers on paper. As you write each answer, tape the top of each piece of chart paper with the corresponding sentence and question over the answer. Then reread the top page and flip it up to see the answer.

- **Is there anything else we should add to our story?**

- **Are the words written in the right way for each page?**

- **Would you like to change any of the words we used?**

- **Who would like to help me write the title?**

Make Revisions   Use correction tape and a marker to replace words that children suggest should be changed. After the changes are made on each page, reread it to children.

I pass a porch
and I see
something move.

What can it be?

Butterflies

Journal Writing   Have children write and draw about a place where they see insects.

WRAP UP # Share Time

Author's Chair   Have children talk about the part of today's lesson they most enjoyed.

S.S.R. Sustained Silent Reading   Have children read silently from a book of their choice.

Centers   ART

Insect Models

Have children make clay models of their favorite insect from the theme. Children can look at the pictures in *Look Closer, Butterfly* and *Wonderful Worms* to review the details of the insect they want to make. When their insect model is complete, have children write the name of the insect on an index card and place it next to their clay model.

Materials

- books and magazines about insects
- modeling clay
- index cards
- crayons

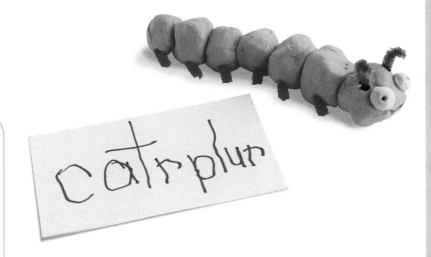

WARM UP

Phonemic Awareness
Phoneme Substitution

Sharing Literature
Big Book of Rhymes and Songs: "Eency Weency Spider"

Read

Big Book of Rhymes and Songs

Respond to Literature

Literature Focus: Matching Words

Reading
Decodable Book 3: What Can Hop?

Interactive Writing ✏️
Writing Process: Proofread

MORNING MESSAGE

Kindergarten News

The date today is _____.

(Child's name) likes to wear _____.

Write Kindergarten News Talk with children about their favorite things to wear.

Use prompts such as the following to guide children as you write the news:

- **What are some of your favorite things to wear?**
- **Who can show me spaces between words?**
- **What letter should I write first in the word *date*?**
- **Who can point to where to begin reading?**

As you write the message, invite children to contribute by writing letters, names, or words they have previously learned. Remind them to use proper spacing, capitalization, and punctuation.

Calendar Language

Point to the numbers on the calendar. Tell children that the numbers tell the date. Point to and read aloud today's date. Name the month and the date.

Sunday	Monday	Tuesday	Wednesday	Thursday	Friday	Saturday
		1	2	3	4	5
6	7	8	9	10	11	12
13	14	15	16	17	18	19
20	21	22	23	24	25	26
27	28	29	30	31		

Phonemic Awareness

PHONEME SUBSTITUTION

Substitute Final Sounds   Tell children that you are going to play a word game. Show them how the game is played. Say:

Log. **Say the word with me:** *log.*

What word would we have if we changed the /g/ in *log* **to /t/?** *Lot.* **The new word is** *lot.* **Say it with me:** *lot.*

Use the following examples and ask children to say the new words.

Say *rug.* **Change the /g/ to /n/.** (*run*)

Say *dog.* **Change the /g/ to /t/.** (*dot*)

Say *pen.* **Change the /n/ to /t/.** (*pet*)

Say *sit.* **Change the /t/ to /p/.** (*sip*)

Say *lip.* **Change the /p/ to /t/.** (*lit*)

Say *sob.* **Change the /b/ to /k/.** (*sock*)

Say *bed.* **Change the /d/ to /t/.** (*bet*)

Say *mat.* **Change the /t/ to /d/.** (*mad*)

Say *hop.* **Change the /p/ to /t/.** (*hot*)

ADVANCED

Have children name the pictures on *Picture Cards bus, cat, hat, pig, rain,* and *seal.* Then have them change the last letter of each name to make a new word.

▲ **Big Book of Rhymes and Songs**

OBJECTIVES

- *To sing a song*
- *To identify rhyming words*
- *To retell the order of events in a song*

Materials

- *Big Book of Rhymes and Songs* p. 20
- *Music CD*
- scissors
- drawing paper
- glue
- crayons
- sentence strips

Sharing Literature

Read "Eency Weency Spider"

READ ALOUD

Before Reading   Display the song "Eency Weency Spider," on page 20 of the *Big Book of Rhymes and Songs*. Read the title aloud as you track the print. Then use these prompts to build background:

- **What do you know about spiders?**
- **How many of you know this song?**

Play the song on the *Music CD* and demonstrate the hand movements.

During Reading   Read the words to the song. As you read,

- track the print.
- emphasize the rhyming words.

Play the song on the *Music CD* as you demonstrate the hand movements again. Sing the song again and have children join in.

Eency Weency
Spider

The eency weency spider
went up the water spout.
Down came the rain
and washed the spider out.
Out came the sun
and dried up all the rain,
And the eency weency spider
went up the spout again.

RESPOND TO LITERATURE

Make Songbooks   Talk with children about the order of events in the song. Have children fold a sheet of drawing paper in half twice and use the four sections to make a book. Have children draw a picture to go with each event: the spider climbing up the spout, the rain washing the spider down, the sun coming out, the spider crawling back up the spout. Help children cut out the four boxes, place them in order, and staple them together to make a book. Children can use their books to sing or recite the rhyme again.

Literature Focus

MATCHING WORDS

Make pairs of sentence strips for the first two lines of "Eency Weency Spider." Cut one strip into individual words and give each word to a child. Then read each sentence strip and have children match their words to those on the strip. Remind children that sentences are made up of separate words.

REACHING ALL LEARNERS

Diagnostic Check: Comprehension

If... children are unable to match words to those in text,

Then... use two sets of word cards and have children match word to word before matching to the word within the text.

ADDITIONAL SUPPORT ACTIVITIES

BELOW-LEVEL	Reteach, p. S54
ADVANCED	Extend, p. S55
ENGLISH-LANGUAGE LEARNERS	Reteach, p. S55

ONGOING ASSESSMENT

As you share "Eency Weency Spider," note whether children

- sing the song.
- can identify rhyming words.
- can retell the order of events in the song.

OBJECTIVE

To decode short vowel /o/o words

Materials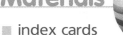

- index cards
- pocket chart
- *High-Frequency Word Card A*
- *Picture Cards fish, kangaroo*
- *Decodable Book 3: What Can Hop?*
- drawing paper
- crayons

ENGLISH-LANGUAGE LEARNERS

Point to the picture on each page and provide the animal name. Have children find the animal name on the page, point to it, and read the word.

Phonics

Short Vowel /o/o  Review

TEACH/MODEL

Decode Words Write the word *hop* on an index card and place it in a pocket chart. Say:

Let's read this word together.

Move your hand under the letters, blend them, and say **/hhoopp/.** Have children blend the sounds to read the word. Repeat the procedure for the word *not*.

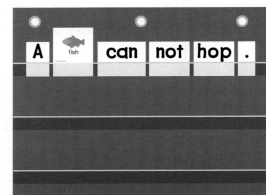

Place the *High-Frequency Word Card A* in the pocket chart, followed by *Picture Card fish*, the word *can* written on an index card, and the words *not* and *hop*. Track the print as you have children read the sentence: **A fish can not hop.** Then replace the *Picture Card fish* with *kangaroo*. Ask children how the sentence will change. Have a child remove the word *not* and read the sentence together: **A kangaroo can hop.**

PRACTICE/APPLY

Read the Book Distribute copies of *What Can Hop?* Have children read the title, encouraging them to point to each word as they read it. Have children read the book, pointing to each word as they read.

Respond Have children fold a piece of drawing paper in half. On one half, have them draw a picture of an animal that can't hop, according to the book, and on the other half, have them draw an insect that can hop. Ask children to label their pictures.

Decodable Book 3: *What Can Hop?*

A cat can not hop.

2

A pig can not hop.

3

A ram can not hop.

4

A snake can not hop.

5

A bat can not hop.

6

Can a frog hop?

7

It can hop!

8

■ **High-Frequency Word**

what

■ **Decodable Words**

See Word List, p. T19.

School–Home Connection

Take-Home Book Version

◀ Decodable Book 3:
What Can Hop?

▲ *Amazing Ants*
Independent Reader 20

OBJECTIVES

- *To improve a group writing project through proofreading*

- *To apply punctuation rules*

Materials

- correction tape

- marker

Writing Process

Write a Wall Book

PROOFREAD

Model Proofreading   Remind children that this is their chance to make the writing better. Direct children's attention to the end mark in each sentence. After reading the first sentence, ask: **Should this sentence end with a question mark or a period?** *(period)* Then read the second and model for children how to know when to use a question mark.

MODEL   I know that this sentence should end with a question mark because *What* is the first word of the sentence. The word *what* is a question word. Listen as my voice rises as I get to the end of the sentence. Repeat the question for children.

Ask children to trace over the end marks that are correct and to fix the end marks that are incorrect with correction tape and a marker.

Self-Selected Writing   Have children write and draw about anything they'd like. If they have difficulty thinking of a topic, have them ask two friends what they're going to write about.

WRAP UP Share Time

Author's Chair Sing and perform the actions for "Eency Weency Spider." Invite children to share their songbooks from today's Literature Response activity.

S.S.R. Have children read silently from a book of their choice.

Centers COOKING

Spider Snacks

Have children make spider snacks by inserting eight pretzel stick pieces into the soft center of a sandwich cookie or a marshmallow. Children can serve the spider snacks on paper plates covered with paper doilies to represent spider webs.

[NOTE: Children with food allergies can suffer potentially dangerous reactions. Check with parents before giving children foods prepared in class.]

Materials

- pretzel sticks
- sandwich cookies
- marshmallows
- paper doilies
- paper plates

Day at a Glance
Day 5

WARM UP

Phonemic Awareness
Rhyme Recognition

Sharing Literature
Read-Aloud Anthology:
"The Ants Came Marching"

Read

KINDERGARTEN
READ-ALOUD
Anthology
Harcourt

Respond to Literature

Literature Focus:
Anticipating Text

Phonics
Blending /o/–/p/

Interactive Writing
Writing Process: Publish

MORNING MESSAGE
Kindergarten News

(Child's name)'s birthday is _____.

(Child's name) special day

is _____.

Write Kindergarten News   Talk with children about special days, such as birthdays. Encourage them to speak in complete sentences.

Use prompts such as the following to guide children as you write the news:

- **Who has a birthday this month?**
- **When is your birthday?**
- **Who can show me the first letter of (child's name)?**
- **Let's clap the syllables for the word *birthday*. How many parts do you clap?**

As you write the message, invite children to contribute by writing letters, names, or words they have previously learned. Remind them to use proper spacing, capitalization, and punctuation.

Calendar Language

Have children identify the day of the week. Then ask them to name class activities for the day.

Sunday	Monday	Tuesday	Wednesday	Thursday	Friday	Saturday
		1	2	3	4	5
6	7	8	9	10	11	12
13	14	15	16	17	18	19
20	21	22	23	24	25	26
27	28	29	30	31		

Phonemic Awareness

PHONEME BLENDING

Blend Phonemes   Use the rabbit for this blending activity. Tell children they can listen to the sounds the rabbit will say and name the word the rabbit is saying.

MODEL   /m/ /o/ /p/ **Say the sounds with the rabbit. /m/ /o/ /p/. Say the sounds more quickly /mmoopp/. Now say the word** *mop* **with the rabbit.**

Ask children to blend the sounds and say the words to finish each sentence the rabbit says:

When I see a red light, I /s/ /t/ /o/ /p/. (*stop*)

I make soup in a /p/ /o/ /t/. (*pot*)

I have two feet, so I wear two /s/ /o/ /k/ /s/. (*socks*)

I help my teacher. I have a classroom /j/ /o/ /b/. (*job*)

To help pull a cart, we could use an /o/ /ks/. (*ox*)

When I climb a ladder, I want to reach the /t/ /o/ /p/. (*top*)

Sharing Literature

Read "The Ants Came Marching"

READ ALOUD

Before Reading   Tell children that they are going to sing a song called "The Ants Came Marching." Use these prompts to build background:

- **Who has seen ants crawling along the ground?**
- **What do they look like?**
- **Do you think the word *marching* tells how ants move? Why or why not?**

During Reading   Play the song on the *Music CD* or sing the song aloud. As you play the song or sing,

- hold up the correct number of fingers to indicate the number of ants in the first verse.
- pause before the second verse to ask children to predict what the next number will be.
- pause occasionally to let children guess the rhyming words in the song.

Read or sing the song again, encouraging children to join in as they recognize the pattern.

▲ **Read-Aloud Anthology**

OBJECTIVES

- *To participate in a counting song*
- *To recognize number words*
- *To make and confirm predictions*
- *To anticipate text*

Materials

- Read-Aloud Anthology p. 140
- Music CD

RESPOND TO LITERATURE

Pantomime the Song Lead children in singing the song again. This time, have children make up actions to go with each of the verses as they sing.

Literature Focus

ANTICIPATING TEXT

Sing with children the first three verses of "The Ants Came Marching." Pause before the fourth verse and model how to figure out what comes next.

MODEL I know what number I should sing next— *four*. The numbers started with *one* and then came *two* and *three*. So that means *four* comes next. The numbers go on up to *ten*.

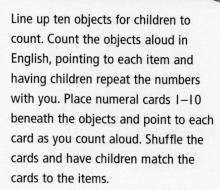

ENGLISH-LANGUAGE LEARNERS

Line up ten objects for children to count. Count the objects aloud in English, pointing to each item and having children repeat the numbers with you. Place numeral cards 1–10 beneath the objects and point to each card as you count aloud. Shuffle the cards and have children match the cards to the items.

ONGOING ASSESSMENT

As you share "The Ants Came Marching," note whether children

- participate in a counting song.
- can recognize number words.
- make and confirm predictions.

LEARNING TO READ

Phonics
Blending /o/ – /p/  Review

OBJECTIVES

- *To build and read simple one-syllable words*

- *To understand that as the letters of words change, so do the sounds*

Materials

- *Alphabet Cards h, n, o, p, p, t*

- *Word Builders*

- *Word Builder Cards h, n, o, p, p, t*

- pocket chart

- chart paper

- marker

- drawing paper

- crayons

REVIEW LETTERS

ACTIVE BEGINNING

Play a Listening Game Explain to children that they are going to play a game in which they listen to words that have the /p/ sound. Ask them to clap if the word begins with the /p/ sound and snap if the word ends with the /p/ sound.

party	camp	stop	pocket	drop
penny	loop	pond	paste	chop

TEACH/MODEL

Blending Words Distribute *Word Builders* and *Word Builder Cards h, n, o, p, p, t* to children. As you place *Alphabet Cards* in a pocket chart, tell children to place the same *Word Builder Cards* in their *Word Builders*.

- Place *Alphabet Cards h, o,* and *p* in the pocket chart. Have children do the same.

- Point to *h*. Say /**hh**/. Point to *o*. Say /**oo**/.

- Slide the *o* next to the *h*. Then move your hand under the letters and blend the sounds, elongating them: /**hhoo**/. Have children do the same.

- Point to the letter *p*. Say /**pp**/. Have children do the same.

- Slide the *p* next to the *ho*. Slide your hand under *hop* and blend by elongating the sounds: /**hhoopp**/. Have children do the same.

- Then have children read the word *hop* along with you.

PRACTICE/APPLY

Guided Practice   Have children build and read new words. Have them place *Word Builder Cards o* and *p* in their *Word Builders.*

- **Add *t* to *op*. What word did you make?**

- **Change *t* to *p*. What word did you make?**

- **Change the last *p* to *t*. What word did you make?**

- **Change *p* to *n*. What word did you make?**

Independent Practice   Write the words *mop, pop,* and *hop* on chart paper. Have children read each word. Then distribute paper with the sentence frame *I can _____* . Have children complete the sentence, using one of the words from the chart. Then have them illustrate their sentence.

ENGLISH-LANGUAGE LEARNERS

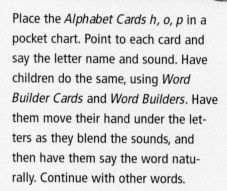

Place the *Alphabet Cards h, o, p* in a pocket chart. Point to each card and say the letter name and sound. Have children do the same, using *Word Builder Cards* and *Word Builders.* Have them move their hand under the letters as they blend the sounds, and then have them say the word naturally. Continue with other words.

ADVANCED

Have children use the *Magnetic Letters h, o, p, t* and *High-Frequency Word Cards I, You, We, on* to build sentences: *I hop on top. You hop on top. We hop on top.*

▲ **Practice Book page 22**

Writing Process

Write a Wall Book

OBJECTIVES

- *To illustrate a group writing project*

Illustrate the Wall Book   Show children the caterpillars on page 11 of the *Big Book*. Remind children that when they illustrate the top page, they need to hide the insect in the picture. Then they can draw the insect big on the answer page underneath. Divide children into eight groups. Distribute to each group a page of the story and crayons. The eighth group can illustrate the title page.

Self-Selected Writing   Have children write and draw about anything they'd like. If they have difficulty thinking of a topic have them ask two friends what they're going to write about.

WRAP UP ## Share Time

Reflect on the Lesson Have children share what they like about "The Ants Came Marching." Have them perform the actions as they sing the verses of the song.

S.S.R. Sustained Silent Reading Have children read silently from a book of their choice.

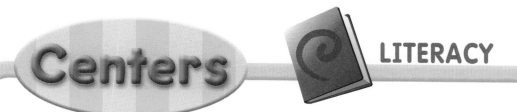

Centers  LITERACY

Reading Time

Place the books in the center. Have children read the books and choose their favorite one. Ask them to draw and label a picture about their favorite book. Have children write the title of the book on their picture. Remind them to write their name on their picture.

Materials

- Decodable Books 1, 2, 3: Kip the Ant; The Big Ram; What Can Hop?

- Little Book: Look Closer

- Library Books: Butterfly; Wonderful Worms

Theme Wrap-Up & Review

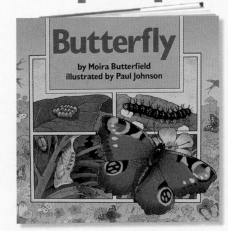

Celebrate *Bug Surprises*

Show children *Look Closer*, *Butterfly*, and *Wonderful Worms*. Help them summarize or retell each story. Invite comments and personal responses; then ask these questions:

- Which of these books about bugs is your favorite? Why?

- What new fact about bugs have you learned in this theme?

- What surprised you most about bugs as you listened to the stories in this theme?

Teacher Self-Evaluation

As you reflect on the theme *Bug Surprises* ask yourself:

- **Which activities best met my goals for this theme? Which ones did not?**

- **Have children become more aware of the small creatures around them?**

- **Which activities worked best for my class and for my teaching style? How might I vary the activities next time?**

THEME PROJECT

Give a Bug Talk!

Summing Up   Have children tell what surprised them about their bug.

REVIEW

Phonics

Sort Words Place *Alphabet Cards Bb* and *Kk* in a pocket chart. *Place Picture Cards baby, bear, boy, bus, kangaroo, key, king,* and *kite* in a pile on a table or desk. Have children take a card, name the picture word, say the sound they hear at the beginning of the word and place the Picture Card under the letter that stands for the beginning sound.

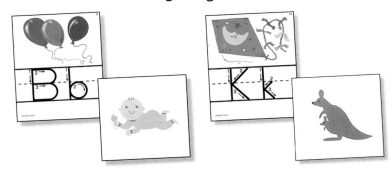

High-Frequency Words

Questions and Answers Place the *High-Frequency Word Cards What do you have* in a pocket chart. Add a question mark. Ask children to read the words. Then have them take turns using a pointer to point to each word as they read it and make up an answer using the sentence frame: *I have a _____.*

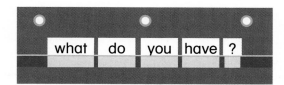

| what | do | you | have | ? |

Comprehension

Main Idea and Details Display *Library Book Wonderful Worms* and ask children to tell the main idea. Page through the book and have them give details about worms.

Writing

Naming Words Have children draw and label insects they have learned about in this theme. Ask them to write the name of the insect next to their drawings.

**Take-Home Book
Theme 7 Practice Book,**
pp. 23–24

ASSESSMENT

Monitoring of Progress

Diagnostic Checks Use the Diagnostic Checks as a point-of-use assessment of children's understanding.

Theme Skills Assessment Use the Theme Skills Assessment to monitor a child's understanding of letter recognition, word recognition, sound-symbol relationships, and decoding skills taught in this theme.

• Assessment Handbook

Animal Adventures

There's imagination at work in reading about fictitious animals and the adventures they have. The various settings of jungle, city, country, and mountains build children's appreciation of the animal's different adventures.

Theme Resources

READING MATERIALS

Big Book
◀ *Walking Through the Jungle*
by Debbie Harter

Library Books

◀ *Elmer* by David Mckee

◀ *So Say the Little Monkeys*
by Nancy Van Laan
illustrated by Yumi Heo

Big Book of Rhymes and Songs

◀ *The Bear Went Over the Mountain*
◀ *The Little Turtle*

Read-Aloud Anthology

◀ *The Rooster Who Went to His Uncle's Wedding*
retold by Alma Flor Ada

◀ *Counting Crocodiles* retold by Judy Sierra

◀ *Going on a Bear Hunt*

◀ *The Strongest One of All*
retold by Mirra Ginsburg

◀ *The Hare and the Tortoise*
retold by Stephanie Calmenson

Independent Readers

▲ *See Me Play*   ▲ *Little Red Hen Bakes a Cake*   ▲ *The Ice Fair*

PHONICS

Theme 8 Practice Book

Phonics Practice Book

Decodable Books

▲ *I Can See It!*   ▲ *What Is In the Box?*   ▲ *Hop on Top*

Alphabet Patterns
wagon, x-ray
page TI8

Phonics Express™ CD-ROM
Level A

TEACHING TOOLS

Big Alphabet Cards
Ww, Xx

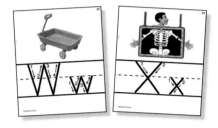

Letter and Sound Charts
Charts 18 and 25

Letter and Sound Chart Sentence Strips
18, and 25

Wish, wash, my gosh.

High-Frequency Word Cards
no, see

Picture/Word Cards

Teacher's Resource Book
pages 68, 63

Oo-pples and Boo-noo-noos

English-Language Learners Kit

Intervention Kit

MANIPULATIVES

Tactile Letter Cards

| w | x |

Word Builder and Word Builder Cards

Magnetic Letters

Write-On/Wipe-Off Board
Letters and Sounds Place Mat

ASSESSMENT

Assessment Handbook
Group Inventory
Theme 8 Test

Big Book ▶

Library Book ▶

Week 1

Week 2

	Week 1	Week 2
• **Sharing Literature** • **Listening Comprehension**	**Big Book:** *Walking Through the Jungle* **Library Book:** *Elmer* **Read-Aloud Anthology:** *"The Rooster Who Went to His Uncle's Wedding"* **Big Book of Rhymes and Songs:** *"The Bear Went Over the Mountain"*	**Big Book:** Walking Through the Jungle **Library Book:** So Say The Little Monkeys **Read-Aloud Anthology:** "Counting Crocodiles" **Big Book of Rhymes and Songs:** "The Little Turtle"
• **Phonemic Awareness** • **Phonics** • **High-Frequency Words**	**Consonant** /w/*w* T **Consonant** /x/*x* T **Review Consonants** *Ww, Xx* T **High-Frequency Words** *no, see* T	**Review Consonant** /ks/ *x*, **Short Vowel** /o/ *o* T **Blending** /o/ - /x/ **Words with** /o/ and /ks/ **Review Blending** /o/ - /x/
• **Reading**	**Decodable Book 4:** *I Can See* **Independent Reader 21:** *See Me Play*	**Decodable Book 5:** *What's in the Box?* **Independent Reader 22:** *Little Red Hen Bakes a Cake*
• **Writing**	**Shared Writing** Word Web **Interactive Writing** Chart **Independent Writing** Message Song Verse Class Book	**Shared Writing** Invitation Class Story **Interactive Writing** Weather Chart **Independent Writing** Class Riddle Book Accordion Book
• **Cross-Curricular Centers**	**ABC Letters and Words** Make Mystery Letters **Math** Animals That Shape Up **ABC Letters and Words** Tic-Tac-Toe **Writing** Would You Believe It? **Art** Patchwork Quilt	**Science** Animal Habitats **Art** Characters on a String Books **Math** More or Less **Art** Favorite Animals **Science** Model Habitats

T = tested skill

Library Book ▶

Week 3

Library Book: *So Say The Little Monkeys*

Big Book: *Walking Through the Jungle*

Read-Aloud Anthology:
"The Strongest One of All"
"Going on a Bear Hunt"
"The Hare and the Tortoise"

Phonogram *-ot*

Phonogram *-op*

Phonogram *-ox*

Build Sentences

Decodable Book 6: *Hop on Top*

Independent Reader 23: *The Ice Fair*

Interactive Writing
Writing Process

✏ **Writing**
Rebus Stories

👑 **Manipulatives**
Rock, Scissors, Paper

🎧 **Listening**
Telling a Story

📖 **Literacy**
Favorite Books

🧱 **Block**
Race the Clock

Theme Organizer
Half-Day Kindergarten

Use the following chart to help organize your half-day kindergarten schedule. Choose independent activities as time allows during your day.

ORAL LANGUAGE

Morning Message
Phonemic Awareness
Sharing Literature
• Big Book:
  Walking Through the Jungle
• Library Book: *Elmer*
• Library Book:
  So Say The Little Monkeys
• *Read-Aloud Anthology*
• *Big Book of Rhymes and Songs*

LEARNING TO READ

Phonics
Decodable Books 4–6
• *I Can See*
• *What's in the Box?*
• *Hop on Top*
High-Frequency Words

Independent Readers 21–23
• *See Me Play*
• *Little Red Hen Bakes a Cake*
• *The Ice Fair*

LANGUAGE ARTS

Shared Writing
Interactive Writing
Independent Writing
Writing Every Day

INDEPENDENT ACTIVITIES

Sharing Literature
Respond to Literature
Phonics
Independent Practice
Handwriting
Practice Book pages
High-Frequency Words
Independent Practice
Practice Book pages

About the
Authors and Illustrators

Debbie Harter

Illustrator of *Walking Through the Jungle*
Debbie Harter creates jewelry and greeting cards, which she sells worldwide, in addition to writing books for children. She lives in North London, England.

David McKee

Author and Illustrator of *Elmer*
David McKee grew up in Devon, England. While he was a student at Plymouth Art College, he began selling his cartoon drawings to newspapers. Since 1964 he has published many books for children, including the *King Rollo* stories which he helped animate for British television. Mr. McKee enjoys traveling and writing books that "leave things unsaid."

Nancy Van Laan

Author of *So Say The Little Monkeys*
Nancy Van Laan was born in Baton Rouge, Louisiana, and received her B.A. from the University of Alabama. In addition to being a playwright and teacher, she is the author of many books for young readers, such as *Rainbow Crow, The Big Fat Worm, This Is the Hat, Buffalo Dance,* and *La Boda: A Mexican Wedding Celebration.* She has three children and lives in Pennsylvania.

Yumi Heo

Illustrator of *So Say The Little Monkeys*
Yumi Heo was born in Korea. Her illustration of *The Lonely Lioness* was awarded the 1996 *New York Times* Best Illustrated Book. Heo now lives in White Plains, New York.

Theme Assessment

MONITORING OF PROGRESS

Assessment Options

Assessment Handbook

- Group Inventory
- Phonemic Awareness Inventory
- Theme Skills Assessment
- Concepts About Print Inventory
- Observational Checklists

After completing the theme, most children should show progress toward mastery of the following skills:

Concepts of Print

- ❑ Follow words from left to right and from top to bottom on the printed page.
- ❑ Recognize and name all uppercase and lowercase letters of the alphabet.

Phonemic Awareness

- ❑ Identify and produce rhyming words in response to an oral prompt.
- ❑ Track and represent changes in simple syllables and words with two and three sounds as one sound is added, substituted, omitted, shifted, or repeated.

Phonics and Decoding

- ❑ Match all consonant sounds and short-vowel sounds to appropriate letters.
- ❑ Read one-syllable and High-Frequency Words.

Vocabulary and High-Frequency Words

- ❑ Read High-Frequency Words *no* and *see.*
- ❑ Identify and sort common words in basic categories.
- ❑ Understand words associated with the calendar.

Comprehension

- ❑ Use pictures and context to make predictions about story content.
- ❑ Connect to life experiences the information and events in texts.

Literary Response

- ❑ Distinguish fantasy from realistic text.
- ❑ Identify characters, settings, and important events.
- ❑ Recognize different genre.

Writing

- ❑ Use letters and phonetically spelled words to write about experiences, stories, people, and objects, or events.
- ❑ Write uppercase and lowercase letters of the alphabet independently, attending to the form and proper spacing of the letters.
- ❑ Use prephonetic knowledge to spell independently.

Listening and Speaking

- ❑ Share information and ideas about literature, speaking audibly in complete, coherent sentences.
- ❑ Sing songs.

Reaching All Learners

■ **BELOW-LEVEL**

Levels of Support

Point-of-use Notes in the Teacher's Edition

pp. 253, 257, 261, 269, 273, 277, 279, 285

Additional Support Activities

High-Frequency Words:
pp. S56–S57

Comprehension and Skills:
pp. S66–S67, S72–S73

Phonemic Awareness:
pp. S58–S59, S64–S65, S68–S69

Phonics:
pp. S60–S61, S62–S63, S70–S71

Intervention Resource Kit

■ **ENGLISH-LANGUAGE LEARNERS**

Levels of Support

Point-of-use Notes in the Teacher's Edition

pp. 257, 261, 263, 265, 279, 281, 287, 289

Additional Support Activities

High-Frequency Words:
pp. S56–S57

Comprehension and Skills:
pp. S66–S67, S72–S73

Phonemic Awareness:
pp. S58–S59, S64–S65, S68–S69

Phonics:
pp. S60–S61, S62–S63, S70–S71

Visit *The Learning Site!* at
www.harcourtschool.com
See Language Support Activities

English-Language Learners Resource Kit

516   **Animal Adventures**

Teacher Notes

Learning Centers

Choose from the following suggestions to enhance your learning centers for the theme *Animal Adventures*.
(Additional learning centers for this theme can be found on pages 584 and 630)

DRAMATIC PLAY

What Am I?

Place the *Picture Cards* in a paper bag. Have one child at a time take a card and pantomime things that the animal on the card might do. The other children in the group should guess what animal the child is imitating. If children cannot guess correctly, the child should show the group the picture and identify it.

Materials

- *Picture Cards: bear, cat, cow, dog, duck, fish, hen, horse, kangaroo, mouse, owl, pig, rabbit, tiger, turtle*
- paper bag

BLOCK CENTER

Adventure Land

Provide a variety of materials in the block center that children can use to create a setting for an animal adventure. Encourage children to use materials to recreate landforms and vegetation. Children can position animals—and if desired people and vehicles—in their settings.

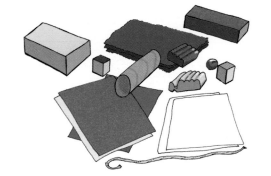

Materials

- blocks
- clay or modeling dough
- recyclable objects: paper tubes, cartons, small cups, plastic bottles
- miniature animals, people, and vehicles
- construction paper
- scraps of cloth or felt
- yarn

Week 1

Animal Adventures

ORAL LANGUAGE

15–30 Minutes

- **Phonemic Awareness**

- **Sharing Literature**

Day 1

Phonemic Awareness, 531
Rhyme Identification

Sharing Literature, 532
 Read

Big Book: *Walking Through the Jungle*

(Skill) **Literature Focus, 533**
Sound Words

Day 2

Phonemic Awareness, 547
Phoneme Isolation

Sharing Literature, 548
 Read

Library Book: *Elmer*

(Skill) **Literature Focus, 549**
Retelling the Story

LEARNING TO READ

45 Minutes

- **Phonics**

- **Vocabulary**

Daily Routines
- **Morning Message**
- **Calendar Language**
- **Writing Prompt**

Phonics, 542 T
Introduce: Consonant *Ww*
Identify/Write **T**

Phonics, 550 T
Review: Consonant *Ww*
Relating /w/ to *w* **T**

High-Frequency Word, 552 T
Introduce: *no*

Words to Remember, 553

LANGUAGE ARTS

15–30 Minutes

- **Writing**
  Daily Writing Prompt

 Interactive Writing, 544
Write a Chart

Writing Prompt, 544
Draw and write about a favorite animal from *Walking Through the Jungle*.

Share Time, 545
Share pictures and sentences about a favorite scene from *Walking Through the Jungle*.

 Writing, 554
Write a Message

Writing Prompt, 554
Draw and write about self-selected topics.

Share Time, 555
Share a favorite part of the lesson.

T = tested skill

Phonics

Consonants *Ww, Xx*

Focus of the Week:
• **HIGH-FREQUENCY WORDS:** *no, see*
• **PHONEMIC AWARENESS**
• **SHARING LITERATURE**
• **WRITING: Word Web, Song Verse, Class Book**

Day 3

Phonemic Awareness, 557
Matching: Final

Sharing Literature, 558
Read-Aloud Anthology: "The Rooster Who Went to His Uncle's Wedding," p. 94

(Skill) **Literature Focus, 559**
Compare Oral Traditions

 **Phonics, 560** T
Introduce: Consonant *Xx*
Identify/Write T

High-Frequency Word, 562 T
Introduce: *see*

Words to Remember, 563

 Shared Writing, 564
Read
Write a Word Web

Writing Prompt, 564
Draw and write about a favorite celebration.

Share Time, 565
Share a favorite part of the story.

Day 4

Phonemic Awareness, 567
Phoneme Isolation

Sharing Literature, 568
Read
Big Book of Rhymes and Songs: "The Bear Went Over the Mountain," p. 21

(Skill) **Literature Focus, 569**
Syllables in Words

 **Phonics, 570** T
Review: Consonant *Xx*
Relating /ks/ to *x*

High-Frequency Words, 572 T
Review: *no, see*

Read
DECODABLE BOOK 4
I Can See It!

 Shared Writing, 574
Write a Song Verse

Writing Prompt, 574
Draw and write about a favorite outdoor activity.

Share Time, 575
Share favorite parts of "The Bear Went Over the Mountain."

Day 5

Phonemic Awareness, 577
Syllable Segmentation

Sharing Literature, 578
Read
Library Book: *Elmer*

(Skill) **Literature Focus, 579**
Making Inferences

 **Phonics, 580** T
Review: Consonants /w/*w*, /x/*x*

 Writing, 582
Write a Class Book

Writing Prompt, 582
Draw and write about self-selected topics.

Share Time, 583
Share a favorite part of the lesson.

Day at a Glance

Day 1

WARM UP

Phonemic Awareness
Rhyme Identification

Sharing Literature
Big Book:
Walking Through the Jungle

Read

Develop Listening Comprehension

Respond to Literature

Literature Focus:
Sound Words

Phonics
Consonant *Ww*

Interactive Writing
Chart

MORNING MESSAGE

Kindergarten News

(Child's name) took (or would like to take) a trip to _____.

Write Kindergarten News Talk with children about trips they have taken or would like to take. Ask them to tell about some of the things they did or would like to do.

Use prompts such as the following to guide children as you write the news:

• **Who can show me a letter *t*?**

• **Who can show me the high-frequency words *to* and *a*?**

• **Who can point to where to begin reading the sentence? Where to end?**

As you write the message, invite children to contribute by writing letters, words, or names they have previously learned. Remind them to use proper spacing, capitalization, and punctuation.

Calendar Language

Point to and read aloud the days of the week. Tell children you will name the school days. Point to and read aloud *Monday* through *Friday*. Ask children to repeat the names of the school days.

Sunday	Monday	Tuesday	Wednesday	Thursday	Friday	Saturday
		1	2	3	4	5
6	7	8	9	10	11	12
13	14	15	16	17	18	19
20	21	22	23	24	25	26
27	28	29	30	31		

Phonemic Awareness

RHYME IDENTIFICATION

Identify Rhyming Words   Have children listen as you say the following:

Pen, me, see. **Say the words with me:** *pen, me, see.* **Two of the words end with the same sound:** *me* **and** *see.* **That means** *me* **and** *see* **are rhyming words.**

Have children repeat the rhyming words. Then tell children that you are going to say three words at a time. Have them identify the two rhyming words in each group.

wink, pink, jungle
(*wink, pink*)

float, river, boat
(*float, boat*)

slip, trip, iceberg
(*slip, trip*)

you, ocean, blue
(*you, blue*)

wax, tax, map
(*wax, tax*)

bear, wear, snake
(*bear, wear*)

lion, walk, talk
(*walk, talk*)

crocodile, I, why
(*I, why*)

chase, wolf, face
(*chase, face*)

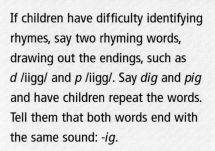

BELOW-LEVEL

If children have difficulty identifying rhymes, say two rhyming words, drawing out the endings, such as *d* /iigg/ and *p* /iigg/. Say *dig* and *pig* and have children repeat the words. Tell them that both words end with the same sound: *-ig*.

ADVANCED

Provide children with *Picture Cards* *cat, hen, key, nail, sun,* and *yak*. Have them say the picture name and as many rhyming words as they can think of.

▲ **Big Book**

OBJECTIVES

- *To listen and respond to a story*

- *To understand that written words represent sounds*

- *To use pictures and context to make predictions*

- *To identify setting*

- *To identify sound words*

Materials

- *Big Book: Walking Through the Jungle*

- *Audiotext*

- drawing paper

- crayons or markers

Sharing Literature

Read Walking Through the Jungle

READ ALOUD

Before Reading   Display the cover of *Walking Through the Jungle* and track the words in the title as you read it aloud. Point to the word *walking* and explain that it is an action word. Then point to *jungle* and tell children that *jungle* is a naming word for a place. Then use these prompts to help children make predictions:

- **What do you think the girl might be doing?** (Possible response: walking through the jungle)

- **What can you tell about a jungle from looking at the cover?** (Possible response: It has lots of plants, trees, and animals.)

Page through the *Big Book*, pointing to the girl in each place. Have children predict what this book might be about.

During Reading   Read the story aloud. As you read,

- pause for children to look at the illustrations and to predict which animal will come next.

- say the sound words expressively.

- model how to identify the setting in each part of the story.

MODEL **I want to figure out the setting, or where and when the story takes place. In the first part of the story, the words say the girl is walking through the jungle. I see jungle plants and animals. It looks as if it is daytime. So this part of the story happens in the jungle during the day.**

DEVELOP LISTENING COMPREHENSION

After Reading   Have children answer these questions:

- **What is the book about?** (Possible responses: a girl being chased by animals; a girl going from place to place around the world)
- **Why does the girl go from place to place?** (Possible response: Animals are chasing after her.)
- **Who chases after the girl?** (lion, whale, wolf, crocodile, snake, polar bear)

RESPOND TO LITERATURE

Draw Events from the Story   Have children draw a picture of their favorite setting from the story. Ask children to write or dictate a sentence about their picture.

Literature Focus

SOUND WORDS

Remind children that sound words are words that name a sound they can hear. Page through *Walking Through the Jungle*, and point out the sound words *roar, whoosh, howl, snap, hiss,* and *growl*. Have children repeat them after you, and using the story pictures, identify the animal that makes each sound. Then have children listen to the story on the *Audiotext*. Have them clap each time they hear a word that names an animal sound.

ADVANCED

Challenge children to extend the skill they have just learned. Have them think of sound words for other animals.

ENGLISH-LANGUAGE LEARNERS

To give children practice with identifying the animals, point to each animal and say its name. Have children repeat the animal name with you several times. Then have them listen to the *Audiotext* to become familiar with animal names and sounds.

ONGOING ASSESSMENT

As you read *Walking Through the Jungle*, note whether children

- listen and respond to a story.
- understand that written words represent sounds.
- use pictures and context to make predictions.
- identify setting.

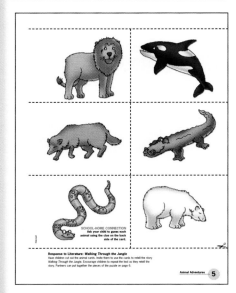

▲ **Practice Book pages 5–6**

WALKING THROUGH THE JUNGLE

Debbie Harter

WALKING THROUGH THE JUNGLE

Walking through the jungle,
Walking through the jungle,

What do you see?
What do you see?

4

5

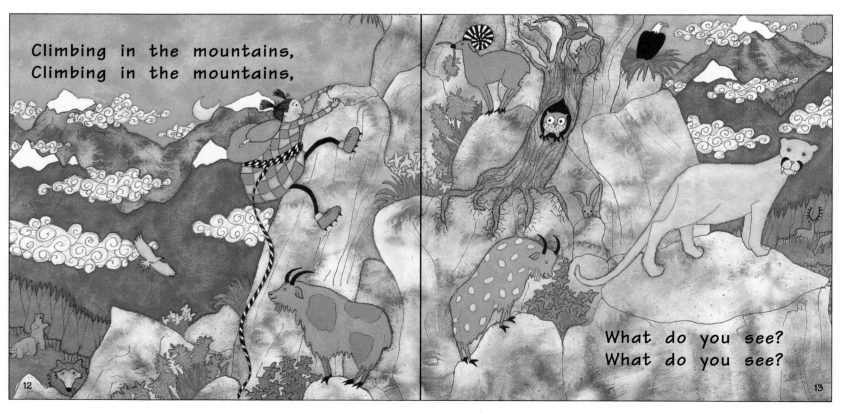

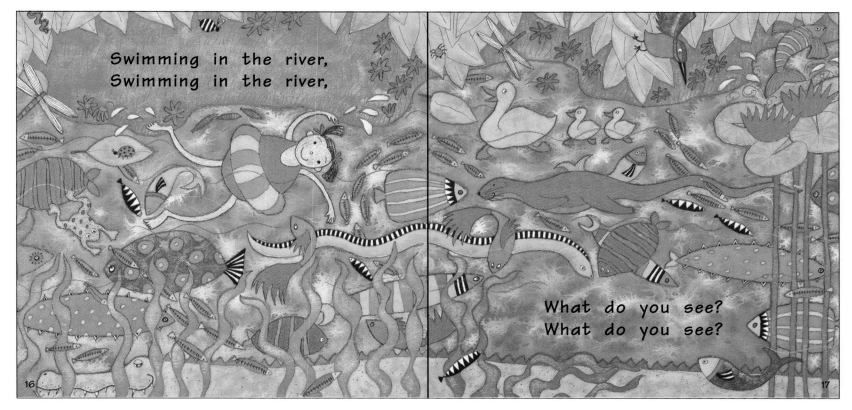

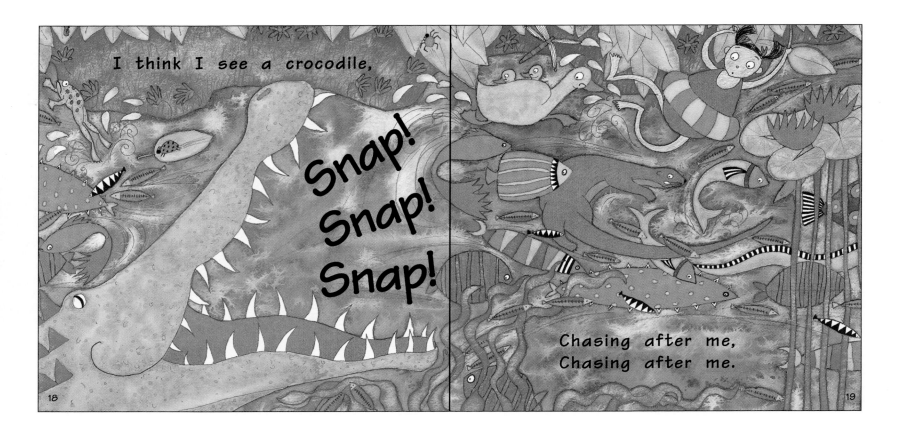

I've been around the world and back,
I've been around the world and back,

And guess what I've seen,
And guess what I've seen.

30

31

OBJECTIVES

- *To recognize W and w*
- *To write uppercase and lowercase Ww independently*

Materials

- *Big Book of Rhymes and Songs* pp. 2–3
- *Music CD*
- *Big Book: Walking Through the Jungle*
- *Big Alphabet Card Ww*
- *Write-On/Wipe-Off Boards*
- drawing paper
- crayons

Phonics
Consonant Ww ✔ Introduce

ACTIVE BEGINNING

Sing "The Alphabet Song" Display "The Alphabet Song" in the *Big Book of Rhymes and Songs*. Play the *Music CD*, and point to each letter as you sing the song with children.

▲ **Big Book of Rhymes and Songs, pp. 2-3**

TEACH/MODEL

Introduce the Letter Name Hold up the *Big Alphabet Card Ww*.

The name of this letter is *w*. Say the name with me.

Point to the uppercase *W*. **This is the uppercase *W*.**

Point to the lowercase *w*. **This is the lowercase *w*.**

Point to the *Big Alphabet Card* again. **What is the name of this letter?**

Point to the *W* in "The Alphabet Song." **What is the name of this letter?**

Display the cover of *Walking Through the Jungle*.

Follow along as I read the title.

Point to the letter *W*. **What is the name of this letter?**

Handwriting

Writing *W* and *w* Write uppercase *W* and lowercase *w* on the board.

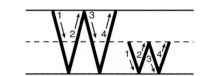

Point to the uppercase *W*. **What letter is this?**

Point to the lowercase *w*. **What letter is this?**

MODEL **Watch as I write the letter *W* so that everyone can read it.**

As you give the Letter Talk, trace the uppercase *W*. Use the same modeling procedure for lowercase *w*.

Letter Talk for *W*

Slanted line down. Slanted line up. Slanted line down. Slanted line up again.

Letter Talk for *w*

Shorter slanted line down. Slanted line up. Slanted line down. Slanted line up again.

D'Nealian handwriting models are on pages R12–13.

PRACTICE/APPLY

Guided Practice Help children find *Ww* on their *Write-On/Wipe-Off Board*. Have them trace the uppercase *W* with a finger and then write the letter several times. Then have them do the same for lowercase *w*.

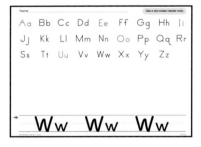

Independent Practice Distribute drawing paper and have children fill the page with *Ww*s. Then have children circle the best *W* and *w* on the page.

BELOW-LEVEL

Guide children in writing the letter. Put your hand over their hand and write the letter with each child. Then have children try on their own.

ENGLISH-LANGUAGE LEARNERS

As you introduce children to *Ww* letter formation, model each step of the Letter Talk to make sure children understand the ideas of slanted line, up, and down.

Phonics Resources

Phonics Express™ **CD-ROM, Level A,** Roamer/Route 3/Park

Phonics Practice Book pages 85–86

▲ **Practice Book page 7**

Interactive Writing

Write a Chart

OBJECTIVES

- To identify sound words

- To write a chart

- To connect life experiences to the text

- To follow words from left to right on a page

- To recognize uppercase and lowercase letters

Writing Every Day

Day 1: Chart
Work with children to write a chart of animal sound words.

Day 2: Message
Children write a message for a sign.

Day 3: Word Web
Work with children to write a word web of story characters.

Day 4: Song Verse
Work with children to write ideas for new verses to "The Bear Went over the Mountain."

Day 5: Class Book
Children draw and label a page for a class book.

SOUND WORDS

Talk About Animal Sounds   Page through *Walking Through the Jungle* and have children identify the animals and the sounds they make. Ask children to tell where they have seen real animals like the ones in the story.

Write a Chart   Tell children that together they are going to make a chart of sound words. Ask: **What should the title be? Who can help me write *S* in Sound?** Have children help you write the title. Write an animal name from *Walking Through the Jungle* on the chart paper. Then, as children name the sound word for the animal, have them help you record it in a second column on the chart. Have children suggest other animals and things that make noise.

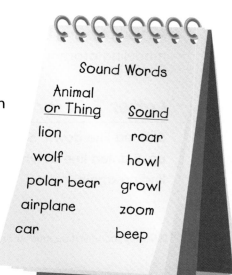

Sound Words	
Animal or Thing	Sound
lion	roar
wolf	howl
polar bear	growl
airplane	zoom
car	beep

SHARE

Read the Chart   Read the completed chart, tracking words from left to right. Have children identify any letters they recognize in the words. Ask children to point to the letter *w* in words. Ask if the letters are uppercase or lowercase *w*.

Journal Writing Ask children to draw and write about their favorite animal from *Walking Through the Jungle.*

WRAP UP # Share Time

Reflect on the Lesson Invite children to share their picture and sentence about their favorite scene from *Walking Through the Jungle*. Ask them to name the letter they learned today.

S.S.R. *Sustained Silent Reading* Have children read silently from a book of their choice.

Centers  ABC LETTER AND WORD

Make Mystery Letters

Fold sheets of construction paper in half. Draw half of a block letter *W*, with the center of the letter on the fold. Have children keep the paper folded as they cut along the lines through two thicknesses of paper. Have children open the paper and identify their *Ww*s. Have children decorate their mystery letters with different color designs.

Materials

- construction paper
- scissors
- crayons or markers

WARM UP

Phonemic Awareness
Phoneme Isolation

Sharing Literature
Library Book: Elmer

Read

ELMER
David McKee

Develop Listening Comprehension

Respond to Literature

Literature Focus:
Retelling the Story

Phonics

Relating /w/ to *w*

High-Frequency Word
no

Writing
Message

MORNING MESSAGE

Kindergarten News

It is fun to watch a parade. It is fun to be in a parade. (Child's name) likes parades because _____.

Write Kindergarten News Talk with children about parades they have seen or been in. Have them tell what they like best about parades.

Use prompts such as the following to guide children as you write the news:

- **Who can show me the beginning of the word *parades*?**
- **How many letters are in the word *parades*?**
- **What letter do you see two times in *parade*?**
- **Who can show me two sentences that begin with the same words?**

As you write the message, invite volunteers to contribute by writing letters, words, or names they have previously learned. Remind them to use proper spacing, capitalization, and punctuation.

Calendar Language

Point to and read aloud the months of the year. Tell children there are twelve months in a year. Point to and name the current month. Ask: *What month is it?*

Sunday	Monday	Tuesday	Wednesday	Thursday	Friday	Saturday
		1	2	3	4	5
6	7	8	9	10	11	12
13	14	15	16	17	18	19
20	21	22	23	24	25	26
27	28	29	30	31		

Phonemic Awareness

PHONEME ISOLATION

Listen for /w/ Tell children you will say some words and they will listen to the beginning sounds in the words. Sing the following to the tune of "A Hunting We Will Go".

Water starts with /w/

Water starts with /w/

I hear /w/ in water

Water starts with /w/

Tell children that you will say a new word and they can say the sound. Use the following words in the rhyme:

warthog	went	waiting
with	wolves	walrus
wigs	watches	week
window	wagons	Wednesday

▲ **"Willoughby, Wallaby, Woo,"** *Oo-pples and Boo-noo-noos: Songs and Activities for Phonemic Awareness,* pages 124–125.

BELOW-LEVEL

As you introduce children to the beginning sound /w/, have them repeat the following routine to help them identify beginning sound /w/. *Wind /w/,* wind *begins with /w/; warm /w/,* warm *begins with /w/; wave /w/,* wave *begins with /w/.* Wind, warm, wave *all begin with /w/.*

▲ **Library Book**

OBJECTIVES

- *To listen and respond to a story*
- *To use pictures and context to make predictions*
- *To recall story events*

Materials

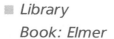

- *Library Book: Elmer*
- drawing paper
- crayons or markers
- chart paper

Sharing Literature

Read Elmer

READ ALOUD

Before Reading Display the cover of *Elmer*. Track the print of the title and the name of the author while reading them aloud. Tell children that David McKee wrote the story and drew the pictures. Page through the book. Then use these prompts to help children make predictions about Elmer:

- **Does Elmer look like the other elephants?** (No) **How is he different?** (He is all different colors.)

- **Why might Elmer be sad?** (Possible response: He wants to look like the other elephants.)

During Reading Read the story aloud. As you do so,

- have children identify colors in the illustrations.
- model for children how to keep track of story events.

MODEL First, Elmer is unhappy about being a patchwork elephant. Then, he rolls himself in berry juice and turns gray. Next, the rain washes away the berry juice. I wonder how the elephants will act towards Elmer.

DEVELOP LISTENING COMPREHENSION

After Reading   Have children answer these questions:

- **How does Elmer feel about being different?** (He doesn't like it.)
- **Why do the other elephants like Elmer?** (Possible responses: Elmer makes up games and jokes; he keeps the other elephants happy.)
- **How does Elmer feel at the end of the story? Why?** (Possible response: happy because his friends like him not for how he looks but because he is a good friend)

RESPOND TO LITERATURE

Solve Riddles   Invite children to answer riddles, using a color word.

- **I'm the color of a stop sign.** (red)
- **I'm the color of the sky on a sunny day.** (blue)
- **I'm the color of a pumpkin.** (orange)
- **I'm the color of a leaf on a tree.** (green)

Have children use different colors to draw pictures of Elmer.

ADVANCED

Challenge children to extend the skill. Ask them to retell another story they have heard or read.

ONGOING ASSESSMENT

As you read *Elmer*, note whether children

- listen and respond to the story.
- use pictures and context to make predictions.
- recall story events.

Literature Focus

RETELLING THE STORY

Ask children to help you retell the story *Elmer*.

MODEL **If I wanted to tell what this story is about, I would think about who is in the story and what happens at the beginning, middle, and ending of the story.**

Lead children to name the characters in *Elmer* and tell what happens. Record their ideas on chart paper and review the events to confirm the order.

1. Elmer wants to look like the other elephants.

2. He rubs himself with berry juice.

3. The berry juice washes off.

4. The elephants have an Elmer's Day parade.

Phonics
Relating /w/ to w

OBJECTIVE
To match consonant w to its sound

Materials

- Letter and Sound Chart 18
- Tactile Letter Cards w
- Picture/Word Cards watch, watermelon
- pocket chart
- Wagon Pattern (page T18)
- marker
- scissors
- craft stick

ACTIVE BEGINNING

Recite the Rhyme
Teach children the rhyme "Wading in the Water." Tell children to listen for the sound /w/ as they learn the rhyme. Then have them recite the rhyme again as they pretend to wind up the boat.

Wading in the Water

I'm wading in the water

Wearing water wings.

I brought along a wind-up boat

And some other water things.

By Susan Little

TEACH/MODEL

W w

Wish, wash,
My gosh,
Walrus washes _____
In his washing machine.

▲ **Letter and Sound Chart 18**

Introduce Letter and Sound   Display Letter and Sound Chart 18.

Touch the letter W. **What is the name of the letter?**

This letter stands for the /w/ sound. When you say /w/, your lips pucker. Say /ww/.

Read aloud the rhyme on the Letter and Sound Chart, tracking the print.

Read the Ww words in the rhyme aloud. Then point to each W and w and have children say the /w/ sound.

Point to the blank. **What Ww word will I write?**

Have children join in as you read the rhyme again. Ask them to make their lips pucker as they say the /w/w words.

PRACTICE/APPLY

Guided Practice Distribute *Tactile Letter Cards w.* Then place *Picture/Word Cards watch* and *watermelon* in the pocket chart. Say the name of the picture as you point to the *w* in each. Have children repeat the words.

Tell children: **Some words begin with *w.***

Point to the *w* in *watch*. **The /w/ sound is at the beginning of *watch*.**

Point to the *w* in *watermelon*. **The /w/ sound is at the beginning of *watermelon*.**

I'm going to say some words. If the word begins with the /w/ sound, hold up your *w* card. If the word doesn't begin with the /w/ sound, don't hold up your *w* card.

sand   wave   fish   weed   wing   wolf

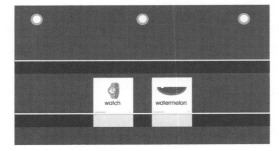

Independent Practice Distribute copies of the Wagon Pattern (page T18). Have children draw and label on the wagon a picture of something whose name begins with the /w/ sound. Ask children to whisper the name to you before they draw. Children can cut out the pattern and tape their wagon to a craft stick. Encourage them to take turns naming other things whose names begin with the /w/ sound.

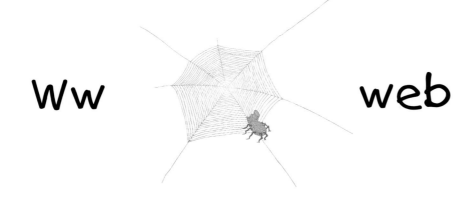

BELOW-LEVEL

Provide children with a set of *Picture Cards*, including some whose names begin with /w/. Have children sort the pictures by naming each one and deciding if the picture name begins with the /w/ sound.

Phonics Resources

Phonics Express™ CD-ROM, **Level A,** Roamer/Route 3/ Building Site, Market

Phonics Practice Book pages 87–88

▲ **Practice Book page 8**

OBJECTIVE

To read high-frequency word no

Materials

- *Big Book: I Read Signs*

- *High-Frequency Word Card* | no |

- *Teacher's Resource Book* p. 139

- drawing paper

- crayons

High-Frequency Word *no* ✔ *Introduce*

TEACH/MODEL

Display these signs from *I Read Signs*, and track the print as you read them aloud: **NO SMOKING, NO STANDING, NO LEFT TURN, NO PARKING.**

Point to the word *NO* and say: **This is the word NO.** Have children say the word with you. Display *High-Frequency Word Card no.* Ask: **What word is this?** Have children follow along as you track the print and reread the signs. Then have a child match the *High-Frequency Word Card no* to the *NO* in each sign.

PRACTICE/APPLY

Guided Practice Make copies of the *High-Frequency Word Card no* in the *Teacher's Resource Book*. Give each child a word card and tell children to point to and say the word *no*. Then, ask each child the question below and tell children to point to their word card as they say the word *no* and finish the response.

Do you roar?	No, I ___.
Do you howl?	No, I ___.
Do you hiss?	No, I ___.

Independent Practice Have children write a rule beginning with the word *NO* on a sign for school or home. Have them glue the *High-Frequency Word Card no* onto drawing paper and write and draw about the rule.

Word Wall

Reading Words Hold up the *High-Frequency Word Card no* and have children read it aloud. Place the *Word Card* under the letter *Nn* on the classroom word chart.

Find Similarities Have children look very closely at their new word *no.* Encourage them to find similarities to other words posted on the chart. Ask the following questions to guide them appropriately:

- *No* **has two letters. Do any of our other words have two letters? Let's read the other words that have two letters.** (do, on, to, my, go, we)

- *No* **has the letters *n* and *o*. Do any of the other words have the same two letters in a different order? Let's read the other word.** (on)

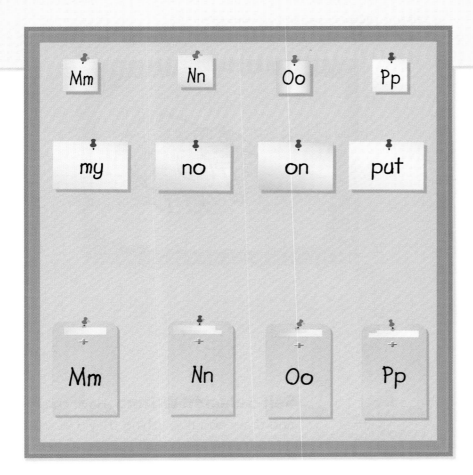

BELOW-LEVEL

Have children trace the letters on their individual *Word Card* with a finger. Then have them write the word with a finger on the top of their desk.

ADVANCED

Have children look in the book *Elmer* to find the word *no.*

▲ **Practice Book page 9**

Animal Adventures 553

OBJECTIVES

- To write a message
- To make a sign
- To connect life experiences to text
- To write by moving from left to right and from top to bottom

Materials

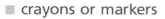

- poster board
- crayons or markers

teaching tip

Before children write, point out that their message should be short so it is quick and easy to read.

Writing

Write a Message

Talk About Messages Remind children that the story *Elmer* ends with the elephants having an Elmer's Day parade. Ask children if they have ever seen people carrying signs in a parade. Talk about the kinds of messages that would be on a sign. Ask them to imagine what messages might be on signs in an Elmer's Day parade.

Write a Sign Tell children that they are going to write a message for a sign in an Elmer's Day Parade. On chart paper, model for children how to write a message on a sign.

> **MODEL** **If I was in an Elmer's Day Parade, I would want to carry a sign. It would show my favorite colors and it would say something nice about Elmer. I will write *Elmer is fun*. Everyone at the parade will read my sign and will know that Elmer is fun.**

Distribute drawing paper to each child and have them write a message. Ask children to use their favorite colors to decorate their signs with a picture, border, or designs.

Self-Selected Writing Have children write and draw about anything they'd like. If they have difficulty thinking of a topic have them ask two friends what they're going to write about.

WRAP UP Share Time

Read the Signs When the signs are finished, have children take turns sharing their work with classmates. Have them track the words as they read them aloud. Invite children to stage a parade, carrying their Elmer signs as they march around the classroom.

S.S.R. *Sustained Silent Reading* Have children read silently from a book of their choice.

Centers MATH

Animals That Shape Up

Display the cover of *Elmer* for children to see. Ask children to identify the shapes that were used to form the picture. Supply the Math Center with pom-poms and construction paper cut into squares, circles, triangles, and rectangles of various sizes for children to use to form another version of Elmer or any other animal of their choice. Suggest that they draw an outline of an animal, fill in the outline by gluing different shapes, and write a caption for their creation.

Materials

- construction paper cut into circles, squares, triangles, and rectangles of various sizes
- pom-poms
- glue
- crayons

WARM UP

Phonemic Awareness
Phoneme Matching: Final

Sharing Literature
Read-Aloud Anthology:
"The Rooster Who Went to His Uncle's Wedding"

Read

Develop Listening Comprehension

Respond to Literature

Literature Focus:
Compare Oral Traditions

Phonics
Consonant *Xx*

High-Frequency Word
see

Shared Writing
Word Web

MORNING MESSAGE

Kindergarten News

This month is _____.

(Child's name) celebrates _____

with (his or her) family.

Write Kindergarten News   Talk with children about experiences they have had going to a family celebration, such as a wedding or birthday party.

Use prompts such as the following to guide children as you write the news:

- **Who can show me the name of the month?**
- **Who can name the beginning sound in (name of month)?**
- **What letter is at the beginning of (name of month)?**

As you write the message, invite children to contribute by writing letters, words, or names they have previously learned. Remind them to use proper spacing, capitalization, and punctuation.

Calendar Language

Point to the numbers on the calendar and have children say them with you. Point to and read aloud the date. Name the month and the date.

Sunday	Monday	Tuesday	Wednesday	Thursday	Friday	Saturday
		1	2	3	4	5
6	7	8	9	10	11	12
13	14	15	16	17	18	19
20	21	22	23	24	25	26
27	28	29	30	31		

Phonemic Awareness

PHONEME MATCHING: FINAL

Matching Final Sounds Say the words *fox* and *Max* slowly several times, emphasizing the end sound. Model for children how to listen for the last sound.

MODEL *Fox, Max.* **I listen for the last sound in each word.** *Fox* **ends with the /ks/ sound.** *Max* **ends with the /ks/ sound.** *Fox* **and** *Max* **have the same ending sound.**

Then say *fix* and *cap* slowly several times, emphasizing the end sound. Have children repeat the words. Say:

Fix, cap. **I listen for the last sound in each word.** *Fix* **ends with the /ks/ sound.** *Cap* **ends with the /p/ sound.** *Fix* **and** *cap* **have different ending sounds.**

Tell children you will say two words at a time and ask them to raise a hand if the words have the same end sound.

will, all (*same*)	**then, rain** (*same*)	**corn, berry** (*not same*)
box, mix (*same*)	**Rex, fox** (*same*)	**sled, cloud** (*same*)
run, old (*not same*)	**set, keep** (*not same*)	**six, tax** (*same*)

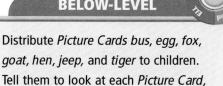

Distribute *Picture Cards bus, egg, fox, goat, hen, jeep,* and *tiger* to children. Tell them to look at each *Picture Card,* name the picture, and tell the sound they hear at the end of the word.

Day 3

LEARNING TO READ

Sharing Literature

Read "The Rooster Who Went to His Uncle's Wedding"

READ ALOUD

Before Reading Turn to page 94 in the *Read-Aloud Anthology*, and read the title "The Rooster Who Went to His Uncle's Wedding." Explain that different versions of this story are told in many Spanish-speaking countries. Then use these prompts to set a purpose for reading:

- **Who do you think the story is about?** (a rooster)
- **Why do you think this story might be make-believe?** (Roosters don't go to weddings.)

During Reading Read the story. As you read,

- invite children to join in when they figure out the pattern of the story.
- use a different voice as you read characters' parts.
- pause to point out the problem.

MODEL What is the problem in this story? The rooster gets his beak dirty on the way to his uncle's wedding and can't get it clean.

▲ **Read-Aloud Anthology**

OBJECTIVES

- *To listen and respond to a folktale*
- *To identify problem and solution*
- *To understand text patterns*

Materials

- *Read-Aloud Anthology, pp. 94–98*

DEVELOP LISTENING COMPREHENSION

After Reading Have children answer these questions:

- **How does the rooster get his beak dirty?** (He eats a kernel of corn that is lying in a mud puddle.)

- **What did the rooster want the other story characters to do for him?** (clean his beak)

- **How does the rooster fix his problem?** (The grass cleans his beak.)

RESPOND TO LITERATURE

Identify the Story Characters Have children identify the story characters using these clues:

- **velvety and grows near the road** (grass)

- **a woolly animal that grazes in the field** (lamb)

- **an animal that can bite** (dog)

- **hard and can be found lying by the road** (stick)

- **bright and lit by shepherds** (fire)

- **something clear that is found in a brook** (water)

- **appears among the clouds in the morning sky** (sun)

Literature Focus

COMPARE ORAL TRADITIONS

Tell children that folktales like "The Rooster Who Went to His Uncle's Wedding" have been told for many years. Explain that one way a storyteller makes a folktale interesting to listeners is to repeat words over and over. Read the repeated words in the story. Then recall the folktale "The Terrible Tragadabas," and have children repeat the words *"Don't you come inside. I'm the Tragadabas, And I'll swallow you alive!"* Ask children to recite the words that are repeated in "The Gingerbread Man."

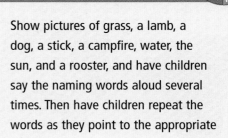

ENGLISH-LANGUAGE LEARNERS

Show pictures of grass, a lamb, a dog, a stick, a campfire, water, the sun, and a rooster, and have children say the naming words aloud several times. Then have children repeat the words as they point to the appropriate picture.

ONGOING ASSESSMENT

As you read "The Rooster Who Went to His Uncle's Wedding," note whether children

- listen and respond to the folktale.

- identify the story's problem

Phonics

Consonant Xx  Introduce

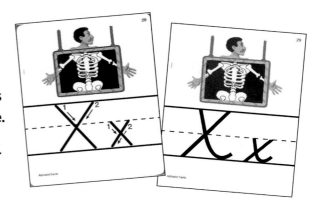

ACTIVE BEGINNING

Review the Letters   Have children name each letter as you display the *Alphabet Cards Bb, Oo, Pp, Tt, Ww.* Ask children whose names begin with any of those letters to stand and say their name.

TEACH/MODEL

Introduce the Letter Name   Hold up the *Big Alphabet Card Xx.*

The name of this letter is *x*. Say the name with me.

Point to the uppercase *X*. **This is the uppercase *X*.**

Point to the lowercase *x*. **This is the lowercase *x*.**

Point to the *Alphabet Card* again. **What is the name of this letter?**

Display page 34 of *From Anne to Zach.*

Follow along as I read the page.

Point to the letter *X*. **What is the name of this letter?**

▲ **Big Book**

OBJECTIVES

• *To recognize X and x*

• *To write uppercase and lowercase Xx independently*

Materials

■ *Alphabet Cards Bb, Oo, Pp, Tt, Ww*

■ *Big Book: From Anne to Zach*

■ *Big Alphabet Card Xx*

■ *Write-On/Wipe-Off Boards*

■ *drawing paper*

■ *crayons*

Phonics Resources

Phonics Express™ **CD-ROM, Level A,** Sparkle/Route 5/ Fire Station

Handwriting

Writing *X* and *x* Write uppercase *X* and lowercase *x* on the board.

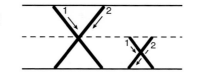

Point to the uppercase *X*. **What letter is this?**

Point to the lowercase *x*. **What letter is this?**

MODEL **Watch as I write the letter *X* so that everyone can read it.**

As you give the Letter Talk, trace the uppercase X. Use the same modeling procedure for lowercase x.

Letter Talk for *X*

Slanted line down to the right. Slanted line down to the left.

Letter Talk for *x*

Draw a shorter slanted line down to the right. Slanted line down to the left.

D'Nealian handwriting models are on pages R12–13.

PRACTICE/APPLY

Guided Practice Help children find *Xx* on their *Write-On/Wipe-Off Board*. Have them trace the uppercase *X* with a finger and then write the letter several times. Then have them do the same for lowercase *x*. Tell children to circle the best *X*.

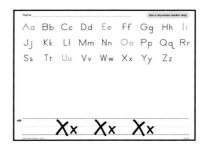

Independent Practice
Distribute drawing paper and have children fill the page with *Xx*s. Then have children circle the best *X* and *x* on the page.

Phonics Practice Book pages 89–90

▲ **Practice Book page 10**

High-Frequency Word *see* ✔*Introduce*

OBJECTIVE

To read high-frequency word see

Materials

■ pocket chart

■ *High-Frequency Word Cards*

■ *Picture/Word Cards* dinosaur, fish, gorilla, helicopter, kangaroo, lamb, rabbit, wagon

■ *Teacher's Resource Book* pp. 138–139

■ drawing paper

■ crayons

■ glue

TEACH/MODEL

Write *I see a* on chart paper. Use *Picture/Word Cards* to complete the sentence.

Point to the word *see* and say: **This is the word *see*.** Have children say the word. Display *High-Frequency Word Card see.* Ask: **What word is this?** Have children read the sentence. Then have a child match the *High-Frequency Word Card see* to the word *see* in the sentence.

PRACTICE/APPLY

Guided Practice Make copies of the *High-Frequency Word Card see* in the *Teacher's Resource Book.* Give each child a card and tell children to point to and say the word *see.* On a sentence strip, write *I see a* _____. Read the sentence, tracking each word. Ask a child to point to the word *see* and then choose a *Picture/Word Card* and read the whole sentence. Repeat the activity with other *Picture/Word Cards.*

Independent Practice Make copies of the *High-Frequency Word Cards I, see, a* in the *Teacher's Resource Book.* Have children draw a picture of something they see and then glue their words *I see a* above their picture. Have them write the picture name to complete the sentence.

Words to Remember

Word Wall

Reading Words Hold up the *High-Frequency Word Card see* and have children read it aloud. Have a child place the *Word Card* under the letter *Ss* of the classroom word chart.

Words in Sentences Have children look closely at their new word *see*. Ask them to name the letters in the word. Then have them read the other high-frequency words. Encourage children to find similarities to other words posted on the chart. Ask the following questions to guide them appropriately:

- *See* has three letters. **What other word do you see that has three letters?**

- **What else is the same about the words *the* and *see*?** (They both have the letter *e*.)

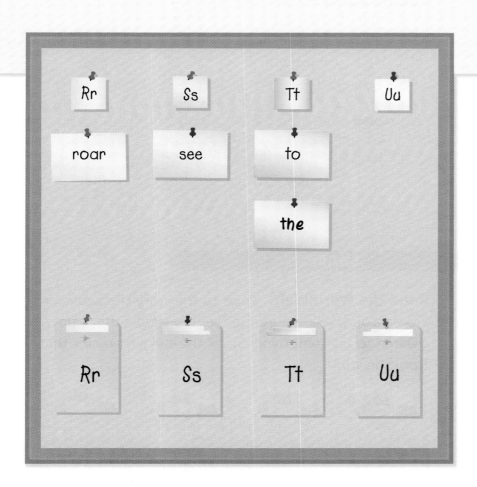

Diagnostic Check: Vocabulary

If... children have difficulty recognizing the word *see*,

Then... have them trace over the letters in the word *see* on their individual *Word Cards*. Then have them write the word *see* with a finger on their desktop as they say it.

ADDITIONAL SUPPORT ACTIVITIES

BELOW-LEVEL	Reteach, p. S56
ADVANCED	Extend, p. S57
ENGLISH-LANGUAGE LEARNERS	Reteach, p. S57

Name _____

What do we s e e ?

We s e e the bird.

We s e e the lion.

We s e e the _____.

Box for children to draw an animal.

High-Frequency Word: see
Have children read the question and trace the word see. Have children write see to complete each sentence and draw another animal they see at the zoo to complete the last sentence.

Animal Adventures **11**

▲ **Practice Book page 11**

OBJECTIVES

- *To identify and sort common words in basic categories*

- *To write a word web*

- *To identify story characters*

Materials

- chart paper

- crayons or markers

Shared Writing

Write a Word Web

STORY CHARACTERS

Talk About a Word Web   Remind children that a word web is a kind of chart that helps group things or ideas together. Tell children that story characters can be grouped together on a word web. Draw a large oval on chart paper and write the words *Story Characters* in the middle oval. Then draw eight spokes with smaller ovals attached to them.

Write a Word Web   Tell children that together they will write a word web for the characters in the story "The Rooster Who Went to His Uncle's Wedding." Ask children to name the characters. (rooster, grass, lamb, dog, stick, fire, water, sun) As children respond, write a character name in each oval.

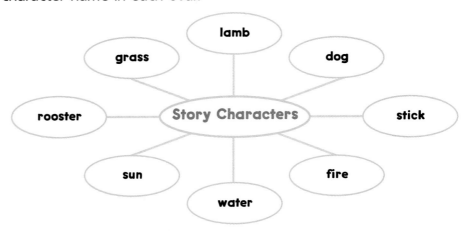

SHARE

Read the Word Web   Point to the story characters and read the words aloud. Ask children to identify letters they know. Invite other children to tell something about the story character that they recall from the story.

Journal Writing Have children draw and write about their favorite celebration.

WRAP UP Share Time

Reflect on the Lesson Have children discuss their favorite part of the story "The Rooster Who Went to His Uncle's Wedding." Have individuals retell the story.

S.S.R. Have children read silently from a book of their choice.

Centers ABC LETTER AND WORD

Tic-Tac-Toe

Draw a Tic-Tac-Toe grid on paper and make copies. Place a copy for each pair of children in the Letter and Word Center. Pairs of children can play together. Tell them to take turns writing the *X*. Remind children to form an *X* by beginning at the top left corner.

Materials

- copies of tic-tac-toe grid on paper
- crayons or markers

Day at a Glance

Day 4

WARM UP

Phonemic Awareness

Phoneme Isolation

Sharing Literature

Big Book of Rhymes and Songs:
"The Bear Went over the Mountain"

Read
Big Book of Rhymes and Songs

Develop Concept Vocabulary

Respond to Literature

Literature Focus: Rhythm of a piece

Phonics

Relating /ks/ to *x*

Reading

Decodable Book 4: *I Can See It!*

Shared Writing

Song Verse

MORNING MESSAGE

Kindergarten News

Today is _____.

Tomorrow is _____.

(Child's name) likes to visit _____.

Write Kindergarten News Talk with children about visiting new places. Ask them to tell the best part of visiting a place they have never been to before.

Use prompts such as the following to guide children as you write the news:

- **Who can show me the letter *w*?**
- **Let's clap syllables for *tomorrow*. How many parts do you clap?**
- **Who can show me two words that name days of the week?**

As you write the message, invite children to contribute by writing letters, words, or names they have previously learned. Remind them to use proper spacing, capitalization, and punctuation.

Calendar Language

Ask what day today is. Ask children what day comes after today. Point to the name of the day and say, *Tomorrow is _____.* Invite volunteers to name today and tomorrow.

Sunday	Monday	Tuesday	Wednesday	Thursday	Friday	Saturday
		1	2	3	4	5
6	7	8	9	10	11	12
13	14	15	16	17	18	19
20	21	22	23	24	25	26
27	28	29	30	31		

Phonemic Awareness

PHONEME ISOLATION

Listen for /ks/ Use a stuffed animal for this isolation activity. Hold up the stuffed animal and say *Max*. Have children repeat it, listening for the ending sound.

Model for children how to listen for the final sound.

> **MODEL** *Max* ends with the /ks/ sound. Max likes words that end with the /ks/ sound. *ta* /x/, tax. Say it with me. *Tax* ends with the /ks/ sound. Does Max like the word *tax*? Yes. *Tax* ends with the /ks/ sound.

Have children answer the following questions with *yes* or *no*.

Does Max like the word *fish*? *(no)*

Does Max like the word *tax*? *(yes)*

Does Max like the word *box*? *(yes)*

Does Max like the word *hat*? *(no)*

Does Max like the word *fox*? *(yes)*

Does Max like the word *fix*? *(yes)*

Does Max like the word *six*? *(yes)*

Does Max like the word *tack*? *(no)*

REACHING ALL LEARNERS

Diagnostic Check: Phonemic Awareness

If... children have difficulty isolating the final phoneme in words,

Then... segment each word for children: *ta*–/ks/. Ask them to segment the word with you and then say the word naturally. Have them repeat the word and then its final sound: *tax* /ks/.

ADDITIONAL SUPPORT ACTIVITIES

BELOW-LEVEL	Reteach, p. S58
ADVANCED	Extend, p. S59
ENGLISH-LANGUAGE LEARNERS	Reteach, p. S59

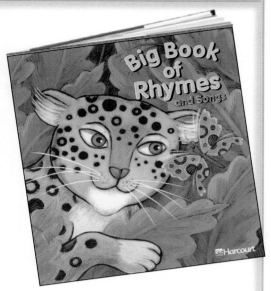

▲ **Big Book of Rhymes and Songs**

OBJECTIVES

• *To listen and respond to a song*

• *To understand text patterns*

• *To clap syllables for spoken words*

Materials

■ *Big Book of Rhymes and Songs, p. 21*

■ *Music CD*

■ construction paper

■ chart paper

■ crayons or markers

Sharing Literature

Read "The Bear Went over the Mountain"

READ ALOUD

Before Reading Point to the title "The Bear Went over the Mountain" on page 21 in the *Big Book of Rhymes and Songs.* Then read the title aloud, tracking the print. Use these prompts to help children make predictions:

• **Why do you think the bear wants to go over the mountain?** (Possible responses: to find other bears, to get food to eat)

• **What do you think he does when he gets there?** (Possible response: He looks for birds.)

During Reading Sing or play the song on the *Music CD.* As you sing,

• track the print.

• emphasize the word *see.*

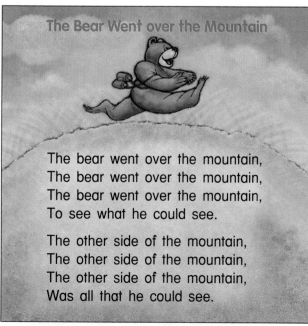

The bear went over the mountain,
The bear went over the mountain,
The bear went over the mountain,
To see what he could see.

The other side of the mountain,
The other side of the mountain,
The other side of the mountain,
Was all that he could see.

▲ **Big Book of Rhymes and Songs, page 21**

DEVELOP CONCEPT VOCABULARY

After Reading Ask children to supply the song words that answer these questions:

- **What word names an animal?** (*bear*)
- **What word names a place?** (*mountain*)
- **What word tells in what direction the bear went?** (*over*)
- **What word means "to look at"?** (*see*)

RESPOND TO LITERATURE

Innovate on the Text Encourage children to tell where they would go to see what they could see. List children's names on a chart, with a place beside each name. Call on a child to find his or her name on the chart and read the line. Then help children make up two lines to substitute for the repeated lines in "The Bear Went over the Mountain." Sing the new song together. For example:

Tonya went to the circus, (etc.)

To see what she could see.

A big, red nose on a
clown (etc.)

Was all that she could see.

Names	Places	
Tonya	circus	
Jason	forest	
Suzy	castle	

Literature Focus

RHYTHM OF A PIECE

Sway your shoulders side to side to keep the beat as you say the first verse of the rhyme "The Bear Went over the Mountain." Tell children when you say the words of a rhyme or a song, you don't want to say some fast and some slow, you want to say them the same. Have children sway their shoulders as you repeat the verse. Then have children say the words and clap the rhythm with you.

OBJECTIVE

To match consonant Xx to its sound

Materials

- Letter and Sound Chart 25
- Tactile Letter Cards x
- Picture/Word Cards fox, X ray
- X ray Pattern (page T18)
- marker
- scissors
- craft stick

X x

Can you find the x in fox, X-ray, exit, and in box? Extra large and extra small, Extra short and extra tall?

▲ **Letter and Sound Chart 25**

Phonics

Relating /ks/ to x

ACTIVE BEGINNING

Recite the Rhyme   Teach children the rhyme "Fox and Ox." Tell children to listen for the sound /ks/ as they learn the rhyme. After they learn the rhyme, encourage them to take turns being the ox and the fox and play Tic-Tac-Toe.

Fox and Ox

A fox and an ox

Played Tic-Tac-Toe,

The fox with *X*

And the ox with *O*.

by Susan Little

TEACH/MODEL

Introduce Letter and Sound   Display *Letter and Sound Chart 25.*

Touch the letter *X.* **What is the name of the letter?**

This letter stands for the /ks/ sound. Say /ks/.

Read the rhyme on the *Letter and Sound Chart* aloud, tracking the print.

Read the *Xx* words in the rhyme aloud. Then point to each *x* and have children say the /ks/ sound.

Have children join in as you read the rhyme again.

PRACTICE/APPLY

Guided Practice Distribute *Tactile Letter Cards x*. Then place *Picture/Word Cards X ray* and *fox* in a pocket chart. Say the names of the pictures as you point to the *x* in each. Have children repeat the words.

Tell children: **Some words begin with *x*, but most words have the /ks/ sound at the end.**

Point to the *X* in *X ray*. **The /ks/ sound is at the beginning of the word *X ray*.**

Point to the *x* in *fox*. **The /ks/ sound is at the end of the word *fox*.**

Tell children: **I'm going to say some words. If the word ends with /ks/, hold up your *x* card. If the word doesn't end with /ks/, don't hold up your card.**

jump	tax	box	pen	six	wax

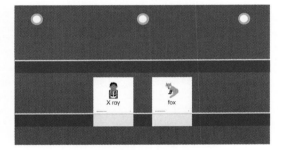

Independent Practice Distribute drawing paper and copies of the X ray Pattern (page TI8) to children. Have children color, cut out, and glue the pattern to the drawing paper. Ask children to draw the number six on the pattern.

BELOW-LEVEL

Show children pictures of a fox, a six, a box. Have children name each picture and tell the ending sound.

Phonics Resources

Phonics Express™ **CD-ROM, Level A,** Sparkle/Route 5/ Harbor, Train Station

Phonics Practice Book pages 91–92

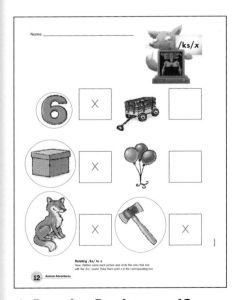

▲ **Practice Book page 12**

OBJECTIVE

To read high-frequency words no, see

Materials

- *Decodable Book 4: I Can See It!*
- *High-Frequency Word Cards*

no

see

- sentence strip
- drawing paper
- crayons

High-Frequency Words
no, see

Decodable Book ✔ Review

TEACH/MODEL

Review *no* and *see* Place the *High-Frequency Word Cards no* and *see* in a pocket chart. Point to each word and have children read. Then write *Can you see it? No.* on a sentence strip and put it in the pocket chart. Have children read the question and answer, pointing to each word. Point to each word again, and have children read the question. Ask a child to choose a *High-Frequency Word Card* and match it to the same word in the question.

no   see

PRACTICE/APPLY

Read the Book Distribute copies of *I Can See It!* Have children read the title, pointing to each word as they read it. Have children read the book, pointing to each word as they read.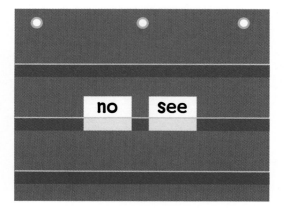

Respond Have children draw and label a picture of something they might see at a circus.

Read

Decodable Book 4: *I Can See It!*

I can see a big top!

2

I can see a man sit!

3

I can see a dog sit!

4

Can you see it?

5

No, I can not see it.

6

You can sit on a box.

7

I can see it!

8

High-Frequency Words

see, no, you

Decodable Words

See Word List on page T19.

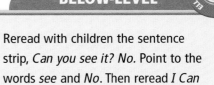

School-Home Connection

Take-Home Book Version

◀ **Decodable Book 4:** *I Can See It!*

BELOW-LEVEL

Reread with children the sentence strip, *Can you see it? No.* Point to the words *see* and *No.* Then reread *I Can See It!* with children. Have them frame the words *see* and *no.*

ADVANCED

Have children use the frame *Can you see a _____?* to write a question. Have them ask a partner their question. The partner can write *No, I can not see a _____.*

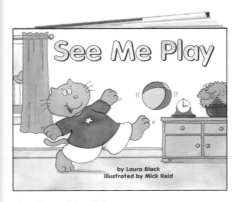

▲ **See Me Play**
Independent Reader 21

Shared Writing

Write a Song Verse

OBJECTIVES

- *To brainstorm a list*
- *To write new song verses*
- *To understand text patterns*
- *To follow words from left to right on a page*

Materials

■ *Big Book of Rhymes and Songs,* p. 21

CREATE A CHART

Talk About the Song   Have children sing "The Bear Went Over the Mountain." Explain that the title tells where the bear went to see what he could see. Have children talk about other places the bear might go. List their responses on the board.

Write New Verses   Tell children that together they are going to write new verses for the song. Read the list of suggestions on the board. Ask children to tell what the bear might see in each place. Record their responses on the list next to the appropriate place. Have children use the suggestions to make up the new verses.

The Bear Went	The Bear Could See
in the ocean	a whale swimming around
up in the sky	an airplane flying high
through a forest	an owl sleeping in a tree
around a tree	the other side of the tree
into a classroom	children reading books

SHARE

Read the Verses   Read the list of suggestions, tracking the words. Have a child point to the word *see.* Have children show spaces between words. Then point to one of the suggestions on the list, and have children sing the song, using the new words.

Writing Every Day

My Journal

Journal Writing Have children write and draw about a favorite outdoor activity.

WRAP UP # Share Time

Reflect on the Lesson Have children tell what they liked about the song "The Bear Went Over the Mountain." Ask them to name some words they learned that have the letter *x*.

S.S.R. *Sustained Silent Reading* Have children read silently from a book of their choice.

 **Centers**  **WRITING**

Would You Believe It?

Display magazine pictures or *Picture Cards* of animals in the Writing Center. Have children look through the pictures to select an animal. Children can work independently to draw a picture of the animal on an imaginary adventure and write a caption that tells where the animal went and what it saw. Encourage them to be creative, explaining that the adventure does not have to be something that could happen in real life.

Materials

- magazine pictures or *Picture Cards* of animals

- drawing paper

- crayons or markers

WARM UP

Phonemic Awareness
Syllable Segmentation

Sharing Literature
Library Book:
Elmer

Read

ELMER
David McKee

Develop Concept Vocabulary

Respond to Literature

Literature Focus:
Making Inferences

Phonics
Consonants /w/w, /x/x

Writing
Class Book

MORNING MESSAGE

Kindergarten News

Today is _____. Yesterday was _____. (Child's name) likes to _____ on a rainy day.

Write Kindergarten News Talk with children about things they like to do on rainy days.

Use prompts such as the following to guide children as you write the news:

- **Let's clap syllables for the word *Yesterday*. How many parts do you clap?**
- **Let's clap syllables for the name of (day).**
- **Let's clap syllables for the name of (yesterday).**
- **Who can show me the uppercase letters?**

As you write the message, invite children to contribute by writing letters, words, or names they have previously learned. Remind them to use proper spacing, capitalization, and punctuation.

Calendar Language

Point to and read aloud the names of the days of the week. Ask what day today is. Ask what day came before today. Invite children to name yesterday and today.

Sunday	Monday	Tuesday	Wednesday	Thursday	Friday	Saturday
		1	2	3	4	5
6	7	8	9	10	11	12
13	14	15	16	17	18	19
20	21	22	23	24	25	26
27	28	29	30	31		

Phonemic Awareness

SYLLABLE SEGMENTATION

Track Syllables in a Word   Remind children that words like *mountain* and *over* have two word parts, or syllables.

MODEL   *Mountain.* **Say *mountain* with me. I can break it into parts: *moun–tain.* Now, let's clap once for each part.** (clap two times as you say it) **I clapped two times. *Mountain* has two parts. Clap the syllables and say the word *mountain* with me.**

Repeat the following words, having children say the words with you and clap the word parts.

patchwork *(patch-work)*	**color** *(col-or)*	**something** *(some-thing)*
helpless *(help-less)*	**himself** *(him-self)*	**purple** *(pur-ple)*
berries *(ber-ries)*	**yellow** *(yel-low)*	**Elmer** *(El-mer)*
walking *(walk-ing)*	**jungle** *(jun-gle)*	**lion** *(li-on)*

ADVANCED

Have children listen for and clap only on the last syllable of each word. Then have them listen for and clap on the middle syllable of longer words.

▲ **Library Book**

OBJECTIVES

- *To recall story events*

- *To understand characters*

- *To make inferences*

Materials

- *Library Book: Elmer*

- chart paper

- marker

- *Audiotext*

Sharing Literature

Read Elmer

Before Reading   Page through *Elmer,* showing children the pictures to help them remember what happens in the story. Model for children how to set a purpose for rereading the story:

MODEL I remember that Elmer is unhappy about his patchwork colors. I want to reread the story so I can remember exactly how Elmer solves his problem.

During Reading   Read the story aloud. As you read,

- pause for children to look at the pictures and tell what is happening.

- change your tone of voice to reflect Elmer's varying emotions.

- have children identify both happy and sad parts of the story.

- point out how the other animals react to Elmer.

MODEL When Elmer is covered with berry juice, his friends don't recognize him. I don't think Elmer expected that to happen. Maybe he doesn't want to be gray after all.

DEVELOP CONCEPT VOCABULARY

After Reading Write the words *elephant, parade, color,* and *berries* on the board. Frame and read each word with children. Ask children to respond to the following questions by using the words in complete sentences.

- **What does an <u>elephant</u> look like?**
- **What would you wear in an Elmer's Day <u>parade</u>?**
- **What <u>color</u> does Elmer want to be?**
- **What does Elmer hope the <u>berries</u> will do?**

RESPOND TO LITERATURE

Describe a Character Ask children to describe Elmer. Then ask them whether he is someone they would want as a friend and to explain why.

MAKING INFERENCES

Page through *Elmer* again so that children can recall the story by looking at the pictures. Then read the last page of text aloud. Discuss with children whether they think Elmer will be happy from now on. Model how to use story information to make an inference about Elmer:

MODEL I think Elmer will be happy because he knows that his friends like him. They think he is fun to be with. They don't really care what color he is. Also, they are going to have a parade to honor him every year.

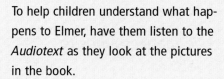

ENGLISH-LANGUAGE LEARNERS

To help children understand what happens to Elmer, have them listen to the *Audiotext* as they look at the pictures in the book.

ONGOING ASSESSMENT

As you reread *Elmer*, note whether children

- recall story events.
- understand characters.

OBJECTIVES

- *To recognize uppercase and lowercase Ww and Xx*
- *To match sounds to letters*

Materials

- pocket chart
- *Big Alphabet Cards Ww, Xx*
- *Alphabet Cards W, X*
- *Picture Cards fox, wagon, watch, water, watermelon, X ray*
- *Tactile Letter Cards w, x*

Phonics Resources

Phonics Express™ CD-ROM, Level A, Roamer/Route 3/ Harbor; Sparkle/Route 5/ Building Site

Consonants /w/w, /x/x ✔ Review

Recite the Rhymes
Display *Big Alphabet Cards Ww* and *Xx*. Ask children to name each letter and to trace the letter with a finger in the palm of a hand. Then have children recite "Wading in the Water" (page 550) and "Fox and Ox" (page 570).

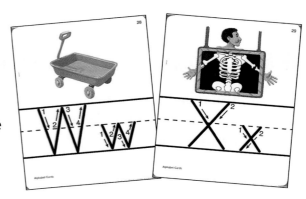

TEACH/MODEL

Discriminate *W* and *X* Hold up *Big Alphabet Card Ww* in a pocket chart and ask what letter this is. Point to the picture and say its name. Have children repeat it. (wagon) **What sound do you hear at the beginning of *wagon*?** (/w/) **What letter stands for the /w/ sound in *wagon*?** Touch the letter and say /w/. Touch the letter again and have children say /w/.

Follow the same procedure for *Big Alphabet Card Xx*.

Place in a pocket chart *Alphabet Cards W* and *X* and *Picture Cards watermelon* and *X ray*. Say each picture name and tell children you need to decide where to put each *Picture Card*.

MODEL I'll start with the watermelon. *W—atermelon* begins with the /w/ sound. So I'll put the picture of the watermelon below *W*.

Model the same process with *Picture Card X ray*.

PRACTICE/APPLY

Guided Practice Place these *Picture Cards* on the chalk ledge: *water, fox, watch, wagon.* Tell children that they will now sort some pictures.

Say the picture name. If the beginning sound is /w/, let's put the card below the *W*. If the ending sound is /ks/, let's put the card below the *X*.

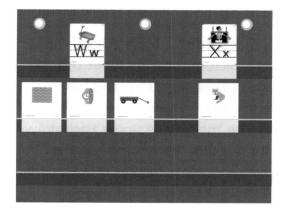

Independent Practice Give each child *Tactile Letter Cards* w and x.

I'm going to say some words. Listen carefully to the sound you hear at the beginning of the word. If it begins with the /w/ sound, hold up the *Letter Card* w.

well	waiter	queen	sunny	wonderful
window	beach	wig	week	warm

I'm going to say some words. Listen carefully to the sound you hear at the end of the word. If it ends with the /ks/ sound, hold up the *Letter Card* x.

dish	fix	wax	six	cage
box	ax	look	Max	ox

REACHING ALL LEARNERS

Diagnostic Check: Phonics

If... children have difficulty identifying letter-sound for /w/w and /x/x patterns in words,

Then... focus on one letter-sound at a time, saying the names of the pictures, saying the initial sound, and tracing the letter on the *Tactile Letter Cards.*

ADDITIONAL SUPPORT ACTIVITIES

BELOW-LEVEL	Reteach, p. S60
ADVANCED	Extend, p. S61
ENGLISH-LANGUAGE LEARNERS	Reteach, p. S61

Phonics Practice Book pages 93–94

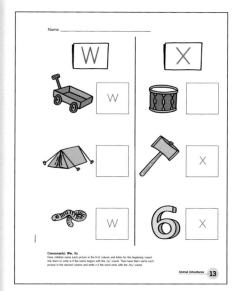

▲ **Practice Book page 13**

Day at a Glance
Day 1

WARM UP

Phonemic Awareness
Syllable Deletion

Sharing Literature
Big Book:
Walking Through the Jungle

Read

Develop Concept Vocabulary

Respond to Literature

Literature Focus: Picture Details

Phonics
Consonant /ks/*x*,
Short Vowel /o/*o*

Writing ✏️
Class Riddle Book

MORNING MESSAGE

Kindergarten News

Today is _____.

(Child's name) likes to eat

_____ for supper.

Write Kindergarten News Talk with children about suppertime in their home. Ask what they like to eat and how they help prepare supper.

Use prompts such as the following to guide children as you write the news:

- **How many letters are in (child's name)?**
- **Let's listen for the beginning sound in (child's name).**
- **What letter will I write first in (child's name)?**
- **What other names begin with the same letter and sound?**

As you write the message, invite children to contribute by writing letters, words, or names they have previously learned. Remind them to use proper spacing, capitalization, and punctuation.

Calendar Language

Point to and read aloud the days of the week. Name the days of the week, inviting children to join in and clap syllables for the name of each day. Ask what today is.

Sunday	Monday	Tuesday	Wednesday	Thursday	Friday	Saturday
		1	2	3	4	5
6	7	8	9	10	11	12
13	14	15	16	17	18	19
20	21	22	23	24	25	26
27	28	29	30	31		

Phonemic Awareness

SYLLABLE DELETION

Delete Syllables from a Word   Say the word *window*, clapping the syllables. Have children repeat the word and clap it with you. Model for children how to delete syllables.

MODEL *Window* has two syllables. Now I'm going to say *window* without the *win*. *dow* Say it with me: *dow*. Now you try. Say *doghouse* without the *dog*. (*house*)

Then say the following, asking children to tell you what syllable is left.

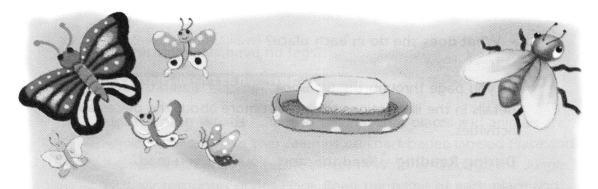

Say *butterfly* without *butter*. (*fly*)   **Say *bathtub* without *bath*.** (*tub*)

Say *classroom* without *class*. (*room*)   **Say *doughnut* without *nut*.** (*dough*)

Say *sailboat* without *sail*. (*boat*)   **Say *seaweed* without *sea*.** (*weed*)

Say *airplane* without *air*. (*plane*)   **Say *railroad* without *rail*.** (*road*)

Say *hotdog* without *hot*. (*dog*)   **Say *firefly* without *fire*.** (*fly*)

Writing

Write a Class Riddle Book

BUILD BACKGROUND

Talk About Story Animals Page through *Walking Through the Jungle*. Have children identify the animals and tell things they know about them, such as where they live, what they look like, and things they do.

Write a Riddle Write the following riddle on the board:

I live in the jungle. I like to swing from trees and eat bananas. What am I?

Read the riddle aloud, and have children guess the answer. On chart paper write these sentence frames: *I live in the ____.* and *I like ____.* Have children complete the sentences and illustrate them. On the back of the paper, have children draw and label the answer. Then write the title "Class Riddle Book" on a cover, and ask a child to draw a cover illustration. Assemble children's pages, add the cover, and staple.

I live in the osn. I like to swm.

OBJECTIVES

- *To write a class riddle book*
- *To describe common objects and events*
- *To write by moving left to right and top to bottom*
- *To recognize uppercase and lowercase letters*

Writing Every Day

Day 1: Class Riddle Book
Children complete sentence frames to create a page for a class riddle book.

Day 2: Weather Chart
Children work together to show on a chart the weather for a week.

Day 3: Invitation
Children work together to write a dinner invitation.

Day 4: Accordion Book
Children draw pictures and write captions to create an accordion book.

Day 5: Class Chart
Children work together to compose chart of places to visit.

Writing Every Day

Self-Selected Writing Have children write and draw about anything they'd like. If they have difficulty thinking of a topic have them ask two friends what they're going to write about.

WRAP UP # Share Time

Author's Chair After the book is assembled, display the cover and have children point to the uppercase letters in the title. Have children identify the letters they recognize. Then ask each child to share his or her own riddle and call on another child to give the answer. The child who gives the answer can turn the page to check the answer.

S.S.R. *Sustained Silent Reading* Have children read silently from a book of their choice.

Centers   SCIENCE

Animal Habitats

Have children make one of the animals from *Walking Through the Jungle* out of modeling clay. Then have them make a display mat for the animal, using a sheet of construction paper. Tell children to decorate their mats by showing things that would be found where the animal lives, such as trees, plants, other animals, and rivers. Direct children to write on the mat their own name, the animal name, and where the animal lives.

 **Materials**

■ modeling clay

■ construction paper

■ crayons and pencils

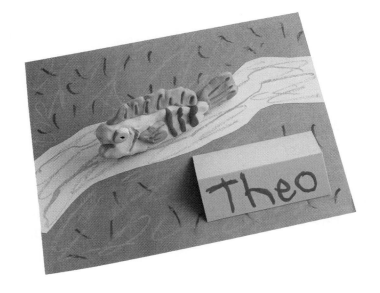

WARM UP

Phonemic Awareness
Phoneme Blending

Sharing Literature
Library Book:
So Say the Little Monkeys

Read

Develop Listening Comprehension

Respond to Literature

Literature Focus: Rhyming Words

Phonics
Blending /o/-/ks/

Interactive Writing
Weather Chart

MORNING MESSAGE

Kindergarten News

There are many houses in our neighborhood.

(Child's name)'s house is _____.

Write Kindergarten News   Talk with children about houses in their neighborhood. Have them describe their own house.

Use prompts such as the following to guide children as you write the news:

- **Let's clap syllables for the word *neighborhood*. How many parts do you clap?**
- **What letter will I write first in the word *house*?**
- **How many words are in the second sentence?**

As you write the message, invite volunteers to contribute by writing letters, words, or names they have previously learned. Remind them to use proper spacing, capitalization, and punctuation.

Calendar Language

Have children identify the day of the week. Then ask them to name class activities for each day.

Sunday	Monday	Tuesday	Wednesday	Thursday	Friday	Saturday
		1	2	3	4	5
6	7	8	9	10	11	12
13	14	15	16	17	18	19
20	21	22	23	24	25	26
27	28	29	30	31		

Phonemic Awareness

PHONEME BLENDING

Blend Sounds   Use the rabbit puppet for this blending activity. Tell children to listen to the sounds the rabbit says, blend the sounds and say the word.

MODEL /p/ /o/ /t/, **The rabbit likes to break words into parts. Listen as he blends the sounds: /ppoott/. Blend the sounds with the rabbit and name the word: /ppoott/, pot.**

Repeat the same procedure with the following words:

▲ *Oo-pples and Boo-noo-noos: Songs and Activities for Phonemic Awareness,* pages 74–75.

/b/ /o/ /ks/ (*box*)   /t/ /e/ /n/ (*ten*)   /f/ /o/ /ks/ (*fox*)

/d/ /o/ /k/ (*dock*)   /h/ /o/ /t/ (*hot*)   /g/ /a/ /s/ (*gas*)

/f/ /i/ /ks/ (*fix*)   /b/ /e/ /l/ (*bell*)   /m/ /a/ /ks/ (*Max*)

/t/ /a/ /k/ (*tack*)   /s/ /o/ /k/ (*sock*)   /o/ /ks/ (*ox*)

/a/ /ks/ (*ax*)

REACHING ALL LEARNERS

Below   On-Level   Advanced   ELL

Diagnostic Check: Phonemic Awareness

If... children have difficulty blending sounds to build words,

Then... segment the beginning sound from each word and have children repeat after you and name the word. For example, /b/–*ox*, /d/–*ock* and so on.

ADDITIONAL SUPPORT ACTIVITIES

BELOW-LEVEL	Reteach, p. S64
ADVANCED	Extend, p. S65
ENGLISH-LANGUAGE LEARNERS	Reteach, p. S65

▲ **Library Book**

OBJECTIVES

- *To listen and respond to a folktale*

- *To use pictures and context to make predictions*

- *To retell the story*

- *To identify rhyming words*

Materials

■ *Library Book:*
So Say the Little Monkeys

Sharing Literature

Read So Say the Little Monkeys

READ ALOUD

Before Reading Display the cover of *So Say the Little Monkeys*, and ask children to predict what kind of animals the story will be about. When children predict monkeys, repeat the word, emphasizing the /m/ sound. Have a child point to the word in the title that he or she thinks is *Monkeys* and explain why. Then read the title aloud as you track the print. Have children look at the cover to make predictions about what the monkeys will do. Use these prompts to guide children as they predict:

- **What do you see in the picture on the cover?** (monkeys eating bananas, a monkey holding a baby monkey, monkeys climbing in trees)

- **What do you think the monkeys will do in the story?** (Possible response: swing on trees)

- **Where do you think the story takes place?** (Possible response: in a jungle)

Tell children that this story happens far away from where they live. The story takes place in a rainforest.

During Reading Read the story aloud. As you read,

- use a lively, singsong rhythm.

- emphasize out the sound words in the text.

- pause to model how to make and confirm predictions.

MODEL Every time a new day comes, the monkeys play instead of building a home. I don't think they will ever build a home!

DEVELOP LISTENING COMPREHENSION

After Reading Have children answer these questions about the story:

- **Where do the monkeys sleep?** (in the thorny trees)
- **Where do the other animals sleep?** (Possible responses: in nests, in tree holes, underground)
- **Why do the monkeys want to build a home?** (because the thorns are uncomfortable, and they are wet and cold at night)
- **Do you think the monkeys will ever build a home? Why?** (Possible response: No, because they are too busy playing and having a fun time.)

RESPOND TO LITERATURE

Retell the Story Display *So Say the Little Monkeys*, and tell children that it is a folktale, a story that has been told many times.

Have children sit in their own "storytelling circle." Show the first picture in the book, and ask a child to say a sentence about it. Then ask another child to continue the story. Repeat with the other illustrations.

Literature Focus

RHYMING WORDS

Remind children that rhyming words sound the same at the end, such as *day* and *play*. Page through the story, and ask children to supply rhyming story words. Give children word clues to help them guess the words. Use the following words and clues:

fun	Clue: **Something you do with your legs.** (*run*)
creep	Clue: **Something you do at night.** (*sleep*)
should	Clue: **Something you use to make a fire.** (*wood*)
hole	Clue: **An animal that lives underground.** (*mole*)
said	Clue: **A place where a person sleeps.** (*bed*)

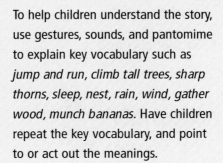

ENGLISH-LANGUAGE LEARNERS

To help children understand the story, use gestures, sounds, and pantomime to explain key vocabulary such as *jump and run, climb tall trees, sharp thorns, sleep, nest, rain, wind, gather wood, munch bananas.* Have children repeat the key vocabulary, and point to or act out the meanings.

ONGOING ASSESSMENT

As you read *So Say the Little Monkeys,* note whether children

- listen and respond to the folktale.
- use pictures and context to make predictions.
- recall story events.

OBJECTIVES

- *To identify and recognize the initial sound of a spoken word*

- *To blend o and x*

Materials

- *Big Alphabet Cards Oo and Xx*

- *Alphabet Cards o, x, b, f*

- pocket chart

- sentence strips

Phonics

Blending /o/ - /ks/  Introduce

ACTIVE BEGINNING

Word Hunt Have children sit in a circle. As you read the following verse, have children echo. Establish a beat and keep it going throughout the verse.

Going on a word hunt.

What's this word?

/b/ /o/ /ks/

Together: *box*!

Continue with the words /f/ /o/ /ks/ (*fox*), /o/ /ks/ (*ox*).

TEACH/MODEL

Recognize *o* and *x* Display *Big Alphabet Card Oo* on the chalk ledge or in a pocket chart. Ask: **What letter is this?** (*o*) **What sound does this letter stand for?** (/o/)

Have children say /o/ with you as you point to the letter.

Do the same procedure for *Big Alphabet Card Xx*.

Word Blending Explain to children that they are going to blend the two letters together to read words.

- Place the *Alphabet Cards o* and *x* in the pocket chart, separate from each other.

- Point to *o*. Say **/o/**. Have children repeat the sound after you.
- Point to *x*. Say **/kkss/**. Have children repeat the sound after you.

- Slide the *x* next to the *o*. Move your hand under the letters and blend the sounds, elongating them—**/okss/**. Have children repeat after you.

- Then have children blend and read *ox* with you.

PRACTICE/APPLY

Guided Practice Place the letters *f*, *o*, and *x* in the pocket chart.

- Point to *f* and say **/ff/**. Point to the letter *o* and say **/o/**. Slide the *o* next to *f*. Move your hand under the letters and blend the sounds, elongating them—**/ffoo/**. Have children blend the sounds after you.

- Point to *x*. Say **/kkss/**. Have children say the sound.

- Slide the *x* next to the *fo*. Slide your hand under *fox* and blend the sounds. Have children blend the sounds as you slide your hand under the word.

- Then have children read the word *fox* along with you.

Follow the same procedure to build and blend *box* with children.

Independent Practice Write on sentence strips the sentence frame *I have a ___ in the box.* Place one strip in the pocket chart and work with children to read the sentence frame. Then pass the sentence strips to children. Have them complete the sentence. When they have finished, ask them to read their sentence.

BELOW-LEVEL

Have children use their *Word Builder* and *Word Builder Cards* to build and blend *fox, box, ox.*

ENGLISH-LANGUAGE LEARNERS

Before giving each child a sentence strip to complete the Independent Practice activity, practice reading the sentence frame together. Then, have children say the sentence and fill in a word orally.

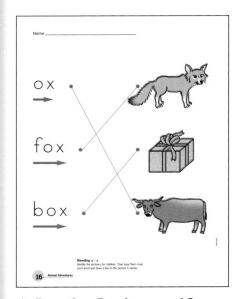

▲ **Practice Book page 16**

Animal Adventures 603

Interactive Writing

Write a Weather Chart

OBJECTIVES

- *To write a weather chart*
- *To recall story events*
- *To connect life experiences to text*
- *To follow words left to right on a page*

Materials

- poster board
- crayons or markers

teaching tip

Before making the chart, explain to children that sometimes people use symbols or pictures instead of words to give information.

WEATHER WORDS

Talk About Weather   Have children recall how the monkeys in the story act when it is rainy and windy and when it is sunny. Tell they will write a chart to show what one week of weather is like for the monkeys in the story.

Write a Weather Chart   Have children help write a weather chart for one week. On poster board, ask children to help you write the title *Monkey Weather Chart,* and list the days for the week across the top. Discuss what picture they can draw on the chart and what word they can write to show the weather, such as *rain* and rain drops for a rainy day, *sun* and a picture of the sun for a sunny day, *cloud* and a picture of a cloud for a cloudy day, and the word *wind* and curly lines for a windy day.

Monday	Tuesday	Wednesday	Thursday	Friday	Saturday	Sunday
sunny	cloudy	cloudy	rainy	sunny	windy	sunny

SHARE

Read the Chart   When the chart is completed, have children read the chart to determine the following:

- **How many rainy days were there?**
- **What kind of weather happened most often in the rain forest?**
- **What kind of weather was there on Wednesday?**

Journal Writing   Have children draw and write about their favorite weather.

WRAP UP **Share Time**

Reflect on the Lesson Ask children to tell about their favorite part of *So Say the Little Monkeys*. Ask them if they would recommend this book to a friend and to tell why.

S.S.R. *Sustained Silent Reading* Have children read silently from a book of their choice.

Centers  ART

Character-on-a-String Books

Make blank books by stapling together several sheets of drawing paper and a long piece of yarn. Have each child draw and cut out a little monkey to tape onto the end of the yarn so that it hangs out below the book. Have children draw pictures of more monkeys in different settings on the book pages. When they read their book, have children use the monkey on the yarn as a bookmark, moving it from page to page and telling a story about what the monkey might do with the other monkeys.

Materials

- drawing paper
- tape
- yarn
- crayons or markers
- scissors

WARM UP

Phonemic Awareness
Phoneme Matching: Initial

Sharing Literature
Read-Aloud Anthology:
"Counting Crocodiles"

Read

KINDERGARTEN
READ-ALOUD
Anthology
Harcourt

Develop Listening Comprehension

Respond to Literature

Literature Focus: Problem-Solution

Phonics
Words with /o/ and /ks/

Shared Writing
Invitation

MORNING MESSAGE

Kindergarten News

Today is (day of week). There are seven days in a week.

This month is (name of month).

There are (number of days) days in (name of month).

Write Kindergarten News   Talk with children about things they can count, such as days in a week, months in a year, crayons in a box, children in a class.

Use prompts such as the following to guide children as you write the news:

- **Who can show me the name of a day? The name of a month?**
- **What sound do you hear at the beginning of (name of month)?**
- **What letter is at the beginning of (name of month)?**

As you write the message, invite children to contribute by writing letters, words, or names they have previously learned. Remind them to use proper spacing, capitalization, and punctuation.

Calendar Language

Name the days of the week, inviting children to join in and clap for each day. Tell children to count the days of the week as you point to each one. Ask how many days are in a week.

Sunday	Monday	Tuesday	Wednesday	Thursday	Friday	Saturday
		1	2	3	4	5
6	7	8	9	10	11	12
13	14	15	16	17	18	19
20	21	22	23	24	25	26
27	28	29	30	31		

Phonemic Awareness

PHONEME MATCHING: INITIAL

Match Initial Sounds Model for children how to match the initial sounds in words:

> **MODEL** *Mouse, monkey.* I listen for the first sound in each word. *Mouse* begins with the /m/ sound. *Monkey* begins with the /m/ sound. *Mouse* and *monkey* have the same beginning sound. Now I'll say two more words. Listen for the beginning sound. Show me thumbs up if both words have the same beginning sound. *Six, seven.* (Children should show thumbs up.)

Tell children you will say some more words. Ask them to show thumbs up each time they hear two words with the same beginning sound.

round, rice	live, low	shout, hop
jungle, jump	dinner, sand	food, friend
tail, leaf	tide, today	deer, king
long, line	wonderful, water	palace, put

BELOW-LEVEL

Elongate the beginning sounds in word pairs, such as *went/wish*, *sea/same*, *river/lion*. Have children repeat the words, elongating the beginning sounds.

ADVANCED

Say word pairs such as *high/help*, *goat/gas*, *top/tame*, and have children produce a third word with the same beginning sound.

OBJECTIVES

- *To build and read simple one-syllable words*

- *To understand that as the letters of words change, so do the sounds*

Materials

- *Alphabet Cards b, f, m, i, o, x*

- *Word Builders*

- *Word Builder Cards b, f, m, i, o, x*

- pocket chart

- *Magnetic Letters*

- cookie sheet

REVIEW LETTERS

Phonics

Words with /o/ and /ks/

ACTIVE BEGINNING

Action Rhyme   Teach children this rhyme and the actions that go with it:

The fox is in a box.
(Outline box with fingers in each sentence.)

The box is on the ox.

The fox and box are on the ox.

TEACH/MODEL

Blending Words   Distribute *Word Builders* and *Word Builder Cards b, f, m, i, o, x* to children. As you place *Alphabet Cards* in a pocket chart, tell children to place the same *Word Builder Cards* in their *Word Builder*.

- Place *Alphabet Cards f, o,* and *x* in the pocket chart. Have children do the same.

- Point to *f*. Say **/ff/**. Point to *o*. Say **/oo/**.

- Slide the *o* next to the *f*. Then move your hand under the letters and blend the sounds, elongating them—**/ffoo/**. Have children do the same.

- Point to the letter *x*. Say **/kkss/**. Have children do the same.

- Slide the *x* next to the *fo*. Slide your hand under *fox* and blend by elongating the sounds—**/ffookkss/**. Have children do the same.

- Then have children blend and read the word *fox* along with you.

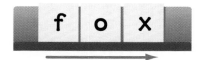

PRACTICE/APPLY

Guided Practice   Have children place *Word Builder Cards i* and *x* in their *Word Builder.*

- **Add *m* to *ix*. What word did you make?**

- **Change *m* to *f*. What word did you make?**

- **Change *i* to *o*. What word did you make?**

- **Change *f* to *b*. What word did you make?**

Independent Practice   Have children use *Magnetic Letters a, b, f, i, p, o, s, t, w, x* and a cookie sheet in the Letters and Words Center to build and read *wax, fix, six, fox, box, pot,* and *top.*

BELOW-LEVEL

Have children name the letters as they place them in their word builders. Say the sound and have them repeat the sound. Have them move their hands under the letters in the word builders as they blend the sounds with you.

ADVANCED

Have children use the *Magnetic Letters b, o, x* and *High-Frequency Word Cards You, I, have, a* to build sentences: *You have a box. I have a box.*

Name _____

box

ox

fox

Words with /x/ and /ks/
Have children read each word and then circle the picture that the word names.

Animal Adventures 17

▲ **Practice Book page 17**

OBJECTIVES

- *To understand the purpose of an invitation*
- *To write an invitation*
- *To connect speech to print*
- *To understand how time is written*

Materials

■ chart paper

■ marker

Shared Writing

Write an Invitation

EXTEND THE FOLKTALE

Talk About the Folktale   Have children recall that Mouse-Deer tells the crocodiles the king will send them a dinner invitation. Ask: **What is an invitation? What do you think the dinner invitation from the king to the crocodiles would say? Let's work together to write it.**

Tell children there are things you must write in an invitation so that the crocodiles will know what it is for. As children suggest ideas for the invitation, write the words on the chart paper. Say the words aloud as you write them. Use the following prompts to guide children as you write their responses on chart paper:

- **What is the invitation for? In an invitation, you usually write the words *Please come*. Where should I start writing?**
- **What are the crocodiles invited to? What letter does *dinner* begin with?**
- **Where is the dinner?**
- **What time is the dinner?**
- **Who is sending the invitation?**

Journal Writing   Have children draw and write about what they think the crocodile would have for dinner.

WRAP UP # Share Time

Read the Invitation   When the invitation is finished, read it with children. Ask children to point to the uppercase letter that starts the sentence. Show them how the time is written, with the hour followed by a colon and two zeros. Repeat the questions from the writing activity and have children check to be sure all of the important information is there.

S.S.R. *Sustained Silent Reading*   Have children read silently from a book of their choice.

 **Centers**   **MATH**

More or Less

Put the animal figures or other small objects in the box and place in the Math Center. Children work with a partner. Each child uses a cup to scoop some figures out of the box. Partners look into the two cups and guess which cup has more figures. Then children take the figures out of each cup and count them to see whether their prediction was correct. Remind children to return the figures to the box to start again or to give others a turn.

 Materials

■ shoe box or other container

■ twenty or more small (1-inch) plastic animal figures, or other small objects

■ small plastic or paper cups

WARM UP

Phonemic Awareness

Onset and Rime: Blending

Sharing Literature

Big Book of Rhymes and Songs: "The Little Turtle"

Read

Develop Concept Vocabulary

Respond to Literature

Literature Focus: Action Words

Phonics

Short vowel /o/o

Reading

Decodable Book 5: *What Is in the Box?*

Writing ✎

Accordion Book

MORNING MESSAGE

Kindergarten News

Today is _____. The month is _____.

(Child's name) was surprised when

_____.

Write Kindergarten News   Talk with children about a time when they were surprised by something that happened. Have them tell how they felt.

Use prompts such as the following to guide children as you write the news:

- **Who can point to a person's name?**
- **Who can show me the name of a day of the week?**
- **Who can show me the name of a month in the year?**
- **What kind of letter do the names begin with?**

As you write the message, invite children to contribute by writing letters, words, or names they have previously learned. Remind them to use proper spacing, capitalization, and punctuation.

Calendar Language

Point to the numbers on the calendar. Have children count the numbers with you. Stop on the day's date. Point to and read it aloud. Have children name the month and the date.

Sunday	Monday	Tuesday	Wednesday	Thursday	Friday	Saturday
			1	2	3	4	5
6	7	8	9	10	11	12
13	14	15	16	17	18	19
20	21	22	23	24	25	26
27	28	29	30	31		

Phonemic Awareness

ONSET AND RIME: BLENDING

Blend Letters in Words   Use the rabbit puppet for this blending activity. Model for children how to blend letters in words.

MODEL   **Listen to the rabbit: /f/–*in*. Say /f/–*in* with the rabbit. He can blend the sounds: /ffiinn/. Blend the sounds with the rabbit. Now say the word.** *fin*

Ask children to listen as the rabbit says the following words, emphasizing the beginning sound. Have children blend the sounds with the rabbit and name the word.

/b/-*ox* (box)	**/t/-*op*** (top)	**/w/-*ax*** (wax)
/k/-*atch* (catch)	**/r/-*ock*** (rock)	**/d/-*ip*** (dip)
/m/-*ud* (mud)	**/s/-*ack*** (sack)	**/p/-*op*** (pop)
/l/-*ist* (list)	**/b/-*ell*** (bell)	**/w/-*et*** (wet)

ADVANCED

Ask children to blend words with consonant blends and digraphs, such as /b/ /r/ – *eak* /s/ /l/ – *ow* /k/ /r/ – *eam* /d/ /r/ – *ink*.

Sharing Literature

Read "The Little Turtle"

READ ALOUD

Before Reading   Display the *Big Book of Rhymes and Songs*. Ask a child to find the table of contents that lists all the rhymes and songs in the book. Point to and read aloud the title "The Little Turtle," and tell children that the poem starts on page 24.

Ask children to share what they know about turtles. Use these prompts to help build background:

- **What do turtles do?** (Possible responses: swim, climb on rocks, sun themselves, catch bugs to eat, snap at things, lay eggs)

- **Where do turtles live?** (in and near water)

- **What sizes do turtles come in?** (Possible responses: There are little turtles and giant sea turtles.)

Tell children that you are going to read the poem with the actions that go along with the words. Have them listen and watch as you demonstrate the actions. (See *Read-Aloud Anthology* page 13 for actions.)

During Reading   Read the poem aloud. As you read,

- pause to model the text pattern.

   MODEL   **I see and hear the words *We snapped at* over and over in the poem. This shows me that turtles snap a lot. Now let's listen for more words that tell us over and over what he likes to do in the poem.**

▲ **Big Book of Rhymes and Songs**

OBJECTIVES

- *To recognize the table of contents in a book*

- *To identify a poem*

- *To listen and respond to a poem*

- *To understand text patterns*

- *To describe objects*

- *To identify action words*

Materials

- *Big Book of Rhymes and Songs* pp. 24–25

- *Read-Aloud Anthology* p. 13

There was a little turtle.
He lived in a box.
He swam in a puddle.
He climbed on the rocks.

He snapped at a mosquito.
He snapped at a flea.
He snapped at a minnow.
And he snapped at me.

He caught the mosquito.
He caught the flea.
He caught the minnow.
But he didn't catch me.

Vachel Lindsay

DEVELOP CONCEPT VOCABULARY

After Reading Ask children to name the things the turtle caught. (mosquito, minnow, flea) Then use the following procedure to discuss the words:

Say *mosquito*. A mosquito is a flying bug that bites.
What is a mosquito? (Possible responses: A mosquito is a flying bug that bites. Its bite makes you itchy.)

Say *flea*. A flea is a jumping bug that bites.
What is a flea? (Possible responses: A flea is a jumping bug that bites. It can bite cats and dogs.)

Say *minnow*. A minnow is a very small fish.
What is a minnow? (Possible responses: A minnow is a very small fish. It swims in water.)

RESPOND TO LITERATURE

Innovate on the Text Remind children that the turtle snapped at things and tried to catch them, such as a mosquito, a flea, a minnow, and a person. Have children make up new lines by supplying new words for the lines:

He snapped at a _____.

He caught the _____.

Say the poem again several times, each time substituting words suggested by children.

★ Literature Focus

ACTION WORDS

Remind children that action words tell what a person or animal is doing. Tell children that *swam, climbed, snapped,* and *catch* are action words in the poem "The Little Turtle." Frame and say each word, one at a time, and have children act out its meaning. Whisper other action words, such as *run, hop, throw, dance,* to individuals, and have them act out the words for the group to guess.

REACHING ALL LEARNERS

Below / On-Level / Advanced / ELL

Diagnostic Check: Comprehension

If... children have difficulty identifying and demonstrating the meanings of action words,

Then... show children *Picture Cards turtle, boy, kangaroo,* and *owl*. Model actions to go with each picture. Turtle-snaps, boy-runs, kangaroo-hops, and owl-flies. Have children repeat the action as you hold up each picture. Ask: *What is the action?*

ADDITIONAL SUPPORT ACTIVITIES

BELOW-LEVEL Reteach, p. S66

ADVANCED Extend, p. S67

ENGLISH-LANGUAGE LEARNERS Reteach, p. S67

Short Vowel /o/o ✔Review

Materials

- *Alphabet Cards b, o, x*

- pocket chart

- *Decodable Book 5: What Is in the Box?*

- a box with a cover

- classroom objects

BELOW-LEVEL

Reread the story with children. Pause and point to the words *no* and *see* when they appear in the story. Have children read the words aloud.

ADVANCED

Have children innovate on the text by adding other animals to the story, using the text pattern.

TEACH/MODEL

Review Blending   Place *Alphabet Cards o* and *x* next to each other in the pocket chart. Move your hand under the letters, blend them, and say the word. **/ookkss/–ox.** Have children blend the sounds and say the word.

Place *Alphabet Card b* in front of *o* and *x*. Slide your hand under the letters, blend them, and say the word: **/bbookkss/–box.** Have children blend the sounds and say the word.

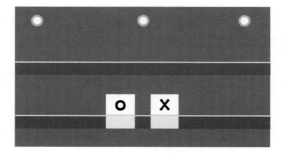

PRACTICE/APPLY

Read the Book   Distribute copies of *What Is in the Box?* Have children read the title. Encourage them to point to each word as they read it.

Have children read the book, pointing to each word as they read it.

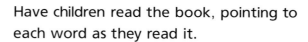

Respond   Have children take turns placing an object in the box, without classmates seeing what it is. The rest of the group asks questions to guess what is in the box.

Decodable Book 5: *What Is in the Box?*

Is a cat in the box?

2

No, it is not a cat.

3

Is a pig in the box?

4

No, it is not a pig.

5

Is a fox in the box?

6

No, it is not a fox.

7

We see it.
A dog is in the box!

8

■ **High-Frequency Words**

what, the, no, see, we

■ **Decodable Words**

See list on page T19.

School–Home Connection

Take-Home Book Version

◀ Decodable Book 5
What Is in the Box?

▲ **Little Red Hen Bakes a Cake**
Independent Reader 22

Animal Adventures **619**

OBJECTIVES

• *To write an accordion book*

• *To write from left to right and top to bottom*

• *To recall sequence*

• *To distinguish letters from words*

Materials

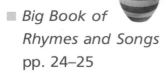

■ *Big Book of Rhymes and Songs* pp. 24–25

■ drawing paper

■ crayons or markers

teaching tip

Before children begin to write their books, have them review the sequence of actions in the poem.

Writing

Write an Accordion Book

BUILD BACKGROUND

Talk About the Poem   Read "The Little Turtle" with children, encouraging them to join in. Explain that the little turtle snapped at things in the poem. Have children talk about the things he tried to catch. List their responses on the board.

a mosqito

a flea

a minnow

me

Write an Accordion Book   Tell children that they are going to write an accordion book that shows the things the turtle tried to catch. Help them fold a strip of drawing paper accordion style into four sections. Frame the title of the poem in the *Big Book of Rhymes and Songs,* and write the title "The Little Turtle" on the board. Have children write the title on the cover of their book. Then have children draw the sequence of actions. Have them write a caption for each scene.

SHARE

Read the Accordion Books   Point to the title on the board, and ask how many words are in the title. Ask the class to count along with you as you point to each word to see how many there are. Ask children if they have three words in the title they wrote for their books. Then have children share their accordion books, reading the captions on each page.

Self-Selected Writing   Have children write and draw about anything they'd like. If they have difficulty thinking of a topic have them ask two friends what they're going to write about.

WRAP UP Share Time

Reflect on the Lesson Ask children to tell about the book they read, *What Is in the Box?* Have them tell what the story was about. Ask them to tell what they thought was in the box.

S.S.R. *Sustained Silent Reading* Have children read silently from a book of their choice.

 Centers  ART

Favorite Animals

Place a variety of magazine pictures of animals on a table. Have children sort through the pictures and identify the animals they like best. Have children cut out three of the animal pictures and glue them onto a sheet of construction paper. Have them label their pictures with the animal name and an action word to describe what each animal does, such as climb, swim, swing, crawl, hop.

 Materials

- magazine pictures of animals
- scissors
- glue
- construction paper
- crayons or markers

Day at a Glance
Day 5

WARM UP

Phonemic Awareness
Phoneme Matching: Final

Sharing Literature
Big Book:
Walking Through the Jungle

Read

WALKING THROUGH THE JUNGLE
Debbie Harter

Respond to Literature
Literature Focus: Setting

Phonics
Blending /o/–/ks/

Shared Writing
Class Story

MORNING MESSAGE

Kindergarten News

The first day of the week is _____.

The last day of the week is _____.

(Child's name) likes to walk _____.

Write Kindergarten News Talk with children about their favorite places to take a walk. Have them tell about the things they see on their walk.

Use prompts such as the following to guide children as you write the news:

- Let's clap syllables for the word *Saturday*. How many parts do you clap?
- Who can tell me the last word part in the word *Saturday*?
- What letter should I write first in the word *walk*?

As you write the message, invite children to contribute by writing letters, words, or names they have previously learned. Remind them to use proper spacing, capitalization, and punctuation.

Calendar Language

Point to and read aloud the days of the week. Have children identify the first day of the week. (Sunday) Have children identify the last day of the week. (Saturday)

Sunday	Monday	Tuesday	Wednesday	Thursday	Friday	Saturday
		1	2	3	4	5
6	7	8	9	10	11	12
13	14	15	16	17	18	19
20	21	22	23	24	25	26
27	28	29	30	31		

Phonemic Awareness

PHONEME MATCHING: FINAL

Match Final Sounds Say the words *guess* and *hiss* slowly several times, emphasizing the ending sound. Have children repeat the words. Say:

Guess, *hiss.* **I listen for the end sound in each word.** *Guess* **ends with the /s/ sound.** *Hiss* **ends with the /s/ sound.** *Guess* **and** *hiss* **have the same ending sound.**

Now I'll say two more words. Listen for the ending sound. Show me thumbs up if both words have the same ending sound. *Toad*, *bed.* (Children should show thumbs up.)

Tell children you will say some more words. Ask them to show thumbs up each time they hear two words with the same ending sound.

ADVANCED

Say pairs of words with the same final sound and ask children to provide more words with the same ending sound; for example, *cut/rat, ham/rim, hood/feed.*

out, **keep**

soap, cup (thumbs up)

cloud, seed (thumbs up)

wag, log (thumbs up)

drum, star

drag, **van**

look, bike (thumbs up)

leaf, roof (thumbs up)

mail, wheel (thumbs up)

▲ **Big Book**

OBJECTIVES

- *To listen and respond to a story*

- *To recall story events*

- *To recognize setting*

Materials

- *Big Book: Walking Through the Jungle*

- *Teacher's Resource Book p. 150*

- crayons or markers

- scissors

- glue or tape

Sharing Literature

Read Walking Through the Jungle

READ ALOUD

Before Reading Display the *Big Book*, and read the title aloud. Point to the word *jungle,* and remind children that the word names a place. Help children set a purpose for listening to the story before you reread it.

> **MODEL** I can remember the animals the girl sees in the story. I want to reread the story to remember the place where she meets each animal.

During Reading Read the story aloud. As you do so,

- allow time for children to comment on the settings shown in the illustrations.

- point out what the girl does in each setting.

> **MODEL** When the girl sees the lion in the jungle, and hears it roar, she swings away on a rope. Her eyes look big. I think she's afraid.

RESPOND TO LITERATURE

Retell the Story   Give children copies of the finger puppets on page 150 of the *Teacher's Resource Book*. Have children draw a picture of a story character, cut it out, glue or tape it, and place it on a finger. Have children retell the story with their puppet, or let them work in small groups, taking turns playing each part.

★ **Literature Focus**

SETTING

Remind children that the setting of a story is when and where the story happens. Explain that many stories happen in one place. Remind children that *Elmer* takes place in the jungle. Point out that the activities in *Walking Through the Jungle* happen in different places. Ask children to name the different settings as you page through the story.

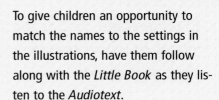
ONGOING ASSESSMENT

As you reread *Walking Through the Jungle*, note whether children

- listen and respond to the story.
- notice changes in the settings and in the character's actions.

OBJECTIVES

- *To build and read simple one-syllable words*
- *To understand that as the letters of words change, so do the sounds*

Materials

- ■ *Alphabet Cards b, f, o, p, t, x*
- ■ *Word Builders*
- ■ *Word Builder Cards b, f, o, p, t, x*
- ■ pocket chart
- ■ index cards
- ■ drawing paper
- ■ crayons

REVIEW LETTERS

Phonics
Blending /o/ - /x/ ✔ *Review*

ACTIVE BEGINNING

Riddles Have children answer these riddles with words that end with /ks/:

- **What is a red animal with a tail?** (*fox*)
- **What is something you put things in?** (*box*)

TEACH/MODEL

Blending Words Distribute *Word Builders* and *Word Builder Cards b, f, p, t, o, x* to children. As you place *Alphabet Cards* in a pocket chart, tell children to place the same *Word Builder Cards* in their *Word Builder.*

- Place *Alphabet Cards b, o,* and *x* in the pocket chart. Have children do the same.
- Point to *b.* Say **/bb/.** Point to *o.* Say **/oo/.**
- Slide the *o* next to the *b.* Then move your hand under the letters and blend the sounds, elongating them—**/bboo/.** Have children do the same.

- Point to the letter *x.* Say **/kkss/.** Have children do the same.
- Slide the *x* next to the *bo.* Slide your hand under *box* and blend by elongating the sounds—**/bbookkss/.** Have children do the same.

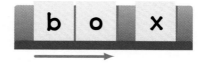

- Then have children read the word *box* along with you. Follow the same procedure with these words: *ox, fox, top.*

PRACTICE/APPLY

Guided Practice   Have children place the *Word Builder Cards* o and *p* in their *Word Builder*.

• **Add *t* to *op*. What word did you make?**

• **Change *t* to *b*. What word did you make?**

• **Change *p* to *x*. What word did you make?**

• **Change *b* to *f*. What word did you make?**

Independent Practice   Write the words *top, box,* and *fox* on index cards and place them in a pocket chart. Have children read the words. Then have them choose one of the words to write and illustrate on drawing paper.

▲ **Practice Book page 18**

Animal Adventures   627

OBJECTIVES

- *To write a class story*

- *To identify and sort common words into basic categories*

- *To follow words from left to right on a page and from top to bottom*

- *To recognize setting*

Materials

■ chart paper

■ markers

Shared Writing

Write a Chart

VISIT PLACES

Talk About the Story   Remind children that the girl in *Walking Through the Jungle* visits different places. Have children suggest other places the girl could visit, animals she might see, and things she could do there. Record their responses on the board.

Places	Animals	Action
farm	horses	ride a horse
city	dog	go to a park
forest	owls	take a walk
lake	fish	swim

Write a Class Story   Tell children that together they are going to write a class story about the girl. Have them choose one of the places on the list and think about the animals the girl sees and the things she does in that place. Call on a child to begin the story by saying a sentence, and have other children add sentences. Record the class story on chart paper.

SHARE

Read the Class Story   After the story is finished, read it to the class. Have children decide on a title for their story. Ask children to show you where sentences begin and end.

Journal Writing   Have children draw and write about a favorite place.

 **Share Time**

Reflect on the Lesson Have children tell about the part of today's lesson they liked most. Have them tell about the puppets they made for *Walking Through the Jungle.*

 Have children read silently from a book of their choice.

 **Centers** **SCIENCE**

Model Habitats

Have small groups construct a model of a mountain, a forest, a river, a desert, or a jungle habitat. Provide them with books and magazines that show how the environments look and animals that live there. Display the *Big Book* for ideas. Have children use natural materials, such as twigs, leaves, and pebbles, to make the models inside box lids. When they have finished, have them add plastic animals or make clay animals that would be found in the habitat they created.

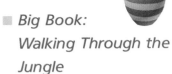 **Materials**

- *Big Book: Walking Through the Jungle*

- magazines and books with pictures of animals in their environments

- box lids

- leaves, twigs, pebbles

- modeling clay

Learning Centers

Choose from the following suggestions to enhance your learning centers for the theme Animal Adventures.
(Additional learning centers for this theme can be found on pages 522–524 and 584)

20 Minutes

SCIENCE CENTER

Animal Groups

Give partners the following *Picture Cards:*
alligator, bear, cat, cow, dog, duck, fish, fox,
goat, gorilla, hen, horse, kangaroo, lamb,
mouse, owl, rabbit, raccoon, seal, tiger, turtle,
and *zebra.* Have partners sort the cards into
the following categories: Animals that Fly,
Animals that Swim, and Animals that Live on
Land. Then have children sort the animals into
the categories Farm Animals and Wild Animals.

Materials

- *Picture Cards alligator, bear,*
  cat, cow, dog, duck, fish,
  fox, goat, gorilla, hen, horse,
  kangaroo, lamb, mouse,
  owl, rabbit, raccoon, seal,
  tiger, turtle, zebra

20 Minutes

SOCIAL STUDIES CENTER

Places for Adventures

Have partners look through magazines to find
and cut out pictures of animals in different environments and settings. Then have partners sort
their pictures into categories based on settings,
such as jungle animals, ocean animals, farm
animals, and pets. Have them arrange and
glue their pictures by category onto a sheet
of paper to make a collage featuring places
for animal adventures.

Materials

- old magazines
- safety scissors
- paper
- glue stick

Teacher Notes

Teacher Notes

THEME 8

Week 3
Animal Adventures

ORAL LANGUAGE
15-30 Minutes

- **Phonemic Awareness**

- **Sharing Literature**

LEARNING TO READ
45 Minutes

- **Phonics**

- **Vocabulary**

Daily Routines
- Morning Message
- Calendar Language
- Writing Prompt

LANGUAGE ARTS
15-30 Minutes

- **Writing**
  Daily Writing Prompt

Day 1

Phonemic Awareness, 637
Phoneme Matching: Medial

Sharing Literature, 638
Read
Library Book: *So Say
the Little Monkeys*

(Skill) **Literature Focus, 639**
Sound Words

Phonics, 640 T
Introduce: Phonogram -*ot*

 Interactive Writing, 642
Writing Process: Prewrite

Writing Prompt, 642
Draw and write about self-selected
topics.

Share Time, 643
Share a favorite part of the lesson.

Day 2

Phonemic Awareness, 645
Phoneme Blending

Sharing Literature, 646
Read
Read-Aloud Anthology:
"The Strongest One of All,"
p. 80

(Skill) **Literature Focus, 647**
Fact and Fantasy

Phonics, 648 T
Introduce: Phonogram -*op*

 Interactive Writing, 650
Writing Process: Draft

Writing Prompt, 650
Draw and write about a favorite way
to exercise.

Share Time, 651
Share a favorite part of "The Strongest
One of All."

T = tested skill

 **Phonics**

Focus of the Week:
- PHONEMIC AWARENESS
- SHARING LITERATURE
- WRITING: (Writing Process)

Phonograms *-ot, -op, -ox*

Day 3

Phonemic Awareness, 653
Phoneme Segmentation

Sharing Literature, 654
Big Book: *Walking Through the Jungle*

(Skill) **Literature Focus, 655**
Text Pattern

 Phonics, 656 T
Introduce: Phonogram *-ox*

 Interactive Writing, 658

Read
Writing Process: Respond and Revise

Writing Prompt, 658
Draw and write about self-selected topics.

Share Time, 659
Share animals and verses from the class poem.

Day 4

Phonemic Awareness, 661
Phoneme Deletion

Sharing Literature, 662
Read-Aloud Anthology: "Going on a Bear Hunt," p. 20

(Skill) **Literature Focus, 663**
Position Words

 Phonics, 664 T
Review: Short Vowel /o/*o*

Read
DECODABLE BOOK 6
Hop on Top

 Interactive Writing, 666
Writing Process: Edit

Writing Prompt, 666
Draw and write about things seen on a neighborhood walk.

Share Time, 667
Discuss the Decodable Book *Hop on Top*.

Day 5

Phonemic Awareness, 669
Phoneme Deletion

Sharing Literature, 670
Read
Read-Aloud Anthology: "The Hare and the Tortoise," p. 34

(Skill) **Literature Focus, 671**
Beginning, Middle, Ending

Phonics, 672 T
Build Sentences

 Interactive Writing, 674
Writing Process: Publish

Writing Prompt, 674
Draw and write about fast and slow things.

Share Time, 675
Act out the parts of the animals in the poem.

Day at a Glance
Day 1

WARM UP

MORNING MESSAGE

Kindergarten News

It is (name of season).

Today is a (type of weather) day.

Phonemic Awareness

Phoneme Matching: Medial

Sharing Literature

Library Book:
So Say the Little Monkeys

Read

Respond to Literature

Literature Focus: Sound Words

Phonics

Phonogram *-ot*

Interactive Writing

Writing Process: Prewrite

Write Kindergarten News Talk with children about the weather where they live. Have them tell the things they like to do on days like today.

Use prompts such as the following to guide children as you write the news:

- **Who can tell me where to start writing?**
- **What is the first letter in (name of season)?**
- **Who can show me a word that describes the weather?**

As you write the message, invite volunteers to contribute by writing letters, words, or names they have previously learned. Remind them to use proper spacing, capitalization, and punctuation.

Calendar Language

Display the names of the four seasons. Point to and read aloud the seasons of the year. Have children repeat the season name with you. Ask: *What season is it?*

Sunday	Monday	Tuesday	Wednesday	Thursday	Friday	Saturday
			1	2	3	4	5
6	7	8	9	10	11	12
13	14	15	16	17	18	19
20	21	22	23	24	25	26
27	28	29	30	31		

Phonemic Awareness

PHONEME MATCHING: MEDIAL

Match Middle Sounds   Say the following sentence: *Tom Fox got a box.* Have children repeat it with you. Then say:

What is the same about the words *Tom*, *Fox*, *got*, *box*? They all have the same middle sound: /o/. Now listen as I say two more words, and tell me if they have the same middle sound: *cab*, *hut*. *Cab* has the /a/ sound in the middle. *Hut* has the /u/ sound in the middle. So *cab* and *hut* have different middle sounds.

Tell children you will say two words at a time. If the words have the same middle sound, children should stand up.

pet, **sell** (same)	**pick**, **mop** (not same)	**such**, **cup** (same)
sad, **has** (same)	**less**, **bug** (not same)	**box**, **job** (same)
bib, **six** (same)	**vet**, **bag** (not same)	**pin**, **dig** (same)

REACHING ALL LEARNERS

Diagnostic Check: Phonemic Awareness

If... children have difficulty identifying words with the same middle sound,

Then... repeat the activity with word pairs beginning with vowel sounds, such as *at/an* and *it/off*.

ADDITIONAL SUPPORT ACTIVITIES

BELOW-LEVEL   Reteach, p. S68

ADVANCED   Extend, p. S69

ENGLISH-LANGUAGE LEARNERS   Reteach, p. S69

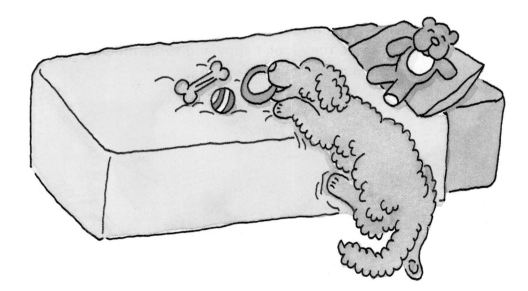

▲ **Library Book**

OBJECTIVES

- *To listen and respond to a folktale*
- *To retell the story*
- *To identify sound words*
- *To understand that written words can represent sounds*

Materials

- *Library Book: So Say the Little Monkeys*
- rhythm instruments

Sharing Literature

Read So Say the Little Monkeys

READ ALOUD

Before Reading Display, *So Say the Little Monkeys*. Use the illustrations to help children retell the story. Then use these prompts to help children recall story events:

- **Why do the monkeys get cold and wet?** (because they don't have a home)
- **Why is it uncomfortable to sleep in the trees?** (They have sharp thorns.)
- **What do the monkeys like to do best?** (Possible responses: have a good time; swing, jump, climb, sing)

As you page through the book, remind children to look at the details in the illustrations to find out more about the places and activities.

During Reading Read the story aloud. As you read,

- emphasize the sound words by modifying the volume and tone of your voice.
- point out that the sound words in the text have all uppercase letters to show that they should be read loudly.
- pause after the sound words for children to repeat them after you.
- react to the pictures and characters.

MODEL When the monkeys find the bananas, I can tell they like them because they look happy and some monkeys even have more than one banana.

RESPOND TO LITERATURE

Retell the Story Show children the rhythm instruments, identify each one, and demonstrate how they are used. Have children listen to the sound each one makes and suggest which part of the story it would fit with best. Write a list on the board.

So Say the Little Monkeys	
WHEEEE, WHEEEE	bells
JABBA JABBA	rhythm sticks
OW OW OW	cymbals
PLINKA PLINKA	rain stick
WOOYA WOOYA	children's whistles
MUNCH MUNCH MUNCH	sand blocks

Distribute the instruments, and review the list on the board for children to practice their parts. Then reread the story, pausing at each sound word to give children time to play their instrument.

Literature
Focus

SOUND WORDS

Remind children that some words name sounds they hear. As children repeat the following sound words from the story, talk about what they mean:

JABBA JABBA (the sound of happy monkeys)

OW OW OW (what the monkeys say when the thorns prick)

PLINKA PLINKA (sound of the rain)

WOOYA WOOYA (sound of the wind)

MUNCH MUNCH MUNCH (sound of monkeys eating bananas)

GURR-YUH GURR-YUH (the sound of the jaguar)

ONGOING ASSESSMENT

As you read *So Say the Little Monkeys,* note whether children

- listen and respond to the folktale.

- can retell the story.

- can identify sound words.

- understand that written words can represent sounds.

Phonics

Phonogram -ot  Introduce

OBJECTIVES

- To find letter patterns in words

- To blend letter patterns to read words

Materials

- ■ *Write-On/ Wipe-Off Boards*

- ■ chart paper

- ■ marker

- ■ *Word Builder Cards*

- ■ *Word Builders*

ACTIVE BEGINNING

Say a Rhyme Teach children the following rhyme. Have them clap as they say the words.

We got a pot.

The pot is on a cot.

It is not a hot pot!

TEACH/MODEL

Discriminate Sounds Say the words *spot* and *lot* and have children repeat them. Ask how the two words are the same. (They both have /ot/; they rhyme.) Tell children that you are going to say some words and that they are to give a thumbs-up when they hear a word that rhymes with *spot*:

| not | fan | trot | dot | mat | got |

Build -ot Words Write the word *pot* on chart paper. Track the print as children read the word. Then write the word *dot*. Again, track the print as children read the word. Ask children to read the two words and have them tell how they are the same. (They have o and t; they rhyme.) Continue by writing the word *not* and having children read the word.

pot
dot
not

PRACTICE/APPLY

Guided Practice Tell children that you will say some words. If a word rhymes with *spot*, they write the word on their *Write-On/Wipe-Off Board*. Have them use the chart with *-ot* words as a reference.
Use these words:

dot, not, pot

dot   cap   not   hog   ham   pot   red

Independent Practice Have children use their *Word Builder Cards* and *Word Builder* to make the words *cot, lot, got, not,* and *pot*. Refer them to the chart with *-ot* words as a starting point.

g o t

ADVANCED

Encourage children to write in their spelling journal other words that belong in the *-ot* family.

early spelling

Have children write in their spelling journal one of the *-ot* words from their *Write-On/Wipe-Off Board*.

The log is h o t.

The p o t is hot.

D o t is hot.

I am n o t hot.

Phonogram: -ot
Have children look at the first picture, read the sentence, and trace over the letters *ot* to finish the word *hot*. Then have children continue by looking at each picture, writing *ot* to complete the sentence, and reading the sentences.

Animal Adventures **19**

▲ **Practice Book page 19**

Day at a Glance

Day 2

Phonemic Awareness
Phoneme Blending

Sharing Literature
Read-Aloud Anthology:
"The Strongest One of All"

Read

**Develop Listening
Comprehension**

Respond to Literature

Literature Focus: Fact and
Fantasy

Phonics
Phonogram *-op*

Interactive Writing
Writing Process: Draft

MORNING MESSAGE

Kindergarten News

Today is _____.

We keep our bodies healthy and

strong by _____.

Write Kindergarten News Talk with children about things around them
that are strong. Have them tell about strong people they know.

Use prompts such as the following to guide children as you write the news:

- **Who can show me three words that begin with an uppercase letter?**
- **Who can point to and read the word *We*?**
- **How many words are in the second sentence?**

As you write the message, invite volunteers to contribute by writing letters,
words, or names they have previously learned. Remind them to use proper
spacing, capitalization, and punctuation.

Calendar Language

Point to and read aloud the days
of the week. Name the days of the
week again, inviting children to
join in and clap syllables for the
name of each day. Ask: *What day
is it?*

Sunday	Monday	Tuesday	Wednesday	Thursday	Friday	Saturday
		1	2	3	4	5
6	7	8	9	10	11	12
13	14	15	16	17	18	19
20	21	22	23	24	25	26
27	28	29	30	31		

Phonemic Awareness

PHONEME BLENDING

Blend Sounds   Tell children they can listen to the sounds you will say and guess the word you are saying.

Say: **/s/ /u/ /n/** slowly, emphasizing each sound. Say it again, blending the sounds: **/ssuunn/**. Have children blend the sounds with you and name the word: **/ssuunn/**, **sun**.

Follow the same procedure with the following words.

/p/ /a/ /t/ *(pat)*	**/r/ /a/ /n/** *(ran)*	**/k/ /o/ /b/** *(cob)*
/t/ /u/ /b/ *(tub)*	**/m/ /i/ /ks/** *(mix)*	**/n/ /e/ /t/** *(net)*
/m/ /o / /p/ *(mop)*	**/w/ /e/ /b/** *(web)*	**/h/ /o/ /p/** *(hop)*
/d/ /u/ /k/ *(duck)*	**/h/ /i/ /l/** *(hill)*	**/d/ /o/ /l/** *(doll)*

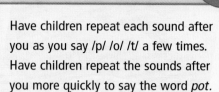

BELOW-LEVEL

Have children repeat each sound after you as you say /p/ /o/ /t/ a few times. Have children repeat the sounds after you more quickly to say the word *pot*.

ADVANCED

Have children try blending words with consonant blends, such as /k/ /r/ /a/ /b/ *(crab)*, /s/ /t/ /e/ /m/ *(stem)*, /g/ /l/ /a/ /s/ *(glass)*.

Day at a Glance

Day 3

WARM UP

Phonemic Awareness
Phoneme Segmentation

Sharing Literature
Big Book: *Walking Through the Jungle*

Read

WALKING THROUGH THE JUNGLE
Debbie Harter

Develop Concept Vocabulary

Respond to Literature

Literature Focus: Text Pattern

Phonics
Phonogram *-ox*

Interactive Writing
Writing Process: Respond and Revise

MORNING MESSAGE

Kindergarten News

(Child's name) likes to read stories.

His (or her) favorite story character

is _____.

Write Kindergarten News Talk with children about their favorite story character. Have them tell the name of the story the character is in, and some of the things the character does.

Use prompts such as the following to guide children as you write the news:

- **Who can show me the name of a story character?**
- **What kind of letter does the name begin with?**
- **Who can show me two names that begin with an uppercase letter?**

As you write the message, invite volunteers to contribute by writing letters, words, or names they have previously learned. Remind them to use proper spacing, capitalization, and punctuation.

Calendar Language

Have children identify the day of the week. Then ask them to name class activities for the day.

Sunday	Monday	Tuesday	Wednesday	Thursday	Friday	Saturday
		1	2	3	4	5
6	7	8	9	10	11	12
13	14	15	16	17	18	19
20	21	22	23	24	25	26
27	28	29	30	31		

Phonemic Awareness

PHONEME SEGMENTATION

Identify the Number of Sounds in a Word   Say the word *hop* and have children repeat it. Then say:

Hop. **Watch while I hold up one finger for each sound: /h/ /o/ /p/. The word *hop* has three sounds. Now you try it. Hold up one finger for each sound you hear.** Say the sounds /d/ /o/ /t/ slowly. **How many sounds did you hear? Count your fingers.** (three)

As you provide the following words, ask children, **What sounds do you hear in ___? How many sounds do you hear in ___?** Encourage children to repeat the sounds as they count.

yes /y/ /e/ /s/, 3	**hit** /h/ /i/ /t/, 3	**nut** /n/ /u/ /t/, 3
in /i/ /n/, 2	**mat** /m/ /a/ /t/, 3	**no** /n/ /o/, 2
cub /k/ /u/ /b/, 3	**bet** /b/ /e/ /t/, 3	**at** /a/ /t/, 2
job /j/ /o/ /b/, 3	**wet** /w/ /e/ /t/, 3	**mom** /m/ /o/ /m/, 3

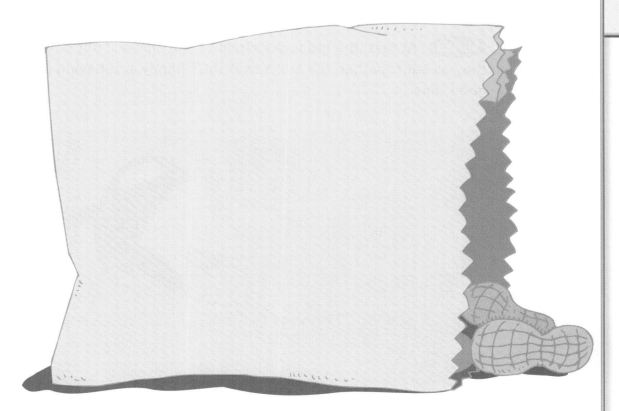

Sharing Literature

Read Walking Through the Jungle

READ ALOUD

Before Reading   Display the *Big Book*, and explain that many words and sentences are repeated. Track and read the first sentence on a page, and have children join in on the repeated sentence. Then use these prompts to set a purpose for reading:

- **What is an example of a sentence that is repeated in the story?** (Possible response: *What do you see? What do you see?*)

- **What words are repeated?** (Possible responses: *Hiss! Hiss! Hiss!*)

Tell children that you are going to reread the story. Have them join in on the repeated words and sentences.

During Reading   Read the story. As you read,

- pause to allow time for children to say repetitive sentences and words.

- track the print of the repetitive sentences and words.

- use expression to read the questions.

   MODEL   **At first, the girl looks afraid of the animals. But when they all eat together, she looks as if she's happy and having a good time.**

▲ **Big Book**

OBJECTIVES

- *To listen and respond to a story*

- *To recall story events*

- *To understand text patterns*

Materials

- *Big Book: Walking Through the Jungle*

- chart paper

- marker

DEVELOP CONCEPT VOCABULARY

After Reading Write the words *jungle, ocean, mountain, river, desert,* and *iceberg* on chart paper. Point to and read each word. Then use the word in a sentence and ask children to respond by using the name of another animal and place in a new sentence. Have children look at the pictures of the settings to help them with their answers.

- I see a monkey in the <u>jungle</u>. What do you see?
- I see a crab in the <u>ocean</u>. What do you see?
- I see a goat on the <u>mountain</u>. What do you see?
- I see an eel in the <u>river</u>. What do you see?
- I see a lizard in the <u>desert</u>. What do you see?
- I see a white fox on the <u>iceberg</u>. What do you see?

RESPOND TO LITERATURE

Share Ideas Have children pretend to go on a trip around the world, visiting a jungle, an ocean, a mountain, a river, a desert, and an iceberg. Ask a child to tell where he or she would go first, and have everyone pretend to walk to the first place. Tell children to think about the sights, sounds, and smells of that place. Have children describe the scene and tell what they would do there. Then go to the next stop on the trip.

Literature Focus

TEXT PATTERNS

Read aloud pages 4–7 of *Walking Through the Jungle*. Point out that on pages 4, 5, and 7, the first line is the same as the second line. Tell children that the whole book has this same pattern of words: First we find out where the girl is, then we see the question *What do you see?*, and the girl tells what she sees chasing her. Read aloud pages 8–11 to show children how the pattern continues.

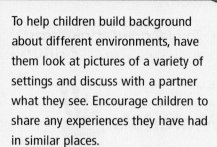

BELOW-LEVEL

To help children build background about different environments, have them look at pictures of a variety of settings and discuss with a partner what they see. Encourage children to share any experiences they have had in similar places.

ONGOING ASSESSMENT

As you read *Walking Through the Jungle,* note whether children

- listen and respond to the story.
- can recall story events.

OBJECTIVE

To improve writing through rereading and revision

Materials

- correction tape
- markers
- chart paper

Writing Process

Write a Flip-Book Poem

RESPOND AND REVISE

Reread the Poem Verses Display the chart paper with the poem verses written in the Day 2 Writing activity (page 650). Read each verse to children, inviting them to recite portions of the poem that they remember. Tell children that the next step in writing their poem is to decide how to improve the verses they wrote.

Make Revisions Ask children questions such as the following:

- **Do all the animal noises match the animals in our poem verses?**
- **Is there a better way to write one of the animal noises?**
- **Are there any animal noises we should add to our poem?**
- **Are there any animal noises we do not want to include in our poem?**

Use correction tape and a marker to replace words that children suggest should be changed. Create verses from new suggestions on new sheets of chart paper. After the changes are made, reread the verses to children.

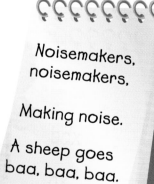

Noisemakers,
noisemakers,

Making noise.

A sheep goes
baa, baa, baa.

Writing Every Day

My Journal

Self-Selected Writing Have children draw and write about self-selected topics in their journal.

WRAP UP Share Time

Revisit the Class Poem   Ask volunteers to name an animal from the class poem. Recite the animal's verse as a group. Repeat until each verse is recited.

S.S.R. *Sustained Silent Reading*   Have children read silently from a book of their choice.

Centers — LISTENING

Telling a Story

Arrange to have children work in small groups to record their own version of *So Say the Little Monkeys* or *Elmer*. Before children begin, have them retell the story together as they page through the book. Have children include sound effects or music in their recording. Make the tape available in the Listening Center for everyone to enjoy.

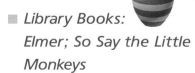

Materials

- *Library Books: Elmer; So Say the Little Monkeys*
- tape recorder
- blank audiocassette

WARM UP

MORNING MESSAGE

Kindergarten News

(Child's name) lost a _____.

He (or she) went on a hunt to find it.

Phonemic Awareness
Phoneme Deletion

Sharing Literature
Read-Aloud Anthology:
"Going on a Bear Hunt"

Read

Respond to Literature

Literature Focus: Concept Words

Phonics
Short Vowel /o/o

Reading
Decodable Book 6: *Hop on Top*

Interactive Writing
Writing Process: Proofread

Write Kindergarten News Talk with children about a time when they lost something or helped someone else find something that was lost. Ask whether the item was found and where it was.

Use prompts such as the following to guide children as you write the news:

- **Who can point to the words *a* and *on*?**
- **What letter should I write first in the word *lost*?**
- **What does *hunt* mean?**

As you write the message, invite volunteers to contribute by writing letters, words, or names they have previously learned. Remind them to use proper spacing, capitalization, and punctuation.

Calendar Language

Point to and read aloud the days of the week. Tell children you will name the school days. Point to and read aloud *Monday* through *Friday*. Ask children to repeat the names of the school days.

Sunday	Monday	Tuesday	Wednesday	Thursday	Friday	Saturday
		1	2	3	4	5
6	7	8	9	10	11	12
13	14	15	16	17	18	19
20	21	22	23	24	25	26
27	28	29	30	31		

Phonemic Awareness

PHONEME DELETION

Delete Phonemes Say the word *wait* and have children repeat it. Say:

Listen while I say *wait* without the /w/: *ait*. Say it with me: *ait*.

Tell children you are going to ask them to say some words without certain sounds. Use the following:

Say *bean* without the /b/. (*ean*)

Say *mat* without the /m/. (*at*)

Say *night* without the /n/. (*ight*)

Say *fit* without the /f/. (*it*)

Say *moon* without the /m/. (*oon*)

Say *pail* without the /p/. (*ail*)

BELOW-LEVEL

If children have difficulty deleting phonemes, say *heel*, elongating the beginning sound and emphasizing the rest of the word. /hhhheel/. Repeat /hhhheel/ several times, each time saying /hh/ more softly until you eliminate it all together.

ADVANCED

Place *Picture Cards bus, hat, jeep, nail, rain,* and *seal* face down on a table. Ask children to take turns choosing a *Picture Card*. Have them name the picture and then say the word without the beginning sound. Have them repeat the process, saying each word without the ending sound.

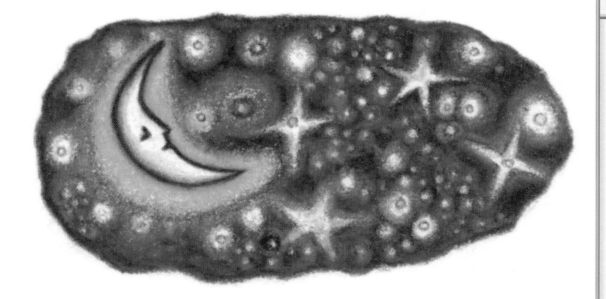

KINDERGARTEN
**READ-ALOUD
Anthology**
Harcourt

▲ **Read-Aloud Anthology**

OBJECTIVES

- *To listen and respond to a poem*
- *To use pictures and context to make predictions*
- *To understand concept words*

Materials

■ *Read-Aloud Anthology, pp. 20–21*

Sharing Literature

Read "Going on a Bear Hunt"

READ ALOUD

Before Reading   Turn to pages 20–21 in the *Read-Aloud Anthology*, and read aloud the title of the poem, "Going on a Bear Hunt." Ask children to share what they know about bears. Then use these prompts to help children make predictions:

- **Where do you think the bear hunt might take place?**
- **Do you think it would be exciting to go along? Why?**
- **Do you think the people in the poem catch a bear?**

Tell children that they will go on an imaginary bear hunt with you as you read and act out the poem. Have children sit cross-legged so they can pat their knees in rhythm with the words throughout the poem.

During Reading   Read the poem aloud. As you read,

- ask children to recall and confirm predictions.

> **MODEL** **I know that bears like to sleep in caves at night and walk around the woods during the day. So I think the hunt is going to take place in the woods.**

- pause to allow time for children to echo the lines of the poem.
- encourage children to tap the rhythm.

Reread the poem, inviting children to join in on both the actions and the words.

RESPOND TO LITERATURE

Recognize Rhythm Tell children that rhythm is the beat they hear in a piece of music. Sometimes a group of words also has a strong rhythm, as in the poem "Going on a Bear Hunt." Designate some children to be Echoers, and have them repeat the words as you read the poem aloud. Designate other children to be Clappers, and have them clap in rhythm as you read the poem. Then have the two groups switch roles as you reread the poem.

Literature Focus

CONCEPT WORDS

Tell children that some words are direction words. Place a book on the table and say: **The book is on the table.** Then put the book under the table and say: **The book is under the table**. Tell children that *on* and *under* are examples of direction words. Say the following directions for children to follow. Identify the direction word in each.

- **Walk <u>through</u> the door.**
- **Look <u>under</u> the desk.**
- **Step <u>over</u> the pencil.**
- **Reach <u>up</u> to the ceiling.**
- **Look <u>down</u> at the floor.**

REACHING ALL LEARNERS

Diagnostic Check: Comprehension

If… children have difficulty understanding the meaning of direction words,

Then… model each example before asking children to follow directions.

ADDITIONAL SUPPORT ACTIVITIES

BELOW-LEVEL	Reteach, p. S72
ADVANCED	Extend, p. S73
ENGLISH-LANGUAGE LEARNERS	Reteach, p. S73

ONGOING ASSESSMENT

As you read "Going on a Bear Hunt," note whether children

- listen and respond to the poem.
- make and confirm predictions.

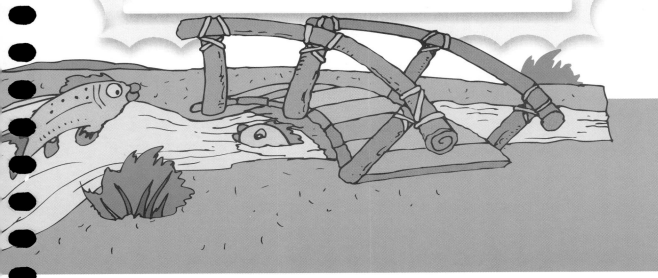

OBJECTIVE
To decode short vowel /o/o words

Materials

- *Alphabet Cards h, o, p*
- pocket chart
- *Decodable Book 6: Hop on Top*
- drawing paper
- crayons

BELOW-LEVEL

Reread the story with children. Have them frame and read the words *my* and *you*.

ADVANCED

Have children read *Hop on Top* with a partner. Ask them to track the print as they read. Then have them read *Independent Reader 23: The Ice Fair*.

Phonics

Short Vowel /o/o  Review

TEACH/MODEL

Review Blending Place *Alphabet Cards h, o,* and *p* next to one another in the pocket chart. Remind children how to blend the letters by sliding your hand under the word as you say **/hhoopp/**, **hop**. Have children blend the sounds and read the word.

PRACTICE/APPLY

Read the Book Distribute copies of *Hop on Top*. Read the title with children, encouraging them to point to each word as they say it.

Have children read the book, pointing to each word as they read.

Respond Have children think of another way Little Fox could have gotten his cap out of the tree. Have children draw and label their solutions.

Decodable Book 6: *Hop on Top*

My cap is on top.
Can you tap it, Pop?

2

I can not.

3

My cap is on top.
Can you tap it, Mom?

4

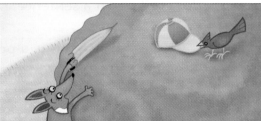

I can not.

5

Hop on top, Mom.

6

Hop on top, Fox.

7

I got it! I got my cap!

8

■ High-Frequency Words

my, you

■ Decodable Words

See list on page T19.

School-Home Connection

Take-Home Book Version

◄ Decodable Book 6:
Hop on Top

▲ **Independent Reader 23:**
The Ice Fair

Animal Adventures 665

OBJECTIVES

- *To apply rules of capitalization*

- *To apply rules of punctuation*

Materials

- correction tape

- markers

Writing Process

Write a Flip-Book Poem

PROOFREAD

Check Capitalization and Punctuation Display the poem verses created in the previous Writing activities. Tell children that this is their chance to make their writing better. Direct children to the end mark in the two sentences of each verse. Ask children **Should these sentences end with a question mark or a period?** Then tell children that, in poetry, each line begins with a capital letter, even if the line does not begin a sentence. Model checking for proper capitalization.

MODEL **Since this is a poem, each line should begin with a capital letter. I look at the first line to see if we used a capital N. Yes, we did. Now I look at the next line.**

Ask children to suggest whether or not other lines and verses use capital letters correctly. Use correction tape and a marker to fix capital letters and punctuation that are incorrect. Reread the verses to children and tell them they are almost ready to finish their poem.

Noisemakers,
noisemakers,

Making noise.

A sheep goes
baa, baa, baa.

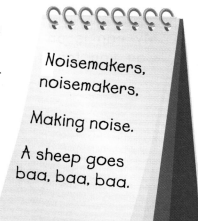

Journal Writing Have children draw and write about things they would see on a walk in their neighborhood.

WRAP UP Share Time

Reflect on the Lesson Ask children to tell about the book they read, *Hop on Top*. Have them tell what the story was about. Then ask them to share the pictures they drew of Little Fox getting his cap.

S.S.R. *Sustained Silent Reading* Have children read silently from a book of their choice.

 **Centers**  **LITERACY**

Favorite Books from Animal Adventures

Place the books in the Literacy Center. Invite children to read the books and to choose their favorite one. Ask them to draw and label a picture about their favorite book. Have them write the title of the book on their picture. Remind them to write their name on their picture.

 Materials

- *Big Book: Walking Through the Jungle; Library Books: Elmer; So Say the Little Monkeys; Decodable Books 4, 5, 6: I Can See It!; What Is in the Box?; Hop on Top*
- drawing paper
- crayons or markers

WARM UP

Phonemic Awareness
Phoneme Deletion

Sharing Literature
Read-Aloud Anthology: "The Hare and the Tortoise"

Read

KINDERGARTEN
READ-ALOUD
Anthology
Harcourt

Develop Listening Comprehension

Respond to Literature

Literature Focus: Beginning, Middle, Ending

Phonics
Build and Read Sentences

Interactive Writing
Writing Process: Publish

MORNING MESSAGE

Kindergarten News

(Child's name) likes running in a race. He (or she) can run from

_____ to _____.

Write Kindergarten News Talk with children about running in races or about races they have watched.

Use prompts such as the following to guide children as you write the news:

- **Let's clap syllables for the word *running*. How many claps do you hear?**
- **Who can point to the word *can*?**
- **How many sentences do you see? Who can show where the first sentence begins? Where does it end?**

As you write the message, invite volunteers to contribute by writing letters, words, or names they have previously learned. Remind them to use proper spacing, capitalization, and punctuation.

Calendar Language

Point to the numbers on the calendar. Tell children that the days of each month are numbered and the numbers tell the date. Point to and read aloud the date. Name the month and the date.

Sunday	Monday	Tuesday	Wednesday	Thursday	Friday	Saturday
		1	2	3	4	5
6	7	8	9	10	11	12
13	14	15	16	17	18	19
20	21	22	23	24	25	26
27	28	29	30	31		

Phonemic Awareness

PHONEME DELETION

Listen while I say *pay* **without the /p/:** *ay.* **Say it with me:** *ay.*

Tell children you are going to ask them to say some words without certain sounds. Use the following:

Say *boot* **without the /b/.** (*oot*)

Say *fat* **without the /f/.** (*at*)

Say *tick* **without the /t/.** (*ick*)

Say *pan* **without the /p/.** (*an*)

Say *nail* **without the /n/.** (*ail*)

Say *soon* **without the /s/.** (*oon*)

▲ "Howdido," *Oo-pples and Boo-noo-noos: Songs and Activities for Phonemic Awareness,* pages 85–87.

BELOW-LEVEL

Physical demonstrations can reinforce the skill for children. Assign three children the sounds in the word *cap.* Have the first child say /k/, the second child say /a/, and the third child say /p/. Have children say their sounds to produce *cap.* Then ask the first child to remain silent as the other two say their sounds to produce *ap.*

▲ **Read-Aloud Anthology**

OBJECTIVES

- *To listen and respond to a fable*

- *To understand characters*

- *To retell the story*

- *To identify beginning, middle, and ending*

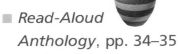

Materials

- *Read-Aloud Anthology*, pp. 34–35

- *Teacher's Resource Book*, p. 92

- crayons or markers

- scissors

- glue or tape

- craft sticks

Sharing Literature

Read "The Hare and the Tortoise"

READ ALOUD

Before Reading   Turn to page 34 in the *Read-Aloud Anthology*, read the title "The Hare and the Tortoise" to children, and ask them if they have heard this story before. Tell children that a hare is an animal like a rabbit and a tortoise is a kind of turtle. Explain that the two animals are going to have a race. Then use these prompts to help children make predictions:

- **Who do you think is going to win the race?**

   MODEL   **The hare and the tortoise are going to race. I know that a hare is like a rabbit, and rabbits run fast. The tortoise is a kind of turtle, and turtles move very slowly. So, I think the hare is going to win the race.**

- **Which character do you think expects to win? Why?**

Explain that this kind of story is called a fable and a fable teaches a lesson. Tell children that they should listen to the story to find out who wins and what the story teaches.

During Reading   Read the story aloud. As you read,

- allow time for children to recall and confirm their predictions.

- point out the things Hare does that help the reader understand him. For example, ask: **Why did Hare laugh when Tortoise wanted to race him?**

- point out what Tortoise does to help the reader understand him. For example, ask: **What does Tortoise do after Hare laughs at him?**

- talk about how the characters feel.

   MODEL   **At the end of the story, Tortoise wins the race. I think he must feel proud that he has beaten Hare, who is faster.**

DEVELOP LISTENING COMPREHENSION

After Reading   Ask children the following questions:

* **Who wins the race? Why?** (Tortoise; because he keeps on going and never gives up.)

* **Why does Hare lose the race?** (He stops running and takes a nap because he is so sure that he is going to win.)

* **What lesson does this story teach?** (Possible responses: You don't always have to be the fastest to win a race; you should always keep trying your best.)

* **Who is your favorite character in this story? Why?** (Accept reasonable answers.)

RESPOND TO LITERATURE

Retell the Fable   Distribute copies of the Character Cutouts from page 92 of the *Teacher's Resource Book*. Have children color them, cut them out, and glue or tape each cutout to a craft stick. Then have children work with a partner to retell the story.

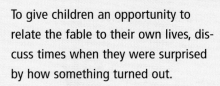

ADVANCED

To give children an opportunity to relate the fable to their own lives, discuss times when they were surprised by how something turned out.

ONGOING ASSESSMENT

As you read "The Hare and the Tortoise," note whether children

* listen and respond to the fable.
* understand characters.
* retell the story.

Literature Focus

BEGINNING, MIDDLE, ENDING

Review Talk about how every story has a beginning, a middle, and an ending. Ask children to tell what happens at the beginning of the story. (Hare and Tortoise decide to have a race.) Say: **This is the beginning of the story.** Then ask what happens next. (Hare gets way ahead of Tortoise so he stops to take a nap.) Say: **This is the middle of the story.** Finally, have children describe the ending of the story. (Hare wakes up to find that Tortoise has already crossed the finish line to win the race.) Say: **This is the ending of the story.** Together, retell the beginning, middle, and ending of the story.

First
Hare and Tortoise start the race.

↓

Next
Hare takes a nap.

↓

Last
Tortoise wins the race.

Day 5

OBJECTIVE

To use knowledge of letters, words, and sounds to read simple sentences

Materials

- chart paper
- marker
- index cards
- pocket chart
- *Decodable Book 6 :Hop on Top*

Phonics

Build Sentences

ACTIVE BEGINNING

Act Out a Nonsense Rhyme   Teach children the following rhyme and actions.

The hot-hot-hot fox-fox-fox,
(Fan yourself with your hand.)

Got-got-got a box-box-box,
(Outline a square with your fingers.)

And went hop-hop-hop.
(Hop around in a circle.)

TEACH/MODEL

Review *-ot, -op, -ox*   Copy the chart below onto chart paper. Read aloud the words and remind children that the words in each column belong to the same word family—the *-ot* family, the *-op* family, and the *-ox* family.

pot	mop	fox
hot	top	box

Model reading the word *pot* first by elongating the sounds, **/ppoott/**, and then reading it naturally. Then have children elongate the sounds */hhoott/* and read the word. Continue with the remaining words. Frame the words *pot* and *hot* and ask how the two words are alike. (Possible responses: They rhyme; they both have *o* and *t*.) Do the same for *mop* and *top*; *fox* and *box*.

PRACTICE/APPLY

Guided Practice Write the following words on index cards: *pot, box, A, is, in, the, fox, lot, mop.* Display the words in a pocket chart as shown.

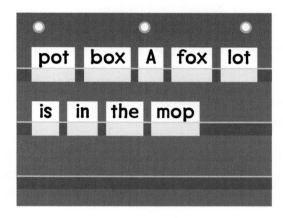

Point to each word and have children read it. If necessary, remind them to blend the sounds together to read the word. Then rearrange the cards to make the following sentence:

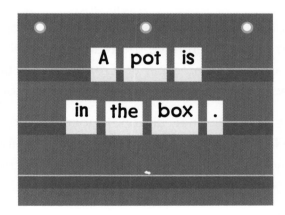

Track the words as you assist children in reading the sentence. Then replace *pot* with the word *fox* and have children read the sentence. Continue by replacing one of the words to provide many opportunities for children to read the sentence.

Independent Practice Have children reread *Decodable Book 6: Hop on Top* for more practice reading connected text.

early spelling

Early Spelling Have children write in their spelling journal one of the words from the Guided Practice sentences. Ask them to draw a picture to illustrate that word.

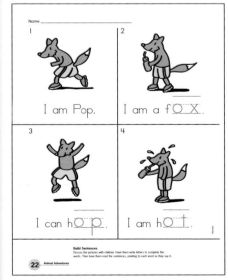

▲ **Practice Book page 22**

Writing Process

Write a Flip-Book Poem

PUBLISH

Distribute Materials   In advance, write the following on several sheets of white paper:

**Noisemakers, noisemakers,
Making noise.**

Read aloud to children the verses of the "Noisemakers" poem the group has written during the previous Writing activities. Divide the group into teams, and give each team a prepared "Noisemakers" sheet, a blank sheet of white paper, and a large sheet of colored paper.

Write and Illustrate   Have each team select a verse, write the final line of the verse on the blank paper *(A _____ goes _____, _____, _____.),* and draw a picture of the animal above the line they wrote. Staple together the top edges of each team's two pages. Then have the teams glue their illustrations to the center of their colored paper. Create a cover page that says *Noisemakers* and staple it on top of the teams' colored paper.

Share   Read the finished flip-book poem to the class, inviting volunteers to lift the flaps to revel the illustrations and the verses' final line. Display the book in the Literacy Center for children to enjoy during center time and Sustained Silent Reading.

Journal Writing Have children write and draw about some things that are fast and slow.

WRAP UP Share Time

Share the Class Flip Book   Reread the poem "Noisemakers" the group just completed. Invite volunteers to act out the parts of the animals in the poem.

S.S.R.   Have children read silently from a book of their choice.

 **Centers**   **BLOCK**

Race the Clock

Have children work by themselves or with a partner to race the clock. Have them set the timer for one minute and see how tall a block tower they can make before the time is up. Have them then stop building and count the blocks in their towers. Have children make towers several times to see if they get faster at beating the clock.

Materials

■ minute timers

■ blocks

■ container for blocks

Theme Wrap-Up & Review

Celebrate *Animal Adventures*

Show children *Walking Through the Jungle, Elmer,* and *So Say the Little Monkeys.* Help them summarize or retell each story. Invite comments and personal responses; then ask these questions:

- **What question would you like to ask the girl in Walking Through the Jungle?**

- **In the story Elmer, how does Elmer's adventure help him learn about himself?**

- **What was your favorite animal adventure? Why did you like it?**

Teacher Self-Evaluation

As you reflect on the theme *Animal Adventures*, ask yourself:

- **Which activities best met my goals for this theme? Which ones did not?**

- **Have children become more aware of how stories bring enjoyment to their lives?**

- **Have I helped children make connections between thematic activities at school and events in their personal life?**

THEME PROJECT

Animal Parade

Summing Up During the parade, have children take turns telling about the animal they have made a mask for.

REVIEW

Phonics

Bingo Distribute a 9 square grid game board and 9 counters to each child. Have children write a *W* in four boxes, an *X* in one box, and the words *fox, box, hop,* and *dot* in the remaining boxes. Place *Picture Cards wagon, watch, watermelon, X-ray* and word cards *fox, box, hop, dot* in a paper bag.

Have chldren take turns reaching into the bag and pulling out a card. Tell them to identify the first letter of the picture name or to read the word. The class can cover that letter or word on their grid with a counter. The first one to cover a row, column, or diagonal row wins the game.

Ww	Xx	fox
hop	Ww	dot
box	Ww	Ww

High-Frequency Words

What Do You See? Place *Picture Cards alligator, bear, dinosaur* and *fox* in a pocket chart. Place *High-Frequency Word Cards Do you see a* _____? *No* in the pocket chart. Ask children to read the words and invite one child to place a *Picture Card* after *a*. Have children read the sentence and answer. Continue with the other *Picture Cards*.

Comprehension

Beginning, Middle, End Display *Library Book Elmer* and have children retell the story. Ask them to tell what happens at the beginning of the story, the middle of the story, and at the end of the story.

Writing

Write Questions Remind children that an asking sentence ends with a question mark. Ask them to name the places the girl in *Walking Through the Jungle* visits. (jungle, ocean, mountains, river, desert) Tell them to draw a picture of the place they liked best and to write an asking sentence about it.

**Take-Home Book
Theme 8 Practice Book**, pp. 23–24

ASSESSMENT

Monitoring of Progress

Diagnostic Checks Use the Diagnostic Checks as a point-of-use assessment of children's understanding.

Theme Skills Assessment Use the Theme Skills Assessment to monitor a child's under-standing of letter recognition, word recognition, sound-symbol relationships, and decoding skills taught in this theme.

• Assessment Handbook

These benchmark statements represent a continuum of learning. The highlighted column describes observable behaviors most of your children should exhibit by the end of the school year.

CONCEPTS ABOUT PRINT

Grade K

Identify the front cover, back cover, and title page of a book.

Follow words from left to right and from top to bottom on the printed page.

Understand that printed materials provide information.

Recognize that sentences in print are made up of separate words.

Distinguish letters from words.

Recognize and name all uppercase and lowercase letters of the alphabet.

Grade 1

Match oral words to printed words.

Identify the title and author of a reading selection.

Identify letters, words, and sentences.

PHONEMIC AWARENESS

Grade K

Track and represent the number of two and three isolated phonemes.

Track and represent the sameness/difference of two and three isolated phonemes.

Track and represent the order of two and three isolated phonemes.

Track (move sequentially from sound to sound) and represent changes in simple syllables and words with two and three sounds as one is added, substituted, shifted, or repeated.

Blend vowel-consonant sounds orally to make words or syllables.

Identify rhyming words in response to an oral prompt.

Produce rhyming words in response to an oral prompt.

Separate words into beginning sounds.

Separate words into ending sounds.

Track auditorily each word in a sentence and each syllable in a word.

Count the number of sounds in syllables.

Count the number of syllables in words.

Sequentially segment individual sounds in 2–3 phoneme words.

Grade 1

Distinguish initial, medial, and final sounds in single-syllable words.

Distinguish long- and-short-vowel sounds in orally stated single-syllable words.

Create and state a series of rhyming words, including consonant blends.

Add, delete, or change target sounds to change words.

Blend two to four phonemes into recognizable words.

These benchmark statements represent a continuum of learning. The highlighted column describes observable behaviors most of your children should exhibit by the end of the school year.

VOCABULARY AND CONCEPT DEVELOPMENT

Grade K

Identify and sort common words in basic categories (e.g., color, shapes, foods).

Describe common objects and events in both general and specific language.

Grade 1

Classify grade-appropriate categories of words (e.g., concrete collections of animals, foods, toys).

STRUCTURAL FEATURES, COMPREHENSION, AND TEXT ANALYSIS

Grade K

Locate the title, table of contents, name of author, and name of illustrator.

Use pictures and context to make predictions about story content.

Connect to life experiences the information and events in texts.

Retell familiar stories.

Ask and answer questions about essential elements of a text.

Distinguish fantasy from realistic text.

Identify types of everyday print materials (e.g., storybooks, poems, newspapers, signs, labels).

Identify characters, settings, and important events.

Grade 1

Identify text that uses sequences or other logical order.

Respond to who, what, when, where, and how questions.

Follow one-step written instructions.

Use context to resolve ambiguities about word and sentence meanings.

Confirm predictions about what will happen next in a text by identifying key words.

Relate prior knowledge to textual information.

Retell the central ideas of simple expository or narrative passages.

Identify and describe the elements of plot, setting, and character(s) in a story, as well as the story's beginning, middle, and ending.

Describe the roles of authors and illustrators and their contributions to print materials.

Talk about books read during the school year.

Write about books read during the school year.

WRITING

Grade K

Use letters and phonetically spelled words to write about experiences, stories, people, objects, or events.

Write consonant-vowel-consonant words (i.e., demonstrate the alphabetic principle).

Write by moving from left to right and from top to bottom.

Write uppercase and lowercase letters of the alphabet independently, attending to the form and proper spacing of the letters.

Grade 1

Select a focus when writing.

Use descriptive words when writing.

Print legibly and space letters, words, and sentences appropriately.

Write brief narratives (e.g., fictional, autobiographical) describing an experience.

Write brief expository descriptions of a real object, person, place, or event, using sensory details.

These benchmark statements represent a continuum of learning. The highlighted column describes observable behaviors most of your children should exhibit by the end of the school year.

ENGLISH LANGUAGE CONVENTIONS

Grade K

Recognize and use complete, coherent sentences when speaking.

Spell independently by using pre-phonetic knowledge, sounds of the alphabet, and knowledge of letter names.

Grade 1

Speak in complete, coherent sentences.

Write in complete, coherent sentences.

Identify and correctly use singular and plural nouns in speaking and writing.

Identify and correctly use contractions in writing and speaking.

Identify and correctly use singular possessive pronouns in writing and speaking.

Distinguish between declarative, exclamatory, and interrogative sentences.

Use a period, exclamation point, and question mark at the end of sentences.

Use knowledge of the basic rules of punctuation and capitalization when writing.

Capitalize the first word of a sentence, names of people, and the pronoun I.

Spell three- and four-letter short-vowel words and grade-level-appropriate sight words correctly.

LISTENING, SPEAKING, AND VIEWING

Grade K

Understand and follow one- and two-step oral directions.

Share information and ideas, speaking audibly in complete, coherent sentences.

Describe things, people, places/locations, actions, and experiences.

Recite rhymes, songs, and poems.

Make up a creative story.

Relate an experience in sequence.

Relate a creative story in sequence.

Grade 1

Listen attentively.

Ask questions for clarification and understanding.

Give, restate, and follow simple two-step directions.

Stay on the topic when speaking.

Use descriptive words when speaking about people, places, things, and events.

Recite poems, rhymes, songs, and stories.

Retell stories using basic story grammar and relating the sequence of story events by answering who, what, when, where, why, and how questions.

Relate an important life event or personal experience in a simple sequence.

Provide descriptions with careful attention to sensory detail.

Additional
Support Activities

Additional Support Activities

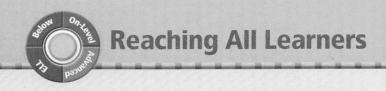
Additional Support Activities
High-Frequency Words

■ BELOW-LEVEL

Reteach: Match Words

Write the word *to* on three self-stick notes and the word *on* on three self-stick notes. Distribute one word to each child. Then write the following sentences on chart paper.

We go to school.

I read to my sister.

I am on the bus.

Please give the book to me.

The computer is on the desk.

Put your coat on the hook.

Read the sentences aloud, tracking the print. Then reread the first sentence and call on a child who has the word *to* to place the self-stick note over the word *to* in the sentence. Follow the same procedure with the other sentences.

For More Intensive Instruction

See Intervention Resource Kit, Lesson 12 for additional **preteach** and **reteach** activities.

■ ADVANCED

Extend: Concentration®

Have partners shuffle two sets of the *High-Frequency Word Cards a, my, the, I, like, go, we, on*, and *to*. Have them place the cards face down on the table and play Concentration, keeping word cards that match after they have read the word.

a	my	the	I

like	go	we	on	to

■ ENGLISH-LANGUAGE LEARNERS

Reteach: Say a Sentence

Display the *High-Frequency Word Card to* and read it with children. Use the word in a sentence, such as *I go to the store*. Then pass the card to a child. The child should use the word *to* in a sentence, and then pass the card on to the next child. Allow each child to have a turn sharing a sentence. Then follow the same procedure with the high-frequency word *on*.

on

to

For More Language Development

See English-Language Learners Resource Kit, Lesson 12 for additional **reteach** activities.

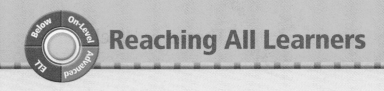
Additional Support Activities
Phonemic Awareness

■ BELOW-LEVEL

Reteach: Listen for /f/

Tell children that you will say some words and each time they hear a word that begins with the /f/ sound, they should stamp their feet. Say these words: *finger, heart, follow, favorite, milk, football, dinner, fudge.*

For More Intensive Instruction

See Intervention Resource Kit, Lesson 12 for additional **preteach** and **reteach** activities.

■ ADVANCED

Extend: Naming Words with /f/

Tell children that Franny Fox is going to the farm and she will only take things with her whose names begin with the /f/ sound. Say: *Franny Fox is taking a fork to the farm.* Then ask each child to repeat the sentence, substituting another *f* word for *fork.*

■ ENGLISH-LANGUAGE LEARNERS

Reteach: Which Word Begins with /f/?

Tell children you will say some words and you want them to listen for the /f/ sound at the beginning of the words. Say: *fish, juice. Which word begins with /f/?* Follow the same procedure using these word pairs: *feet/mask, food/hurry, buckle/fan, funny/soup, vest/fence, giant/fix.*

For More Language Development

See English-Language Learners Resource Kit, Lesson 12 for additional **reteach** activities.

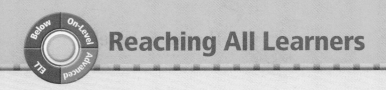
Additional Support Activities
Phonics

**For More
Intensive Instruction**

**See Intervention
Resource Kit, Lesson 12**
for additional **preteach**
and **reteach** activities.

■ BELOW-LEVEL

Reteach: **Write the Letter**

Have children work with their *Write-on/Wipe-off Boards*.
Display the *Picture Card fox*, name it, and ask children to
write the beginning letter of the picture name on their board.
Have children show you what letter they wrote. One at a time,
display the *Picture Cards girl, gorilla, fork,
fish, goat, firefighter, gate*. Have children
say the picture name to themselves quietly, write the beginning letter on their
board, and hold it up.

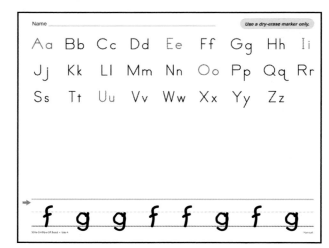

■ ADVANCED

Extend: Picture Puzzles

Create simple picture puzzles for these words: *goat, game, fan, gum, farm, feet*. Have partners work to put the puzzle together and write the word that names the picture.

■ ENGLISH-LANGUAGE LEARNERS

Reteach: Is It *g* or *f*?

Distribute *Tactile Letter Cards g* and *f* to each child. Then display the *Picture Card girl*. Ask a child to name the picture and the beginning letter. Have all children hold up the *g* card. As you display the *Picture Cards firefighter, fox, gorilla, goat, fork, gate, fish*, have children say the picture name quietly to themselves and hold up the card that shows the beginning letter of the picture name.

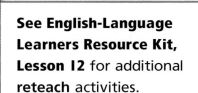

For More Language Development

See English-Language Learners Resource Kit, Lesson 12 for additional **reteach** activities.

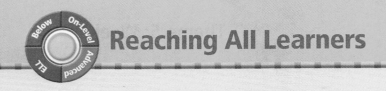
Additional Support Activities
Phonics

For More Intensive Instruction

See Intervention Resource Kit, Lesson 13 for additional **preteach** and **reteach** activities.

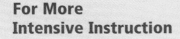

■ BELOW-LEVEL

Reteach: Recognizing *i*

Distribute *Tactile Letter Cards i*. Tell children you will say two words and they should hold up their letter card *i* when they hear a word that begins with the /i/ sound. Say *otter* and *into*. Repeat the procedure with *apple/inside, insect/elephant, itch/opera*. Then follow the same procedure for medial *i*, using these word pairs: *wind/cap, hut/tip, bug/sit*.

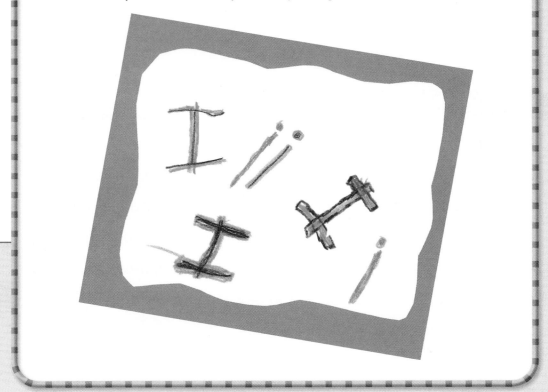

■ ADVANCED

Extend: Name *i* Words

Hold up the *Big Alphabet Card i* and ask children to identify the letter. Tell them that as you pass the card to each one of them, they should say a word that begins with *i* or has *i* in the middle. Record children's words on chart paper and then have individuals come to the chart and circle the *i* in each word.

inch
wig
list
into
whisper

■ ENGLISH-LANGUAGE LEARNERS

Reteach: Write *i*

Have children work with their *Write-on/Wipe-off Boards*. Say the word *igloo* and ask: *Does* igloo *begin with the /i/ sound?* When children respond *yes*, have them write the letter *i* on their board. Say some more words and if they hear the /i/ sound at the beginning, they are to write the letter *i*. Say the words: *inch, interesting, under, ink, addition.* Repeat the procedure for words with medial *i*: *pin, lot, yes, mix, dig.*

For More Language Development

See English-Language Learners Resource Kit, Lesson 13 for additional **reteach** activities.

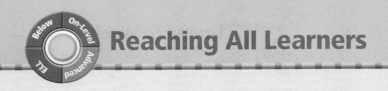
Additional Support Activities
Phonemic Awareness

For More Intensive Instruction

See Intervention Resource Kit, Lesson 13 for additional **preteach** and **reteach** activities.

■ BELOW-LEVEL

Reteach: Blend the Sounds

Ask children to listen carefully to the following sounds and name the word you are trying to say: /f/ /i/ /t/. Continue with the following words.

/s/ /e/ /t/	/m/ /a/ /n/
/l/ /i/ /p/	/w/ /i/ /n/
/t/ /o/ /p/	/r/ /u/ /g/
/b/ /i/ /t/	/d/ /e/ /n/

■ ADVANCED

Extend: *Picture Card* Riddles

Place the *Picture Cards cat, egg, hen, jet, lamb, pig, sun,* and *van* in a large box. Choose a card from the box, and without showing it to children, say *You see this in the sky. It is the /s/ /u/ /n/.* After children guess the answer, allow them to take turns giving clues for the rest of the *Picture Cards.*

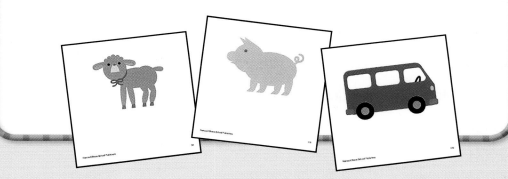

■ ENGLISH-LANGUAGE LEARNERS

Reteach: Blending Sounds

Ask children to repeat these sounds after you (pause after each phoneme): /y/ /e/ /s/. Then say the sounds a little more quickly, again having children repeat them after you, until you say the word *yes.* Follow the same procedure for the words *pin, dip, bag, run, leg, him.*

For More Language Development

See English-Language Learners Resource Kit, Lesson 13 for additional **reteach** activities.

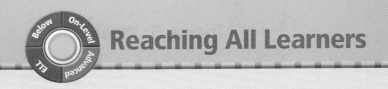

Additional Support Activities
Comprehension and Skills

■ BELOW-LEVEL

Reteach: **Family Questions**

Read aloud a simple nonfiction book about families to children. Then write these question words on the board and read them: *What, When, Where, Why, How.* Encourage children to state questions they would like to have answered about the book, using one of the question words on the board.

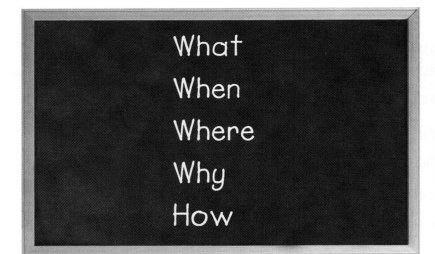

For More Intensive Instruction

See Intervention Resource Kit, Lesson 13 for additional **preteach** and **reteach** activities.

■ ADVANCED

Extend: Writing Questions

Have pairs reread a familiar nonfiction book. Ask children to take turns writing questions they would like to find the answers to. If possible, provide resources for or assistance in finding the answers.

Why do fish liv undrwatur?

How do fish breth?

■ ENGLISH-LANGUAGE LEARNERS

Reteach: Asking Questions

Write these question words on the board and read them aloud: *What, When, Where, Why, How.* Explain that questions often begin with these words. Then have children think of questions they would like to ask about families and state them, using one of the question words to begin.

What

When

Where

For More Language Development

See English-Language Learners Resource Kit, Lesson 13 for additional **reteach** activities.

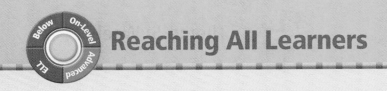
Additional Support Activities
Phonemic Awareness

■ BELOW-LEVEL

Reteach: Listen for *g*

Tell children that you will say some words and each time they hear a word that ends with the /g/ sound, they should give themselves a hug. Say these words: *plug, jig, read, flag, clean, log, big, leg.*

For More Intensive Instruction

See Intervention Resource Kit, Lesson 14 for additional **preteach** and **reteach** activities.

■ **ADVANCED**

Extend: How Does It End?

Divide the group into two teams. Ask the first team member to listen carefully as you say three words: *fig, wet, tug.* Ask: *Which two words end with the same sound? What is the last sound you hear in* tug? Award one point for each correct answer. Continue with sets of words such as those shown.

> hit, bug, sag
> fox, wig, leg
> dog, red, jig
> log, wag, run
> jet, big, mug
> lip, tag, pig

■ **ENGLISH-LANGUAGE LEARNERS**

Reteach: Does It End the Same Way?

Ask children to listen carefully to the ending sound as you say *rug.* Then ask: *Does* pig *end like* rug? Have children indicate a thumbs up if the answer is *yes.* Continue focusing on *rug* (*Does* tag *end like* rug? *Does* ten *end like* rug?) and then move on to other final *g* words.

For More Language Development

See English-Language Learners Resource Kit, Lesson 14 for additional **reteach** activities.

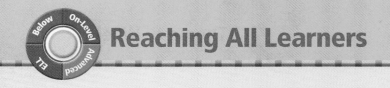
Additional Support Activities
Phonics

■ BELOW-LEVEL

Reteach: Read the Words

Write the following words on index cards: *pig, dig, fig, gap, pit, dip, fit*. Display each card, ask a child to read the word, and have the child use the word in a sentence.

dig

pit

dip

**For More
Intensive Instruction**

**See Intervention
Resource Kit, Lesson 14**
for additional **preteach**
and **reteach** activities.

■ ADVANCED

Extend: Build Words

Distribute *Word Builder Cards a, d, f, g, i, p, t* and *Word Builders*. Ask a child to spell the word *dig* using the *Word Builder Cards*. Have the child show the word to the group. Then have all children spell the following words, calling on one child to display his or her word: *fig, dip, fit, pig, pit, gap*.

■ ENGLISH-LANGUAGE LEARNERS

Reteach: Words with *i* and *g*

Distribute one *Alphabet Card p, i, g* to each of three children and ask them to stand side by side. Then point to the letters as you read the word, *pig*. Have children read the word with you. Follow the same procedure for *dig, pit, fit, dip, fig*.

For More Language Development

See English-Language Learners Resource Kit, Lesson 14 for additional **reteach** activities.

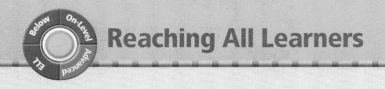
Additional Support Activities
Comprehension and Skills

For More Intensive Instruction

See Intervention Resource Kit, Lesson 14 for additional **preteach** and **reteach** activities.

■ **BELOW-LEVEL**

Reteach: Nursery Rhyme Pictures

Recite a familiar nursery rhyme, such as "Hickory Dickory Dock." Ask children to tell what pictures they "see" in their mind when they hear the words to the rhyme.

■ ADVANCED

Extend: Drawing Pictures

Distribute drawing paper and crayons to children. Then reread the poem "The Very Nicest Place" on page 22 of the *Big Book of Rhymes and Songs*. As children listen, ask them to draw the pictures they "see" in their mind. Encourage children to share their pictures and describe them in words.

■ ENGLISH-LANGUAGE LEARNERS

Reteach: Visualizing a Poem

Reread the poem "A Long Way" on page 14 of the *Big Book of Rhymes and Songs*. Then read it again, pausing at the words *car, airplane, bus, subway, ferryboat*. Ask children to describe the picture they "see" in their mind for each of the words.

For More Language Development

See English-Language Learners Resource Kit, Lesson 14 for additional **reteach** activities.

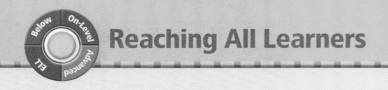

Additional Support Activities
High-Frequency Words

**For More
Intensive Instruction**

**See Intervention
Resource Kit, Lesson 15**
for additional **preteach**
and **reteach** activities.

■ BELOW-LEVEL

Reteach: Complete the Sentence

Place the *High-Frequency Word Cards You have a* in a pocket
chart and read them with children. Then display the *Picture
Cards carrot, fork, hat, key, lemon*, and *ring* on the chalk
ledge. Ask children to read the *High-Frequency Words You
have* a and then, as you point to a *Picture Card*, have children
orally complete the sentence; for example, *You have a carrot*.

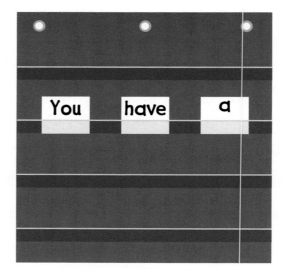

■ ADVANCED

Extend: Write a Sentence

Distribute copies of the *High-Frequency Word Cards You, have, a* from page T21. Have children read the words aloud. Then ask them to glue the words onto drawing paper and complete the sentence, adding a picture to illustrate their work.

■ ENGLISH-LANGUAGE LEARNERS

Reteach: Using the Word *have*

Distribute a classroom object, such as a book, a pen, an eraser, to each child. Display the *High-Frequency Word Card have* and read the word. Then point to a child and say *You have a (book, pen, eraser)*, pointing to the word card as you say the word *have*. Have the group repeat each sentence with you.

For More Language Development

See English-Language Learners Resource Kit, Lesson 15 for additional **reteach** activities.

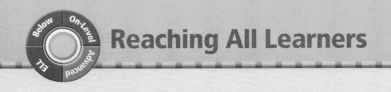
Additional Support Activities
Phonemic Awareness

For More Intensive Instruction

See Intervention Resource Kit, Lesson 15 for additional **preteach** and **reteach** activities.

■ BELOW-LEVEL

Reteach: Listen for /h/

Tell children that you will say some words and each time they hear a word that begins with the /h/ sound, they should smile and show a happy face. Say these words: *kitchen, hamster, hello, radio, high, heat, lemon, hear.*

■ ADVANCED

Extend: Naming /h/ Words

Have children chant the following rhyme with you:

Hip, hip, hooray,

What word with /h/ can you say?

Provide an *h* word, such as *horse*. Ask children to repeat the rhyme with you and call on individuals to name a new *h* word.

■ ENGLISH-LANGUAGE LEARNERS

Reteach: Which Word Begins with /h/?

Say the following words. Call on a child to tell you which word in each pair begins with the /h/ sound.

hungry/lock	poem/hand
gym/happy	heart/vest
hippo/duck	wheel/hero
heavy/school	ham/night

For More Language Development

See English-Language Learners Resource Kit, Lesson 15 for additional **reteach** activities.

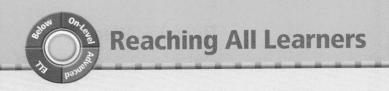
Additional Support Activities
Phonics

For More Intensive Instruction

See Intervention Resource Kit, Lesson 15 for additional **preteach** and **reteach** activities.

■ BELOW-LEVEL

Reteach: Picture Hunt

Divide children into two groups. Have one group cut out magazine pictures whose names begin with *h* and the other group cut out magazine pictures whose names begin with *l*. Write *h* on one sheet of chart paper and *l* on the other, and have children tape the pictures below the letter that stands for the beginning sound.

■ ADVANCED

Extend: Draw and Label *Hh* and *Ll* Pictures

Have children fold a large sheet of drawing paper in half. On the top of the left side of the paper, have them print *Hh* and on the top of the right side, have them print *Ll*. Then ask children to draw two pictures whose names begin with *h* and two whose names begin with *l*. Encourage children to label their pictures.

■ ENGLISH-LANGUAGE LEARNERS

Reteach: Picture Sort

Display the *Picture Cards* hen, horse, ladder, helicopter, lunch box, lemon, hat, lamb on the chalk ledge. Label two boxes with self-stick notes, *h* and *l*. Ask children to help you put the pictures in the correct boxes. Have a child name the first picture, name the beginning letter, and place the *Picture Card* in the correct box. Repeat the procedure until all the *Picture Cards* have been sorted into the appropriate boxes.

For More Language Development

See **English-Language Learners Resource Kit, Lesson 15** for additional **reteach** activities.

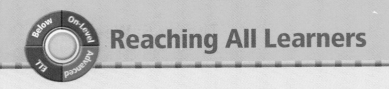
Additional Support Activities
Phonics

For More Intensive Instruction

See Intervention Resource Kit, Lesson 16 for additional **preteach** and **reteach** activities.

■ BELOW-LEVEL

Reteach: Identify Beginning Letters

Distribute *Tactile Letter Cards p* and *i*. Tell children you will say two words. If the two words have the same beginning sound, they should hold up the letter that stands for that beginning sound. Use these word pairs: *paint/park, lunch/pail, inch/igloo, post/deer, into/ax, inside/if, peel/puppy*.

■ ADVANCED

Extend: Name a Word

Place multiple sets of *Tactile Letters i* and *p* in a big hat or box. Have children sit in a circle. Pass the hat to the first child and have him or her reach into the hat and pull out a letter. Ask the child to name the letter and say a word that begins with that letter. Continue around the circle until every child has had a turn.

i

p

■ ENGLISH-LANGUAGE LEARNERS

Reteach: Write Beginning Letters

Say the word *peach* and ask children to repeat it with you. Ask: *Who can write the beginning letter in* peach? Have a child write the letter on the board. Then continue the procedure with these words: *pocket, insect, iguana, party, into, patch, ill, pond.*

For More Language Development

See English-Language Learners Resource Kit, Lesson 16 for additional **reteach** activities.

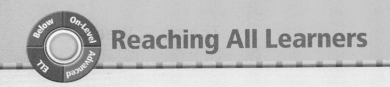
Additional Support Activities
Phonemic Awareness

**For More
Intensive Instruction**

**See Intervention
Resource Kit, Lesson 16**
for additional **preteach**
and **reteach** activities.

■ **BELOW-LEVEL**

Reteach: Word Cheer

Divide children into three groups and tell them that they are
going to cheer a word together. Tell the first group that their
part of the word is /b/. Have them practice it, /b/ /b/ /b/. Tell the
second group that their part of the word is /i/. Have them practice it, /i/ /i/ /i/. Tell the third group that their part of the word is
/g/. Have them practice it, /g/ /g/ /g/. Tell children you will lead
them in the cheer; that as you point to each group, they are to
say their part of the word. Point from the first group to the
second group to the third group so that children cheer the
word *big*. Follow the same procedure for other words.

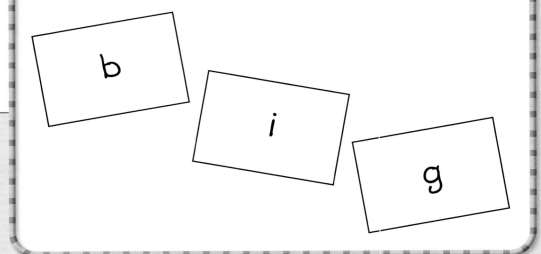

■ ADVANCED

Extend: Act Out Words

Tell children you are going to say a word and you want them to act it out. Say: /s/ /i/ /t/. After children have acted out the word, call on an individual to name it. Follow the same procedure for the words *dig, pack, kick, lock.*

■ ENGLISH-LANGUAGE LEARNERS

Reteach: Blending Sounds

Ask children to repeat these sounds after you (pause after each phoneme): /w/ /i/ /n/. Then say the sounds a little more quickly, again having children repeat them after you, until you say the word *win.* Follow the same procedure for the words *dig, fill, pan, hot, set, lip.*

For More Language Development

See English-Language Learners Resource Kit, Lesson 16 for additional **reteach** activities.

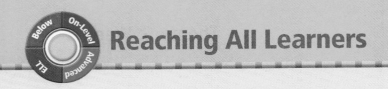
Additional Support Activities
Comprehension and Skills

For More Intensive Instruction

See Intervention Resource Kit, Lesson 16 for additional **preteach** and **reteach** activities.

■ BELOW-LEVEL

Reteach: Make a Picture Card

Distribute one of the following *Picture Cards* to each child: *cat, fox, goat, mouse, nail, socks*. Have children identify their picture name and then create a rhyming picture card by drawing and writing a word that rhymes with their *Picture Card*.

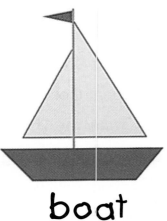

boat

■ ADVANCED

Extend: Write a Rhyming Sentence

Write the following rhyming word pairs on chart paper: *cat/hat, big/dig, pen/hen*. Read aloud the list of words. Have each child choose a rhyming pair and write a sentence using both words. Children can illustrate their sentences.

cat/hat
big/dig
pen/hen

■ ENGLISH-LANGUAGE LEARNERS

**For More
Language Development**

Reteach: Listen for Rhyming Words

Ask children to stand. Tell them that you will say two words and if the two words rhyme, they should sit. Use word pairs such as the following: *win/fin, pig/hat, run/fun, hot/not, mat/rug, vet/jet*.

**See English-Language
Learners Resource Kit,
Lesson 16** for additional
reteach activities.

win

fin

hot

not

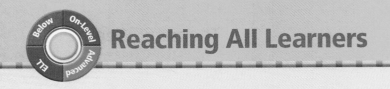
Additional Support Activities
Phonemic Awareness

For More Intensive Instruction

See Intervention Resource Kit, Lesson 17 for additional **preteach** and **reteach** activities.

■ BELOW-LEVEL

Reteach: Beginning Sounds

Divide children into two groups. Tell them you will say three words. Explain to the first group that their job is to tell you which two words begin with the same sound. The job of the second group is to name the first sound in the two words. Then say: *leaf, lost, cake*. Have the first group name the two words that begin with the same sound and have the second group name that sound. After several turns, switch the jobs of the groups.

point, hippo, hill

rabbit, lettuce, loose

karate, open, kite

baby, basket, yellow

lemon, white, lunch

sand, handle, hero

■ ADVANCED

Extend: Matching Pairs

Distribute the *Picture Cards carrot, cow, gate, girl, helicopter, horse, ladder, lamb, pineapple, puzzle, water,* and *watermelon*. Have children shuffle the cards and then make pairs by matching those cards whose names have the same beginning sounds.

■ ENGLISH-LANGUAGE LEARNERS

Reteach: Listen for Beginning Sounds

Ask children: *What is the beginning sound you hear in* table? *Does* drum *begin like* table? *Does* tub *begin like* table? *Does* teacher *begin like* table? Follow the same procedure with other sets of words.

For More Language Development

See English-Language Learners Resource Kit, Lesson 17 for additional **reteach** activities.

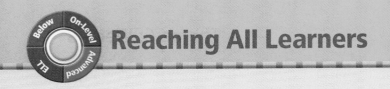
Additional Support Activities
Phonics

■ BELOW-LEVEL

Reteach: Read Words with *-ip*

Place the *Alphabet Cards s, i, p* in a pocket chart and ask children to read the word. Continue the procedure with these words: *nip, tip, rip, hip, lip, dip*.

For More Intensive Instruction

See Intervention Resource Kit, Lesson 17 for additional **preteach** and **reteach** activities.

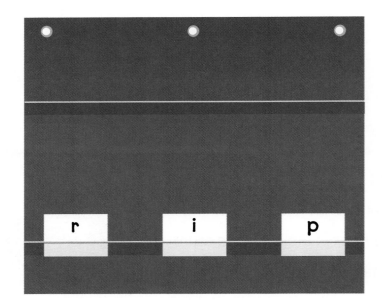

■ ADVANCED

Extend: Concentration®

Write each of the following words on two index cards: *rip, tip, sip, lip, dip, hip, nip*. Have partners shuffle the cards and place them face down on a table to play Concentration. Children keep the matches they make.

■ ENGLISH-LANGUAGE LEARNERS

Reteach: Read -*ip* Words

Place the *Alphabet Cards i, p* in a pocket chart and read the phonogram with children. Then as you place each of the following letters in front of -*ip*, call on children to read the words: *t (tip), n (nip), s (sip), h (hip), r (rip)*.

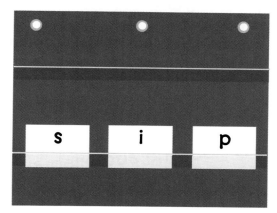

For More Language Development

See English-Language Learners Resource Kit, Lesson 17 for additional reteach activities.

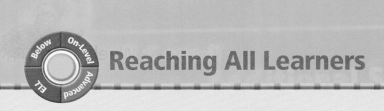
Additional Support Activities
Phonemic Awareness

For More Intensive Instruction

See Intervention Resource Kit, Lesson 18 for additional **preteach** and **reteach** activities.

■ **BELOW-LEVEL**

Reteach: Which Word Begins with /k/?

Say the following pairs of words. Ask children to name the word in each pair that begins with the /k/ sound.

kick/laundry	barn/keep
kayak/panda	zoo/kit
elephant/kitchen	key/whale
koala/dive	name/kangaroo

■ ADVANCED

Extend: Naming Words with *k*

Tell children that Kelly Kangaroo is buying birthday presents for her friends and she will only buy things whose names begin with the /k/ sound. Ask: *Will Kelly Kangaroo buy a kite?* After children respond, ask the same question again, using these objects: *dog, key, kettle, piano, kitten, basket, koala, ketchup.*

■ ENGLISH-LANGUAGE LEARNERS

Reteach: Does It Begin the Same Way?

Ask children to listen carefully to the beginning sound as you say *kitten*. Then ask: *Does* kite *begin like* kitten? Have children indicate a thumbs up if the answer is *yes.* Continue focusing on *kitten* (*Does* key *begin like* kitten? *Does* mail *begin like* kitten?) and then move on to other initial *k* words.

For More Language Development

See English-Language Learners Resource Kit, Lesson 18 for additional **reteach** activities.

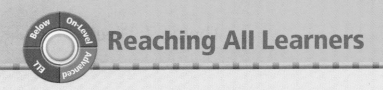
Additional Support Activities
Phonics

**For More
Intensive Instruction**

**See Intervention
Resource Kit, Lesson 18**
for additional **preteach**
and **reteach** activities.

■ **BELOW-LEVEL**

Reteach: Write the Letter

Have children work with their *Write-on/Wipe-off Boards*. Say
the word *bounce* and ask a child to name the beginning letter
in the word. Have each child write the letter *b* on their board.
Ask children to listen carefully to the following words (as you
say them one at a time) and write the beginning letter on their
board: *kite, band, birthday, king, boots, koala, kid, best.* Have
children hold up their board after each word so you can
confirm their answers.

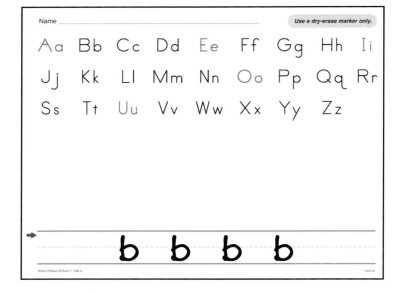

■ ADVANCED

Extend: *B* and *K* Pictures

Assign each child in a pair the letter *b* or *k*. Have children write their letter at the top of a large sheet of paper. Then have children cut out magazine pictures of objects whose names begin with their target letter and glue them onto their paper. Encourage children to write a label for each picture.

■ ENGLISH-LANGUAGE LEARNERS

Reteach: Is It *b* or *k*?

Divide children into two groups. Give one group the *Big Alphabet Card b* and the other the *Big Alphabet Card k*. Have each group name their letter. Then ask children to listen carefully as you display the *Picture Card boy* and name it. Ask: *Which group gets this picture—the* b *group or the* k *group?* Continue with the *Picture Cards king, bus, bear, kangaroo, baby, kite, key.*

For More Language Development

See English-Language Learners Resource Kit, Lesson 18 for additional **reteach** activities.

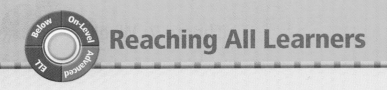

Additional Support Activities
Phonics

For More Intensive Instruction

See Intervention Resource Kit, Lesson 19 for additional **preteach** and **reteach** activities.

■ **BELOW-LEVEL**

Reteach: Recognizing *o*

Distribute *Tactile Letter Cards o*. Tell children you will say two words and they should hold up their letter card *o* when they hear a word that begins with the /o/ sound. Say *opera* and *under*. Repeat the procedure with *alley/ox, ostrich/egg, otter/inch*. Then follow the same procedure for medial *o*, using these word pairs: *pop/dig, mat/fog, well/stop*.

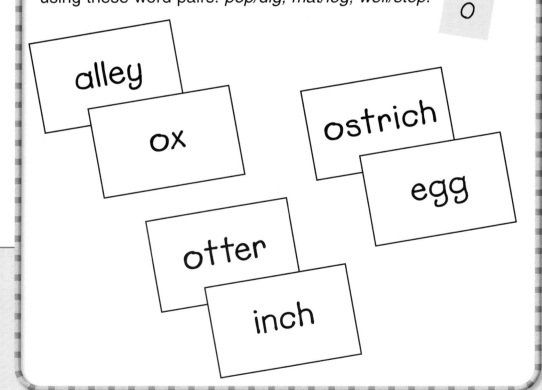

■ ADVANCED

Extend: Make Picture Cards

Have children make their own picture cards for the letter *o*. On four blank index cards, ask them to draw two pictures whose names begin with *o* and two pictures whose names have *o* in the middle. Have children write the picture name on the back of each card.

log

■ ENGLISH-LANGUAGE LEARNERS

Reteach: Listen for *o*

Tell children you will say some words and you want them to listen for the beginning sound. If the word begins with the /o/ sound, children should raise their hand. Say the following words, recording those with initial *o* on chart paper (after children have identified them): *otter, ant, up, ox, edge, on, opera*. Read the words on the chart paper and ask individuals to circle the letter *o* in each word. Follow the same procedure for words with medial *o*, using these words: *mop, log, sad, fun, job, spot, pin.*

otter
ox
on
opera

**For More
Language Development**

See **English-Language Learners Resource Kit, Lesson 19** for additional **reteach** activities.

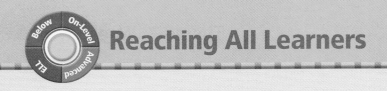

Additional Support Activities
Phonemic Awareness

■ BELOW-LEVEL

Reteach: Word Cheer

Divide children into three groups and tell them that they are going to cheer a word together. Tell the first group that their part of the word is /j/. Have them practice it, /j/ /j/ /j/. Tell the second group that their part of the word is /o/. Have them practice it, /o/ /o/ /o/. Tell the third group that their part of the word is /g/. Have them practice it, /g/ /g/ /g/. Tell children you will lead them in the cheer; that as you point to each group, they are to say their part of the word. Point from the first group to the second group to the third group so that children cheer the word *jog*. Follow the same procedure for other words.

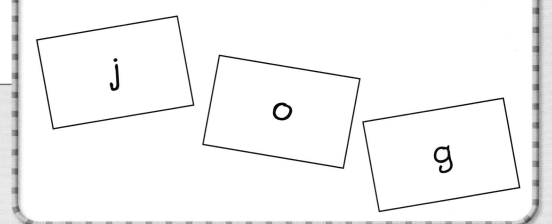

For More Intensive Instruction

See Intervention Resource Kit, Lesson 19 for additional **preteach** and **reteach** activities.

■ ADVANCED

Extend: *Picture Card* Riddles

Place the *Picture Cards bus, dog, fox, hat, van,* and *yak* in a large box. Choose a card from the box, and without showing it to children, say *You can wear this. It is a /h/ /a/ /t/.* After children guess the answer, allow them to take turns giving clues for the rest of the *Picture Cards.*

■ ENGLISH-LANGUAGE LEARNERS

Reteach: Blending Sounds

Have children say the following chant with you:

/h/ /o/ /t/, /h/ /o/ /t/,

The sounds /h/ /o/ /t/ make hot.

Repeat the chant, using the following words: *hop, big, sun, fit, can, tell.*

/h/ /o/ /t/, /h/ /o/ /t/,

For More Language Development

See English-Language Learners Resource Kit, Lesson 19 for additional reteach activities.

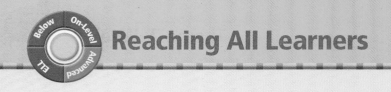
Additional Support Activities
Comprehension and Skills

**For More
Intensive Instruction**

**See Intervention
Resource Kit, Lesson 19**
for additional **preteach**
and **reteach** activities.

■ BELOW-LEVEL

Reteach: What Will Happen?

Ask children to watch carefully as you perform the following
actions: pick up a book, sit in a chair, and open the book in
your lap. Ask: *What do you think I will do next?* After children
respond that you will read, ask them to tell what clues helped
them figure this out. Repeat
the procedure with the
following actions: pick up
a piece of chalk and walk
to the board; put on
your coat or sweater
and walk toward the
door.

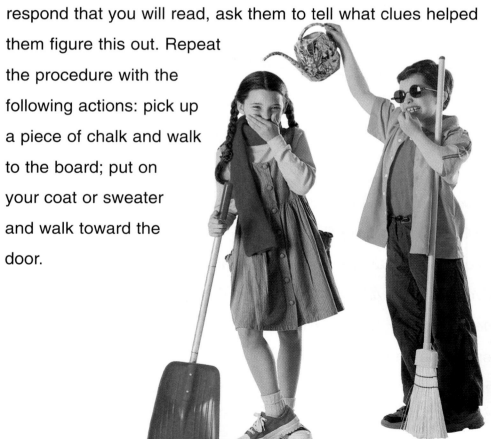

■ ADVANCED

Extend: Think About the Story

Recall the story "The Ants and the Grasshopper" with children. Ask the following questions and have children explain their answers:

- How do you think Grasshopper felt at the beginning of the story? How did he feel at the end?
- How do you think the ants felt when they saw Grasshopper playing while they were working?
- How do you think the ants felt when Grasshopper came to their door looking for food in the winter?

■ ENGLISH-LANGUAGE LEARNERS

Reteach: How Do They Feel?

Gather pictures that clearly show different emotions in people. Display one picture at a time and ask children how they think the people feel. Ask them to tell what clues in the picture helped them figure out the feelings.

For More Language Development

See English-Language Learners Resource Kit, Lesson 19 for additional reteach activities.

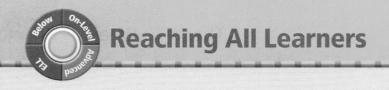
Additional Support Activities
Phonemic Awareness

■ BELOW-LEVEL

Reteach: Segment Picture Names

Display the *Picture Card van* and *ask* children to identify it.
Then ask: *Who can tell me the sounds you hear in* van? Have
a child respond. Follow the same procedure with the *Picture
Cards bus, cat, fox, hat, hen, jet, pig, sun.*

**For More
Intensive Instruction**

**See Intervention
Resource Kit, Lesson 20**
for additional **preteach**
and **reteach** activities.

■ ADVANCED

Extend: What Are the Sounds?

Divide children into two teams. Show the first team member the *Picture Card hen*. Ask the child to name the picture and then tell you the sounds he or she hears in the word. Alternate between teams, using the *Picture Cards bus, cat, dog, duck, egg, jet, lamb, sun, van, yak.* Each correct answer scores a point.

■ ENGLISH-LANGUAGE LEARNERS

Reteach: Listen for the Sounds

Ask children to listen to the sounds in this word as you elongate them: */mmmaaappp/. The sounds in* map *are /m/ /a/ /p/.* Then say the following words, elongating the sounds, and ask individuals to tell you what sounds they hear in each word: *rock, net, fun, hat, wig, got.*

For More Language Development

See English-Language Learners Resource Kit, Lesson 20 for additional **reteach** activities.

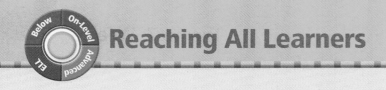

Reaching All Learners

Additional Support Activities
Phonics

■ BELOW-LEVEL

Reteach: Read Words with *o* and *p*

Place the *Alphabet Cards m, o, p* in a pocket chart. Ask children to read the word with you. Repeat the procedure with the words *top, hop, pot, pan, pig*.

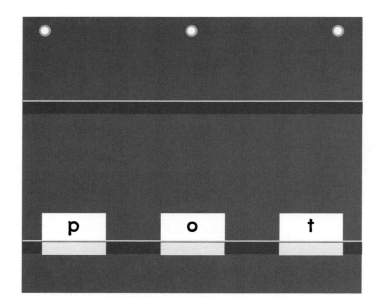

**For More
Intensive Instruction**

**See Intervention
Resource Kit, Lesson 20**
for additional **preteach**
and **reteach** activities.

■ ADVANCED

Extend: Build Words

Distribute *Word Builder Cards a, g, h, i, m, n, o, p, t* and *Word Builders*. Ask a child to spell the word *top* using the *Word Builder Cards*. Have the child show the word to the group. Then have all children spell the following words, calling on one child to display his or her word: *pan, pig, hop, mop, pot, pat*.

■ ENGLISH-LANGUAGE LEARNERS

Reteach: Write Words with *o* and *p*

Have children work with their *Write-on/Wipe-off Boards*. Tell children that together you are going to write words with the letters *o* and *p*. Say the word *hop* and ask: *Who can tell me the first sound you hear in* hop? When a child responds, have all the children write *h* on their board. Continue in the same manner to elicit the second and third sounds in *hop*, having children write each letter to complete the word. Follow the same procedure for the words *mop, top, pad, pot*.

For More Language Development

See **English-Language Learners Resource Kit, Lesson 20** for additional **reteach** activities.

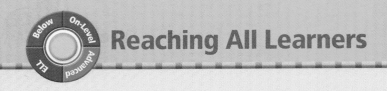
Additional Support Activities
Comprehension and Skills

■ BELOW-LEVEL

Reteach: Find the Match

Write a sentence from the *Big Book Look Closer* on a sentence strip. Read the sentence aloud and have children repeat it with you. Cut apart the words on the sentence strip and give each word to a child. Then display the corresponding page in the *Big Book*. Have children match their word cards to the word in the book. You can follow the same procedure with other sentences.

I passed wild roses and saw something move.

I

wild

passed

roses

and

something

saw

move.

**For More
Intensive Instruction**

**See Intervention
Resource Kit, Lesson 20**
for additional **preteach**
and **reteach** activities.

■ ADVANCED

Extend: Word Hunt

Write these words on index cards: *creepy, caterpillar, funny, will, butterfly, days, yellow, once*. Then display and read aloud "Fuzzy Wuzzy, Creepy Crawly" on pages 18–19 of the *Big Book of Rhymes and Songs*. Hold up the word card *funny* and read it. Ask: *Who can match this card to the word* funny *on the page?* Hand the card to a child and have the child hold it up below the corresponding word. Continue with the other word cards.

■ ENGLISH-LANGUAGE LEARNERS

Reteach: Match the Words

Write the following sentence on two sentence strips: *The eency weency spider went up the water spout.* Read the sentence aloud, tracking the print. Then cut one strip into individual words and mix up the cards. Set the sentence strip on the chalk ledge. Call on children to take a word card and place it in front of the matching word on the sentence strip.

The eency weency spider went up the water spout.

For More Language Development

See English-Language Learners Resource Kit, Lesson 20 for additional **reteach** activities.

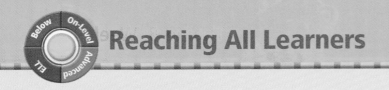
Additional Support Activities
Phonemic Awareness

■ BELOW-LEVEL

Reteach: Words in a Box

Tell children that you would like to put words with the same ending sounds they hear in *box* into an imaginary box. Ask: *Could I put the word* mix *in the box*? ax? cat? fox? wax? six? bell? fix? shop?

For More Intensive Instruction

See Intervention Resource Kit, Lesson 21 for additional **preteach** and **reteach** activities.

■ ADVANCED

Extend: Draw /ks/ Pictures

Tell children you are going to say three words and that they should listen carefully to the ending sound in each word. Say: *When you hear a word that ends with /ks/, I want you to draw a picture showing that word on your paper.* Say the words *pig, box, carrot.* Allow time for children to draw a quick picture. Then repeat the procedure with the words *coat, ball, fox.*

■ ENGLISH-LANGUAGE LEARNERS

Reteach: Does It End the Same Way?

Ask children to listen carefully to the ending sounds as you say *box.* Then ask: *Does* six *end like* box? Have children indicate a thumbs up if the answer is *yes.* Continue focusing on *box* (*Does* cup *end like* box? *Does* wax *end like* box?) and then move on to other final *x* words.

For More Language Development

See English-Language Learners Resource Kit, Lesson 21 for additional **reteach** activities.

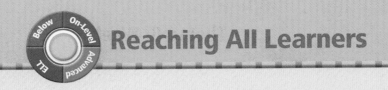
Additional Support Activities
Phonics

**For More
Intensive Instruction**

**See Intervention
Resource Kit, Lesson 21**
for additional **preteach**
and **reteach** activities.

■ BELOW-LEVEL

Reteach: Write the Letter

Have children work with their *Write-on/Wipe-off Boards*. Ask
them to write the letter that stands for the beginning sound
they hear in each of these words (as you say them one at a
time): *window, x-ray, well, wind*. Follow the same procedure,
having children write the ending sound they hear in each of
these words: *box, fix, tax*.

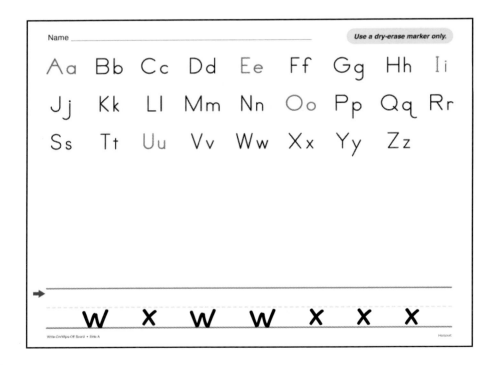

■ ADVANCED

Extend: Picture Puzzles

Create simple picture puzzles for these words: *fox, box, wagon, six, watch, wolf.* Have partners work to put the puzzle together and write the word that names the picture.

■ ENGLISH-LANGUAGE LEARNERS

Reteach: Letters and Sounds

Write the letter *w* on the board, saying the Letter Talk as you write: *Slant down right, up right, down right, up right.* Have children write several *w*s on a sheet of paper. Then say: *Willie Walrus wiggles!* Have children repeat *Willie Walrus wiggles!* with you. Follow the same procedure for *x*, using the sentence *Max Fox is six.*

For More Language Development

See English-Language Learners Resource Kit, Lesson 21 for additional **reteach** activities.

Additional Support Activities
Phonics

■ BELOW-LEVEL

Reteach: Identify Beginning and Ending Letters

Distribute *Tactile Letter Cards o* and *x*. Tell children you will say two words. If the two words have the same beginning sound, they should hold up the letter *o*. Use these word pairs: *odd/flowers, ox/otter, olive/object, attic/octopus*.

Then tell children you will say two words. If the words have the same ending sound, children should hold up the letter *x*. Use these word pairs: *mix/ox, wax/rip, fox/ax, six/box*.

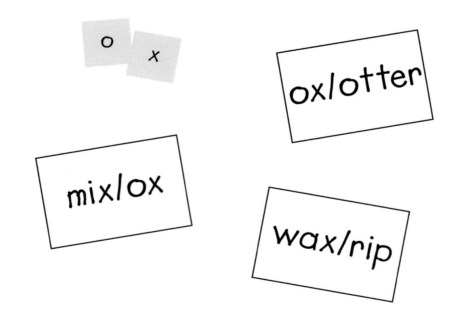

For More Intensive Instruction

See Intervention Resource Kit, Lesson 22 for additional **preteach** and **reteach** activities.

■ ADVANCED

Extend: Name a Word

Place multiple sets of *Tactile Letters o* and *x* in a big hat or box. Have children sit in a circle. Pass the hat to the first child and have him or her reach into the hat and pull out a letter. Ask the child to name the letter and say a word that begins with *o* or ends with *x*. Continue around the circle until every child has had a turn.

o   x

■ ENGLISH-LANGUAGE LEARNERS

Reteach: Is It *o* or *x*?

Distribute *Tactile Letter Cards o* and *x* to each child. Then say: octopus. Octopus *begins with the letter* o. *Hold up the letter* o. Follow the same procedure using the words *on, otter, Oscar*. Then use these words to work with final *x* in the same way: *wax, box, mix*.

For More Language Development

See English-Language Learners Resource Kit, Lesson 22 for additional **reteach** activities.

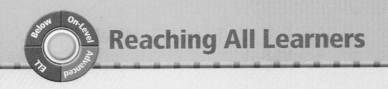
Additional Support Activities
Phonemic Awareness

**For More
Intensive Instruction**

**See Intervention
Resource Kit, Lesson 22**
for additional **preteach**
and **reteach** activities.

■ BELOW-LEVEL

Reteach: Blend the Sounds

Ask children to listen carefully to the following sounds and
name the word you are trying to say: /s/ /o/ /k/. Continue with
the following words.

/m/ /u/ /d/	/w/ /a/ /ks/
/h/ /o/ /p/	/d/ /o/ /g/
/z/ /i/ /p/	/r/ /a/ /t/
/f/ /a/ /n/	/t/ /e/ /l/

■ ADVANCED

Extend: Act Out Words

Tell children you are going to say a word and you want them to act it out. Say: /n/ /o/ /k/. After children have acted out the word, call on an individual to name it. Follow the same procedure for the words *mix, hug, rip, hop*.

■ ENGLISH-LANGUAGE LEARNERS

Reteach: Blending Sounds

Have children say the following chant with you:

/b/ /o/ /ks/, /b/ /o/ /ks/,

The sounds /b/ /o/ /ks/ make box.

Repeat the chant, using the following words: *man, win, pet, dig, run, top.*

For More Language Development

See English-Language Learners Resource Kit, Lesson 22 for additional **reteach** activities.

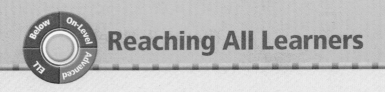
Additional Support Activities
Comprehension and Skills

■ BELOW-LEVEL

Reteach: Who Can Act It Out?

Ask the group: *Who can dance?* Call on an individual to perform the action. Follow the same procedure for words such as *bend, smile, wave, throw*, and *paint*, allowing each child to act out a word.

For More Intensive Instruction

See Intervention Resource Kit, Lesson 22 for additional **preteach** and **reteach** activities.

■ ADVANCED

Extend: Animal Actions

Brainstorm with children action words that might tell about a monkey; for example, *jump, swing, eat*. Record children's ideas in a list under the animal's name and continue with other animals. When the lists are finished, read the action words for each animal and encourage children to act them out.

<u>bird</u>
fly
sing
peck

<u>snake</u>
crawl
hiss
rattle

■ ENGLISH-LANGUAGE LEARNERS

Reteach: What Am I Doing?

Perform various actions, such as sit, walk, jump, read. Ask children to name each of the actions, providing support as necessary.

For More Language Development

See English-Language Learners Resource Kit, Lesson 22 for additional **reteach** activities.

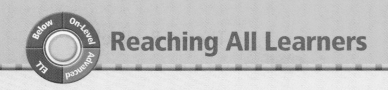
Additional Support Activities
Phonemic Awareness

For More Intensive Instruction

See Intervention Resource Kit, Lesson 23 for additional **preteach** and **reteach** activities.

■ BELOW-LEVEL

Reteach: Listen for Middle Sounds

Say the following pairs of words. Ask children to clap twice when they hear two words with the same middle sound.

cot/mop	dip/can
run/bus	bed/let
wig/pin	tap/hut
gum/shut	bag/sit

■ ADVANCED

Extend: Name Words with the Same Middle Sound

Say the word *top.* Go around the group and ask each child to name another word that has the same sound they hear in the middle of *top.* Follow the same procedure with the words *jam, quick, net, bug.*

■ ENGLISH-LANGUAGE LEARNERS

Reteach: Naming Middle Sounds

Say the words *not* and *hop* and have children repeat them with you. Say: not *and* hop *have the same middle sound—/o/. Say the middle sound with me—/o/, /o/, /o/.* Follow the same procedure using the words *fan/pat, run/tug, men/get, sit/fin.*

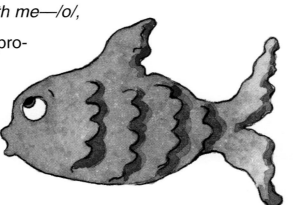

For More Language Development

See English-Language Learners Resource Kit, Lesson 23 for additional **reteach** activities.

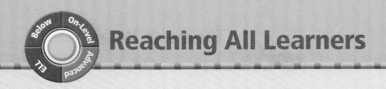

Additional Support Activities
Phonics

■ BELOW-LEVEL

Reteach: Build and Read Words

Distribute *Word Builder Cards b, f, l, o, x* and *Word Builders* to children. Ask them to build and read the following words: *box, fox, ox, lox.*

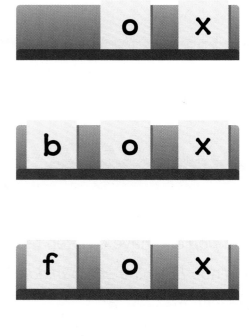

For More Intensive Instruction

See Intervention Resource Kit, Lesson 23 for additional **preteach** and **reteach** activities.

■ ADVANCED

Extend: -ox Riddles

Write these words on the board: *box, ox, fox.* Then give the following clues and have children read the answer from the board:

- This animal has reddish fur.
- This is a place where you might find cereal.
- This animal works in the fields.

■ ENGLISH-LANGUAGE LEARNERS

Reteach: Read -ox Words

Place the *Alphabet Cards o, x* in a pocket chart and read the phonogram with children. Then as you place each of the following letters in front of -ox, call on children to read the words: b (ox), f (ox), l (ox).

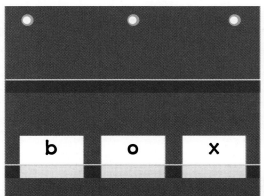

**For More
Language Development**

See English-Language Learners Resource Kit, Lesson 23 for additional **reteach** activities.

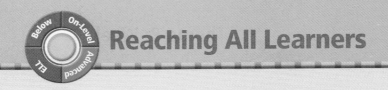
Additional Support Activities
Comprehension and Skills

**For More
Intensive Instruction**

**See Intervention
Resource Kit, Lesson 23**
for additional **preteach**
and **reteach** activities.

■ **BELOW-LEVEL**

Reteach: **Following Directions**

Ask the following questions, emphasizing the concept words, and
call on individuals to respond:

• Who can reach both hands *up*?

• Who can turn *around*?

• Who can look *under* the table?

• Who can walk *through* the door?

■ ADVANCED

Extend: Act Out the Words

Write the following concept words on index cards: *up, down, in, out, over, under*. Place the cards in a box. One at a time, ask children to choose an index card. Help them read the word and then have them perform an action that demonstrates their word; for example, reach up, sit down, place a pencil in their desk, and so on.

■ ENGLISH-LANGUAGE LEARNERS

Reteach: Simon Says

Play Simon Says with children, emphasizing the concept words as you give directions. Use commands such as *Simon says sit* down, *Simon says look* out *the window, Simon Says* put your hand on *your head*.

"Simon says wiggle your toes."

For More Language Development

See English-Language Learners Resource Kit, Lesson 23 for additional reteach activities.

Theme Resources

Theme Resources

Consonant *Gg*

Review the Letter Name

Hold up *Alphabet Card Gg.* Tell children the following:

The name of this letter is *Gg*. Say the name with me.

(Point to the uppercase *G*.) **This is the uppercase *G*.**
(Point to the lowercase *g*.) **This is the lowercase *g*.**
(Point to the *Alphabet Card* again.) **What is the name of this letter?**

Write the Letter

Write uppercase *G* and lowercase *g* on the board. Tell children the following:

(Point to the uppercase *G*.) **What letter is this?**
(Point to the lowercase *g*.) **What letter is this?**
Watch as I write the letter *Gg* so that everyone can read it. (Write *G* and *g*.)

Guided Practice

Distribute *Tactile Letter Cards Gg.* Have students trace the letter *Gg* on the card. Then have them write the letter several times and circle their best *G* and *g*.

Review the Letter Sound

Hold up *Alphabet Card Gg.* Tell children

The letter *g* stands for the /g/ sound. Say /gg/.
(Point to the *Alphabet Card*.) **The letter *g* stands for /gg/.**
(Point to the *Alphabet Card*.) **What sound does this letter make? Say the sound each time I touch the card.** (Touch the card several times, each time having children say /gg/.)

Guided Practice

Give each child a *Gg Word Builder Card.* Tell children that you will say a word, and that, if the word starts with /g/, they should hold up their card. If it does not, they should not hold up their card.

guitar	gorilla	gate	dinosaur	goat
milk	gobble	raccoon	dog	garden

Sorting *Gg's*

Place *Word Builder Cards Gg* and *Dd* in a paper bag. Place *Picture Cards doctor, dinosaur, duck, gate, girl, goat* in another paper bag. Tell children to empty the paper bags and to match the pictures to the letters. Tell them to name the letter of the word each picture name begins with and to say the sound the letter stands for. VISUAL/AUDITORY

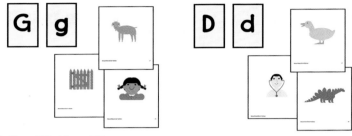

"Gg" Ball

Mark the letters *Gg* on a large ball with washable marker. Have students sit in a circle. Give the ball to one child. Tell children you will say a word and if the word begins with the /g/ sound they can repeat the word and pass the ball to the next child. If the word doesn't begin with the /g/ sound, they say, "Stop the G-Ball!" Use these words:

gate	game	gorilla	gallop	gift
sand	good	nest	guess	goose
gold	nail	girl	goat	gum

AUDITORY

"Gg" Puzzles

Have students cut out from magazines objects whose names begin with *Gg*. Have them glue their pictures to drawing paper and write the name of the object as a caption. Cut the pictures into four parts to make a puzzle and have children put the pieces back together. VISUAL/AUDITORY/KINESTHETIC

ALTERNATIVE TEACHING STRATEGIES

Consonant *Ff*

Review the Letter Name

Hold up *Alphabet Card Ff.* Tell children the following:

The name of this letter is *Ff.* Say the name with me.

(Point to the uppercase *F.*) **This is the uppercase *F.***
(Point to the lowercase *f.*) **This is the lowercase *f.***
(Point to the *Alphabet Card* again.) **What is the name of this letter?**

Write the Letter

Write uppercase *F* and lowercase *f* on the board. Tell children the following:

(Point to the uppercase *F.*) **What letter is this?**
(Point to the lowercase *f.*) **What letter is this?**
Watch as I write the letter *Ff* so that everyone can read it. (Write *F* and *f.*)

Guided Practice

Distribute *Tactile Letter Cards Ff.* Have students trace the letter *Ff* on the card. Then have them write the letter several times and circle their best *F* and *f.*

Review the Letter Sound

Hold up *Alphabet Card Ff.* Tell children the following:

The letter *f* stands for the /f/ sound. Say /ff/.
(Point to the *Alphabet Card.*) **The letter *f* stands for /ff/.**
(Point to the *Alphabet Card.*) **What sound does this letter make? Say the sound each time I touch the card.** (Touch the card several times, each time having children say /ff/.)

Guided Practice

Give each child an *Ff Word Builder Card.* Tell children that you will say a word, and that, if the word starts with /f/, they should hold up their card. If it does not, they should not hold up their card.

fish	fork	fox	car	milk
fog	seal	fun	fair	mitten
family	finger	goat	carrot	fox

Sorting *Ff's*

Place *Word Builder Cards Ff, Pp,* and *Cc* in a paper bag. Place *Picture Cards fish, firefighter, fork, fox, peanut, pig, pineapple, puzzle, car, carrot, cat, cow* in another paper bag. Tell children to empty the paper bags and to match the pictures to the letters. Tell them to name the letter of the word each picture name begins with and to say the sound the letter stands for. VISUAL/AUDITORY

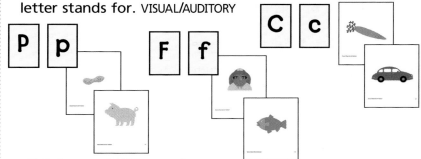

Ff Card Match

Distribute to each child four index cards. Tell children you will say some words and if the word you say begins with the /f/ sound they can write *Ff* on one of their cards. Say the following words: **fox, feet, dog, fingers, fence, gate.** Tell children to turn the *Ff* cards over and draw a picture of an object whose name begins with *Ff.* If necessary, help them name objects that begin with /f/. (fork, fish, feather, fan) Have students work with a partner to place the cards face down and take turns flipping them over and matching pictures. VISUAL/AUDITORY/KINESTHETIC

Fancy Fox

Distribute drawing paper. Have students draw a large fox. Ask them to fill the fox with *Ff*s and to draw a fancy outfit on the fox. Have them brainstorm what kinds of clothes a fancy fox might wear. (hat with feathers, jacket and tie, gown, ribbons, sequins, stars, shoes)

Short Vowel *Ii*

Review the Letter Name

Hold up *Alphabet Card Ii.* Tell children the following:

The name of this letter is *Ii*. Say the name with me.

(Point to the uppercase *I*.) **This is the uppercase *I*.**

(Point to the lowercase *i*.) **This is the lowercase *i*.**

(Point to the *Alphabet Card* again.) **What is the name of this letter?**

Write the Letter

Write uppercase *I* and lowercase *i* on the board. Tell children the following:

(Point to the uppercase *I*.) **What letter is this?**

(Point to the lowercase *i*.) **What letter is this?**

Watch as I write the letter *Ii* so that everyone can read it. (Write *I* and *i*.)

Guided Practice

Distribute *Tactile Letter Cards Ii.* Have students trace the letter *Ii* on the card. Then have them write the letter several times and circle their best *I* and *i*.

Review the Short Vowel Letter Sound

Hold up *Alphabet Card Ii.* Tell children the following:

The letter *i* stands for the /i/ sound. Say /i/ /i/.

(Point to the *Alphabet Card*.) **The letter *i* stands for /i/.**

(Point to the *Alphabet Card*.) **What sound does this letter make? Say the sound each time I touch the card.** (Touch the card several times, each time having children say /i/.)

Guided Practice

Give each child an *Ii Word Builder Card.* Tell children that you will say a word, and that, if the word starts with /i/, they should hold up their card. If it does not, they should not hold up their card.

igloo	inch	ink	apple
inchworm	ant	in	astronaut

Inch Along

Draw a game board pattern on the board. The game board shows 7 sections, each one inch long. Have students take turns writing *Ii* in each section as they say: *i stands for /i/.* Tell children they can be inchworms and inch along the board. Have them say this counting rhyme as they take turns pointing to the section: *one inch, two inch, three inch, four inch; five inch, six inch, seven inch more.* Have them count backwards and point to each section. VISUAL/AUDITORY/KINESTHETIC

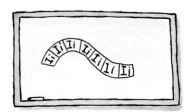

Inside Igloos

Distribute drawing paper. Have students draw an igloo. Tell them you will say some words. If the word begins with the /i/ sound, they can write *Ii* inside their igloos. Use these words:

in   inch   alligator   inside   igloo   apple

VISUAL/AUDITORY

Modeling Ii

Distribute *Tactile Letter Cards I* and *i* and modeling dough to each child. Have them place the cards on their desks and trace the upper and lowercase letters with their fingers chanting /i/, /i/, /i/ as they work. Then ask them to roll their dough into long snakes and make uppercase *I*s and lowercase *i*s with their modeling dough. VISUAL/AUDITORY/KINESTHETIC

ALTERNATIVE TEACHING STRATEGIES

Consonant *Ll*

Review the Letter Name

Hold up *Alphabet Card Ll.* Tell children the following:

The name of this letter is *Ll*. Say the name with me.

(Point to the uppercase *L.*) **This is the uppercase *L.***
(Point to the lowercase *l.*) **This is the lowercase *l.***
(Point to the *Alphabet Card* again.) **What is the name of this letter?**

Write the Letter

Write uppercase *L* and lowercase *l* on the board. Tell children the following:

(Point to the uppercase *L.*) **What letter is this?**
(Point to the lowercase *l.*) **What letter is this?**
Watch as I write the letter *Ll* so that everyone can read it. (Write *L* and *l.*)

Guided Practice

Distribute *Tactile Letter Cards Ll.* Have students trace the letter *Ll* on the card. Then have them write the letter several times and circle their best *L* and *l.*

Review the Letter Sound

Hold up *Alphabet Card Ll.* Tell children the following:

The letter *l* stands for the /l/ sound. Say /ll/.
(Point to the *Alphabet Card.*) **The letter *l* stands for /ll/.**
(Point to the *Alphabet Card.*) **What sound does this letter make? Say the sound each time I touch the card.** (Touch the card several times, each time having children say /ll/.)

Guided Practice

Give each child an *Ll Word Builder Card.* Tell children that you will say a word, and that, if the word starts with /l/, they should hold up their card. If it does not, they should not hold up their card.

lace	ladder	lamb	duck	igloo
telephone	lamp	leaves	moon	legs
list	lock	nurse	fish	log

Sorting *Ll*'s

Place *Word Builder Cards Ll, Ff,* and *Gg* in a paper bag. Place *Picture Cards ladder, lamb, lemon, lunch box, fish, fork, firefighter, fox, gate, girl, goat,* and *gorilla* in another paper bag. Tell children to empty the paper bags and to match the pictures to the letters. Tell them to name the letter of the word each picture name begins with and to say the sound the letter stands for. VISUAL/AUDITORY

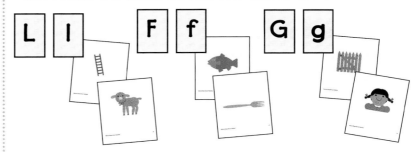

Leaf Creatures

Distribute drawing paper. Tell children to draw the outline of a large leaf. Have them add arms, legs, and other details to make a leaf creature. Ask children to write *Ll*'s on their leaf creatures. Have them write a name that begins with /l/ for their leaf creature. Tell children to cut out their leaf creatures and help them attach a piece of yarn to the creature. Ask them to have their puppet leaf creature tell its name and where it lives. VISUAL/AUDITORY/KINESTHETIC

Lunchbox *Ll*'s

Have students name foods that begin with the /l/ sound: *lettuce, lime, lemon, lollipops, lasagna, liverwurst, licorice, lentils.* Provide drawing paper and have children draw the outline of a lunchbox. Tell them to fill their lunch box with foods that begin with /l/. Have them label the *Ll* foods.
VISUAL/AUDITORY

Consonant *Hh*

Review the Letter Name

Hold up *Alphabet Card Hh.* Tell children the following:

The name of this letter is *Hh.* Say the name with me.

(Point to the uppercase *H.*) **This is the uppercase *H.***
(Point to the lowercase *h.*) **This is the lowercase *h.***
(Point to the *Alphabet Card* again.) **What is the name of this letter?**

Write the Letter

Write uppercase *H* and lowercase *h* on the board. Tell children the following:

(Point to the uppercase *H.*) **What letter is this?**
(Point to the lowercase *h.*) **What letter is this?**
Watch as I write the letter *Hh* so that everyone can read it. (Write *H* and *h.*)

Guided Practice

Distribute *Tactile Letter Cards Hh.* Have students trace the letter *Hh* on the card. Then have them write the letter several times and circle their best *H* and *h.*

Review the Letter Sound

Hold up *Alphabet Card Hh.* Tell children the following:

The letter *h* stands for the /h/ sound. Say /hh/.
(Point to the *Alphabet Card*.) **The letter *h* stands for /hh/.**
(Point to the *Alphabet Card*.) **What sound does this letter make? Say the sound each time I touch the card.** (Touch the card several times, each time having children say /h/.)

Guided Practice

Give each child an *Hh Word Builder Card.* Tell children that you will say a word, and that, if the word starts with /h/, they should hold up their card. If it does not, they should not hold up their card.

hat	helicopter	hen	inchworm
hammer	nest	horse	horn
lemon	hive	lunchbox	hand

Happy Hats

Distribute hat-shaped drawing paper. Tell children you will say some words and they can write *Hh* on their hats each time they hear a word that begins with the /h/ sound. Say these words: *house, happy, hit, ring, ladder, hop, gate, hospital.* Tell children to draw a happy face on their hats. Ask them to take turns pointing to the *Hh*'s on their hats and saying a word that begins with the /h/ sound.
AUDITORY/VISUAL

Hand Words

Distribute drawing paper. Tell children to place their hand on the paper and to trace around it. Then ask them to draw two or three pictures of objects whose names begin with the /h/ sound on their "hands." Tell them to label their drawings.
VISUAL/AUDITORY/KINESTHETIC

Hh Puzzles

Provide each child with a uppercase *H* and a lowercase *h.* Make the letters large enough so they are easy to trace and cut. Have students trace the patterns onto construction paper and cut them out. Tell them to use one color construction paper for the uppercase *H* and a different color for the lowercase *h.* Then have them cut each letter into three or four parts to make puzzles. Have students put the puzzles together. AUDITORY/VISUAL/KINESTHETIC

Consonant *Bb*

Review the Letter Name

Hold up *Alphabet Card Bb.* Tell children the following:

The name of this letter is *Bb.* Say the name with me.

(Point to the uppercase *B.*) **This is the uppercase *B.***
(Point to the lowercase *b.*) **This is the lowercase *b.***
(Point to the *Alphabet Card* again.) **What is the name of this letter?**

Write the Letter

Write uppercase *B* and lowercase *b* on the board. Tell children the following:

(Point to the uppercase *B.*) **What letter is this?**
(Point to the lowercase *b.*) **What letter is this?**
Watch as I write the letter *Bb* so that everyone can read it. (Write *B* and *b.*)

Guided Practice

Distribute *Tactile Letter Cards Bb.* Have students trace the letter *Bb* on the card. Then have them write the letter several times and circle their best *B* and *b.*

Review the Letter Sound

Hold up *Alphabet Card Bb.* Tell children the following:

The letter *b* stands for the /b/ sound. Say /bb/.
(Point to the *Alphabet Card.*) **The letter *b* stands for /bb/.**
(Point to the *Alphabet Card.*) **What sound does this letter make? Say the sound each time I touch the card.** (Touch the card several times, each time having children say /b/.)

Guided Practice

Give each child an *Bb Word Builder Card.* Tell children that you will say a word, and that, if the word starts with /b/, they should hold up their card. If it does not, they should not hold up their card.

baby	bear	boy	dog	carrot
ball	duck	lemon	basket	buckle
pineapple	boot	pig	bunch	bag

Sorting *Bb*'s

Place *Word Builder Cards Bb, Dd,* and *Pp* in a paper bag. Place *Picture Cards baby, bear, boy, bus, dinosaur, doctor, dog, duck, pig, peanut, pineapple,* and *puzzle* in another paper bag. Tell children to empty the paper bags and to match the pictures to the letters. Tell them to name the letter of the word each picture name begins with and to say the sound the letter stands for. AUDITORY/VISUAL/KINESTHETIC

B Squares

Provide each child with a square piece of paper divided into nine three-inch squares. Tell children you will say a word and they can write the letter that stands for the sound they hear at the beginning of the word. Say the following words: **bat, ball, pig, dog, bird, pot, dot, big, bus.** Tell them to color all the squares with *Bb*'s blue. AUDITORY/VISUAL

Bb	Bb	Pp
Dd	Bb	Pp
Dd	Bb	Bb

B Game

Ask children to stand in a straight line on one side of the room. Tell them to take one step forward if the word you say begins with /b/ and to take one step backward if the word does not begin with /b/. When the line has moved to the other side of the room, the game is over. Use these words:

ball	baseball	bat	bear	basket
lemon	boy	bus	lunch	bike
hat	bench	band	mouse	nail

AUDITORY/KINESTHETIC

Consonant *Kk*

Review the Letter Name

Hold up *Alphabet Card Kk.* Tell children the following:

> **The name of this letter is *Kk*. Say the name with me.**
>
> (Point to the uppercase *K*.) **This is the uppercase *K*.**
>
> (Point to the lowercase *k*.) **This is the lowercase *k*.**
>
> (Point to the *Alphabet Card* again.) **What is the name of this letter?**

Write the Letter

Write uppercase *K* and lowercase *k* on the board. Tell children the following:

> (Point to the uppercase *K*.) **What letter is this?**
>
> (Point to the lowercase *k*.) **What letter is this?**
>
> **Watch as I write the letter *Kk* so that everyone can read it.** (Write *K* and *k*.)

Guided Practice

Distribute *Tactile Letter Cards Kk.* Have students trace the letter *Kk* on the card. Then have them write the letter several times and circle their best *K* and *k*.

Review the Letter Sound

Hold up *Alphabet Card Kk.* Tell children the following:

> **The letter *k* stands for the /k/ sound. Say /kk/.** (Point to the *Alphabet Card*.) **The letter *k* stands for /kk/.**
>
> (Point to the *Alphabet Card*.) **What sound does this letter make? Say the sound each time I touch the card.** (Touch the card several times, each time having children say /k/.)

Guided Practice

Give each child an *Kk Word Builder Card.* Tell children that you will say a word, and that, if the word starts with /k/, they should hold up their card. If it does not, they should not hold up their card.

kangaroo	key	goat	kite	duck
kitten	bear	box	kettle	dog
fish	fork	king	kick	mitten

Kk Kites

Give each child six "kites" cut out of construction paper. Tell children you will say some words and they can write an *Kk* on the kite when they hear a word that begins with /k/. Say these words: **king, gate, kitten, key, lamb, kiss.** Have students draw pictures of objects whose name begins with the /k/ sound on the remaining kites. VISUAL/AUDITORY

Kk Card Match

Distribute four index cards to each child. Have them draw the following on the cards: a kitten, a kite, a king, a key. Tell them to work with a partner and to place their cards face down and take turns flipping them over to match the pictures. As they turn over the cards, have them name the picture and say the sound they hear at the beginning of the picture name. AUDITORY/VISUAL/KINESTHETIC

Sorting *Kk*'s

Place *Word Builder Cards Kk, Ss, Rp, Pp* in one paper bag. Place *Picture Cards kangaroo, key, king, kite, sandwich, seal, socks, sun, rabbit, raccoon, rain, ring, peanut, pig, pineapple, puzzle* in another paper bag. Tell children to empty the paper bags and to match the pictures to the letters. Tell them to say the sound each picture name begins with and name the letter that stands for the sound. VISUAL/AUDITORY/KINESTHETIC

ALTERNATIVE TEACHING STRATEGIES

Short Vowel *Oo*

Review the Letter Name

Hold up *Alphabet Card Oo.* Tell children the following:

The name of this letter is *Oo.* Say the name with me.

(Point to the uppercase *O.*) **This is the uppercase *O.***
(Point to the lowercase *o.*) **This is the lowercase *o.***
(Point to the *Alphabet Card* again.) **What is the name of this letter?**

Write the Letter

Write uppercase *O* and lowercase *o* on the board. Tell children the following:

(Point to the uppercase *O.*) **What letter is this?**
(Point to the lowercase *o.*) **What letter is this?**
Watch as I write the letter *Oo* so that everyone can read it. (Write *O* and *o.*)

Guided Practice

Distribute *Tactile Letter Cards Oo.* Have students trace the letter *Oo* on the card. Then have them write the letter several times and circle their best *O* and *o.*

Review the Short Vowel Letter Sound

Hold up *Alphabet Card Oo.* Tell children the following:

The letter *o* stands for the /o/ sound. Say /o/ /o/.
(Point to the *Alphabet Card.*) **The letter *o* stands for /o/ /o/.**
(Point to the *Alphabet Card.*) **What sound does this letter make? Say the sound each time I touch the card.** (Touch the card several times, each time having children say /o/.)

Guided Practice

Give each child an *Oo Word Builder Card.* Tell children that you will say a word, and that, if the word starts with /o/, they should hold up their card. If it does not, they should not hold up their card.

ox	otter	octopus	alligator	inchworm
October	olive	igloo	omelet	opera

Otter *Oo*'s

Draw a game board pattern on the board. The game board shows seven sections, each one shaped like an *O.* Tell children they can be otters and bounce along the board. Have students take turns saying a word that begins with the /o/ sound and writing *Oo* in each section as they say: *My O word is ____. It begins with /o/.* Have one child point to the filled in *O*'s as the rest of the children say this counting rhyme: *One otter, two otters, three otters, four; five otters, six otters, seven otters more.* Have them count backwards as another child points to each section.
VISUAL/AUDITORY/KINESTHETIC

Octopus

Distribute drawing paper. Have students draw an octopus. Tell them to write *Oo* on its tentacles. Ask them to name the octopus and to write its name on their picture. VISUAL/AUDITORY

Modeling *Oo*

Distribute *Tactile Letter Cards Oo* and modeling dough to each child. Have them place the cards on their desks and trace the upper and lowercase letters with their fingers chanting /o/, /o/, /o/ as they work. Then ask them to roll their dough into long snakes and make uppercase *O*s and lowercase *o*s with their modeling dough. VISUAL/AUDITORY/KINESTHETIC

Correlating Your Themes

Theme	Big Books	Library Books	Pre-decodable/ Decodable Books	Center Activities
Animals/Pets	*Does a Kangaroo Have a Mother, Too?* *Walking Through the Jungle*	*Are You There, Baby Bear?* *Elmer* *So Say the Little Monkeys*	*My Pig* *The Big Ram* *What Can Hop?*	Animal Parents and Animal Babies Pop-Up Joey Clay Animal Families All About Animals Write About an Animal Baby
Bears		*Are You There, Baby Bear?*	*I Have, You Have*	Animal Parents and Animal Babies
Birthdays	*Does a Kangaroo Have a Mother, Too?*	*A Birthday Basket for Tia*		
Bugs	*Look Closer*	*Butterfly* *Wonderful Worms*	*Kip the Ant* *The Big Ram* *What Can Hop?*	Surprising Bugs Ant March Anthills and Worm Tunnels Make a Butterfly Flying Bugs, Crawling Bugs
Day and Night		*A Time for Playing*	*To the Park*	
Families	*Does a Kangaroo Have a Mother, Too?*	*Dear Juno* *Are You There, Baby Bear?*	*To the Park* *Sit on My Chair* *I Have, You Have* *Soup* *Hop on Top*	Make a Family Tree How Many People Are in Your Family? Family Portrait Animal Parents and Animal Babies
Food			*Soup* *The Dig*	Animal Snacks
Friendships		*Dear Juno*	*Soup*	Write About a Friend Friends and Helpers
Garden/Plants	*Walking Through the Jungle*		*To the Park*	
Helping/Cooperation			*Soup* *The Dig* *The Big Ram* *I Can See It!* *Hop on Top*	May I Help You? Friends and Helpers Helping Others Building Together "Helpers" Collage
Imagination	*Walking Through the Jungle*		*I Have, You Have* *The Big Ram* *What's In the Box?*	Who's Playing? Animal Stick Puppets Adventure Land Puppet Show
Neighborhoods	*Walking Through the Jungle*		*To the Park* *The Big Ram* *Is It for Me?*	
Special Me			*Sit on My Chair*	Make a Family Tree May I Help You? Something I Learned To Do
Travel	*Off We Go!* *Walking Through the Jungle*		*To the Park*	Adventureland Places for Adventures

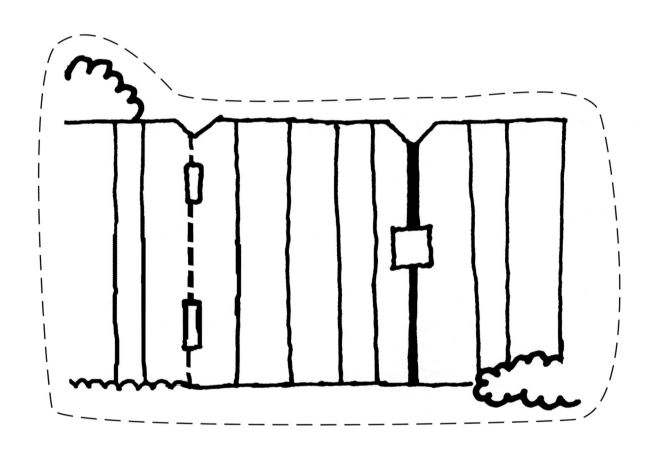

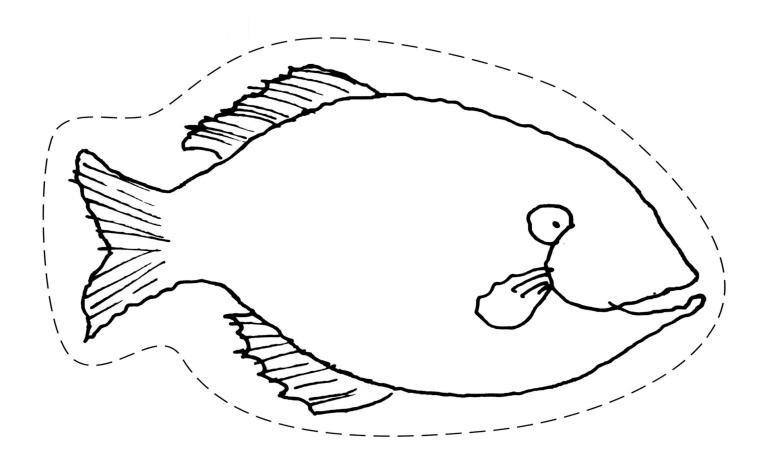

Harcourt

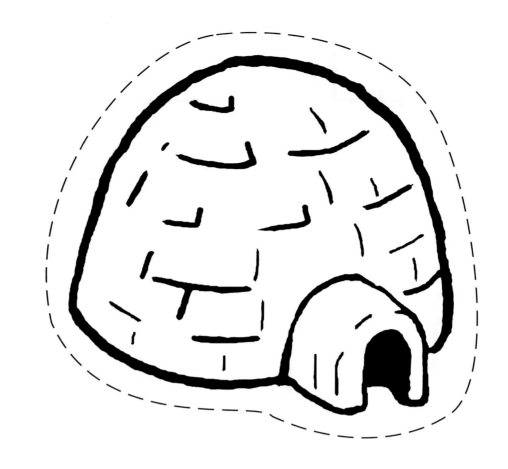

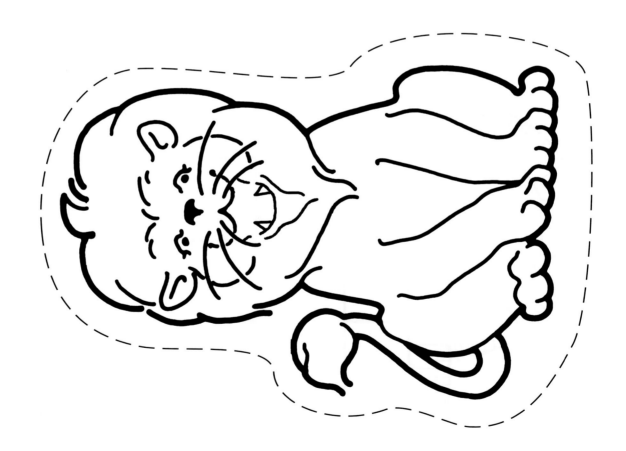

Harcourt

ALPHABET PATTERNS

ALPHABET PATTERNS

Story-by-Story Word Lists

The following words appear in the *Pre-decodable* and *Decodable Books* in Themes 5–8.
New High-Frequency Words are followed by an asterisk. New Story Words are printed in italics.
All other words listed are decodable or have been previously taught. Words appearing for the
first time in that story are in red.

The Park

go*
like*
on*
the*
to*
we*

Sit on My Chair

my*
on*
sit

My Pig

can
dig
my*
pig

I Have, You Have

I
have*
a
you*

Soup

a
have*
lid
like*
sip
the*
we*

The Dig

a
dig
have*
lid
map
the*
we*

Kip the Ant

ant
can
dig
do*
go*
hit
Kip
nap
pat
tap
the*
what*

The Big Ram

am
big
can
go*
I
not
on
ram
the*
top
you*

What Can Hop?

a
bat
can
cat
frog
hop
it
not
pig
ram
snake
what*

I Can See It!

a
big
box
can
dog
him
I
it
man
no*
not
on
see*
sit
top
you*

What Is in the Box?

a
box
cat
dog
fox
in
is
it
no*
not
pig
see*
the*
we*
what*

Hop on Top

can
cap
fox
got
hop
I
is
it
mom
my*
not
on
pop
tap
top
you*

Harcourt

Cumulative Word List: Themes 1–8

The following words appear in the *Pre-decodable* and *Decodable Books* in Themes 1–8.
High-Frequency Words are followed by an asterisk. Story Words are printed in italics. All other
words listed are decodable. Words appearing for the first time in this volume are in red.

a	*frog*	like*	ram
am	go	man	sat
ant	got	map	see*
bat	have*	mat	sip
big	him	mom	sit
box	hit	my*	*snake*

Phonics Sequence and High-Frequency Words

THEME 1: Getting To Know You

Phonics Skills Alphabet Introduction, Early Literacy Skills

High-Frequency Words (none)

Pre-decodable Book 1
First Day at School

Pre-decodable Book 2
Where's My Teddy?

THEME 2: I Am Special

Phonics Skills Consonant *Mm*, Consonant *Ss*, Consonant *Rr*, Consonant *Tt*

High-Frequency Words a, my, the

Pre-decodable Book 3
Pet Day

Pre-decodable Book 4
My Bus

Pre-decodable Book 5
The Party

THEME 3: Around the Table

Phonics Skills Consonant *Pp*, Consonant *Cc*, Short Vowel *Aa*

High-Frequency Words I, like

Pre-decodable Book 6
The Salad

Pre-decodable Book 7
I Am

Pre-decodable Book 8
The Mat

THEME 4: Silly Business

Phonics Skills Consonant *Nn*, Consonant *Dd*

High-Frequency Words go, we

Pre-decodable Book 9
We Go

Pre-decodable Book 10
I Nap

Pre-decodable Book 11
Tap, Tap, Tap

THEME 5: Family Ties

Phonics Skills Consonant *Gg*, Consonant *Ff*, Short Vowel *Ii*

High-Frequency Words on, to

Pre-decodable Book 12
The Park

Pre-decodable Book 13
Sit on My Chair

Pre-decodable Book 14
My Pig

THEME 6: Animal Families

Phonics Skills Consonant *Ll*, Consonant *Hh*

High-Frequency Words you, have

Pre-decodable Book 15
I Have, You Have

Pre-decodable Book 16
Soup

Pre-decodable Book 17
The Dig

THEME 7: Bug Surprises

Phonics Skills Consonant *Bb*, Consonant *Kk*, Short Vowel *Oo*

High-Frequency Words *do, what*

Decodable Book 1
Kip the Ant

Decodable Book 2
The Big Ram

Decodable Book 3
What Can Hop?

THEME 8: Animal Adventures

Phonics Skills Consonant *Ww*, Consonant *Xx*

High-Frequency Words *no, see*

Decodable Book 4
I Can See It

Decodable Book 5
What's in the Box?

Decodable Book 6
Hop on Top

THEME 9: Around the Town

Phonics Skills Consonant *Vv*, Consonant *Jj*, Short Vowel *Ee*

High-Frequency Words *look, come*

Decodable Book 7
A Big, Big Van

Decodable Book 8
Come In

Decodable Book 9
Hop In!

THEME 10: Neighborhood Helpers

Phonics Skills Consonant *Yy*, Consonant *Zz*

High-Frequency Words *for, me*

Decodable Book 10
Is It for Me?

Decodable Book 11
We Can Fix

Decodable Book 12
A Hat I Like

THEME 11: Exploring Our Surroundings

Phonics Skills Consonant *Qq*, Short Vowel *Uu*

High-Frequency Words *one, little*

Decodable Book 13
Little Cat, Big Cat

Decodable Book 14
But I Can

Decodable Book 15
Up, Up, Up

THEME 12: Under the Ocean

Phonics Skills Short Vowels a, i, o, e, u

High-Frequency Words *are, here*

Decodable Book 16
Is It a Fish?

Decodable Book 17
It Is Fun

Decodable Book 18
A Bug Can Tug

Decodable Book 19
Sid Hid

Decodable Book 20
In a Sub

Harcourt

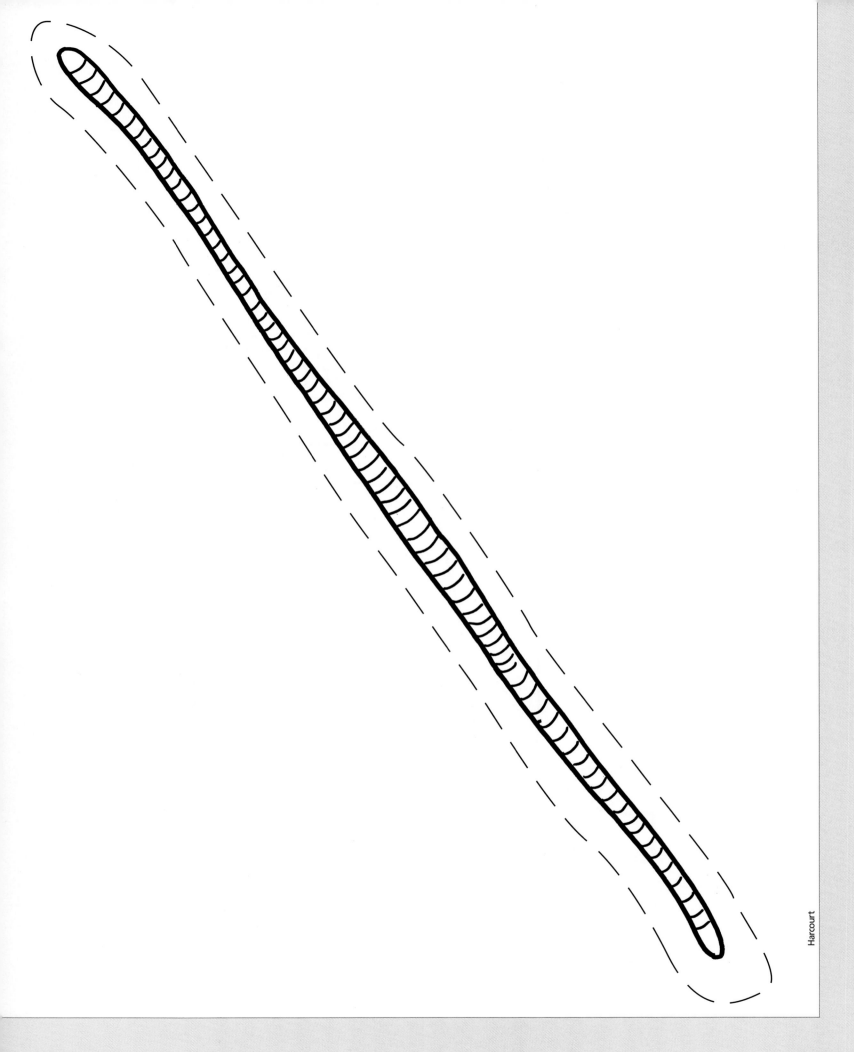

Harcourt

Harcourt

Harcourt

Harcourt

Additional Resources

Additional Resources

Managing the Classroom
Setting the Stage

Designing a Space

One of the keys to productive learning is the physical arrangement of your classroom. Each classroom has unique characteristics, but the following areas should be considered in your floor plan.

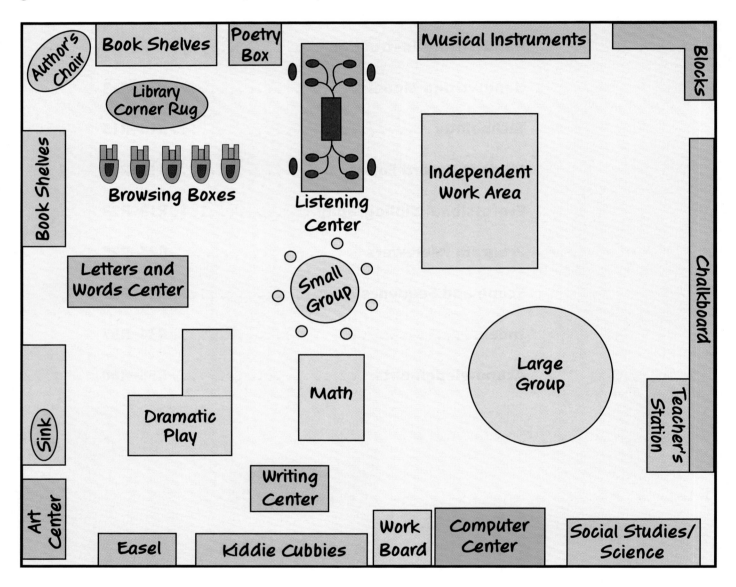

When arranging your classroom, consider traffic patterns and usage of areas. Place quiet centers near small group and independent work areas. Provide some private spaces for children to work.

Tip: A three-sided cardboard divider can instantly become a "private office" or a portable learning center.

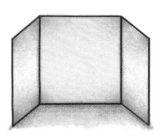

Organizing Materials

- Make certain each work area has the supplies needed to perform the required tasks. Add new supplies as activities change.

- Plan for the accommodation of complete and incomplete tasks and materials storage.

three-sided box for supplies or work

bins, tins, and plastic storage bags

Tips

Keeping the Room Organized

- Clean and resupply each center as needed.

- Get children into the habit of returning materials to their proper places.

- Determine the placement of items and centers by usage. For example, you'll need a wastebasket in the Art Center. Art Centers need to be located nearest the sink.

- Set aside time once a day for room cleaning. Assign specific tasks for each child.

Introducing the Centers

Before beginning a routine, acquaint children with procedures for and use of each area.

- Label each center with its name, its icon (see pages T22–T27 in Volume 1), and a symbol to indicate the number of children who can use the center.

- Help children understand how much time they will spend in a center. For example, they can read several books from the Browsing Boxes, listen to one tape recording in the Listening Center, and play one phonics game in the Letters and Words Center.

- Show children how to use the tape recorder, computer, headphones, and overhead projector. Demonstrate proper usage of art supplies.

Managing the Classroom

Beginning a Routine

Establish Flexible Work Groups

In order for you to work with small groups without interruption, the other class members must clearly understand what they are to do. To plan a series of tasks that the other children can do independently, establish small work groups. These are heterogeneous groups of children who are scheduled for the same center activities on a daily basis. You can change these groups as often as you like.

Introduce a Work Board

One way to schedule classroom activity is with a Work Board. A typical Work Board includes the names of small group members and icons that represent independent tasks. This sample Work Board is a pocket chart with cards. The Work Board can also be a cork board, a peg board with hooks, or a magnetic board. Its design should be flexible, enabling you to move cards on a daily basis.

Carrie Joshua Derek Suwanna Dillon	Mickey Dante Maritza Ty Karla
ABC Letters and Words Center	Science Center
Science Center	1 2 3 Math Center
Art Center	ABC Letters and Words Center

Introduce the Icons Icons are simple shapes that children can easily recognize and connect with a center in the classroom. Make icons consistent throughout the year. Label each activity center with the icon.

Organize the Work Board One way to set up your Work Board is to place groups of names as shown in the sample above. Near each group, place icons to represent activities for the day. Rotate group cards each day, giving each group a new set of activities. Further options are provided by using an icon that represents "free choice" of three or more additional activities. At the end of the week, change the icons to provide a new set of activities for the next week.

Tips

Using the Work Board

- If a child is working on a task in a center and is called to a small group session, he or she can return to that same center once instruction is finished.

- Children not engaged in a teacher-directed small-group activity who have completed their other assignments should check the Work Board to follow the routine listed for them.

- If the maximum number of children is using a center, a child can move to the next task shown on the Work Board and return to the previous one at a later time.

Tracking Progress

There are various ways to keep track of what children are doing during the course of a day.

Kid Watching   Observe children throughout the day. Determine which children are unable to finish all the activities for the day, but are working to capacity, and which children are not completing tasks because they are spending too much time in one center. Visit the centers. Note activities that work well and those that do not.

Portfolios   Have children store products they take from center activities in a portfolio created from a file folder, carton, or even a paper bag with handles. These products can be shared during conferences with children.

Conferencing   Set up a conference schedule to spend ten minutes each week looking through children's portfolios and talking with them about activities they have enjoyed, books they have read, games they have played, art they have created, and so on.

Setting Up Centers

Planning Activities for Classroom Centers

Many of the materials for ongoing centers are at your fingertips. Base center activities on literacy skills children are learning throughout the year. The following are suggestions for particular centers.

Reading Center

This center is a large area in your classroom that can include the following:

Listening Station   Include a tape recorder and headsets. Provide *Audiotexts* and a variety of commercial tapes and tapes recorded by volunteers and children. If you are providing text with a tape, make multiple copies and store the tape and books in a plastic bag. Suggest an extension activity following listening.

Poetry Box   Arrange a large box with copies of poems, rhymes, and finger plays that have been shared during reading time. The poems can be presented as large or small posters, in small books, as puzzles, or as copies for children to illustrate and take home.

Browsing Boxes   Provide boxes of books for each small reading group. Use color-coded boxes or bins that hold fifteen or more books. Provide multiple copies if possible. Books can include those that have been shared during group sessions and books that are appropriate for independent reading. Children can choose books to read from their assigned box.

Classroom Library   One corner of your room can house books children can freely choose and enjoy on their own. Include books of all kinds: Big Books, library books, and books children have made.

ABC Letters and Words Center

Organize this center on a table in one corner of the classroom. Include activities for building and reading words. Children can use an overhead projector and plastic or cardboard letter shapes to form words to project on the wall. Provide write-on/wipe-off boards for writing words and word building pocket charts with letters and cards. Provide supplies for making rhyming words flip books, word slides, word wheels, and phonics game boards.

Computer Center

Children can write with the computer by using word processing software, interact with literature software, or practice phonics activities with the *Phonics Express*™ CD-ROM. See references throughout the lessons.

Writing Center

This should be a clearly defined space where writing materials are stored. Your classroom display of learned words might also be nearby for handy reference. Organize all materials in labeled containers.

Other materials might include an alphabet chart and picture dictionaries.

blank books	a variety of paper	stationery and envelopes
stickers	rubber stamps	poster board
pencils	markers	staplers and staple remover
glue	hole punch and yarn	date stamp

Curriculum Centers

Provide reading and writing activities in curriculum centers. Ideas are suggested with each day's instruction and before each theme. Provide materials as needed for children to

- create graphs in the Math Center.

- perform an experiment in the Science Center.

- make a map in the Social Studies Center.

- create new verses to perform a song in the Music Center.

- create artwork in the Art Center in response to stories.

Handwriting

Individual children come to kindergarten at various stages of readiness for handwriting, but they all have the desire to communicate effectively. To learn correct letter formation, they must be familiar with concepts of:

- **position (top, middle, bottom, etc.).**
- **size (tall, short).**
- **direction (left, right, up, down, etc.).**
- **order (first, next, last).**
- **color (red, yellow, green).**
- **same and different.**

Getting to Know You, the first theme in *Trophies*, includes lessons that teach and practice these skills in familiar contexts so that children learn this vocabulary before formal handwriting lessons begin.

Stroke and Letter Formation

The shape and formation of the letters in *Trophies* are based on the way experienced writers write their letters. Most letters are formed with a continuous stroke, so children do not often pick up their pencils when writing a single letter. Letter formation is simplified through the use of letter talk—an oral description of how the letter is formed. Models for manuscript and D'Nealian handwriting are used in this program to support different writing systems.

Learning Modes

A visual, kinesthetic, tactile, and auditory approach to handwriting is used throughout *Trophies.* To help children internalize letter forms, each letter is taught in the context of how it looks, the sound that it stands for, and how it is formed. Suggested activities also include opportunities for children to use their sense of touch to "feel" a letter's shape before and after they practice writing the letter.

Position for Writing

Establishing the correct posture for writing, pencil grip, and paper position will help children form letters correctly and help prevent handwriting problems later on.

Posture   Children should sit with both feet on the floor and with hips to the back of the chair. They can lean forward slightly but not slouch. The writing surface should be smooth and flat and at a height that allows the upper arms to be perpendicular to the surface and the elbows to be under the shoulders.

Writing Instrument   An adult-sized number two lead pencil is a satisfactory writing tool for most children. However, use your judgment in determining what type of instrument is most suitable for a child, given his or her level of development.

Paper Position and Pencil Grip   To determine each child's hand dominance, observe him or her at play and note which hand is the preferred hand. Activities such as stringing beads, rolling a ball, building a block tower, or turning the pages in a book will help you note hand dominance.

Left Hand   A left-handed child slants the paper  from right (top) to left (bottom) so that the paper is slanted along the line of the left arm toward the elbow. While writing, the child puts his or her right hand toward the top of the paper to hold it in place. The child holds the pencil slightly above the paint line—about 1 1/2 inches from the lead tip—between the thumb and index finger. The other fingers curve slightly to form a pad on which to slide across the paper. The pencil rests in the crook between.

Right Hand A right-handed child slants the paper from the left (top) to right (bottom) so that the paper is slanted along the line of the right arm toward the elbow. While writing, the child places the left hand on the left, toward the top of the paper to hold it still. He or she holds the pencil at the paint line—about 1 inch from the lead tip. The pencil is held between the thumb and index finger and rests against the third finger. The last two fingers curve slightly under to form a pad on which to slide across the paper. The pencil rests in the crook between the thumb and index finger.

Reaching All Learners

Excellent instruction builds on what children already know and can do. Given the tremendous range of children's access to writing materials and experiences prior to kindergarten, a variety of approaches are suggested throughout *Trophies* as viable alternatives for reaching all learners.

Extra Support For children with limited print concepts, one of the first and most important understandings is that print carries meaning and that writing has real purpose. Whenever possible, include opportunities for writing in natural settings such as learning centers. For example, children can:

- make shopping lists in the creative dramatics center.
- record observations in the science center.
- write and illustrate labels for materials in the art area.

ELL English-Language Learners can participate in the same kinds of meaningful print experiences as their classmates. These might include

- writing signs, labels, and simple messages.
- labeling pictures.
- writing or dictating stories about one's own picture.
- shared writing experiences.

Challenge To ensure children's continued rapid advancement as confident writers, give them:

- exposure to a wide range of reading materials.
- opportunities for independent writing on self-selected and assigned topics.
- explicit instruction in print conventions (punctuation, use of capital letters, and so on) when children need them.

The handwriting strand in *Trophies* teaches correct letter formation using a variety of materials to help all children become fluent, confident writers. These materials include:

- multi-modal activities in the *Teacher's Edition*
- *Big Alphabet Cards* showing correct stroke
- *Write-On/Wipe-Off Board*
- *Tactile Letter Cards*
- *Magnetic Letters,* capital and lowercase
- handwriting practice in *Practice Books* and the *Phonics Practice Book*

Handwriting
Capital Manuscript Alphabet

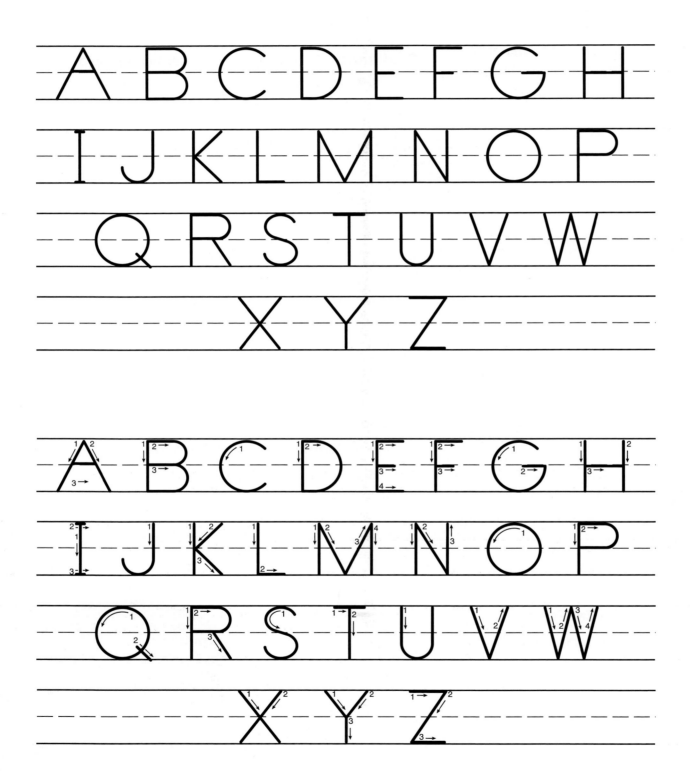

A B C D E F G H
I J K L M N O P
Q R S T U V W
X Y Z

Handwriting
Lowercase Manuscript Alphabet

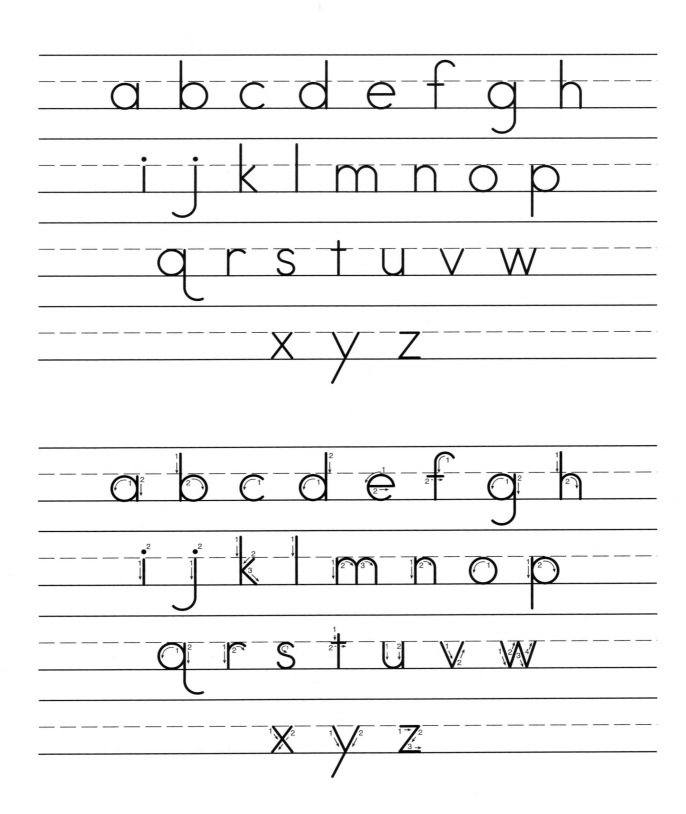

Handwriting
D'Nealian Capital Alphabet

A B C D E F G H

I J K L M N O P

Q R S T U V W

X Y Z

Handwriting
D'Nealian Lowercase Alphabet

a b c d e f g h

i j k l m n o p

q r s t u v w

x y z

My Rules for Internet Safety

I agree that

- **I will never give out private information,** such as my last name, my address, my telephone number, or my parents' work addresses or telephone numbers on the Internet.

- **I will never give out the address or telephone number** of my school on the Internet without first asking an adult's permission.

- **I understand which sites I can visit** and which ones are off-limits.

- **I will tell an adult right away** if something comes up on the screen that makes me feel uncomfortable.

- **I will never agree to meet in person** with anyone I meet online.

- **I will never e-mail a person any pictures** of myself or my classmates without an adult's permission.

- **I will tell an adult** if I get an inappropriate e-mail message from anyone.

- **I will remember that going online** on the Internet is like going out in public, so all the safety rules I already know apply here as well.

- **I know the Internet is a useful tool,** and I will always use it as a responsible person.

- **I will follow these same rules when I am at home,** in school, at the library, or at a friend's.

_X_ _____   _____
　　　　(Student signs here)　　　　　　　　　(Parent/Guardian signs here)

Visit *The Learning Site*
www.harcourtschool.com

Harcourt

Traveling on the Internet

There are so many things to see and do on the Internet that new users may wish they had a "tour guide" to help them see the most interesting sites and make sure they don't miss anything. There are many ways to become a savvy Web traveler—one is by learning the language. Here are some common terms.

bookmark A function that lets you return to your favorite Web sites quickly.

browser Application software that allows you to navigate the Internet and view a Web site.

bulletin board/newsgroup Places to leave an electronic message or to share news that anyone can read and respond to.

chat room A place for people to converse online by typing messages to each other. Once you're in a chat room, others can contact you by e-mail. Some online services monitor their chat rooms and encourage participants to report offensive chatter. Some allow teachers and parents to deny children access to chat rooms altogether.

cookie When you visit a site, a notation known as a "cookie" may be fed to a file in your computer. If you revisit the site, the cookie file allows the Web site to identify you as a return guest—and offer you products tailored to your interests or tastes. You can set your online preferences to limit or let you know about cookies that a Web site places on your computer.

cyberspace Another name for the Internet.

download To move files or software from a remote computer to your computer.

e-mail Messages sent to one or more individuals via the Internet.

filter Software that lets you block access to Web sites and content that you may find unsuitable.

ISP (Internet Service Provider) A service that allows you to connect to the Internet.

junk e-mail Unsolicited commercial e-mail; also known as "spam."

keyword A word you enter into a search engine to begin the search for specific information or Web sites.

links Highlighted words on a Web site that allow you to connect to other parts of the same Web site or to other Web sites.

listserv An online mailing list that allows individuals or organizations to send e-mail to groups of people at one time.

modem An internal or external device that connects your computer to a phone line that can link you to the Internet.

password A personal code that you use to access your Internet account with your ISP.

privacy policy A statement on a Web site describing what information about you is collected by the site and how this information is used.

search engine A function that helps you find information and Web sites. Accessing a search engine is like using the catalog in a library.

URL (Uniform Resource Locator) The address that lets you locate a particular site. For example, **http://www.ed.gov** is the URL for the U.S. Department of Education. All government URLs end in **.gov**. Nonprofit organizations and trade associations end in **.org**. Commercial companies now end in **.com**, and non-commercial educational sites end in **.edu**. Countries other than the United States use different endings.

virus A file maliciously planted in your computer that can damage files and disrupt your system. Antivirus software is available.

Web site An Internet destination where you can look at and retrieve data. All the Web sites in the world, linked together, make up the World Wide Web or the "Web."

Visit *The Learning Site*
www.harcourtschool.com

Harcourt

Using the Student Record Form

Using the Student Record Form

The record form on the following pages is a tool for tracking each student's progress toward grade-level standards. In addition to formal records on assessment results and instructional plans, you may also wish to complete this form several times yearly for each student. Make one copy of the form for each student. Record the date at the top of the column, and use the codes provided to record student progress. You may wish to add comments at the bottom or on the back of the form.

Sharing Student Progress with Family Members

The record form can be one vehicle for communicating with families about how students are making progress toward grade-level standards. Explain that students are expected to master the standards toward the end of the school year. Therefore, a code of B, or Beginning, at the start of the year is expected for most students. After that time, most students should be receiving a P for Making Progress, and by the end of the year they should meet or exceed each standard.

Students who are not making progress, of course, require intervention and frequent assessment to monitor progress and adapt instruction. Explain to family members the levels of support offered by *Trophies* and how you are using these tools to help their students succeed. On the other hand, some students may begin to meet or exceed the standards early in the year. For these families, you can explain how you are using *Trophies* to extend and accelerate progress. (For more information about levels of support in *Trophies*, see Theme Assessment to Plan Instruction at the beginning of each theme.)

Encouraging Family Involvement

Besides explaining student progress, there are several things you can do to encourage parents and guardians to support their students' achievement:

- Use the School-Home Connections pages in the Theme Resources section to suggest activities and reading materials on a weekly basis.
- Copy the Additional Homework Ideas pages at the beginning of each theme, and send them home with students. Encourage family members to use at least one activity per day.
- Have students use My Reading Log (provided in this tabbed section) daily, to record their reading outside of class. Stress repeatedly that sustained daily reading is essential to student growth. Request that parents or guardians sign off on the My Reading Log form, to encourage them to monitor students' reading.
- Above all, offer praise and recognition for all efforts that family members make to support students' literacy.

Student Record Form

Student _____ Teacher _____ Grade _____

	Date_____	Date_____	Date_____	Date_____	Date_____	Date_____
WORD ANALYSIS, FLUENCY, AND SYSTEMATIC VOCABULARY DEVELOPMENT						
Identify the front cover, back cover, and title page of a book.						
Follow words from left to right and from top to bottom on the printed page.						
Understand that printed materials provide information.						
Recognize that sentences in print are made up of separate words.						
Distinguish letters from words.						
Recognize and name all uppercase and lowercase letters of the alphabet.						
Track (move sequentially from sound to sound) and represent the number, sameness/difference, and order of two and three isolated phonemes.						
Track (move sequentially from sound to sound) and represent changes in simple syllables and words with two and three sounds as one sound is added, substituted, omitted, shifted, or repeated.						
Blend vowel-consonant sounds orally to make words or syllables.						
Identify and produce rhyming words in response to an oral prompt.						
Distinguish orally stated one-syllable words and separate into beginning or ending sounds.						
Track auditorily each word in a sentence and each syllable in a word.						
Count the number of sounds in syllables and syllables in words.						
Match all consonant and short-vowel sounds to appropriate letters.						
Read simple one-syllable and high-frequency words.						
Understand that as letters of words change, so do the sounds.						
Identify and sort common words in basic categories.						
Describe common objects and events in both general and specific language.						
READING COMPREHENSION						
Locate the title, table of contents, name of author, and name of illustrator.						
Use pictures and context to make predictions about story content.						
Connect to life experiences the information and events in texts.						
Retell familiar stories.						
Ask and answer questions about essential elements of a text.						
LITERARY RESPONSE AND ANALYSIS						
Distinguish fantasy from realistic text.						
Identify types of everyday print materials.						
Identify characters, settings, and important events.						

Harcourt

WRITING STRATEGIES

Use letters and phonetically spelled words to write about experiences, stories, people, objects, or events.						
Write consonant-vowel-consonant words.						
Write by moving from left to right and from top to bottom.						
Write uppercase and lowercase letters of the alphabet independently, attending to the form and proper spacing of the letters.						

WRITTEN AND ORAL ENGLISH LANGUAGE CONVENTIONS

Recognize and use complete, coherent sentences when speaking.						
Spell independently by using pre-phonetic knowledge, sounds of the alphabet, and knowledge of letter names.						

LISTENING AND SPEAKING STRATEGIES

Understand and follow one- and two-step oral directions.						
Share information and ideas, speaking audibly in complete, coherent sentences.						
Use descriptive words when speaking about people, places, things, and events.						

SPEAKING APPLICATIONS
(Genres and Their Characteristics)

Describe people, places, things, locations, and actions.						
Recite short poems, rhymes, and songs.						
Relate an experience or creative story in a logical sequence.						

Comments:

Key:

B = Beginning

P = Making Progress

M = Meets Standard

E = Exceeds Standard

Harcourt

STUDENT RECORD FORMS

Professional Bibliography

Adams, M. J. 1990. *Beginning to Read: Thinking and Learning About Print.* Cambridge: Massachusetts Institute of Technology Press.

Adams, M. J., et al. 1998. "The Elusive Phoneme: Why Phonemic Awareness Is So Important and How to Help Children Develop It," *American Educator: The Unique Power of Reading and How to Unleash It,* Vol. 22, Nos. 1 and 2, 18–29.

Adams, M. J.; R. Treiman; and M. Pressley. 1998. "Reading, Writing, and Literacy," in *Handbook of Child Psychology: Child Psychology in Practice* (Fifth edition). Vol. 4. Edited by I. E. Sigel and K. A. Renninger. New York: Wiley.

Allen, L. 1998. "An Integrated Strategies Approach: Making Word Identification Instruction Work for Beginning Readers," *The Reading Teacher,* Vol. 52, No. 3, 254–68.

American Association of School Librarians and the Association of Educational Communications and Technology. 1998. *Information Power: Building Partnerships for Learning.* Chicago: American Library Association.

Anderson, R. C., et al. 1985. *Becoming a Nation of Readers: The Report of the Commission on Reading.* Washington, D.C.: National Academy of Education, Commission on Education and Public Policy.

Anderson, R. C.; P. T. Wilson; and L. G. Fielding. 1988. "Growth in Reading and How Children Spend Their Time Outside of School," *Reading Research Quarterly,* Vol. 23, No. 3, 285–303.

Anderson, R. C., and W. E. Nagy. 1991. "Word Meanings," in *Handbook of Reading Research.* Vol. 2. Edited by R. Barr, et al. New York: Longman.

Ball, E. W., and B. A. Blachman. 1991. "Does Phoneme Awareness Training in Kindergarten Make a Difference in Early Word Recognition and Developmental Spelling?" *Reading Research Quarterly,* Vol. 26, No. 1, 49–66.

Barinaga, M. 1996. "Giving Language Skills a Boost," *Science,* Vol. 271, 27–28.

Baumann, J. F., and E. J. Kame'enui. 1991. "Research on Vocabulary Instruction: Ode to Voltaire," in *Handbook of Research on Teaching the English Language Arts.* Edited by J. Flood, J. J. D. Lapp, and J. R. Squire. New York: Macmillan.

Beck, I., et al. 1996. "Questioning the Author: A Year-Long Classroom Implementation to Engage Students with Text," *The Elementary School Journal,* Vol. 96, 385–414.

Beck, I., et al. 1998. "Getting at the Meaning: How to Help Students Unpack Difficult Text," *American Educator: The Unique Power of Reading and How to Unleash It,* Vol. 22, Nos. 1 and 2, 66–71, 85.

Beck, I., et al. 1997. *Questioning the Author: An Approach for Enhancing Student Engagement with Text.* Newark, Del.: International Reading Association.

Berninger, V. W., et al. 1994. "Developmental Skills Related to Writing and Reading Acquisition in the Inter-mediate Grades," *Reading and Writing: An Interdisciplinary Journal,* Vol. 6, 161–96.

Berthoff, A. E. 1984. "Recognition, Representation, and Revision," in *Rhetoric and Composition: A Sourcebook for Teachers and Writers.* Edited by R. Graves. Portsmouth, N.H.: Boynton Cook.

Blachman, B. A., et al. 1994. "Kindergarten Teachers Develop Phoneme Awareness in Low-Income, Inner-City Classrooms," *Reading and Writing: An Interdisciplinary Journal,* Vol. 6, 1–18.

Blachowicz, C. L. Z., and P. Fisher. 1996. *Teaching Vocabulary in All Classrooms.* Englewood Cliffs, N.J.: Merrill/Prentice Hall.

Bloom, B. S., ed. 1985. *Developing Talent in Young People.* New York: Ballantine Books.

Bus, A. G.; M. H. van IJzendoorn; and A. D. Pellegrini. 1995. "Joint Book Reading Makes for Success in Learning to Read: A Meta-Analysis on Inter-generational Transmission of Literacy," *Review of Educational Research,* Vol. 65, 1–21.

Byrne, B., and R. Fielding-Barnsley. 1995. "Evaluation of a Program to Teach Phonemic Awareness to Young Children: A One- and Three-Year Follow-Up and a New Preschool Trial," *Journal of Educational Psychology,* Vol. 87, No. 3, 488–503.

California Department of Education. 1996c. *Connect, Compute, and Compete: The Report of the California Education Technology Task Force.* Sacramento: California Department of Education.

California Department of Education. 1994. *Differentiating the Core Curriculum and Instruction to Provide Advanced Learning Opportunities.* Sacramento: California Department of Education.

California Department of Education. 1998a. *English-Language Arts Content Standards for California Public Schools, Kindergarten Through Grade Twelve.* Sacramento: California Department of Education.

California Department of Education. 1995. *Every Child a Reader: The Report of the California Reading Task Force.* Sacramento: California Department of Education.

California Department of Education. 1998b. *Fostering the Development of a First and a Second Language in Early Childhood.* Sacramento: California Department of Education.

California Department of Education. 1999c. *Reading/Language Arts Framework for California Public Schools: Kindergarten Through Grade Twelve.* Sacramento: California Department of Education.

California Department of Education. 1996a. *Recommended Readings in Literature, Kindergarten Through Grade Eight* (Revised annotated edition). Sacramento: California Department of Education.

Calkins, L. 1996. "Motivating Readers," ERIC Clearinghouse on Assessment and Evaluation (No. SP525606), *Instructor,* Vol. 106, No. I, 32–33.

Campbell, F. A., and C. T. Ramsey. 1995. "Cognitive and Social Outcomes for High-Risk African American Students at Middle Adolescence: Positive Effects of Early Intervention," *American Educational Research Journal,* Vol. 32, 743–72.

Carlisle, J. F., and D. M. Nomanbhoy. 1993. "Phonological and Morphological Awareness in First-Graders," *Applied Psycholinguistics,* Vol. 14, 177–95.

Carnine, D.; J. Silbert; and E. J. Kame'enui. 1990. *Direct Instruction Reading.* Columbus, Ohio: Merrill Publishing Company.

Chall, J.; V. Jacobs; and L. Baldwin. 1990. *The Reading Crisis: Why Poor Children Fall Behind.* Cambridge: Harvard University Press.

Cornwall, A., and H. Bawden. 1992. "Reading Disabilities and Aggression: A Critical Review," *Journal of Learning Disabilities,* Vol. 25, 281–88.

Corson, D. 1995. *Using English Words.* Dordrecht, Netherlands: Kluwer.

Cunningham, A. E., and K. E. Stanovich. 1993. "Children's Literacy Environments and Early Word Recognition Subskills," *Reading and Writing: An Interdisciplinary Journal,* Vol. 5, 193–204.

Cunningham, A. E., and K. E. Stanovich. 1998. "What Reading Does for the Mind," *American Educator: The Unique Power of Reading and How to Unleash It,* Vol. 22, Nos. 1 and 2, 8–15.

Cunningham, P. M. 1998. "The Multisyllabic Word Dilemma: Helping Students Build Meaning, Spell, and Read 'Big' Words," *Reading and Writing Quarterly,* Vol. 14, 189–218.

Daneman, M. 1991. "Individual Differences in Reading Skills," in *Handbook of Reading Research* (Vol. 2). Edited by R. Barr, M. L. Kamil, P. B. Mosenthal, and P. D. Pearson. New York: Longman.

Defior, S., and P. Tudela. 1994. "Effect of Phonological Training on Reading and Writing Acquisition," *Reading and Writing,* Vol. 6, 299–320.

Delpit, L. D. 1986. "Skills and Other Dilemmas of a Progressive Black Educator," *Harvard Educational Review,* Vol. 56, 379–85.

Dickinson, D. K., and M. W. Smith. 1994. "Long-Term Effects of Preschool Teachers' Book Readings on Low-Income Children's Vocabulary and Story Comprehension," *Reading Research Quarterly,* Vol. 29, No. 2, 104–22.

Dillard, A. 1998. "What Reading Does for the Soul: A Girl and Her Books," *American Educator: The Unique Power of Reading and How to Unleash It,* Vol. 22, Nos. 1 and 2, 88–93.

Ediger, M. 1988. "Motivation in the Reading Curriculum," ERIC Clearinghouse on Assessment and Evaluation (No. CS009424).

Ehri, L. 1994. "Development of the Ability to Read Words: Update," in *Theoretical Models and Processes of Reading.* Edited by R. Ruddell, M. Ruddell, and H. Singer. Newark, Del.: International Reading Association.

Ehri, L. C., and S. McCormick. 1998. "Phases of Word Learning: Implications for Instruction with Delayed and Disabled Readers," *Reading and Writing Quarterly,* Vol. 14, 135–63.

Ehri, L. C. 1991. "Development of the Ability to Read Words," in *Handbook of Reading Research* (Vol. 2). Edited by R. Barr, et al. New York: Longman.

Ehrlich, M. F.; B. Kurtz-Costess; and C. Loridant. 1993. "Cognitive and Motivational Determinants of Reading Comprehension in Good and Poor Readers," *Journal of Reading Behavior,* Vol. 25, No. 4, 365–81.

Eisenberg, M., and R. Berkowitz. 1990. *Information Problem Solving: The Big Six Skills Approach to Library and Information Skills Instruction.* Norwood, N.J.: Ablex.

Englert, C. S., et al. 1995. "The Early Literacy Project: Connecting Across the Literacy Curriculum," *Learning Disability Quarterly,* Vol. 18, 253–75.

Epstein, J. L. 1995. "School-Family-Community Partnerships: Caring for Children We Share," *Phi Delta Kappan,* Vol. 76, No. 9, 701–2.

Felton, R. H., and P. P. Pepper. 1995. "Early Identification and Intervention of Phonological Deficits in Kindergarten and Early Elementary Children at Risk for Reading Disability," *School Psychology Review,* Vol. 24, 405–14.

Fielding, L. G., and Pearson, P. D. 1994. "Synthesis of Research—Reading Comprehension: What Works," *Educational Leadership,* Vol. 51, No. 5, 62–7.

Fielding-Barnsley, R. 1997. "Explicit Instruction in Decoding Benefits Children High in Phonemic Awareness and Alphabet Knowledge," *Scientific Studies of Reading,* Vol. I, No. I, 85–98.

Fitzgerald, J. 1995. "English-as-a-Second-Language Learners' Cognitive Reading Processes: A Review of Research in the U.S.," *Review of Educational Research,* Vol. 65, 145–90.

Flower, L. 1985. *Problem-Solving Strategies for Writing.* New York: Harcourt Brace Jovanovich.

Foorman, B., et al. 1998. "The Role of Instruction in Learning to Read: Preventing Reading Failure in At-Risk Children," *Journal of Educational Psychology,* Vol. 90, 37–55.

Foster, K. C., et al. 1994. "Computer-Assisted Instruction in Phonological Awareness: Evaluation of the DaisyQuest Program," *Journal of Research and Development in Education,* Vol. 27, 126–37.

Fuchs, L. S., et al. 1993. "Formative Evaluation of Academic Progress: How Much Growth Can We Expect?" *School Psychology Review,* Vol. 22, No. 1, 27–48.

Gambrell, L. B., et al. 1996. *Elementary Students' Motivation to Read.* Reading Research Report No. 52. Athens, Ga.: National Reading Research Center.

Gardner, H. 1983. *Frames of Mind: The Theory of Multiple Intelligences.* New York: Basic Books.

Gersten, R., and J. Woodward. 1995. "A Longitudinal Study of Transitional and Immersion Bilingual Education Programs in One District," *Elementary School Journal,* Vol. 95, 223–39.

Giles, H. C. 1997. "Parent Engagement As a School Reform Strategy," ERIC Clearinghouse on Urban Education (Digest 135).

Goldenberg, C. N., and R. Gallimore. 1991. "Local Knowledge, Research Knowledge, and Educational Change: A Case Study of Early [First-Grade] Spanish Reading Improvement," *Educational Researcher,* Vol. 20, No. 8, 2–14.

Goldenberg, C. 1992–93. "Instructional Conversations: Promoting Comprehension Through Discussion," *The Reading Teacher,* Vol. 46, 316–26.

Good, R. III; D. C. Simmons; and S. Smith. 1998. "Effective Academic Interventions in the United States: Evaluating and Enhancing the Acquisition of Early Reading Skills," *School Psychology Review,* Vol. 27, No. 1, 45–56.

Greene, J. F. 1998. "Another Chance: Help for Older Students with Limited Literacy," *American Educator: The Unique Power of Reading and How to Unleash It,* Vol. 22, Nos. 1 and 2, 74–79.

Guthrie, J. T., et al. 1996. "Growth of Literacy Engagement: Changes in Motivations and Strategies During Concept-Oriented Reading Instruction," *Reading Research Quarterly,* Vol. 31, 306–25.

Hanson, R. A., and D. Farrell. 1995. "The Long-Term Effects on High School Seniors of Learning to Read in Kindergarten," *Reading Research Quarterly,* Vol. 30, No. 4, 908–33.

Hart, B., and T. R. Risley. 1995. *Meaningful Differences in the Everyday Experience of Young American Children.* Baltimore: Paul H. Brookes Publishing Co.

Hasbrouck, J. E., and G. Tindal. 1992. "Curriculum-Based Oral Reading Fluency Norms for Students in Grades 2 Through 5," *Teaching Exceptional Children,* Vol. 24, 41–44.

Hiebert, E. H., et al. 1992. "Reading and Writing of First-Grade Students in a Restructured Chapter I Program," *American Educational Research Journal,* Vol. 29, 545–72.

Hillocks, G., Jr. 1986. *Research on Written Composition: New Directions for Teaching.* Urbana, Ill.: National Council for Teachers of English.

Honig, B.; L. Diamond; and L. Gutlohn. 2000. *Teaching Reading Sourcebook for Kindergarten Through Eighth Grade.* Emeryville, CA: CORE, Consortium on Reading Excellence.

Honig, B.; L. Diamond; and R. Nathan. 1999. *Assessing Reading: Multiple Measures for Kindergarten Through Eighth Grade.* Emeryville, CA: CORE, Consortium on Reading Excellence.

Hoover-Dempsey, K. V., and H. M. Sandler. 1997. "Why Do Parents Become Involved in Their Children's Education?" *Review of Educational Research,* Vol. 67, No. 1, 3–42.

Hunter, M., and G. Barker. 1987. "If at First . . . : Attribution Theory in the Classroom," *Educational Leadership,* Vol. 45, No. 2, 50–53.

Jimenez, R. T.; G. E. Garcia; and P. D. Pearson. 1996. "The Reading Strategies of Latina/o Students Who Are Successful Readers: Opportunities and Obstacles," *Reading Research Quarterly,* Vol. 31, 90–112.

Juel, C. 1991. "Beginning Reading," in *Handbook of Reading Research* (Vol. 2). Edited by R. Barr, M. L. Kamil, P. B. Mosenthal, and P. D. Pearson. New York: Longman.

Juel, C. 1988. "Learning to Read and Write: A Longitudinal Study of 54 Children from First Through Fourth Grades," *Journal of Educational Psychology,* Vol. 80, 437–447.

Kame'enui, E. J. 1996. "Shakespeare and Beginning Reading: 'The Readiness Is All,'" *Teaching Exceptional Children,* Vol. 28, No. 2, 77–81.

Kuhn, M. R., and S. A. Stahl. 1998. "Teaching Children to Learn Word Meanings from Context: A Synthesis and Some Questions," *Journal of Literacy Research,* Vol. 30, No. 1, 119–38.

Lance, K. C.; L. Welborn; and C. Hamilton-Pennell. 1993. *The Impact of School Library Media Centers on Academic Achievement.* San Jose, Calif.: Hi Willow Research and Publishing.

Leather, C. V., and L. A. Henry. 1994. "Working Memory Span and Phonological Awareness Tasks as Predictors of Early Reading Ability," *Journal of Experimental Child Psychology,* Vol. 58, 88–111.

Levy, B. A.; A. Nicholls; and D. Kohen. 1993. "Repeated Readings: Process Benefits for Good and Poor Readers," *Journal of Experimental Child Psychology,* Vol. 56, 303–27.

Liberman, I. Y.; D. Shankweiler; and A. M. Liberman. 1991. "The Alphabetic Principle and Learning to Read," in *Phonology and Reading Disability: Solving the Reading Puzzle.* Edited by D. Shankweiler and I. Y. Liberman. Ann Arbor: University of Michigan Press.

Lie, A. 1991. "Effects of a Training Program for Stimulating Skills in Word Analysis in First-Grade Children," *Reading Research Quarterly,* Vol. 26, No. 3, 234–50.

Lipson, M. Y., and K. K. Wixson. 1986. "Reading Disability Research: An Interactionist Perspective," *Review of Educational Research,* Vol. 56, 111–36.

Louis, K. S.; H. M. Marks; and S. Kruse. 1996. "Teachers' Professional Community in Restructuring Schools," *American Educational Research Journal* (Vol. 33).

Lundberg, I.; J. Frost; and O. P. Petersen. 1988. "Effects of an Extensive Program for Stimulating Phonological Awareness in Preschool Children," *Reading Research Quarterly,* Vol. 23, 263–284.

Lyon, G. R. 1995. "Toward a Definition of Dyslexia," *Annals of Dyslexia,* Vol. 45, 3–27.

Lyon, G. R., and V. Chhabra. 1996. "The Current State of Science and the Future of Specific Reading Disability," *Mental Retardation and Developmental Disabilities Research Reviews,* Vol. 2, 2–9.

Markell, M. A., and S. L. Deno. 1997. "Effects of Increasing Oral Reading: Generalization Across Reading Tasks," *The Journal of Special Education,* Vol. 31, No. 2, 233–50.

McCollum, H., and A. Russo. 1993. *Model Strategies in Bilingual Education: Family Literacy and Parent Involvement.* Washington, D.C.: United States Department of Education.

McGuinness, D.; C. McGuinness; and J. Donahue. 1996. "Phonological Training and the Alphabetic Principle: Evidence for Reciprocal Causality," *Reading Research Quarterly,* Vol. 30, 830–52.

McWhorter, J. 1998. *The Word on the Street: Fact and Fable about American English.* New York: Plenum.

Moats, L. C. 1995. *Spelling: Development, Disability, and Instruction.* Baltimore: York Press.

Moats, L. C. 1998. "Teaching Decoding," *American Educator: The Unique Power of Reading and How to Unleash It,* Vol. 22, Nos. 1 and 2, 42–49, 95–96.

Moffett, J., and B. J. Wagner. 1991. *Student-Centered Language Arts, K-12.* Portsmouth, N.H.: Boynton Cook.

Morrow, L. M. 1992. "The Impact of a Literature-Based Program on Literacy, Achievement, Use of Literature, and Attitudes of Children from Minority Backgrounds," *Reading Research Quarterly,* Vol. 27, 250–75.

Mosenthal, P. 1984. "The Problem of Partial Specification in Translating Reading Research into Practice," *The Elementary School Journal,* Vol. 85, No. 2, 199–227.

Mosenthal, P. 1985. "Defining Progress in Educational Research," *Educational Researcher,* Vol. 14, No. 9, 3–9.

Mosteller, F.; R. Light; and J. Sachs. 1996. "Sustained Inquiry in Education: Lessons from Skill Grouping and Class Size," *Harvard Educational Review,* Vol. 66, No. 4, 797–842.

National Center to Improve the Tools of Educators. 1997. *Learning to Read, Reading to Learn—Helping Children to Succeed: A Resource Guide.* Washington, D.C.: American Federation of Teachers.

National Research Council. 1998. *Preventing Reading Difficulties in Young Children.* Edited by M. S. Burns, P. Griffin, and C. E. Snow. Washington, D.C.: National Academy Press.

National Research Council. 1999. *Starting Out Right: A Guide to Promoting Children's Reading Success.* Edited by M. S. Burns, P. Griffin, and C. E. Snow. Washington, D.C.: National Academy Press.

Neuman, S. B. 1996. "Children Engaging in Storybook Reading: The Influence of Access to Print Resources, Opportunity, and Parental Interaction," *Early Childhood Research Quarterly,* Vol. 11, 495–513.

O'Connor, R. E.; J. R. Jenkins; and T. A. Slocum. 1995. "Transfer Among Phonological Tasks in Kindergarten: Essential Instructional Content," *Journal of Educational Psychology,* Vol. 87, 202–17.

Pearson, P. D., et al. 1992. "Developing Expertise in Reading Comprehension," in *What Research Says to the Teacher.* Edited by S. J. Samuels and A. E. Farstrup. Newark, Del.: International Reading Association.

Pearson, P. D., and K. Camperell. 1985. "Comprehension in Text Structures," in *Theoretical Models and Processes of Reading.* Edited by H. Singer and R. B. Ruddell. Newark, Del.: International Reading Association.

Perfetti, C. A., and S. Zhang. 1995. "The Universal Word Identification Reflex," in *The Psychology of Learning and Motivation* (Vol. 33). Edited by D. L. Medlin. San Diego: Academic Press.

Phillips, L. M.; S. P. Norris; and J. M. Mason. 1996. "Longitudinal Effects of Early Literacy Concepts on Reading Achievement: A Kindergarten Intervention and Five-Year Follow-Up," *Journal of Literacy Research,* Vol. 28, 173–95.

Pinnell, G. S., and L. C. Fountas. 1997. *Help America Read: A Handbook for Volunteers.* Portsmouth, N.H.: Heinemann.

Pressley, M.; J. Rankin; and L. Yokoi. 1996. "A Survey of Instructional Practices of Primary Teachers Nominated as Effective in Promoting Literacy," *The Elementary School Journal,* Vol. 96, 363–84.

Purcell-Gates, V.; E. McIntyre; and P. Freppon. 1995. "Learning Written Storybook Language in School: A Comparison of Low-SES Children in Skills-Based and Whole-Language Classrooms," *American Educational Research Journal,* Vol. 32, 659–85.

Robbins, C., and L. C. Ehri. 1994. "Reading Storybooks to Kindergartners Helps Them Learn New Vocabulary Words," *Journal of Educational Psychology,* Vol. 86, No. 1, 54–64.

Rosenshine, B., and C. Meister. 1994. "Reciprocal Teaching: A Review of the Research," *Review of Educational Research,* Vol. 64, No. 4, 479–530.

Ross, S. M., et al. 1995. "Increasing the Academic Success of Disadvantaged Children: An Examination of Alternative Early Intervention Programs," *American Educational Research Journal,* Vol. 32, 773–800.

Ruddell, R.; M. Rapp Ruddell; and H. Singer, eds. 1994. *Theoretical Models and Processes of Reading* (Fourth edition). Newark, Del.: International Reading Association.

Ryder, R. J., and M. F. Graves. 1994. "Vocabulary Instruction Presented Prior to Reading in Two Basal Readers," *Elementary School Journal,* Vol. 95, No. 2, 139–53.

Sacks, C. H., and J. R. Mergendoller. 1997. "The Relationship Between Teachers' Theoretical Orientation Toward Reading and Student Outcomes in Kindergarten Children with Different Initial Reading Abilities," *American Educational Research Journal,* Vol. 34, 721–39.

Samuels, S. J. 1979. "The Method of Repeated Reading," *The Reading Teacher,* Vol. 32, 403–08.

Sanacore, J. 1988. "Linking Vocabulary and Comprehension Through Independent Reading," ERIC Clearinghouse on Assessment and Evaluation (No. CS009409).

Shefelbine, J. 1991. *Encouraging Your Junior High Student to Read.* Bloomington, Ind.: ERIC Clearinghouse on Reading, English, and Communication.

Shefelbine, J. L. 1990. "Student Factors Related to Variability in Learning Word Meanings from Context," *Journal of Reading Behavior,* Vol. 22, No. 1, 71–97.

Shore, W. J., and F. T. Durso. 1990. "Partial Knowledge in Vocabulary Acquisition: General Constraints and Specific Detail," *Journal of Educational Psychology,* Vol. 82, 315–18.

Shore, B. M., et al. 1991. *Recommended Practices in Gifted Education: A Critical Analysis.* New York: Teachers College Press.

Simmons, D. C., and E. J. Kame'enui. 1996. "A Focus on Curriculum Design: When Children Fail," in *Strategies for Teaching Children in Inclusive Settings.* Edited by E. Meyen, G. Vergason, and R. Whelan. Denver: Love Publishing.

Simmons, D. C., and E. J. Kame'enui, eds. 1998. *What Reading Research Tells Us About Children with Diverse Learning Needs: Bases and Basics.* Mahwah, N.J.: Lawrence Erlbaum Associates.

Sindelar, P. T.; L. Monda; and L. O'Shea. 1990. "Effects of Repeated Readings on Instructional- and Mastery-Level Readers," *Journal of Educational Research,* Vol. 83, 220–26.

Slavin, R. E.; N. L. Karweit; and B. A. Wasik, eds. 1993. *Preventing Early School Failure: Research, Policy, and Practice.* 1993. Boston: Allyn and Bacon.

Snider, V. E. 1995. "A Primer on Phonological Awareness: What It Is, Why It's Important, and How to Teach It," *School Psychology Review,* Vol. 24, 443–55.

Spear-Swerling, L., and R. J. Sternberg. 1998. "Curing Our 'Epidemic' of Learning Disabilities," *Phi Delta Kappan,* Vol. 79, No. 5, 397–401.

Spear-Swerling, L., and R. J. Sternberg. 1996. *Off Track: When Poor Readers Become Learning Disabled.* Boulder, Colo.: Westview Press.

Stanovich, K. E. 1986. "Matthew Effects in Reading: Some Consequences of Individual Differences in the Acquisition of Literacy," *Reading Research Quarterly,* Vol. 21, 360–407.

Stanovich, K. E. 1994. "Constructivism in Reading Education," *The Journal of Special Education,* Vol. 28, 259–74.

Stanovich, K. E. 1993–94. "Romance and Reality," *The Reading Teacher,* Vol. 47, 280–90.

Sulzby, E., and W. Teale. 1991. "Emergent Literacy," in *Handbook of Reading Research* (Vol. 2). Edited by R. Barr, M. L. Kamil, P. B. Mosenthal, and P. D. Pearson. New York: Longman.

Topping, K. 1998. "Effective Tutoring in America Reads: A Reply to Wasik," *The Reading Teacher,* Vol. 52, No. 1, 42–50.

Torgesen, J. K. 1998. "Catch Them Before They Fall: Identification and Assessment to Prevent Reading Failure in Young Children," *American Educator: The Unique Power of Reading and How to Unleash It,* Vol. 22, Nos. 1 and 2, 32–39.

Treiman, R. 1985. "Onsets and Rimes as Units of Spoken Syllables: Evidence from Children," *Journal of Experimental Child Psychology,* Vol. 39, 161–81.

Treiman, R.; S. Weatherston; and D. Berch. 1994. "The Role of Letter Names in Children's Learning of Phoneme-Grapheme Relations," *Applied Psycholinguistics,* Vol. 15, 97–122.

Vandervelden, M. C., and L. S. Siegel. 1995. "Phonological Recoding and Phoneme Awareness in Early Literacy: A Developmental Approach," *Reading Research Quarterly,* Vol. 30, 854–73.

Vellutino, F. R., et al. 1996. "Cognitive Profiles of Difficult-to-Remediate and Readily Remediated Poor Readers: Early Intervention as a Vehicle for Distinguishing Between Cognitive and Experiential Deficits as Basic Causes of Specific Reading Disability," *Journal of Educational Psychology,* Vol. 88, 601–38.

Wagner, R. K., et al. 1993. "Development of Young Readers' Phonological Processing Abilities," *Journal of Educational Psychology,* Vol. 85, 83–103.

Walberg, H. J. 1984. "Families as Partners in Educational Productivity," *Phi Delta Kappan,* Vol. 65, No. 6, 397–400.

Wasik, B. A., and R. E. Slavin. 1993. "Preventing Early Reading Failure with One-to-One Tutoring: A Review of Five Programs," *Reading Research Quarterly,* Vol. 28, 178–200.

Wells, G. 1986. *The Meaning Makers: Children Learning Language and Using Language to Learn.* Portsmouth, N.H.: Heinemann.

White, T. G.; M. F. Graves; and W. H. Slater. 1990. "Growth of Reading Vocabulary in Diverse Elementary Schools: Decoding and Word Meaning," *Journal of Educational Psychology,* Vol. 82, 281–90.

Whitehurst, G. J., et al. 1994. "Outcomes of an Emergent Literacy Intervention in Head Start," *Journal of Educational Psychology,* Vol. 86, 542–55.

Yopp, H. K. 1988. "The Validity and Reliability of Phonemic Awareness Tests," *Reading Research Quarterly,* Vol. 23, No. 2, 159–77.

Program Reviewers

Dr. Judylynn Baily-Mitchell
Principal
West Salisbury
Elementary School
Salisbury, Maryland

Dr. Judith F. Barry
Coordinator of Reading/
Language Arts
Taunton Public Schools
Taunton, Massachusetts

Carol Berman
Lead Teacher
Crestview Elementary School
Miami, Florida

Angela Berner
Language Arts Staff Developer
Huntington Unified
School District
Administration Offices
Huntington Station, New York

Susan Birch
Teacher
Dunns Corners
Elementary School
Westerly, Rhode Island

Candace Bouchard
Teacher
Sanburg Elementary School
San Diego, California

Sandra Carron
Teacher
Moreno Valley Unified
School District
Moreno Valley, California

Loretta Cudney
Teacher
Riverside Unified School District
Riverside, California

Justyne Davis
Teacher
Wallbridge Community
Education Center
St. Louis, Missouri

Dr. Ann Dugger
Reading Teacher/Title I
Will Rogers Elementary School
Stillwater, Oklahoma

Rosemary Foresythe
Reading Specialist
West Pottsgrove
Elementary School
Pottstown, Pennsylvania

Stanley Foster
Teacher
Magnolia Avenue School
Los Angeles, California

Kimberly Griffeth
Teacher
Fulton Elementary
Aurora, Colorado

Jeffrey Guerra
Teacher
Westchase Elementary School
Tampa, Florida

Anne Henry
Teacher
Northern Hills
Elementary School
Edmond, Oklahoma

Carol Hookway
Teacher
Memorial Elementary School
Natick, Massachusetts

Arlene Horkey
Curriculum-Technology Specialist
Belleair Elementary School
Clearwater, Florida

Carolyn M. Horton
District Reading Facilitator
Cedar Rapids Community
School District,
Educational Service Center
Cedar Rapids, Iowa

Patty Jacox
Teacher
Lansing Elementary
Aurora, Colorado

Beverly Keeley
Teacher
Grant Foreman
Elementary School
Muskogee, Oklahoma

Rebecca L. Kelly
Teacher
Wekiva Elementary School
Longwood, Florida

Lisa Leslie
Teacher
Costello Elementary School,
Troy Public Schools
Troy, Michigan

Arlene D. Loughlin
Student Achievement Specialist
Curlew Creek
Elementary School
Palm Harbor, Florida

Christin Machado
Teacher
Jefferson Elementary School
Burbank, California

Alicia L. Marsh
Teacher
Pearl Sample
Elementary School
Culpepper, Virginia

K. Gale Martin
Teacher
JEB Stuart Elementary School
Richmond, Virginia

Anne M. Merritt
Teacher
Citrus Glen Elementary School
Ventura, California

Joan Miller
Teacher
Carlton Hills Elementary School
Santee, California

Bobbie A. Overbey
Teacher
Carillon Elementary School
Oviedo, Florida

Katherin Pagakis
English Teacher
Washington Elementary School
Waukegan, Illinois

Barbara Pitts
Administrator
Joy Middle School
Detroit, Michigan

Sundee Preedy
Teacher
Aloma Elementary School
Winter Park, Florida

Dr. Carolyn Reedom
Principal
Vanderberg Elementary School
Henderson, Nevada

Dorina Rocas
Teacher
Corono-Norco Unified
School District
Corona, California

Josephine Scott
Language Arts
Curriculum Director
Columbus City School District,
Northgate Center
Columbus, Ohio

Renee Siefert
Teacher
Serrano Elementary School
Moreno Valley, California

Gayle E. Sitter
Mathematics Resource
Teacher
Educational Leadership Center
Orlando, Florida

Linda Smolen
Director of Reading
Buffalo City School District
Buffalo, New York

Gail Soft
Teacher
Vermillion Primary School
Maize, Kansas

Alejandro Soria
Teacher
Leo Politi Elementary
Los Angeles, California

Jan Strege
Vice-Principal
Schlegel Road
Elementary School
Webster, New York

Dahna Taylor
Teacher
Chavez Elementary School
San Diego, California

Dr. Sandra Telfort
Teacher
Palmetto Elementary School
Miami, Florida

Dana Thurm
Teacher
Olivenhain Pioneer
Elementary School
Carlsbad, California

Geralyn Wilson
Literacy Coordinator
James McCosh Intermediate
Chicago, Illinois

John L. York
Teacher
Cedar Heights
Elementary School
Cedar Falls, Iowa

Maureen A. Zoda
Reading Specialist Coordinator
Meadow Brook
Elementary School
East Longmeadow,
Massachusetts

KINDERGARTEN REVIEWERS

Janice Allocco
Teacher
Klem Road South
Elementary School
Webster, New York

Irma A. Barr
Teacher
Embassy Creek
Elementary School
Cooper City, Florida

Dikki Cie Chanski
Teacher
Troy Public Schools,
Martell Elementary School
Troy, Michigan

Rosemary Gaskin
Teacher
Broad Rock Elementary School
Richmond, Virginia

Carol Grenfell
District Language
Arts Specialist
Ventura Unified School District
Ventura, California

Cathleen Hunter
Teacher
Peterson Elementary
Huntington Beach, California

Karen A. Kuritar
Teacher
Allen Elementary School
Dayton, Ohio

Charlotte Otterbacher
Teacher
Hamilton Elementary
Troy, Michigan

Gwendolyn Perkins
Teacher
Ginter Park Elementary School
Richmond, Virginia

Kelly Schmidt
Teacher
Public School #225 Seaside
Rockaway Parkway, New York

Corene Selman
Teacher
Westwood Early
Childhood Center
Woodward, Oklahoma

Laureen B. Stephens
Teacher
Mountainview
Elementary School
Saycus, California

Pam Styles
Teacher
World of Wonder
Community School
Dayton, Ohio

Scope and Sequence

	GR K	GR I	GR 2	GR 3	GR 4	GR 5	GR 6
Reading							
Concepts about Print							
Understand that print provides information	░						
Understand how print is organized and read	░						
Know left-to-right and top-to-bottom directionality	░						
Distinguish letters from words	░						
Recognize name	░						
Name and match all uppercase and lowercase letter forms	░						
Understand the concept of word and construct meaning from shared text, illustrations, graphics, and charts	░						
Identify letters, words, and sentences	░	░					
Recognize that sentences in print are made up of words	░						
Identify the front cover, back cover, title page, title, and author of a book	░						
Match oral words to printed words	░						
Phonemic Awareness							
Understand that spoken words and syllables are made up of sequences of sounds	░						
Count and track sounds in a syllable, syllables in words, and words in sentences	░	░	░	░	░		
Know the sounds of letters	░						
Track and represent the number, sameness, difference, and order of two or more isolated phonemes	░						
Match, identify, distinguish, and segment sounds in initial, final, and medial position in single-syllable spoken words	░	░					
Blend sounds (phonemes) to make words or syllables	░						
Track and represent changes in syllables and words as target sound is added, substituted, omitted, shifted, or repeated	░	░					
Distinguish long- and short-vowel sounds in orally stated words		░					
Identify and produce rhyming words	░						
Decoding: Phonic Analysis							
Understand and apply the alphabetic principle	░	░					
Consonants: single, blends, digraphs in initial, final, medial positions	•	•	•				
Vowels: short, long, digraphs, r-controlled, variant, schwa		•	•				
Match all consonant and short-vowel sounds to appropriate letters	•	•					
Understand that as letters in words change, so do the sounds	•	•					
Blend vowel-consonant sounds orally to make words or syllables	•	•					
Blend sounds from letters and letter patterns into recognizable words	░	░	░				
Decoding: Structural Analysis							
Inflectional endings, with and without spelling changes: plurals, verb tenses, possessives, comparatives-superlatives		•	•				
Contractions, abbreviations, and compound words		•	•				
Prefixes, suffixes, derivations, and root words			•	•	•	•	•
Greek and Latin roots					•	•	•
Letter, spelling, and syllable patterns		░	░	░	░	░	░
Phonograms/word families/onset-rimes	░	░					
Syllable rules and patterns				•			

Key

Shaded area   Explicit Instruction / Modeling / Practice and Application

•   Tested

Assessment resources include: Kindergarten Assessment Handbook; Placement and Diagnostic Assessments, Grades I, 2, and 3–6; Reading and Language Skills Assessments, Grades I–6; Holistic Assessments, Grades I–6; End-of-Selection Tests, Grades I–6; and Oral Reading Fluency Assessment, Grades I–6

	GR K	GR 1	GR 2	GR 3	GR 4	GR 5	GR 6
Decoding: Strategies							
Visual cues: sound/symbol relationships, letter patterns, and spelling patterns							
Structural cues: compound words, contractions, inflectional endings, prefixes, suffixes, Greek and Latin roots, root words, spelling patterns, and word families							
Cross check visual and structural cues to confirm meaning							
Syllabication rules and patterns							
Word Recognition							
One-syllable and high-frequency words	•	•	•				
Common, irregular sight words	•	•	•				
Common abbreviations			•				
Lesson vocabulary		•	•	•	•	•	•
Fluency							
Read aloud in a manner that sounds like natural speech		•	•				
Read aloud accurately and with appropriate intonation and expression			•	•			
Read aloud narrative and expository text with appropriate pacing, intonation, and expression				•	•	•	•
Read aloud prose and poetry with rhythm and pace, appropriate intonation, and vocal patterns							
Vocabulary and Concept Development							
Academic language							
Classify-categorize		•		•		•	
Antonyms			•	•	•		
Synonyms			•	•	•		
Homographs				•	•		
Homophones			•	•	•	•	
Multiple-meaning words			•	•	•		
Figurative and idiomatic language							•
Context/context clues			•	•	•	•	•
Content-area words							
Dictionary, glossary, thesaurus				•	•		
Foreign words							
Connotation-denotation						•	•
Word origins (acronyms, clipped and coined words, regional variations, etymologies, jargon, slang)							
Analogies							
Word structure clues to determine meaning			•	•	•	•	•
Inflected nouns and verbs, comparatives-superlatives, possessives, compound words, prefixes, suffixes, root words			•	•	•	•	•
Greek and Latin roots, prefixes, suffixes, derivations, and root words					•	•	•
Develop vocabulary							
Listen to and discuss text read aloud							
Read independently							
Use reference books							
Comprehension and Analysis of Text							
Ask/answer questions							
Author's purpose				•	•	•	•
Author's perspective						•	•
Propaganda/bias							•

Key

Shaded area — Explicit Instruction / Modeling / Practice and Application

• — Tested

Assessment resources include: Kindergarten Assessment Handbook; Placement and Diagnostic Assessments, Grades 1, 2, and 3–6; Reading and Language Skills Assessments, Grades 1–6; Holistic Assessments, Grades 1–6; End-of-Selection Tests, Grades 1–6; and Oral Reading Fluency Assessment, Grades 1–6

	GR K	GR I	GR 2	GR 3	GR 4	GR 5	GR 6
Background knowledge: prior knowledge and experiences							
Cause-effect			•	•	•	•	•
Compare-contrast			•	•	•	•	•
Details		•	•	•	•	•	•
Directions: one-, two-, multi-step	•	•	•	•	•		
Draw conclusions				•	•	•	•
Fact-fiction							
Fact-opinion				•	•	•	•
Higher order thinking							
Analyze, critique and evaluate, synthesize, and visualize text and information							
Interpret information from graphic aids			•	•	•	•	•
Locate information		•	•	•	•	•	•
Book parts				•			•
Text features				•		•	
Alphabetical order		•					
Main idea: stated/unstated		•	•	•	•	•	•
Main idea and supporting details				•	•	•	•
Make generalizations							
Make inferences			•	•	•	•	•
Make judgments							
Make predictions/predict outcomes							
Monitor comprehension							
Adjust reading rate, create mental images, reread, read ahead, set/adjust purpose, self-question, summarize/paraphrase, use graphic aids, text features, and text adjuncts							
Paraphrase/restate facts and details			•	•	•	•	•
Preview							
Purpose for reading							
Organize information							
Alphabetical order							
Numerical systems/outlines							
Graphic organizers							
Referents							
Retell stories and ideas							
Sequence		•	•	•	•	•	•
Summarize			•	•	•	•	•
Text structure							
Narrative text			•	•	•	•	•
Informational text (compare and contrast, cause and effect, sequence/chronological order, proposition and support, problem and solution)					•	•	•
Study Skills							
Follow and give directions			•	•	•		
Apply plans and strategies: KWL, question-answer-relationships, skim and scan, note taking, outline, questioning the author, reciprocal teaching							
Practice test-taking strategies							

Key

Shaded area   Explicit Instruction/Modeling/Practice and Application

•   Tested

Assessment resources include: Kindergarten Assessment Handbook; Placement and Diagnostic Assessments, Grades 1, 2, and 3–6; Reading and Language Skills Assessments, Grades 1–6; Holistic Assessments, Grades 1–6; End-of-Selection Tests, Grades 1–6; and Oral Reading Fluency Assessment, Grades 1–6

	GR K	GR 1	GR 2	GR 3	GR 4	GR 5	GR 6
Research and Information							
Use resources and references							
Understand the purpose, structure, and organization of various reference materials							
Title page, table of contents, chapter titles, chapter headings, index, glossary, guide words, citations, end notes, bibliography				•			•
Picture dictionary, software, dictionary, thesaurus, atlas, globe, encyclopedia, telephone directory, on-line information, card catalog, electronic search engines and data bases, almanac, newspaper, journals, periodicals			•	•	•	•	•
Charts, maps, diagrams, timelines, schedules, calendar, graphs, photos			•	•			•
Choose reference materials appropriate to research purpose							•
Viewing/Media							
Interpret information from visuals (graphics, media, including illustrations, tables, maps, charts, graphs, diagrams, timelines)			•	•	•	•	•
Analyze the ways visuals, graphics, and media represent, contribute to, and support meaning of text							
Select, organize, and produce visuals to complement and extend meaning							
Use technology or appropriate media to communicate information and ideas							
Use technology or appropriate media to compare ideas, information, and viewpoints							
Compare, contrast, and evaluate print and broadcast media							
Distinguish between fact and opinion							
Evaluate the role of media							
Analyze media as sources for information, entertainment, persuasion, interpretation of events, and transmission of culture							
Identify persuasive and propaganda techniques used in television and identify false and misleading information							
Summarize main concept and list supporting details and identify biases, stereotypes, and persuasive techniques in a nonprint message							
Support opinions with detailed evidence and with visual or media displays that use appropriate technology							
Literary Response and Analysis							
Genre Characteristics							
Know a variety of literary genres and their basic characteristics			•	•	•	•	•
Distinguish between fantasy and realistic text							
Distinguish between informational and persuasive texts							
Understand the distinguishing features of literary and nonfiction texts: everyday print materials, poetry, drama, fantasies, fables, myths, legends, and fairy tales			•	•	•	•	•
Explain the appropriateness of the literary forms chosen by an author for a specific purpose							
Literary Elements							
Plot/Plot Development							
Important events		•	•	•	•	•	•
Beginning, middle, end of story		•	•				
Problem/solution			•				
Conflict				•			
Conflict and resolution/causes and effects					•	•	•
Compare and contrast							
Character							
Identify		•					
Identify, describe, compare and contrast			•	•	•	•	•
Relate characters and events					•	•	•

Key
Shaded area Explicit Instruction / Modeling / Practice and Application
•   Tested
       Assessment resources include: Kindergarten Assessment Handbook; Placement and Diagnostic Assessments, Grades 1, 2, and 3–6;
       Reading and Language Skills Assessments, Grades 1–6; Holistic Assessments, Grades 1–6; End-of-Selection Tests, Grades 1–6; and
       Oral Reading Fluency Assessment, Grades 1–6

	GR K	GR I	GR 2	GR 3	GR 4	GR 5	GR 6
Traits, actions, motives				•	•	•	•
Cause for character's actions					•		
Character's qualities and effect on plot							•
Setting							
Identify and describe		•	•	•	•	•	•
Compare and contrast			•	•	•	•	•
Relate to problem/resolution							
Theme							
Theme/essential message				•	•	•	•
Universal themes							
Mood/Tone							
Identify							•
Compare and contrast							•

Literary Devices/Author's Craft

	GR K	GR I	GR 2	GR 3	GR 4	GR 5	GR 6
Rhythm, rhyme, pattern, and repetition							
Alliteration, onomatopoeia, assonance, imagery							
Figurative language (similes, metaphors, idioms, personification, hyperbole)				•	•	•	•
Characterization/character development				•		•	
Dialogue				•	•	•	•
Narrator/narration					•	•	•
Point of view (first-person, third-person, omniscient)					•	•	•
Informal language (idioms, slang, jargon, dialect)							

Response to Text

	GR K	GR I	GR 2	GR 3	GR 4	GR 5	GR 6
Relate characters and events to own life							
Read to perform a task or learn a new task							
Recollect, talk, and write about books read							
Describe the roles and contributions of authors and illustrators							
Generate alternative endings and identify the reason and impact of the alternatives							
Compare and contrast versions of the same stories that reflect different cultures							
Make connections between information in texts and stories and historical events							
Form ideas about what had been read and use specific information from the text to support these ideas							
Know that the attitudes and values that exist in a time period or culture affect stories and informational articles written during that time period							
Explore origin and historical development of words and changes in sentence patterns over the years							

Self-Selected Reading

	GR K	GR I	GR 2	GR 3	GR 4	GR 5	GR 6
Select material to read for pleasure							
Read a variety of self-selected and assigned literary and informational texts							
Use knowledge of authors' styles, themes, and genres to choose own reading							
Read literature by authors from various cultural and historical backgrounds							

Cultural Awareness

	GR K	GR I	GR 2	GR 3	GR 4	GR 5	GR 6
Connect information and events in texts to life and life to text experiences							
Compare language, oral traditions, and literature that reflect customs, regions, and cultures							
Identify how language reflects regions and cultures							
View concepts and issues from diverse perspectives							
Recognize the universality of literary themes across cultures and language							

Key

Shaded area Explicit Instruction / Modeling / Practice and Application

• Tested

Assessment resources include: Kindergarten Assessment Handbook; Placement and Diagnostic Assessments, Grades 1, 2, and 3–6; Reading and Language Skills Assessments, Grades 1–6; Holistic Assessments, Grades 1–6; End-of-Selection Tests, Grades 1–6; and Oral Reading Fluency Assessment, Grades 1–6

SCOPE AND SEQUENCE

Writing

Writing Strategies

	GR K	GR 1	GR 2	GR 3	GR 4	GR 5	GR 6
Writing process: prewriting, drafting, revising, proofreading, publishing							
Collaborative, shared, timed writing, writing to prompts		•	•	•	•	•	•
Evaluate own and others' writing							
Proofread writing to correct convention errors in mechanics, usage, punctuation, using handbooks and references as appropriate				•	•	•	•

Organization and Focus

	GR K	GR 1	GR 2	GR 3	GR 4	GR 5	GR 6
Use models and traditional structures for writing							
Select a focus, structure, and viewpoint							
Address purpose, audience, length, and format requirements							
Write single- and multiple-paragraph compositions			•	•	•	•	•

Revision Skills

	GR K	GR 1	GR 2	GR 3	GR 4	GR 5	GR 6
Correct sentence fragments and run-ons					•	•	•
Vary sentence structure, word order, and sentence length							
Combine sentences					•	•	•
Improve coherence, unity, consistency, and progression of ideas							
Add, delete, consolidate, clarify, rearrange text							
Choose appropriate and effective words: exact/precise words, vivid words, trite/overused words						•	•
Elaborate: details, examples, dialogue, quotations							
Revise using a rubric							

Penmanship/Handwriting

	GR K	GR 1	GR 2	GR 3	GR 4	GR 5	GR 6
Write uppercase and lowercase letters							
Write legibly, using appropriate word and letter spacing							
Write legibly, using spacing, margins, and indention							

Writing Applications

	GR K	GR 1	GR 2	GR 3	GR 4	GR 5	GR 6
Narrative writing (stories, paragraphs, personal narratives, journal, plays, poetry)		•	•	•	•	•	•
Descriptive writing (titles, captions, ads, posters, paragraphs, stories, poems)		•	•	•	•	•	•
Expository writing (comparison-contrast, explanation, directions, speech, how-to article, friendly/business letter, news story, essay, report, invitation)			•	•	•	•	•
Persuasive writing (paragraph, essay, letter, ad, poster)						•	•
Cross-curricular writing (paragraph, report, poster, list, chart)							
Everyday writing (journal, message, forms, notes, summary, label, caption)							

Written and Oral English Language Conventions

Sentence Structure

	GR K	GR 1	GR 2	GR 3	GR 4	GR 5	GR 6
Types (declarative, interrogative, exclamatory, imperative, interjection)		•	•	•	•	•	•
Structure (simple, compound, complex, compound-complex)		•	•	•	•	•	•
Parts (subjects/predicates: complete, simple, compound; clauses: independent, dependent, subordinate; phrase)		•	•	•	•	•	•
Direct/indirect object							
Word order		•					

Grammar

	GR K	GR 1	GR 2	GR 3	GR 4	GR 5	GR 6
Nouns (singular, plural, common, proper, possessive, collective, abstract, concrete, abbreviations, appositives)		•	•	•	•	•	•
Verbs (action, helping, linking, transitive, intransitive, regular, irregular; subject-verb agreement)		•	•	•	•	•	•
Verb tenses (present, past, future; present, past, and future perfect)		•	•	•	•	•	•
Participles; infinitives							

Key

Shaded area Explicit Instruction/Modeling/Practice and Application

• Tested

Assessment resources include: Kindergarten Assessment Handbook; Placement and Diagnostic Assessments, Grades 1, 2, and 3–6; Reading and Language Skills Assessments, Grades 1–6; Holistic Assessments, Grades 1–6; End-of-Selection Tests, Grades 1–6; and Oral Reading Fluency Assessment, Grades 1–6

	GR K	GR 1	GR 2	GR 3	GR 4	GR 5	GR 6
Adjectives (common, proper; articles; comparative, superlative)		•	•	•	•	•	•
Adverbs (place, time, manner, degree)				•	•	•	•
Pronouns (subject, object, possessive, reflexive, demonstrative, antecedents)		•	•		•	•	•
Prepositions; prepositional phrases					•	•	•
Conjunctions							
Abbreviations, contractions				•	•	•	•
Punctuation							
Period, exclamation point, or question mark at end of sentences		•	•	•	•	•	•
Comma			•	•	•	•	•
Greeting and closure of a letter			•	•	•	•	•
Dates, locations, and addresses			•	•	•	•	•
For items in a series			•	•	•	•	•
Direct quotations							
Link two clauses with a conjunction in compound sentences					•	•	•
Quotation marks			•	•	•	•	•
Dialogue, exact words of a speaker				•	•	•	•
Titles of books, stories, poems, magazines						•	•
Parentheses/dash/hyphen					•	•	•
Apostrophes in possessive case of nouns and in contractions				•	•	•	•
Underlining or italics to identify title of documents					•	•	•
Colon					•	•	•
Separate hours and minutes					•	•	•
Introduce a list					•	•	•
After the salutation in business letters						•	•
Semicolons to connect independent clauses							
Capitalization							
First word of a sentence, names of people, and the pronoun *I*	•	•	•	•	•	•	•
Proper nouns, words at the beginning of sentences and greetings, months and days of the week, and titles and initials of people		•	•	•	•	•	•
Geographical names, holidays, historical periods, and special events							•
Names of magazines, newspapers, works of art, musical compositions, organizations, and the first word in quotations when appropriate							•
Use conventions of punctuation and capitalization							
Spelling							
Spell independently by using pre-phonetic knowledge, sounds of the alphabet, and knowledge of letter names							
Use spelling approximations and some conventional spelling							
Common, phonetically regular words			•	•	•	•	•
Frequently used, irregular words			•	•	•	•	•
One-syllable words with consonant blends			•	•	•	•	•
Contractions, compounds, orthographic patterns, and common homophones				•	•	•	•
Greek and Latin roots, inflections, suffixes, prefixes, and syllable constructions					•	•	•
Use a variety of strategies and resources to spell words							
Listening and Speaking							
Listening Skills and Strategies							
Listen to a variety of oral presentations such as stories, poems, skits, songs, personal accounts, or informational speeches							
Listen attentively to the speaker (make eye contact and demonstrate appropriate body language)							

Key

Shaded area Explicit Instruction / Modeling / Practice and Application

•   Tested

    Assessment resources include: Kindergarten Assessment Handbook; Placement and Diagnostic Assessments, Grades 1, 2, and 3–6; Reading and Language Skills Assessments, Grades 1–6; Holistic Assessments, Grades 1–6; End-of-Selection Tests, Grades 1–6; and Oral Reading Fluency Assessment, Grades 1–6

	GR K	GR 1	GR 2	GR 3	GR 4	GR 5	GR 6
Listen for a purpose							
Follow oral directions (one-, two-, three-, and multi-step)	■	■	■	■	■	■	■
For specific information	■	■	■	■	■	■	■
For enjoyment	■	■	■	■	■	■	■
To distinguish between the speaker's opinions and verifiable facts				■	■	■	■
To actively participate in class discussions					■	■	■
To expand and enhance personal interest and personal preferences					■	■	■
To identify, analyze, and critique persuasive techniques					■	■	■
To identify logical fallacies used in oral presentations and media messages						■	■
To make inferences or draw conclusions					■	■	■
To interpret a speaker's verbal and nonverbal messages, purposes, and perspectives						■	■
To identify the tone, mood, and emotion					■	■	■
To analyze the use of rhetorical devices for intent and effect					■	■	■
To evaluate classroom presentations					■	■	■
To respond to a variety of media and speakers		■	■	■	■	■	■
To paraphrase/summarize directions and information				■	■	■	■
For language reflecting regions and cultures				■	■	■	■
To recognize emotional and logical arguments				■	■	■	■
To identify the musical elements of language				■	■	■	■
Listen critically to relate the speaker's verbal communication to the nonverbal message					■	■	■

Speaking Skills and Strategies

	GR K	GR 1	GR 2	GR 3	GR 4	GR 5	GR 6
Speak clearly and audibly and use appropriate volume and pace in different settings	■	■	■	■	■	■	■
Use formal and informal English appropriately	■	■	■	■	■	■	■
Follow rules of conversation	■	■	■	■	■	■	■
Stay on the topic when speaking	■	■	■	■	■	■	■
Use descriptive words	■	■	■	■	■	■	■
Recount experiences in a logical sequence	■	■	■	■	■	■	■
Clarify and support spoken ideas with evidence and examples		■	■	■		■	■
Use eye contact, appropriate gestures, and props to enhance oral presentations and engage the audience	■	■	■	■	■	■	■
Give and follow two-, three-, and four-step directions		■	■	■	■	■	■
Recite poems, rhymes, songs, stories, soliloquies, or dramatic dialogues	■	■	■	■	■	■	■
Plan and present dramatic interpretations with clear diction, pitch, tempo, and tone				■	■	■	■
Organize presentations to maintain a clear focus				■	■	■	■
Use language appropriate to situation, purpose, and audience				■	■	■	■
Make/deliver							
Oral narrative, descriptive, informational, and persuasive presentations				■	■	■	■
Oral summaries of articles and books					■	■	■
Oral responses to literature					■	■	■
Presentations on problems and solutions					■	■	■
Presentation or speech for specific occasions, audiences, and purposes					■	■	■
Vary language according to situation, audience, and purpose					■	■	■
Select a focus, organizational structure, and point of view for an oral presentation					■	■	■
Participate in classroom activities and discussions	■	■	■	■	■	■	■

Key

Shaded area Explicit Instruction/Modeling/Practice and Application

   •   Tested

       Assessment resources include: Kindergarten Assessment Handbook; Placement and Diagnostic Assessments, Grades 1, 2, and 3–6;
       Reading and Language Skills Assessments, Grades 1–6; Holistic Assessments, Grades 1–6; End-of-Selection Tests, Grades 1–6; and
       Oral Reading Fluency Assessment, Grades 1–6

SCOPE AND SEQUENCE

400–401, 410–411, 424–425, 432–433, 448–449, 470–471

Using prior knowledge, *See* **Comprehension, Focus skills**

Visual discrimination,
See **Concepts of print, Early literacy skills, Lowercase letters, Phonics/Decoding, Uppercase letters.**

Visualizing,
See **Comprehension, Focus skills**

Vocabulary and concept development,
action words, **K-1:** 184, 208–209, 212, 222–223, 230, 238, 258, 299, 308, 406, 409, 430, 431, 533; **K-2:** 25, 158, 221, 263, 266, 450, 469; **K-3:** 155, 158, 389, 409, 447, 572, 576, 577

categories, **K-1:** 198–199, 289, 309, 414–415, 445, 582–583, 612–613, 644–645; **K-2:** 163, 255, 266, 399, 544, 593, 628, 666; **K-3:** 71, 301, 389, 434

color words, **K-1:** 414–415, 553; **K-2:** 485, 549; **K-3:** 139

describe objects and events, **K-1:** 132, 273, 375, 415, 445; **K-2:** 22, 36, 38, 41, 46, 48, 51, 56, 61, 66, 68, 71, 82, 90, 98, 109, 128, 131, 144, 147, 150, 155, 160, 166, 192, 218, 226, 241, 252, 268, 271, 304, 309, 314, 322, 330, 333, 376, 386, 394, 396, 409, 420, 428, 439, 444, 447, 466, 474, 480, 482, 485, 488, 490, 498, 530, 533, 546, 554, 556, 576, 582, 590, 598, 601, 606, 614, 625, 655, 660, 668, 671; **K-3:** 22, 38, 48, 68, 82, 90, 98, 106, 114, 128, 136, 144, 152, 160, 192, 208, 218, 228, 239, 252, 260, 268, 276, 298, 306, 322, 330, 362, 376, 386, 396, 406, 420, 428, 436, 444, 452, 466, 474, 482, 490, 498, 530, 546, 556, 566, 574, 588, 596, 604, 612, 620, 634, 642, 650, 653, 658, 666

describing words, **K-1:** 114, 132, 189, 226, 230, 259, 273, 373, 375, 414, 415, 445, 528, 557; **K-2:** 142, 241, 404, 485, 579; **K-3:** 290, 314, 384, 559, 580

naming words, **K-1:** 28, 44, 75, 115, 126, 132, 134, 176, 244, 259, 309, 312, 373, 378, 414, 422, 423, 445, 518, 583, 624, 648; **K-2:** 36, 67, 71, 85, 207, 216, 244, 258, 271, 274, 365, 374, 384, 423, 447, 485, 564, 593, 617, 628, 655, 666; **K-3:** 101, 163, 255, 389, 590, 637

number words, **K-1:** 116–117, 567; **K-2:** 231, 504; **K-3:** 364, 422

opposites, **K-2:** 104, 674; **K-3:** 469
position words, **K-1:** 239, 434; **K-3:** 423
shape words, **K-3:** 85
size words, **K-2:** 496
sound words, **K-1:** 115, 165, 226, 373, 375, 423, 445, 528, 557, 645; **K-2:** 51, 533, 544, 600, 638–639, 666; **K-3:** 155, 226, 317, 409, 412, 492, 644, 668, 669
word meaning, **K-1:** 132, 189, 208–209, 248–249, 299, 374, 398, 414, 422, 430–431, 445, 477, 508, 583, 613; **K-2:** 25, 36, 40, 51, 60, 61, 71, 85, 92, 101, 104, 131, 146, 154, 158, 163, 216, 220, 221, 231, 241, 255, 263, 266, 271, 301, 308, 336, 365, 384, 399, 404, 409, 412, 423, 438, 446, 447, 450, 468, 469, 476, 477, 485, 496, 500, 532, 533, 549, 559, 569, 579, 593, 617, 639, 655, 663, 674; **K-3:** 51, 131, 221, 241, 271, 548, 614, 607

See also **Listening, Oral language, Speaking**

Vowels,
See **Phonics/Decoding**

Walking Through the Jungle, by Debbie Harter, **K-2:** 532–533, 592–593, 624–625, 654–656

Warthogs in the Kitchen, by Pamela Duncan Edwards, **K-1:** 510–515

What's What? by Mary Serfozo, **K-3:** 430–431, 468–469

Wonderful Worms, by Linda Glaser, **K-2:** 430–431, 468–469

Word and letter center,
See **Learning centers**

Word Builder, K-1: 416–417, 424–425, 432–433, 454–455, 462–463, 470–471, 576–577, 584–585, 592, 593, 600–601, 622–623, 638–639, 646–647; **K-2:** 118–119, 148–149, 164–165, 272–273, 288–289, 318–319, 456–457, 486–487, 502–503, 610–611, 626–627, 640–641; **K-3:** 118–119, 148–149, 164–165, 272–273, 288–289, 456–457, 486–487, 502–503, 560–561, 578–579

Word Builder Cards, K-1: T38–T42

Word families,
See **Phonemic Awareness, Phonics/Decoding**

Word recognition,
See **High-frequency words**

Words,
See **Concepts of print, Vocabulary and concept development**

Words to Remember, K-1: 193, 203, 243, 253, 293, 303, 369, 379, 425, 471, 537,
547, 593, 639; **K-2:** 45, 55, 215, 225, 383, 393, 553, 563; **K-3:** 45, 55, 215, 225, 383, 393, 553, 563

Write-On/Wipe-Off Board, K-1: 132, 175, 191, 225, 275, 347, 365, 400, 516, 535; **K-2:** 34–35, 52–53, 86–87, 204–205, 302–303, 310–311, 318–319, 372–373, 390–391, 424–425, 542–543, 560–561, 640–641, 648–649, 656–657; **K-3:** 35, 53, 69, 87, 205, 223, 302–303, 311, 319, 373, 425, 593, 601, 609

Writer's Workshop,
about an animal/a story about going to Grandma's, **K-2:** 120

Writing,
Interactive Writing,
about animal homes, **K-1:** 176; **K-2:** 632
about the five senses, **K-3:** 434
action words, **K-2:** 450
address a letter, **K-2:** 134
birthday message, **K-2:** 74
chart, **K-2:** 544; **K-3:** 648
describing words, **K-2:** 404; **K-3:** 384
description, **K-3:** 282
directions, **K-1:** 448, 538; **K-3:** 150, 442
food words, **K-1:** 410
grocery lists, **K-2:** 274
labels, **K-1:** 72
list rules, **K-1:** 586
lists, **K-1:** 30, 586; **K-3:** 66, 244, 564, 618
mural, **K-1:** 226
new verses, **K-1:** 244; **K-3:** 112
opposites, **K-2:** 104
poster, **K-3:** 166
questions, **K-2:** 434; **K-3:** 304
recipe, **K-1:** 370
rhymes, **K-2:** 328; **K-3:** 504
sentences, **K-2:** 46
shape treasure hunt, **K-3:** 36
story, **K-1:** 632; **K-2:** 166
story map, **K-3:** 602
thank-you note, **K-2:** 312; **K-3:** 236
weather chart, **K-2:** 604; **K-3:** 236

Shared Writing,
about a job, **K-3:** 216
about a library visit, **K-1:** 578
about animals, **K-2:** 88
about story characters, **K-1:** 128
action words, **K-1:** 184
alphabet poster, **K-1:** 54
animal names, **K-1:** 46
bus rules, **K-3:** 258
character web, **K-2:** 142
chart, **K-1:** 110, 518, 528; **K-2:** 266, 674; **K-3:** 648
description, **K-3:** 580
directions/instructions, **K-1:** 456; **K-3:** 104
facts about kangaroos, **K-2:** 320
graph, **K-1:** 276

Acknowledgments

Big Books

For permission to reprint copyrighted material, grateful acknowledgment is made to the following sources:

Boyds Mills Press, Inc.: From Anne to Zach by Mary Jane Martin, illustrated by Michael Grejniec. Text copyright © 1996 by Mary Jane Martin; illustrations copyright © 1996 by Michael Grejniec.

Candlewick Press Inc., Cambridge, MA: The Shape of Things by Dayle Ann Dodds, illustrated by Julie Lacome. Text © 1994 by Dayle Ann Dodds; illustrations © 1994 by Julie Lacome.

Dutton Children's Books, a division of Penguin Putnam Inc.: Peanut Butter and Jelly: A Play Rhyme, illustrated by Nadine Bernard Westcott. Illustrations copyright © 1987 by Nadine Bernard Westcott.

Harcourt, Inc.: Look Closer by Brian and Rebecca Wildsmith. Copyright © 1993 by Brian and Rebecca Wildsmith. *Moo Moo, Brown Cow* by Jakki Wood, illustrated by Rog Bonner. Text copyright © 1991 by Jakki Wood; illustrations copyright © 1991 by Rog Bonner.

HarperCollinsChildrensBooks, a division of HarperCollins Publishers, Inc.: Does a Kangaroo Have a Mother, Too? by Eric Carle. Copyright © 2000 by Eric Carle. *I Read Signs* by Tana Hoban. Copyright © 1983 by Tana Hoban.

Hyperion Books for Children, an Imprint of Disney Children's Book Group, LLC: Warthogs in the Kitchen: A Sloppy Counting Book by Pamela Duncan Edwards, illustrated by Henry Cole. Text © 1998 by Pamela Duncan Edwards; illustrations © 1998 by Henry Cole. Originally published in the United States and Canada by Hyperion Books for Children.

Little, Brown and Company (Inc.): Off We Go! by Jane Yolen, illustrated by Laurel Molk. Text copyright © 2000 by Jane Yolen; illustrations copyright © 2000 by Laurel Molk.

North-South Books Inc., New York: Five Little Ducks: An Old Rhyme, illustrated by Pamela Paparone. Illustrations copyright © 1995 by Pamela Paparone.

Orchard Books, New York: Walking Through the Jungle by Debbie Harter. Text copyright © 1997 by Barefoot Books; illustrations copyright © 1997 by Debbie Harter.

G. P. Putnam's Sons, a division of Penguin Putnam Inc.: Mice Squeak, We Speak by Arnold Shapiro, illustrated by Tomie dePaola. Text copyright © 1984 by World Book, Inc.; illustrations copyright © 1997 by Tomie dePaola. Originally titled "I Speak, I Say, I Talk."

Jackie Silberg, Miss Jackie Music Co.: Music from "All the Fish" (Retitled: "Splash in the Ocean!"), adapted by "Miss Jackie" Silberg. Music copyright © 1977 by Miss Jackie Music Co.

Simon & Schuster Books for Young Readers, Simon & Schuster Children's Publishing Division: Pass the Fritters, Critters by Cheryl Chapman, illlustrated by Susan L. Roth. Text copyright © 1993 by Cheryl Chapman; illustrations copyright © 1993 by Susan L. Roth.

Library Books and Theme Books

For permission to reprint copyrighted material, grateful acknowledgment is made to the following sources:

Atheneum Books for Young Readers, an imprint of Simon & Schuster Children's Publishing Division: Cover and illustrations by Michael Bryant from *Good-Bye Hello* by Barbara Shook Hazen. Illustrations copyright © 1995 by Michael Bryant. Cover and illustrations by Yumi Heo from *So Say the Little Monkeys* by Nancy Van Laan. Illustrations copyright © 1998 by Yumi Heo.

Boyds Mills Press, Inc.: Cover and illustrations by Michael Grejniec from *From Anne to Zach* by Mary Jane Martin. Illustrations copyright © 1996 by Michael Grejniec.

Candlewick Press Inc., Cambridge, MA: Cover and illustrations by Julie Lacome from *The Shape of Things* by Dayle Ann Dodds. Illustrations © 1994 by Julie Lacome.

Dial Books for Young Readers, a division of Penguin Putnam Inc.: Cover and illustrations from *Bunny Cakes* by Rosemary Wells. Illustrations copyright © 1997 by Rosemary Wells.

DK Publishing, Inc., New York: Cover and illustrations by Nadine Bernard Westcott from *Hello Toes! Hello Feet!* by Ann Whitford Paul. Illustrations copyright © 1998 by Nadine Bernard Westcott.

Dutton Children's Books, a division of Penguin Putnam Inc.: Cover and photographs by Thomas D. Mangelsen from *A Time for Playing* by Ron Hirschi. Photographs copyright © 1994 by Thomas D. Mangelsen. Cover and illustrations from *Are You There, Baby Bear?* by Catherine Walters. Copyright © 1999 by Catherine Walters.

HarperCollinsChildrensBooks, a division of HarperCollins Publishers, Inc.: Cover and illustrations from *Guess Who?* by Margaret Miller. Copyright © 1994 by Margaret Miller. Cover and illustrations by Lizzy Rockwell from *Career Day* by Anne Rockwell. Illustrations copyright © 2000 by Lizzy Rockwell.

Henry Holt and Company, Inc.: Cover and photographs from *Fish Faces* by Norbert Wu. Photographs copyright © 1993 by Norbert Wu.

Hyperion Books for Children, an Imprint of Disney Children's Book Group, LLC: Cover and illustrations by Henry Cole from *Warthogs in the Kitchen: A Sloppy Counting Book* by Pamela Duncan Edwards. Illustrations © 1998 by Henry Cole. Originally published in the United States and Canada by Hyperion Books for Children. Cover and illustrations from *Jazzbo and Googy* by Matt Novak. Copyright © 2000 by Matt Novak.

Alfred A. Knopf, Inc.: Cover and illustrations from *Swimmy* by Leo Lionni. Illustrations copyright © 1963 by Leo Lionni; illustrations copyright renewed 1991 by Leo Lionni.

Little, Brown and Company (Inc.): Cover and illustrations from *Come Along, Daisy!* by Jane Simmons. Copyright © 1998 by Jane Simmons. Originally published in Great Britain by Orchard Books, 1998.

Lothrop, Lee & Shepard Books, a division of William Morrow & Company, Inc.: Cover and illustrations from *Elmer* by David McKee. Illustrations copyright © 1968 by David McKee.

Margaret K. McElderry Books, Simon & Schuster Children's Publishing Division: Cover and illustrations by Keiko Narahashi from *What's What?* by Mary Serfozo. Illustrations copyright © 1996 by Keiko Narahashi.

The Millbrook Press: Cover and illustrations by Loretta Krupinski from *Wonderful Worms* by Linda Glaser. Illustrations copyright © 1992 by Loretta Krupinski.

Penguin Putnam Books for Young Readers, a division of Penguin Putnam Inc.: Cover and illustrations by Tomie dePaola from *Mice Squeak, We Speak* by Arnold Shapiro. Illustrations copyright © 1997 by Tomie dePaola. Reprinted by permission of World Books, Inc. Originally titled "I Speak, I Say, I Talk."

Random House Children's Books, a division of Random House, Inc., New York: Cover and illustrations by Bob Barner from *Benny's Pennies* by Pat Brisson. Illustrations copyright © 1993 by Bob Barner. Cover and illustrations by Michael Letzig from *The Crayon Box that Talked* by Shane DeRolf. Illustrations copyright © 1997 by Michael Letzig.

Scholastic Inc.: Cover and photographs by Shelley Rotner from *The Body Book* by Shelley Rotner and Stephen Calcagnino. Photographs copyright © 2000 by Shelley Rotner. Cover and photographs by Shelley Rotner from *Hold the Anchovies! A Book about Pizza* by Shelley Rotner and Julia Pemberton Hellums. Photographs copyright © 1996 by Shelley Rotner.

Simon & Schuster Books for Young Readers, Simon & Schuster Children's Publishing Division: Cover and illustrations by Paul Johnson from *Nature Chains: Butterfly* by Moira Butterfield. Copyright © 1991 by Teeney Books Limited. Cover and illustrations by Cecily Lang from *A Birthday Basket for Tía* by Pat Mora. Illustrations copyright © 1992 by Cecily Lang.

Viking Children's Books, a division of Penguin Putnam Inc.: Cover and illustrations from *Look Out Kindergarten, Here I Come!* by Nancy Carlson. Copyright © 1999 by Nancy Carlson. Cover and illustrations by Blanche Sims from *I Took My Frog to the Library* by Eric A. Kimmel. Illustrations copyright © 1990 by Blanche Sims. Cover and illustrations by Susan Hartung from *Dear Juno* by Soyung Pak. Illustrations copyright © 1999 by Susan Hartung.

Big Book of Rhymes and Songs

For permission to reprint copyrighted material, grateful acknowledgment is made to the following sources:

Dial Books for Young Readers, a division of Penguin Putnam Inc.: "I Am" from *It's Raining Laughter* by Nikki Grimes. Text copyright © 1997 by Nikki Grimes.

David Higham Associates: "Kitchen Sink-Song" by Tony Mitton from *Poems Go Clang! A Collection of Noisy Verse*. Text © 1997 by Tony Mitton.

Homeland Publishing (CAPAC), a division of Troubadour Records Ltd.: Lyrics by Raffi and D. Pike from "Everything Grows" in *Raffi's Top 10 Songs to Read* by Raffi. Lyrics © 1987 by Homeland Publishing (CAPAC), a division of Troubadour Records Ltd. "Wheels on the Bus" and "Down By the Bay" (traditional) from *Rise and Shine* (1982) and *Singable Songs for the Very Young* (1976) by Raffi.

LADYBUG Magazine: "Winter Birds" by Ben Kenny from *LADYBUG* Magazine, January 1999, Vol. 9, No. 2. Text © 1999 by Benjamin C. Kenny. Lyrics from "Five Speckled Frogs" in *LADYBUG* Magazine, June 1994, Vol. 4, No. 10. Lyrics © 1994 by Carus Publishing Company.

Little, Brown and Company (Inc.): "Los pescaditos" / "The Little Fishes" from *Los pollitos dicen/The Baby Chicks Sing* by Jill Syverson-Stork and Nancy Abraham Hall. Lyrics copyright © 1994 by Jill Syverson-Stork and Nancy Abraham Hall.

Ludlow Music, Inc., New York, NY: From "Mary Was a Red Bird" ("Mary Wore Her Red Dress"), collected, adapted, and arranged by Alan Lomax and John A. Lomax. Lyrics TRO - © copyright 1941 (Renewed) by Ludlow Music, Inc.

The McGraw-Hill Companies: "Fuzzy Wuzzy, Creepy Crawly" from *Hey Bug!* by Lillian Schulz.

Marian Reiner, on behalf of Aileen Fisher: "When It Comes to Bugs" from *I Wonder How, I Wonder Why* by Aileen Fisher. Text copyright © 1962, 1990 by Aileen Fisher.

Westwood Creative Artists, on behalf of Dennis Lee: From "The Kitty Ran Up the Tree" in *Jelly Belly* by Dennis Lee. Text copyright © 1983 by Dennis Lee. Published by Macmillan of Canada.

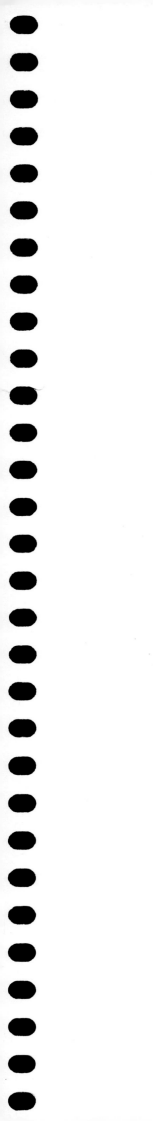